Arthur Machen

Arthur Machen

Critical Essays

Edited by
Antonio Sanna

LEXINGTON BOOKS
Lanham • Boulder • New York • London

Published by Lexington Books
An imprint of The Rowman & Littlefield Publishing Group, Inc.
4501 Forbes Boulevard, Suite 200, Lanham, Maryland 20706
www.rowman.com

6 Tinworth Street, London SE11 5AL, United Kingdom

Copyright © 2021 The Rowman & Littlefield Publishing Group, Inc.

All rights reserved. No part of this book may be reproduced in any form or by any electronic or mechanical means, including information storage and retrieval systems, without written permission from the publisher, except by a reviewer who may quote passages in a review.

British Library Cataloguing in Publication Information Available

Library of Congress Cataloging-in-Publication Data

Library of Congress Control Number: 2021932238

ISBN 978-1-7936-3546-4 (cloth)
ISBN 978-1-7936-3548-8 (pbk)
ISBN 978-1-7936-3547-1 (electronic)

To the people who have experienced London's different facets with me: the flatmates on the fifth floor of Marylebone Road Campus (2002/03), Luca, Catiuscia and Paola, Freya, Lloymore, Roberto, Vickie, Gianni, and Zinzu.

Contents

Introduction—Arthur Machen: His Life, His Work, and His Critics   1
Antonio Sanna

PART I: HUMAN BEINGS AND THEIR ENVIRONMENTS   39

1. "A London *cognita* and a London *incognita*": Mapping London in Arthur Machen's *The London Adventure, or the Art of Wandering*   41
 Amanda M. Caleb

2. The Problem of Agency in Arthur Machen's *The Terror*   59
 Francesco Corigliano

3. Heterotopic Spaces in Machen's Fiction   75
 Antonio Sanna

4. Dead Matter: Posthumanism and Stones   95
 Fernando Gabriel Pagnoni Berns and Emiliano Aguilar

PART II: DARWINISM AND DEGENERATION   113

5. Fear, Fairies, and Fossils: The Legacy of Arthur Machen's "Little People" Stories   115
 Justin Mullis

6. "Dissolution and Change": Reading *The Great God Pan* as Monstrous Adaptation   135
 Jessica George

| 7 | Lucian's *Ornaments in Jade*: Symbolist Decadence in Arthur Machen's Prose Poetry
Kostas Boyiopoulos | 151 |
| 8 | "A Substance as Jelly": Helen Vaughan as Pathogen and *femme fatale* in "The Great God Pan"
Loredana Salis and Laura Mauro | 171 |

PART III: SPIRITUALITY — **191**

9	"[A] Mystic, Ineffable Force and Energy": Arthur Machen and Theories of New Materialism Adrian Tait	193
10	Occult Investigations in Arthur Machen's Detective Stories Deborah Bridle	209
11	Through the Ancient Wood: Envisioning Apophatic Mysticism in *A Fragment of Life* Geoffrey Reiter	225
12	A "Miracle" in No Man's Land? Arthur Machen and the Angels of Mons Andrew R. Lenoir	241

| Index | 259 |
| About the Contributors | 265 |

Introduction
Arthur Machen: His Life, His Work, and His Critics
Antonio Sanna

Gothic novelist, writer of weird fiction, essayist, translator, journalist, and actor: Arthur Machen was a very active (though reserved) figure in the literary landscape of the past decades of the Victorian age and the first half of the twentieth century. Yet, nowadays, in spite of the many (re-)editions of his works, many critics lament his absence from popular recollection in the past century. In 1918, for example, American journalist Vincent Starrett attempted to reevaluate Machen (whom he defined as "a novelist of the soul") in the eyes of the public, justifying the writer's lack of fame as due to the non-ordinariness of his subjects and predicting that "His apotheosis will begin after his death."[1] H.P. Lovecraft in "Supernatural Horror in Literature" (1927) presents Machen as the "author of some dozen tales long and short, in which the elements of hidden horror and brooding fright attain an almost incomparable substance and realistic acuteness."[2] Lovecraft briefly traces Machen's career, praising the "lyrical and expressive" prose style of all of his works, appreciating his "impressionable Celtic heritage," and focusing on the writer's production during the 1890s.[3] Similarly, in 1949, William Francis Genkle affirmed, "Machen remains yet to be properly appreciated and honored by a wider public."[4] In 1963, Aidan Charlton and William Reynolds published a brief biography of the then-deceased Welsh writer, an attempt to popularize his works that has been more subsequently done by Mark Valentine in 1995. In *Arthur Machen*, Valentine offers a succinct but precise biography of the writer along with a brief evaluation of his productions, arguing that Machen "achieved passing notoriety twice, but popular appreciation of his books, never."[5] Yet, in spite of the few academic studies on the subject, Machen has been recognized as a very influential figure among popular writers such as Ray Bradbury (1920–2012), T.E.D. Klein (b. 1947), and Stephen King (b. 1947) as well as directors such as Clive Barker (b. 1952) and Guillermo Del

Toro (b. 1964).[6] In the past few decades, a cult following has been cultivated by societies such as the "Friends of Arthur Machen," and has been facilitated by the repeated publication of different editions of his works by a great variety of publishers.

What emerges from a study of Machen's works and life are some themes and preoccupations recurring throughout his oeuvre. Indeed, from his earliest works (especially the horror stories written during the 1890s), Machen has often dealt with the theme of a reality hidden from human perception and accessible only through a complex (not necessarily scientific) investigation of the phenomena or an inner spiritual revelation. As Genkle argues, indeed, "[in the 1890s] Machen began to postulate the existence of things behind the veil of common appearances. Wells looked forward, Machen backward."[7] According to Genkle, it is for this reason that the Welsh writer "is a master at evoking the willing suspension of disbelief."[8] Such a hidden reality is presented either as demoniacal and haunting or as a spiritual awakening of the single individual. Central to Machen's philosophy, as S.T. Joshi has evidenced, is also a continuous, though feeble, struggle against science and rationalism, which is opposed to "the sense of wonder and mystery into our perception of the world and a disapproval of Protestantism.[9]

Common to many of the writer's fictional and autobiographical works are the settings of London (where Machen spent much of his life) and the Welsh countryside. The former is represented as a metropolis characterized by hidden corners of unexpected beauty as much as by areas of sordid lives and squalor. Machen's characters move in such a milieu, which becomes either a dark labyrinth of gloom and fear in the tales of horror or a place of casual (more or less pleasant) encounters and a cold city, indifferent to the lives of its inhabitants, in the more prosaic stories. Linked to this urban environment is the frequent trope of the loneliness of the artist, forced to a meager existence and to be unwillingly employed in other jobs that distract him from the production of literary works and the cultivation of the arts.[10] However, Machen frequently portrays the landscape of Wales as the background environment for his characters. The Welsh countryside is depicted as a peaceful environment, strong in its associations with folklore, legends, and myths of Arthurian narratives or the historical significance of the Ancient Roman occupation.

Arthur Machen (pen name for Arthur Llewellyn Jones-Machen)[11] was born on March 3, 1863, in the Welsh village of Caerleon-on-Usk, in the heart of Gwent, the only child of John Edward Jones, the Perpetual Curate of Llanddewi Vach, and Janet Robina Machen, daughter of a captain in the Royal Navy, who was an invalid for the greatest part of the writer's life.[12] The family moved to Landdewi Vach Rectory in 1864 (as soon as its construction was completed), in the middle of the Welsh countryside, characterized by wooded hills, brooks, and Ancient Roman ruins (which were fundamental in the formation of the young Machen, whose lonely wanderings in the countryside were later reproduced frequently in his writings).[13] At eleven, the young boy moved with his aunt Maria Jones to Hereford to enter the Cathedral School, but his visits home during the summer breaks were particularly formative for his access to the Rectory's library and his talks about archaeology with his father.[14] In 1876 Machen visited Dublin and, after leaving Hereford, in 1880 he went to London for the first time to begin a career in medicine, but he failed the exams to enter the Royal College of Surgeons. After his return to Gwent, Machen began to work on "Eleusinia" (1881), his first fictional work, privately published in an edition of 100 copies. "Eleusinia" is a 326-line poem about the gathering of a crowd in Ancient Greece's Athens for the celebration of the rites for goddess Demeter, whose glory is praised as bringing fertility to the land and the atonement of sins. The poem is focused specifically on the human cult of the goddesses Demeter and Persephone, the chants sung by the Athenians, the intermingling of "sweet sounds and scents," and the rites' mysterious initiation toward the Truth.[15] "Eleusinia" was sent to Joseph Jones, the Hereford stationer, who returned half dozen copies to Machen, along with a favorable review. This convinced the writer's family of his prospective career in journalism.

Machen was therefore sent back to London in the summer of 1881. In Burlington College near Turnham Green, he experienced many difficulties in mastering shorthand under the tutelage of writer Lewis Sergeant and he began to book review for *The Hereford Times*.[16] Two years later, Machen was employed by Messrs. Marcus Ward (an educational publishing house in Chandos Street) for a £50 annual stipend and moved to a tiny room in Clarendon Road, Notting Hill. In this period, he "wrote feverishly and planned prodigiously and read ravenously" while composing cultural calendars and, after his resignation from Messrs. Ward, tutoring a group of children.[17] Since this early period, Machen, who was living a simple life marked by severe privations, acquired his habit to wander around the metropolis in solitary walks, discovering quiet angles of the capital unknown to its great population, and observing with fascination the almost perennial movement of people and transport vehicles. After losing his last pupil (and, therefore, his only source of income), Machen was forced to return to Wales. However, financial aid from several friends of his family allowed him to work on the final proofs and to publish (with George Redway) *The Anatomy of Tobacco* (1884), a treatise that analyzes in detail both the matter and the manner of smoking.[18] The book traces the origins and kinds of tobacco, the single parts that form pipes, the various schools of pipe philosophers with extravagant names, and the hours of the day and the night most pleasant for smoking. The writer argues that smoking in the dark is not pleasurable and that women are not qualified to sell tobacco because they do not smoke. Machen explains his views on the subject with a rich vocabulary and an empirical method, offering precise definitions (in Latin) of his terms and categories (which could sometimes sound granted or exaggerated in respect to the subject). The volume is also flavored by a lot of footnotes that direct the reader to alternative interpretations of the events or theories narrated in the main text.

Machen was then assigned by Redway to the translation of the *Heptameron* of Marguerite of Navarre, a collection of short stories on romantic and sexual topics originally published in 1558, which he rendered in the rich English of the Restoration period (a linguistic style he admired in the seventeenth-century literati he had studied in the past).[19] He completed the translation in February 1885. That very summer Machen returned to Clarendon Road in London after having been offered a job as a cataloger of volumes on mysticism and the occult for Redway (two of his catalogs, published, respectively, in 1887 and 1888, have become highly prized collector's items), and simultaneously practiced shorthand in the evenings.[20] He was then dismissed from Redway and forced to return home for the imminent death of his mother, where he remained from winter 1885 to summer 1886, working at his next manuscript during the nights. After returning to London in early 1887, he took up a residence in Bloomsbury and was initially employed as a secretary for Redway, but became also the editor of *Walford's Antiquarian*. It was in 1887 that Machen met Arthur Edward Waite (1857–1942), who was to become one of his most enduring friends (and promoters). During this time, he courted and married Amelia "Amy" Hoggs, who was over a decade his senior and whom he had first met when he was living at Burlington College. In September, Machen's father died at fifty-seven, just a few months before the heritage from some maternal relatives in Scotland was granted. Machen thus inherited a conspicuous sum of money that gave him a marginal independence for about fifteen years. He resigned from Redway and soon completed and published (with his friends Harry Spurr and Herbert Jones) *The Chronicle of Clemendy* (1888), a framed collection of tales written in the style of Chaucer's *The Canterbury Tales* (c. 1400) and recalling the romance tales of King Arthur as much as the style of Rabelais. *The Chronicle*, initially conceived as a great romance, contains the depiction of many humorous situations (such as the merry Silurian people's fondness for ale in the town of Uske and the story of the drunken monk Brother Drogo). The narration often purposefully avoids the logical progress of the story, continually introducing secondary irrelevant characters, and lingering on the most trivial particulars (which are described with verbose sentences and long, alliterating lists of nouns and verbs) to create a comical effect through the emphasis on joviality, petty courtship, and facetiousness rather than on religiousness or chivalric values. The text itself seems to define its own tortuous playfulness when, in reference to the dispute between two knights, it says: "the Argument . . . had not been concluded . . . but rather mixed, muddled, confounded, obscured, dedalised, and entangled to an intolerable extent."[21]

In 1888, Machen reprised his work of cataloging, but this time for Messrs Robson and Kerslake in Leicester Square.[22] He was assigned the translation of Beroarde de Belville's *Le Moynen de Parvenir*, a playful and ornate novel dated 1610 that he translated first as *The Way to Attain*, and, in its later modified version, as *Fantastic Tales*. Work on the volume was completed in about a year, but Machen simultaneously translated the twelve volumes of *Casanova's Memoirs*, the autobiographical narration of the famous Venetian adventurer and womanizer's life. In 1890, he began to work as a journalist for *The Globe*, *St. James Gazette*, and *The World*.[23] In these journals, he published several short stories as well, including: "The Town of Long Ago" (1889), which lauds a fictional town where a poet grows before making his fortune; "Over the Gate" (1890), which praises the activity of leaning against a gate and looking at the hills, valleys, and the colorful sky on a summer morning while listening to the birds' songs; and "Rus in Urbe" (1890), which sets London's urban parks against the stillness and beauty of the countryside. Some of the short stories written at this time are focused on imaginary lands, such as "Of the Isle of Shadows, and of the Strange Customs of the Men That Dwell There" (1890), which describes a fictional land where an Uncrowned King presides over a murderous, unlawful, pagan people; "Tales from Barataria" (1890), which depicts the witty tricks of its fictional inhabitants; and "A Further Account of the Academy of Lagado" (1890), which continues in the tradition of Swift's *Gulliver's Travels* (1726) the satirical portrayal of the Academy of letters on Laputa, where various professors engage with animosity on unscientific discussions on subjects such as bookselling, translation, diet, and morality. Other short stories are set in a more present, urban setting, such as "A Remarkable Coincidence" (1890), about two Bohemian friends living in Soho and collaborating to the writing of a novel, published ahead of time by only one of them under a pseudonym; and "An Underground Adventure" (1890), about a young man being mistaken for a pretender by a rich widow who seems initially to be a lonely victim of love, but then proposes abruptly and bluntly, accepting no refusals and thus forcing the male protagonist to literally run away from her. Many of the short stories are generally characterized by long, descriptive sentences rich in adjectives, whereas other narratives, such as "The Lost Club" (1890)—on two friends wandering drunk in London and ending up in a club where a strange ritual leads to the disappearance of a gentleman—present short sentences and a fast pace. Particularly worthy of mention is "A Double Return" (1890), recounting how the protagonist discovers that his look-alike has spent the previous night with his own wife. This narrative created much sensation in the public and brought forth a praise from Oscar Wilde, whom the writer had personally met in early 1890.

After a journey to Touraine (the first in a series of visits to France), and after provisionally living in Guilford Street, Machen moved to a cottage in the Chiltern Hills in March 1891, where he completed what was going to be his most-renowned work, "The Great God Pan." Machen lived in the countryside for two years and returned to London in November 1893, first in Great Russell Street and later in Gray's Inn. In 1894, "The Great God Pan" was published. The novella begins with the depiction of an illicit experiment performed by Dr. Raymond and witnessed by Mr. Clarke, over the brain of a young woman, Mary. The experiment was intended to lift the veil preventing the vision of the world of spirit, which is imperceptible to the human senses. Mary thus becomes apparently able to see the horned Greek god, but she becomes "a hopeless idiot" and dies after giving birth to a girl nine months later.[24] In the subsequent decades, a series of unmotivated suicides by gentlemen of good position in London leads the story's protagonist, Villiers, and Mr. Clarke, to suspect Helen Vaughan, a fascinating yet corrupting and malevolent woman. Near the end of the tale, it is revealed that Helen is actually the product of the union of Mary with Pan and that she has been hiding under false identities, approaching several male victims and leading them alternatively to despair, nervous shock, madness, and self-destruction. "The Great God Pan" stirred much criticism from its Victorian public for its implicit representation of illicit sex and its thematic preoccupation with issues of decadence, forbidden knowledge, and the dissolution of "several boundaries, including those between past and present; science and myth; reason and the supernatural; moral constraint and sexual indulgence; self-control and abandonment."[25] It was further criticized for its depiction of man's hysteria and weakness against the rising New Woman.[26] Contemporary critics defined the novella as "a failure and an absurdity" (*The Echo*), "only succeed[ing] in being ridiculous" (*The Manchester Guardian*), and "an incoherent nightmare of sex and the supposed horrible mysteries behind it, such as might conceivably possess a man who was given to a morbid brooding over these matters, but which would soon lead to insanity if unrestrained."[27]

In Chiltern Hills, Machen wrote two untitled books, which he then destroyed unpublished.[28] However, he had also completed "The Inmost Light," which was paired in 1894 with "The Great God Pan" in John Lane's edition of the story. The short story is a typical detective narrative that slowly unveils its central mystery thanks to the main character's ability to link disparate elements (a piece of paper with meaningless writing, a case reported on the journals, some chance encounters, and a stolen box) in a common explanation. The story introduces Dyson, a recurring character in Machen's early production, as a man of letter prone to reveries, who is composed, even pedantic.[29] As Dyson discovers after several investigations, in the squalid suburban area of Harlesden Dr. Black has privately experimented on his wife. Managing to separate her soul from her body, he has confined the former within a precious stone, leaving the woman's body into the possession of a demonic force. The result of such a brutal experiment is witnessed by chance by Dyson when he sees Mrs. Black looking out the window with a "not human" face.[30] The woman dies, apparently of brain disease, and after several months Dyson makes the acquaintance of the dying doctor, who has become a miserable and wretched man living in abject misery. The tale concludes with Dyson's recovery of the doctor's confession along with the shining jewel containing Mrs. Black's soul, which is released by the story's protagonist. As is the case with "The Great God Pan," "The Inmost Light" deals with the theme of forbidden, obscure knowledge, "a region of knowledge . . . which wise men seeing from afar off shun like the plague."[31] Following the tradition of stories of mad scientists such as Mary Shelley's *Frankenstein* (1818) and Dr. Jekyll in the eponymous 1886 novella by Robert Louis Stevenson, and anticipating figures such as H.G. Wells's *The Island of Doctor Moreau* (1896), the doctor's attempt to bridge "the gulf between the world of consciousness and the world of matter" in "The Inmost Light" has disastrous results, for his relatives, colleagues, and friends as well as for his own conscience and health.[32]

In 1895, Machen published (first in the late-spring issues of A.E. Waite's paper *The Unknown World* and subsequently in book form) "The Shining Pyramid," which reintroduces Dyson, this time accompanied by Mr. Vaughan, who invites the protagonist to solve the enigma of a girl's disappearance on the hills of a Welsh village. Dyson's investigations reveal that several mysterious clues, such as the arrangement of small flint arrowheads in different symbolic patterns and red marks on a stone reproducing an odd oval eye, can be explained through the existence of a cave-dwelling dwarfish race (the "little people" that folklore identifies as fairies), who have kidnapped the innocent girl. Dyson and Vaughan locate the missing girl while she is being sacrificed on a pyramid of fire by the evil and deformed creatures who speak with "strident and horrible hissing" during a ceremony that, as Geoffrey Reiter evidences, "is orgiastic but not ecstatic—it is profoundly physical and by no means spiritual."[33] The tale is notable for its atmosphere of mystery, its haunting of the imagination and destabilizing of the rationality of the protagonists (and the readers), and for the depiction of the "desolate loneliness and strangeness of the land" where "the fantastic limestone rocks hinted horror through the darkness."[34]

In the same year, *The Three Impostors: or, The Transmutations* (1895) was published. It is an episodic novel set in London, where Mr. Dyson and his friend Charles Phillips, a student of physical science, discuss their finding of a gold coin of some antiquity, lost by a gentleman with the spectacles in front of Dyson during a wild chase. The titular impostors, three suspicious weird-mannered individuals, who have been given the task to kill the man with the spectacles and retrieve the gold coin, approach separately Dyson and Phillips on several occasions during the story, hoping to acquire some information on their victim while assuming false identities that are recounted through a series of fantastic tales delivered to the two protagonists. These tales include the unwilling involvement of a man with a group of outlaws in America ("Novel of the Dark Valley"), a professor's disappearance on the Grey Hills—which is caused by the evil actions of the "little people"— ("Novel of the Black Seal"), the death of a collector of instruments of torture by his latter purchase ("Novel of the Iron Maid," the only story that had been written independently and was later incorporated into *The Three Impostors*), and a student's transformation into a dark, putrid, bubbling mass, caused by a medical white powder that is actually Vinum Sabbati—the wine used during witches' Sabbath ("Novel of the White Powder"). As Reiter has noted, the three impostors, whose tales are highly aestheticized, are actually passive (they fail in their mission to retrieve the Gold Tiberius) and the reader is always one step ahead.[35] This volume, published by Keynotes series, was much criticized for its decadent tropes, which came under heavy attack, especially after the trials and conviction of Oscar Wilde (and in spite of the many subsequent protestations by the writer himself), and for its borrowings from Stevenson's *New Arabian Nights* (1882) and *The Dynamiter* (1885).[36] The volume was therefore a commercial failure, although it was reevaluated in the following decades and could now be considered as one of the writer's best works.

The next publication by Machen was "The Red Hand" (1895), a short story whose protagonists are Dyson (always moved by "a fervent curiosity and an innate liking for the obscure") and the skeptical and incredulous Mr. Phillipps.[37] At the beginning of the tale, the two main characters argue over the presence of troglodytes in contemporary London, while having a walk in a derelict area of the city. Here, they find the corpse of Sir Thomas Vivian, apparently murdered with a primitive flint knife. The titular hand, painted with red chalk near the body of the victim and considered to be a sign of the evil eye, is one of the clues (along with a letter bearing a bizarre handwriting and a stone table bearing the same mark of the hand) that lead to the confession of the miserable Mr. Selby, a former friend of the murdered man. Sir Vivian had found the artifacts while searching for a lost race of primitive people in Western England and was then killed by Mr. Selby in self-defense when he revealed the actual discovery of the dwarfish and accursed race.

After spending two years (1895–1897) writing two works that were rejected by several publishers (*The Hill of Dreams* and *Ornaments in Jade*) only to be published over a decade later, in 1898 Machen was employed as a member of the editorial staff of the weekly journal, *Literature*. He produced a lot of unsigned journalism during this year. As soon as he resigned from *Literature* at the beginning of 1899, he worked on three more books: *Hieroglyphics*, "The White People," and *A Fragment of Life*. In 1899, Machen was greatly afflicted by the death of his wife Amy, whom he rarely mentioned in his following writings. This has been considered one of the causes for his subsequent involvement with occultism and mysticism, a move that was also motivated by his personal experience of some occult events at the time (which he later described in detail in the autobiography *Things Near and Far*).[38] He joined his friend A.E. Waite as a member of the Hermetic Order of the Golden Dawn, a hierarchical society founded in the late 1880s with the express intent to promote esoteric philosophy and to study Kabbalah.[39] The Order actually revealed to Machen no secrets or hidden meanings of life and the world and at the turn of the century he converted to Christianity.[40]

Between 1901 and 1903, after his inheritance had been almost depleted, Machen began to act as a bit player in Frank Benson's Repertory Company (the Company performed, among other works, several Shakespearean plays in London and in a tour of the West, but Machen generally had only minor roles). During his theatrical years, Machen completed the manuscript of *Hieroglyphics* and sent it to Grant Richards, who published it in March 1902. The book is a literary tract presented as a series of notes reporting the words of an unnamed "obscure literate Hermit" recorded during some conversations with the author.[41] The main argument of the volume is that "fine literature" is constituted by "ecstacy"—intended also as "rapture, beauty, adoration, wonder, awe, mystery, sense of the unknown, desire for the unknown" and as "the power of exciting a vivid curiosity"—and that art is "the sole channel by which the highest and purest truth can reach us."[42] The hermit favors fine literature as an allegory of life over a realistic and faithful representation of experience. He distinguishes art from artifice and elaborates on several rhetorical devices. He initially explains at length the meaning of all the essential terms he uses, referencing works of world literature as examples of his theories, but also using a pleasant, conversational tone that makes the subject accessible and not strictly theoretical. The hermit himself admits to a tendency to wander continually between examples as different as the *Odyssey*, M. Dupin's detective stories, *Vanity Fair*, *Don Quixote*, and the past and present glorifications of drunkenness. *Hieroglyphics* received mixed reviews, although it went through several editions in the following years.

Machen, who had been engaged in the meantime with Miss Dorothie Purefoy Huddleston (1878–1947), momentarily quitted the company, left his rooms in Soho for Cosway Street, and married on June 25, 1903. He then reprised his acting career for several months during 1904. In the meantime, the writer had been contacted by his friend Waite, who published the short story "The White People" (which had been written in 1899) and the short novel *A Fragment of Life*. The former begins with a discussion between the characters of Ambrose and Cotgrave on sin and the unconsciousness of wickedness. A concrete example is offered through the reading of a diary recounting pagan rituals performed by an adolescent girl in the woods in emulation of those ceremonies enacted by her nurse that she witnessed when she was a child. The diary also reports tales the young girl heard about the titular white people (a race akin to fairies and nymphs) appearing and communing with human beings, especially in implicit acts of a sexual nature. The tale presents mystic knowledge as derived along a female line of women who desire independence from men and cultivate their freedom in the solitude of the forests (the nurse learned the songs from her own grandmother). The descriptions of the secretive woods "where the air was full of whispers and a pale, dead light came out from the rotten trunks that were lying on the ground" are noteworthy, as is the stream-of-consciousness style of the girl's diary, whose thoughts moves smoothly from images and memories to sensations and reverie.[43]

A Fragment of Life (1904) narrates the daily domestic vicissitudes of the Darnells, who live in Shepherd's Bush. One of the story's greatest merits is its ability to recreate, with precision, the atmosphere of serenity (and even boredom) of an affectionate married couple and the milieu of privacy in the home, with its habits, perfumes, and small talk about daily occurrences or neighbor gossip. The story is also an example of how Machen "can invest the ordinary with a sense of numinous wonder."[44] Indeed, on the one hand, the narrative is characterized by uneventful discussions on the possible refurbishing of the spare room, on domestic expenses, on the problems between their servant Alice and her would-be mother-in-law, and on Edward's peregrinations through London's suburbs. On the other, the slow spiritual rebirth of the couple is elaborated gracefully near the end of the narrative through a series of dreams, vigils, memories of childhood, and Edward Darnell's research on his ancestors, which helps the couple to become conscious of a higher meaning in life and urges them to abandon London for the ancient woods of Wales.[45]

One of Machen's less known works is *The House of the Hidden Light*, co-written with Waite and printed in 1904, but only in three copies. The volume is made of thirty-five letters by Machen and Waite (whose pseudonyms are, respectively, "Filius Aquarum" and "Elias Artista"), addressed to each other between 1899 and 1903. Best defined by R.A. Gilbert as "a record of a quest in which two men sought to find their souls by way of earthly love," the cryptic epistolary descriptions of the two men's attempts to find light out of a dark path are conveyed through complex language—filled with occult terminology and characterized by repetitions, Latin mottoes, symbols, and long lists of nouns—that alludes to the rituals of the Hermetic Order of the Golden Dawn.[46] It also simultaneously attempts to conceal references to real places and persons (especially, the two women courted at the time of the correspondence by Machen and Waite: the young actress, Vivienne Pierpont, whom Machen named "The Shepherdess," and Dora Stuart-Menteath).[47] The book, recently re-published by Tartarus Press, has been generally ignored by the critics and has been rarely included in Machen's oeuvre because of its cryptic language and hermetic contents.

In 1905, after several months of rest, Machen toured with Herbert Tree's acting company and then dedicated his time to research (especially on the legend of the Saint Graal) at the British Museum in anticipation of his next literary work. In 1906, he collected, with Grant Richards, his best works in the volume *The House of Souls*, adding a new, personal preface that indicates the genesis of the single works present in the volume and explains the writer's deliberate change of style during the 1890s, from the ornate prose of his translations and earlier works to the journalistic style of his subsequent writing.[48] *The House of Souls* sold well, but it also received further harsh criticism. After being commissioned to a new work by Mr. Francis Griffiths, Machen wrote *Dr. Stiggins: His Views and Principles* as a retort to this criticism. Conceived as an amplification of his preface to *The House of Souls*, the volume—which was published in late 1906, but initially attracted no notice at all by the critics—is a satirical work in the form of a series of six interviews to the titular character, who addresses directly and confidentially the interviewer and presents himself as a minister of the Free Church.[49] The book uses clever dialectics, witty humor, frequent digressions into secondary subjects, and an enormous amount of references to European history and English literature to make fun of subjects such as English Protestantism, corrupt Roman Catholicism, and American Democracy (whose occupation of other countries and massacre of innocents are presented as "necessary and justifiable, for they are the will of the people").[50] *Dr. Stiggins* also draws continuous comparisons between American and English beliefs, diets, and lifestyles, advocates the abolishment of history from schools (because its undemocratic trend leads to forget and despise the common people), and criticizes with a hilarious and inoffensive tone a vast array of subjects, from the dogmatism of Dante's *Divine Comedy*, the obscenity and immorality of Chaucer and the comedy of manners to the contemporary faith in supernatural phenomena and journalism.

In 1907, Grant Richards reconsidered the manuscript of *The Garden of Avallaunius* (which had been written between 1895 and 1897 and had been politely rejected three times) and decided to publish it under the title *The Hill* *of Dreams.*⁵¹ Conceived by Machen as his own *magnum opus* and considered by some critics as the writer's actual best work, it is a novel set in Wales and London. The protagonist is the adolescent Lucian Taylor, who is fond of reading and of visiting the ruins of a Roman fort on the top of a hill near his cottage during his holidays from school. There he falls asleep to "queer, nightmarish dreams" that imprint on him a sensation of mysticism that will haunt him for the rest of his days.⁵² At twenty-three, Lucian attempts to write a manuscript, which is officially rejected by a publisher but is then amply plagiarized by another writer. This occasion provides the reader with the description of the ideal style and meaning of literature and of what is expected from an author by literary critics. The novel alternates Lucian's literary ambitions and his first love for a local girl with vivid and precise descriptions of a landscape characterized by hills, torrents, and the colors of sunsets, while recreating the atmosphere, small talks, and malignancies of Caermaen's country life. All of these themes produce Lucian's reveries and the flights of his imagination, which creates visions of the Roman past. The protagonist's reminiscences of his readings are alternated to his moments of profound isolation and loneliness once he moves to London to cultivate his writing talent. In its second half *The Hill of Dreams* offers great psychological insights on human nature, especially when it lingers on the difficulty for the protagonist to create a literary work, on "the agonies of the artificer who strives and perseveres in vain," and the misery coming from the fear of failure—a failure that is only delayed throughout the narrative until its tragic ending, which offers no redemption in spite of the spiritual renewal of the protagonist.⁵³

In the first half of 1907, the Welsh writer worked on and completed a new novel (*The Secret Glory*). At this time, he had been attending the New Bohemians Club, where he met Richard Middleton (for whose posthumous 1912 collection *The Ghost-Ship* Machen wrote the preface) and Lord Alfred Douglas (who had recently acquired *The Academy* and soon invited Machen to write for the journal).⁵⁴ While resuming his acting career throughout 1908 until his last professional performance in April 1909, Machen wrote as a columnist, reviewer, and reporter for newspapers and literary journals such as *The Neolith*, *T.P.'s Weekly*, and the *Daily Mail*.⁵⁵ He obtained a permanent position at the *Evening News* in autumn 1910, but this occupation forced him to tight schedules and pressing deadlines for several years and to reporting both interesting and tedious events/interviews.⁵⁶ In 1914, Machen published "The Bowmen" in the *Evening News*, a short story about the recent battle of Mons in Belgium between the German and the outnumbered English troops. This later became one of the most popular works in the author's oeuvre. In this narrative, after resigning to an imminent and inevitable death the British troops in the trenches witness the apparition of shining archers whose arrows decimate the enemy lines. The short tale generated immediately an intense debate and was reprinted several times because it was considered to be an authentic testimony of a miraculous occurrence. Machen himself had to repeatedly admit the fictional nature of his story against an obstinate public desirous to believe in angels. "The Bowmen" was then republished in 1915 in the collection *The Angels of Mons, The Bowmen and Other Legends of War*, a collection of short stories about angelic apparitions during World War I. The volume includes "The Soldiers' Rest" (about a soldier who is captured and wounded by the Germans in France and narrates his encounter with some heavenly beings praising his courage and readiness to sacrifice himself), and "The Monstrange" (written in the form of a German soldier's diary, recounting his hearing of a church bell, the vision of a white robe, and the smelling of incense as probable hallucinations dictated by his remorse for the cruelties he had perpetrated). In the volume's introduction and postscript Machen reconstructs the entire debate about the veracity of "The Bowmen" and reiterates that "it had no foundation in fact of any kind or sort."[57]

In 1915, the Faith Press published "The Great Return," an eighty-page short story that narrates the fictional events occurring in Lantrisant, a coastal town in Arfonshire, "a land that seemed to be in a holy, happy dream."[58] The narrator visits the place after reading a newspaper article briefly reporting the strange occurrence of mysterious lights flashing out in the night in the middle of the sea and from the local church. The narrator, initially dismissive of the reporter's article, investigates that the church has been smelling of incense and odors of paradise since the occurrence of the lights. He gathers several testimonies of many of the village people, who have brightened, illuminated faces, "glowing with an ineffable joy," are exalted in their hearts after further miraculous events have taken place (such as a rose of fire appearing over the sea and the hearing of ringing of bells and the chanting of choirs), and have recovered from their illnesses.[59] Alternating between an explanation of the facts relying on the idea of a collective auditory hallucination and an acceptance of the supernatural nature of the events, the narrator finally connects the various tales to the Graal legend and its keeper, the "King Fisherman." He argues that the place has received a visitation from heaven and from the figures populating ancient religious myth. The tale is an epitome of a rational mind's acceptance of the wondrous and supernatural against the habit of thought and the difficulty in making the required "wildest guess as to the nature of the whole picture."[60] Contrary to *The Angels of Mons*, which sold over 55,000 copies by the end of 1915, "The Great Return" sold poorly and received very few reviews.

Machen's subsequent work was *The Terror* (it was first serialized in the *Evening News* in 1916 and then published by Duckworth in 1917), one of his most celebrated works. The short novel begins with the rumors about a series of events that are delaying the British intervention in France during World

War I, events whose dissemination on newspapers has been forbidden by a Secret Circular. These include a plane brought down by a flight of thousands of pigeons and many unexplained deaths in the countryside. The story egregiously traces the cumulative spread of the terror ("there's terror in the air," affirms one of the characters), which infects the inhabitants of the Welsh country (named Meirion), who formulate many different theories to explain the facts (such as the presence of a madman, a double-personality killer, German agents or a Z Ray influencing the psychic ether).[61] In spite of the accumulation of evidence—horses panic, bees and farm dogs become overly aggressive, trees change their shape and are lighted, and people are killed "in an inscrutable manner by some inscrutable means, day after day"—no final explanation is reached by the characters.[62] A good summary of the first three-fourths of the book would be: "Here was horror, there was horror; but there was no link to join one horror with another; no common basis of knowledge from which the connection between this horror and that horror might be inferred."[63] At the end of the narrative, just before the terror suddenly ends, Dr. Lewis plausibly speculates that animals have revolted against humankind because the latter, by being involved in a world war, has renounced its place as the supreme and most righteous species.[64]

In spite of his strenuous work as a journalist, 1917 was a good year for Machen. His daughter, Janet, was born on February 26. He began a correspondence with Vincent Starrett, one of his greatest promoters over the Atlantic, and he was commissioned a series of theological articles—collected in the sixty-page volume *War and The Christian Faith* (1918)—that were well-received.[65] The subsequent years were marked by his work as a journalist, his family's move from Edward House, Lisson Grove, to St John's Wood (in 1919), and his work for *The Lyons Mail* (for which he wrote the essays that later made up the collection *Dog and Duck*, published in book format in 1924). In 1921, Machen left his post at the *Evening News*, but his fortune changed considerably as soon as a new edition of the *Memoirs of Casanova* was issued (with a new introduction by the writer), and when Mr. Alfred Knopf decided to introduce the writer to American readers by re-publishing his works. The specific format of the volumes printed by Knopf, which had a bright yellow binding and a dark blue paper label with golden lettering, made Machen's volumes instantly recognizable in the American market.[66] Simultaneously, many of Machen's earlier volumes were being re-issued in England, including the Caerleon Edition of his works, printed in nine volumes by Martin Secker. The success that Machen enjoyed internationally during the 1920s finally produced a long-awaited (and deserved) period of moderate comfort for the writer.

The 1920s were also marked by the publication of several new volumes, the first of whom was *The Secret Glory* (1922). This novel recounts the story of Ambrose Meyrick, a student at Lupton Public School, where he is bullied by some of his schoolmates. The narrative initially alternates between the actions and thoughts of Ambrose, who loves architecture and dreams of the religious legends of his native West, and the schoolmaster Mr. Horbury, severe, sadistic in his punishments and extremely imaginative in his ambitious plans for the future development of the school. The story focuses then only upon the fifteen-year-old student, his initial resistance to the school's disciplinary and teaching system, and his subsequent mock acceptance of it. *The Secret Glory* also depicts Ambrose's experiences after the end of school, his liberating visit to London with his servant girl Nelly, and his passion for the Celtic cultural heritage, "that great dream of Celtic sanctity that for me had always been *the* dream."[67] Ambrose's oddities culminate with his journey to the East which, according to a very brief (and unsatisfying) epilogue, leads him to the recovery of the Saint Grail. The book is a pleasant work providing readers with an accurate description of life in public schools, especially in some of its negative aspects (such as the lectures of the Classics, which are described as being taught in a nauseating way, and the bullying occurring among the students). According to Joshi, *The Secret Glory* "is too unfocused and too desultory in its narration," a characteristic that partly marred the book's success.[68]

Between 1922 and 1924, Machen published his autobiography in three volumes, which brought him some gratifying critical acclaim and contributed to solidifying his fame.[69] The first volume, *Far Off Things* (1922), had been written in 1914 and recounts the early years of the writer's life amid the natural landscapes of Gwent with its wild hills, Roman forts, and white farms. The book lingers on the countryside's inspiring cityscape and its "vague, indefinable sense of awe and mystery and terror," which is often compared to the landscape and lifestyle of London.[70] Machen does not present the events of his life in a chronological order and until the last third of the book he jumps from past memories and images to literary digressions, anecdotes, and tales of his neighbors. What emerges is the writer's youth as an only child as characterized by loneliness and the curiosity for his country; his heterogeneous readings and literary influences (*The Arabian Nights*, *Don Quixote*, *Confessions of an English Opium Eater*, and Swinburne's *Songs Before Sunrise* are the most prominent); his precarious living conditions in an overwhelming London (which is defined as a "new unknown world"); his first attempts at writing since 1880; his uninteresting journalistic days; and his poverty and solitude in the metropolis.[71]

The second volume of the autobiography, titled *Things Near and Far* (1923),[72] resumes the narrative from winter 1884–1885, during the writer's residence at his native village, where he spent much time "wondering and dreaming and setting my heart on the hopeless endeavor of letters" and continues with Machen's return to London, his work as a cataloger, translator, journalist, and actor as well as his literary production until 1902.[73] Most interesting are those tales offering the genesis of Machen's stories, but, as is the case with *Far Off Things*, the first-person narration of the writer's life and his changes of residence are often interrupted by digressions on matters such as spiritualism and Theosophy, Dorè's paintings of France, his favorite dishes and wines, the activity of indexing, and the connection between material and spiritual things. Such digressions are instrumental for Machen to clearly explain his views and reveal explicitly his beliefs.

The third and last volume of the autobiography, *The London Adventure, or the Art of Wandering* (1924), is equally filled with digressions on various matters up to the point of refusing to talk about Machen's life, indulging instead on peripheral matters such as literary and historical issues, scientific disputes, *poltergeist* phenomena and séances, and the very genesis of the volume at hand. The book recounts the writer's life during the late 1890s and 1900s, but, as the title suggests, it is mainly focused on those errands Machen conducted through the streets and suburbs of the metropolis, which he attempts to catalog in what he calls "my London science."[74] Anecdotes about his life and odd adventures are indeed scattered through the descriptions of the areas of the capital that he visited. Machen does not hide his detestation for modern red brick buildings, whereas he expresses his appreciation for older houses and taverns, the "remnants of a former age."[75] *The London Adventure* thus exemplifies "the study of the specific effects of the geographical environment, consciously organised or not, on the emotions and behaviour of individuals" that over thirty years later (in 1955) the lettrist Guy Debord codified as psychogeography.[76] Machen has been considered as one of the precursors of psychogeography for his imaginative reworking of the city (which occurs also in his Gothic tales, which transform the capital into a haunting, labyrinthic environment) and the unexpected insights gained during the aimless wandering.

Contemporary to his autobiographies, Machen published the collection of two stories *Strange Roads. With The Gods in Spring* (first serialized in 1919, then printed in book form in 1923 by The Classic Press), which includes several illustrations by Joseph Simpson and H. R. Millar. "Strange Roads" describes a series of paths in Wales whose beauty is suggested by the detailed description of the landscape, plants, and trees, and where the narrator can hear an invisible group of people pursuing him that, he wonders, could be the Fairy Folk. In the latter part of the tale, Machen recounts the experience of a friend of his who investigated the Ulster Movement in Ireland as a journalist. "With the Gods in Spring" applies the theme of the "illuminating secret, hidden beneath all the surfaces of things" to a couple of paintings of the head of the Christ allegedly executed by ladies under spirit influence and compares it to the narrator's own experience of the glimpse on the unknown and the divine during a winter walk to Usk.[77]

In 1923, Vincent Starrett edited a collection of tales by Machen titled *The Shining Pyramid*, which includes, along with the titular narrative, some earlier short stories, such as "The Lost Club," "A Wonderful Woman" (1890), on two friends meeting each other after a long time, one of them having recently married with the other gentleman's former lover, who has changed her name and pretends not to recognize him; and "Drake's Drum" (1919), on the titular instrument being heard aboard the British ships during the surrender of the German fleet after the 1918 armistice. Among the more recent pieces in the collection is "The Priest and the Barber," which revisits fictionally Machen's own experience as a cataloger by narrating a priest's exploration of a barber's dusty library, which is endowed with both ancient books on occultism and modern volumes on pseudosciences. The most successful short story in *The Shining Pyramid*, however, is "Out of the Earth" (1923). Its narrative begins with reports of some evil rumors about the misbehavior of children at different watering-places in Wales. Machen, addressing readers as himself, refuses to name such locations to avoid the rumors being considered as evidence, as "sworn truth," as the case with "The Bowmen" five years earlier.[78] As the rumors grow "more monstrous and incredible," the narrator attempts to prove them wrong by spending a pleasant holiday in the area himself, until a friend of his describes his encounter with a group of foul-mouthed, irreverent, and violent children who are revealed to be visible and audible only to other children and childlike people.[79] The rest of the collection is made of essays such as: "The Art of Dickens" and "Unconscious Magic," on literary realism and symbolism and the effects of literature; "Education and the Uneducated," on the connection between "book-learning" and education; "New Lamps for Old," on universal Good Will and progress upward; "Mandatum Novissimum," on socialism and poverty; and "Sad Happy Race," a reflection on acting and theater companies.

The following year saw the publication of *Dog and Duck: A London Calendar Et Cætera* (1924), a collection of twenty-seven essays generally ordered according to festivities and events occurring in chronological order in the calendar year and dealing with subjects as disparate as the observance of the tradition of Valentines ("On Valentines and Other Things"), boat races ("July Sport"), the first autumnal fogs ("The Fogs of Yesteryear"), astrology ("Some February Stars"), and weather talk ("March and a Moral"). The ironic but respectful essays use a placid tone and accessible language, although they are simultaneously erudite in their references to historical and literary sources as well as in their reconstruction of the etymology of the terms (such as the Latin origins of the word "cake" in "On Simnel Cakes"). Some of the essays use long digressions that lead the reader quite off topic, from old English games to an unsolved murder case ("Dog and Duck"), and from jokes to "in camera" fairies ("April Fool").[80]

Machen then published an earlier work of his, *Ornaments in Jade*, which he had begun almost two decades earlier and was finally published in a limited print run.[81] This is a collection of ten elegant prose poems, which use evocative language that lingers on the depictions of the landscape with its colors and perfumes. "Midsummer" is about the magical, soothing atmosphere surrounding a farm-house at dusk and during the night; and "Nature, or, The Splendid Holiday" contains some very poetic descriptions of the countryside's landscape, filled with colors and light during a summer holiday. Such an investment in the poetic description of the setting is equally applied to the urban milieu of the capital in "The Holy Things," describing a moment of epiphany experienced by a man dissatisfied with his life and work during the incessant procession and humming of omnibuses and the voices and cries of people in Holborn. Equally, "Psychology" depicts a writer's observation of a quiet and secluded quarter of West London's inhabitants and sets it against his secret thoughts and fantasies of madness, wickedness, and lust. As Reiter has observed, the poems "share certain overlapping themes: the baseness of shallow materialism, a glorification of ritualism (particularly pagan), a delight in nature."[82] Ritualism is indeed evident in the case of "The Ceremony," the story of a girl remembering a ritual that was performed by her nurse on a grey stone in the wood when she was a child and led to the brief opening of a portal on an alternate world of flames. Ecstatic reverie is also characteristic of "The Rose Garden," a tale about a girl dreamily watching, from her window, a thin and dark stranger boy standing on a pedestal and holding a double flute, the boy who has taught her "the perfect knowledge" of how to reach the world beyond the senses through rapture after rejecting all of her family's teachings.[83] "The Turanians" is another example of a young female protagonist's admiration for the "faun-like grace" of a group of gypsies camping in the wood.[84]

In 1924, Machen also published *The Glorious Mystery*, a collection of five short stories and twenty-one articles made up of contributions to *The Academy*; *The Neolith*; *The Quest*, *John O'London's Weekly*, and *T.P.'s Weekly* that was edited by Vincent Starrett. The short stories included in the collection are: "The Holy Things," "Psychology," "The Rose Garden" (from *Ornaments in Jade*), "The Iron Maid" (from *The Three Impostors*), and the recent "A New Christmas Carol" (1924)—an (unfortunately) very short sequel to Charles Dickens' 1843 tale, which recreates the original story's atmosphere and introduces a new spectral apparition representing Ruin and Despair that visits old, good Scrooge in his dreams. The essays explore the Celtic and pagan origins of the myth of Holy Grail ("The Sangraal"), Christian religion ("Faith and Conduct" and "The Apostolic Ideal"), and literary matters ("Edgar Allan Poe"). They also reveal the writer's interest in Medievalism ("The Dark Ages") and his dislike for Protestantism ("Ecclesia Anglicana").

An atypical work in Machen's oeuvre, *The Canning Wonder* (1925) discusses the enigmatic case of Elizabeth Canning, a domestic servant who disappeared for four weeks in 1753 and, after her return in an emaciated and starved condition, accused a gypsy woman of abducting her and attempting to force her into prostitution. After initially proposing that Canning was an "infernal liar" and her story therefore a fabrication, Machen reports the girl's tale of imprisonment, pointing out, in clear and factual language, the discrepancies, inconsistencies, and contradictions of her story.[85] The writer then criticizes the irregular proceedings of the court, attributing the initial jury's verdict against the gypsy woman to "that disease, obscure and sometimes terrible, called Collective Hallucination or Delusion," and finally reports Canning's charge with perjury at the second trial.[86] The narrative thus assumes the form of a court drama, where the different and contradictory testimonies are portrayed through a continuous sense of injustice, hidden scheming, and deliberate perjurers, and concludes with the statement that in 1773 Canning's "secret died with her."[87]

In 1926, two more collections of essays were published by Machen: *Dreads and Drolls* and *Notes and Queries*. The former comprises twenty-nine accounts (out of the sixty-two originally published in *The Graphic*) of strange, inexplicable cases that in the volume's introduction the writer defines as generally "veridical," although he also admits that "here and there imagination plays a small part."[88] The cases include the jokes played on the famous clown Joe Grimaldi at the beginning of the nineteenth century ("The Man with the Silver Staff"); the return of long-lost relatives and their further sudden disappearance ("The Adventure of the Long-Lost Brother" and "The Strange Case of Emily Weston"); the disturbances created by a ghost ("7B Coney Court"); and the adventures overseas of a kidnapped gentleman, whose wife and children are charged with his murder during his absence ("The Campden Wander"). At the end of the various cases, Machen illustrates the opposing rational and supernatural explanations. Other essays of the collection focus instead on different matters, such as the birth of clubs ("How Clubs Began") and the loss of the inns ("A Lament for London's Lost Inns"), the styles of letter-writing ("Polite Correspondance"), and executions ("Deadly Nevergreen").

Notes and Queries (1926) is a collection of fifteen essays (all originally published in *T.P.'s Weekly* in 1908–1909) on disparate subjects such as a fictional conversation on love between Lancelot and would-be Queen Guinevere and the latter's love for the valiant knight ("Lancelot and Guinevere"), the real paternity of the works of the Bard ("Shakespeare and Shakspere"), the unalterable condition of humankind through the historical ages ("A New Year Meditation"), the immorality of politicians ("Casuistry"), the actual healing powers of the medicines bought by the English people ("Imagination and Health"), the legend of the Graal ("Celtic Magic" and "The Holy Graal"), and Socialism ("Justice, Liberty—and Fallacy"). The essays have a conversational though erudite tone, them being actively engaged in a debate with many literary and critical sources, but they also benefit from the subtle and derisory irony typical of the writer.

By 1927, the Machen boom was waning and the Welsh writer was mainly working on introductions for other people's volumes, articles for some journals, and as a chief reader for Ernest Benn Ltd (a position that he kept for six years). At the end of the year, the Machens moved to 28 Loudoun Road and, in 1929, they moved to Lynwood, Amersham. There Machen, now aged sixty-six, alternated between periods of sickness and serenity. In 1930, the fifty-page book *Tom O'Bedlam and His Song*, an essay on rationalism and humankind's actual lack of reason (inspired by the popular song of a former harmless resident of London's psychiatric asylum), was published. In 1931, Machen composed "Opening the Door" for the anthology of fifteen ghost stories *When Churchyards Yawn*. It recounts the tale of the six-week disappearance of retired scholar Secretan Jones in 1907 from his house in Canonbury. During an interview with the narrator it emerges that Jones, an advocate of "the grave menace of the new mechanical transport," recalls his memory becoming progressively more and more unreliable and objects in his room disappearing (and sometimes reappearing) suddenly.[89] Jones has no recollection of his own absence and, fearing a nervous breakdown, he leaves for a vacation in the Black Mountains, where he finally disappears without leaving any traces.

In the early 1930s, Machen contributed to *The Literary Merit of the English Bible* (1931)—a collection of articles by writers such as Arthur Conan Doyle and Sir Quiller-Couch—he published the little leaflet "In the 'Eighties," and supplied a series of monthly articles to *The Dalton Citizen*.[90] He also worked intensely as reviewer and essayist for *Everyman*, *The Sunday Referee*, *The New Statesman*, *The Sunday Times*, *The Independent*, *Time and Tide*, *The Daily Telegraph*, and *The Observer*. His most notable work from this period, however, though unappreciated by the critics and the public, is *The Green Round* (1933); Machen's last novel. The story initially presents a Smith, of Wimbledon, who complains publicly about the construction of a red brick palace over the peaceful dunes near the picturesque village of Porth, in the West of Wales—in the area known as "the green round"—where dancing and all sorts of entertainment are practiced. However, Smith later discovers, there exists actually no such building. The protagonist of the story, the fifty-five-year-old scholar of fairy legends Mr. Lawrence Hillyer, is introduced after the preface as a solitary man experiencing an existential crisis who is advised by his doctor to visit a seaside village. In Porth, he apparently recovers completely, but he is then accused of being friend with—and possibly an accomplice of—a dwarfish man he is seen him with by other people, who has murdered and mutilated a farmer's wife. When Mr. Hillyer returns to London more people see him in the company of the brutish man, and a series of accidents involving the breaking of objects and furniture occur near him until he convinces himself that he is delusional. Mr. Hillyer's doctor verifies his patient's story, but the protagonist of the novel actually starts seeing his dwarfish nemesis himself and finally expatriates. The novel, defined by Reiter as "a cobbling together of ideas from across Machen's career ... poorly made and unfocused," was poorly received.[91] The supernatural occurrences are alternated to the characters' discussions of matters such as the intermingling of the dreaming and the waking states, statistics, and dreams, which delay the progress of an otherwise suspenseful story.

Among the last works of the writer was the collection *The Children of the Pool and Other Stories* (1936), which comprises six short stories. In the renowned title story, the narrator encounters James Roberts, an old acquaintance of his, while visiting a wooded region of Wales. After a walk to a black pool in the middle of twisted woods, Roberts' nerves are shattered by his encounters with a young unseen female figure haunting him in the woods and at his farm and reminding him loudly of his past sins. The narrator refuses to believe in the existence of the blackmailing girl, whom their tenant Mrs. Morgan believes to be one of the children of the pool. He thinks that his friend's consciousness and guilt have produced a monster out of his imagination after having been influenced by the horrific landscape of the black pool. Wales offers the background landscape also in "Change," which portrays the seaside village of Meirion, where the narrator belittles the "damned superstitious nonsense" of the local people lighting candles in the night to keep fairies away until a visitor's child is exchanged with a fairy creature near a cave as a consequence of a magical incantation performed by the apparently young nursery-governess.[92] The 1936 volume also includes "The Tree of Life," a twice-told tale about Teilo Morgan, last descendant of a wealthy family of the Welsh landed gentry, who invests his energies in the development of experimental farming of his property and plants the Arbor Vitæ on the grounds; and "The Bright Boy," on a young Oxford graduate who is employed as the tutor of a young precocious pupil living in the countryside who is actually a fifty-year-old criminal with a diminutive stature and juvenile appearance. One of the most popular tales in the collection among contemporary fans of Machen's oeuvre is "Out of the Picture," which links two disparate events in a common explanation. The story begins with a discussion about abstract rather than imitative painting (informed by Kabbala teachings) between the narrator and the painter, M'Calmont. The latter, as the protagonist later discovers, has painted the same distorted, "piteous and malignant" human figure again and again in his works.[93] The narrator then tells us about a child surrounded by strange phenomena, and of numerous outrageous attacks committed in London's fog by a malevolent dwarf who is finally identified as the subject of M'Calmont's paintings. A similar structure involving different overlapping tales is present in "The Exalted Omega," in which the apathetic and joyless Mansel experiences a supernatural occurrence when he hears a woman's voice in his room. Simultaneously, the medium Mrs. Ladislaw, the authenticity of whose powers is severely doubted—because her "childish tricks" have been exposed repeatedly—delivers a message from the deceased Mansel warning of the death by poisoning of a lady in the future, which actually occurs in Mansel's flat after the new tenants have settled in.[94] The final, non-definitive explanation of the story remains unsolved, and it could be either merely circumstantial or supernatural (as due to real messages from the dead).[95]

In 1936, the collection *The Cosy Room and Other Stories*, edited by John Gawsworth, was published. This book contains several poems from *Ornaments in Jade*, but also older short stories such as "A Wonderful Woman," "The Double Return," "The Lost Club," "The Hidden Mystery" (1908)—on an art critic's (and the public's) incapacity to recognize, completely appreciate, or explicitly elaborate upon the value of works of art—and "Drake's Drum." More recent stories are: "A New Christmas Carol," "Munitions of War" (originally published in *The Ghost-Book*, edited by Cynthia Asquith, in 1926), about ghost ships appearing during the night in Westpool's quays; "The Islington Mystery" (1927, first published in the collection of detective stories *The Black Cap*)—which depicts the morbid interest of the public in the details of murder cases through the tale of a taxidermist's (Harold Boale) alleged murder of his own wife, and his trial (presented as an unsolved case on which the narrator passes no judgment). "The Gift of Tongues" (1927) is about a minister experiencing an ecstatic moment in which he speaks an unidentified language during Christmas mass in the Welsh village of Treowen. The collection also includes "Awaking" (1930), on the dreams of a young man visiting a medieval fair, and "The Compliments of the Season" (1934), on a flock of birds recreating a religious figure in a cradle of moss. The most renown tales of the collection are the titular "The Cosy Room" (written in 1929), which vividly depicts the paranoia, "bitter agony," and incipient madness experienced by a fugitive murderer hiding in London; and "N" (1936).[96] "N" exemplifies the psychogeographic, imaginative description of the capital by presenting the encounter of three friends who recall their London vicissitudes and discuss about the streets of the metropolis as they were four/five decades earlier. One of the characters mentions a suburban park near Stoke Newington that is unexpectedly unknown to all interlocutors. The matter is momentarily abandoned as unimportant, until Arnold, the story's protagonist, finds mention of such a luxuriant and beatitude-inspiring park in a nineteenth-century text. He therefore visits Stoke Newington and receives a third testimony of the existence of the park when he is told about an escaped lunatic who affirmed to see such a view from his lodging's window.

The Children of the Pool was followed by "Ritual" (1937), a short story set in Whitsun holiday in London that depicts the coincidence witnessed by the narrator and an American friend of his between the pastime of a group of children pretending to kill and bury one of them in North London Square and the actual death of a young boy in the same period. The last collection published during Machen's lifetime is *Holy Terrors* (1946), which includes some of the tales already published in *Ornaments in Jade* and *The Children Of The Pool*, but also older short stories, such as "The Soldiers' Rest," "The Great Return," "The Happy Children" (1920)—about a journalist witnessing a ghostly nocturnal procession of zombie-like children in a Northern district—and "Munitions of War" (1926). Among the more recent stories are "Opening the Door" and "The Cosy Room."[97]

After the war, Machen was put on King George V's list for the annual Civil List Pension, which he received from 1932 (in the amount of 100 pounds, increased to 140 pounds in 1938). By the mid-1930s, the writer's eyesight was almost gone. His second wife, Purefoy, died on March 30, 1947. Machen died on December 15, 1947, in a private hospital in Beaconsfield, at the age of eighty-four, and was buried in St Mary the Virgin churchyard in Amersham. Many collections of his works have been published since the writer's death. Among these, is *Bridles & Spurs* (1951), a collection of twelve essays on the fallibility of human judgment ("A Forgotten Book"), spiritualism and the laws of the unseen ("The Strange Tale of Mount Nephin"), envy ("Mutterings in the Dark Grove"), life's preoccupations and anxieties ("Pictures on the Cards"), grammar schools ("The Old Grammar School"), the origin of the legend of the Holy Grail ("The Holy Grail"), and Charles Dickens and Walter Scott ("Lost Books" and "True to Life"). As is the case of the majority of Machen's essays, to sustain his theories, the writer makes use of disparate examples from literary and philosophical sources as much as he recounts peripheral matters such as card games, personal anecdotes, and myths.[98]

Machen's works have been constantly reprinted in the past two decades. Different editions abound, especially in collections of horror stories and weird fiction which have been published by both University presses and, particularly, by independent publishers, such as DODO Press in 2009, Benediction Classics and Arcane Wisdom in 2011, CreateSpace (assiduously) from 2012 to 2018, Wildpress and Delphi Classics in 2013, Aziloth Books in 2014, Scholar's Choice and Booklassic in 2015, Trieste Publishing, Musaicum Books, and Penguin Classics in 2017. Tartarus Press has been one of the most active publishers in the dissemination of Machen's works through its editions in both printed and ebook forms and has published over twenty books by the Welsh writer. Over twenty editions of Machen's novels, novellas, and short stories have been printed in 2018 alone by different publishers. Among these are Aaron Worth's *The Great God Pan and Other Horror Stories* (Oxford University Press, 2018), Jim Miller's *The Great God Pan & Other Classic Horror Stories* (Dover Thrift, 2018), and Dennis Denisoff's *Decadent and Occult Works by Arthur Machen* (Modern Humanities Research Association, 2018). Only the latter includes both fictional and critical works by the Welsh author. The critical assessment of Machen's production in the aforementioned books is, however, limited to brief introductions that generally evidence some of the main themes of the novels and short stories by the Welsh author, or that merely summarize their publication history.

Critical essays on Machen have been hitherto relegated mainly to the field of Gothic studies or studies of the occult. An example of the former is Kelly Hurley's *The Gothic Body: Sexuality, materialism, and degeneration at the fin de siècle* (Cambridge University Press, 2004), which focuses sparingly on "The Great God Pan," *The Three Impostors*, and "The Inmost Light." Only one chapter is dedicated to Machen in Roger Luckhurst's *The Invention of Telepathy, 1870–1901* (Oxford University Press, 2002)—which includes the writer among the representatives of "late Victorian Gothic." The same is true in Corinna Wagner's *Gothic Evolutions: Poetry, Tales, Context, Theory* (Broadview, 2014)—an anthology that combines texts and their critical interpretations—and in Jane Aaron's *Welsh Gothic* (University of Wales Press, 2013), which focuses on the representation of the Welsh landscape in the writer's works.

Monographs and collections of essays dedicated to Machen are often dated, as is the case of Caroline Alice Lejeune and Anthony Lejeune's *Arthur Machen: Essays* (St Albert's Press, 1960), Aidan Reynolds, William Charlton, and D.B. Wyndham Lewis's *Arthur Machen: A Short Account of His Life and Works* (Dufour, 1964), Wesley D. Sweetser's *Arthur Machen* (Twayne Publishers, 1964), S.T. Joshi's *The Weird Tale: Arthur Machen/ Lord Dunsany/Algernon Blackwood/M.R. James/Ambrose Bierce/H.P. Lovecraft* (Sarnath Press, 1990), and Adam Barry Eckersley's *The Fiction of Arthur Machen: Fantastic Writing in the Context of Materialism* (University of London, 1995). Similarly, John Gawsworth and Roger Dobson's *The Life of Arthur Machen* (Tartarus Press, republished in 2005), which focuses almost exclusively on the life of the Welsh writer, offering minor interpretations of his works, was completed during the writer's lifetime. More recent studies include Richard J. Bleiler's *The Strange Case of "The Angels of Mons": Arthur Machen's World War I Story, The Insistent Believers, and His Refutations* (McFarland, 2015), which sets Machen's fictional account of the apparition of angels against the original counter-narratives that responded to it (such as Phyllis Campbell's, John Garnier's, and Isabelle E. Taylor's). Andrew McCann's *Popular Literature, Authorship and the Occult in Late Victorian Britain* (Cambridge University Press, 2014) and Susan Johnston Graf's *Talking to the Gods: Occultism in the Works of W.B. Yeats, Arthur Machen, Algernon Blackwood, and Dion Fortune* (SUNY Press, 2015) dedicate only one of their chapters to Machen. McCann examines the intersection of the experience of the occult with the development of popular literary aesthetics in Machen as well as in the works of Daphne du Maurier, Marie Corelli, and Rosa Praed. Johnston Graf considers how the membership and practices of the Hermetic Order of the Golden Dawn influenced the four writers mentioned in the title of her volume. The most recent volumes on the subject are James Machin's *Faunus: The Decorative Imagination of Arthur Machen* (MIT University Press, 2019) and Mark Valentine and Timothy J. Jarvis' *The Secret Ceremonies: Critical Essays on Arthur Machen* (Hippocampus Press, 2019). Both volumes are collections of essays, some of whom have been previously published, either during Machen's life or in "Faunus," the journal of the Friends of Arthur Machen.

As the previous list indicates, interest in Machen has been constant in the past decade (as Susan Johnston Graf affirms, "Machen remains a fringe figure with a cult following").[99] A critical analysis of the writer's production will certainly be beneficial for both scholars and fans of his works. This volume, *Arthur Machen: Critical Essays*, is therefore the first completely original study published in the past two decades on an under-researched author that nevertheless is still much appreciated and read around the world. The volume is an edited collection that contains twelve chapters, and is organized into three sections. These center on different aspects of the literary production of Machen and the critical debate that surrounds his work. Section One, "Human Beings and Their Environments," focuses on the representation of human beings and the world in the writer's works, whether it is the omnipresent London or the mysterious nature. The first chapter in the collection, by Amanda M. Caleb, utilizes Mikhail Bakhtin's concept of the chronoscope to argue that Machen's third autobiographical volume, *The London Adventure*, presents time and space as intrinsically connected through the individualized experience of both storytelling and space to contextualize the individual's experience of London's modernization at the turn of the twentieth century.

Francesco Corigliano's chapter applies Mark Fisher's difference between the two modes of the "weird" and the "eerie" to the representation of nature as a "willing agent" in *The Terror*. The third chapter, by Antonio Sanna, analyzes those locations in Machen's fiction such as woods, hills, and even entire villages which open up to an alternative, supernatural reality that can induce alternatively fear, the uncanny, and mystical feelings in the characters or even threaten their lives. This chapter examines the natural and urban locations in which supernatural or extraordinary events occur through the concepts of heterotopia and chronotopia theorized by the French philosopher Michel Foucault during the 1960s. In the fourth chapter, Fernando Gabriel Pagnoni Berns and Emiliano Aguilar, examine how stones and minerals are of the highest importance within Machen's *oeuvre*. According to the two contributors, stones are markers of something beyond humanity and, in Machen's world, they are both language and something that comes before the construction of proper language, thus connecting humans with ulterior realities but also marking the indifference of nature toward humanity.

The second part of the book, "Darwinism and Degeneration," interprets Machen's writings through a series of disciplines and academic theories that were contemporary to the writer (such as paleontology and medicine). The chapters in this section demonstrate how Machen was influenced by the scientific discourses of his time and reproduced them in his works. The fifth chapter, by Justin Mullis, demonstrates that for Machen the influence of paleontology—the study of prehistoric life—can most clearly be seen in his cycle of "little people" tales. Mullis also traces the influence of such stories on subsequent writers and present scientists. In the following chapter, Jessica George explores the ways in which the intertextual motifs and allusions of "The Great God Pan" resonate with the themes of adaptation and monstrosity. The novella could therefore be read, George affirms, as a monstrous adaptation. In the seventh chapter, Kostas Boyiopoulos showcases Machen's prose poetry as a supreme example of Symbolist Decadence by focusing on *Ornaments in Jade* alongside aspects of his exquisite novel *The Hill of Dreams*. By examining the two works' overlapping themes and images as well as Machen's 1890s "Notebook," Boyiopoulos argues that *Ornaments in Jade* is composed by Lucian, the protagonist of the 1907 novel. The chapter that concludes the second section, written by Loredana Salis and Laura Mauro, examines the fin-de-siècle themes of bodily degeneration, revulsion, and disease in "The Great God Pan." Through several comparisons to the works of Robert Louis Stevenson and Oscar Wilde, Salis and Mauro argue that the destructive influence of Helen Vaughan throughout the novella can be likened to an infectious pathology, a venereal disease.

The final section of the volume, "Spirituality," considers an aspect of the writer's literary production complementary to the reproduction of the scientific and medical debates of his time: his interest in the occult and mysticism, and the religious themes present in many of his works. These topics are inextricably bound with scientific and rational interpretations of nature and create therefore a fitting juxtaposition with the previous section's chapters. In the ninth chapter, Adrian Tait explains, in a wide-ranging discussion of works such as *The Terror*, "Out of the Earth," and *A Fragment of Life*, how Machen's eco-spirituality may be interpreted as a monistic vision of a deep ecological totality that is nevertheless rooted in material entanglements of the quantum kind as described in the theories of the New Materialists. The subsequent chapter, by Deborah Bridle, analyzes the episodic novel *The Three Impostors* (1895) and the short stories "The Inmost Light," "The Shining Pyramid," and "The Red Hand," which can all be categorized under the "crime fiction" or "detective fiction" label. In these stories, Bridle demonstrates, rational thinking clashes with the existence of paranormal phenomena and strongly jeopardizes usual techniques of ratiocination: occultism thus works as a literal motif and a metatextual symbol, ultimately leading to the failure of the detective. The eleventh chapter, by Jeoffrey Reiter, examines how in *A Fragment of Life* Machen is faced with the difficult paradox of attempting to communicate the incommunicable experience of ecstasy by means of the *via negative* (apophatic mysticism). Reiter argues that to accomplish this paradoxical task, Machen juxtaposes the imagery of the Welsh countryside and the Eucharistic Grail against the mundane realities of daily life to create an initial sense of mystery before proceeding, finally, to suggest the stripping away of even these symbols to a greater reality. The last chapter of the collection, by Andrew R. Lenoir, examines "The Bowmen" against the environment of spiritualism, occult, religious revival, and wartime desperation that made the United Kingdom susceptible to angel mania. Lenoir's chapter tracks the story's mutation over time and the transformation of Machen's ghost archers into a battalion of winged angels.

The twelve chapters in this collection aim to invite a multidisciplinary discussion of a writer who has often been neglected the critical attention that he deserves. *Arthur Machen: Critical Essays* takes readers into several distinct areas and addresses a large range of topics, including the literary, the artistic, the scientific, the religious, the sociocultural, and the personal. It is the expressed wish of this volume's editor that the Welsh writer will be further read, studied, and appreciated by both the old and young generations in the forthcoming decades and centuries.

NOTES

1. Vincent Starrett, *Arthur Machen: A Novelist of Ecstasy and Sin* (Chicago, IL: Walter M. Hill, 1918), 11.
2. H.P. Lovecraft, "Supernatural Horror in Literature," http://www.hplovecraft.com/writings/texts/essays/shil.aspx (accessed February 12, 2019).
3. Ibid.
4. William Francis Genkle, *Arthur Machen: Weaver of Fantasy* (Millbrook, NY: Round Table Press, 1949), 3.
5. Mark Valentine, *Arthur Machen* (Bridgend: Seren, 1995), 7.
6. Keith McDonald and Roger Clark, *Guillermo del Toro: Film as Alchemic Art* (London: Bloomsbury, 2015), 45.
7. Genkle, *Arthur Machen*, 55.
8. Ibid., 139.
9. S.T. Joshi, *The Weird Tale* (Holicong, PA: Wildside Press, 2003), 16. Joshi divides Machen's works into two phases: the best fiction written during the 1890s and what he considers the tedious works written subsequently "that can be totally dispensed with or ignored without affecting our understanding of him" (17). According to Joshi what mars the entire production of the writer is the "lack of narrative skill" (23), especially in those tales written in the first decades of the twentieth century which spell out explicitly an explanation of the depicted supernatural events in their endings.
10. Several essays and articles published throughout Machen's life further explore London, analyzing different aspects of its urban environment, from the night sky ("The Night Sky of London," 1910), the Thames ("A Night on the Thames," 1912), the slums and back streets ("A Study in Backstreets," 1912), and comparing the capital of his youth to the present city ("When I Was Young in London," 1913). In essays such as "Re-Discovery of London" (1914), Machen guides the reader through his walks, showing him/her the details of the landscape as he strolls from one area of the capital to another, indicating the types of houses and warehouses, noting the colors of the gardens and the river, and the shapes of the porticos.
11. His father adopted his wife's surname to acquire a legacy from the Scottish Machens. See John Gawsworth, *The Life of Arthur Machen*, ed. Roger Dobson (Carlton-in-Coverdale: Tartarus Press, 2017), 588–98. Ebook.
12. Ibid., 449–96.
13. Gawsworth affirms: "He was not exactly unhappy, but he lived a different life from his companions, a life in the mind, a secure life, upon which everyday happenings could in no wise encroach." Ibid., 657–62.
14. Ibid., 688–95.
15. Arthur Machen, "Eleusina" (Hereford: Joseph Jones, 1881), 14.
16. Gawsworth, *The Life of Arthur Machen*, 952–63.
17. Genkle, *Arthur Machen*, 25.
18. According to Gawsworth, *The Anatomy of Tobacco* "was started solely to entertain the author, with no thought at all of publication. It was written as an anodyne, a relief for the troubles and the loneliness of the young man." Gawsworth, *The Life of Arthur Machen*, 1072–82.

19. According to Gawsworth, Machen's translation tempered the original text's eroticism. Ibid., 1385–90.

20. Ibid., 1292–302.

21. Arthur Machen, *The Chronicle of Clemendy; or, The History of the IX Joyous Journeys* (Carbonnek: The Society of Pantagruelists, 1888), 125.

22. The catalog published in this period under the name of Thomas Marvell and titled *Thesaurus Incantatus: The Enchanted Treasure, or The Spagyric Quest of Beroaldus Cosmopolita* is written in the form of a pompous fictional account of a king who discovers several mystical truths. The second part of the booklet contains an annotated list of books on mysticism, occultism, magic, astrology, and alchemy which includes the works of St. Thomas Aquinas, Nicholas Flamel, Paracelsus, and Thomas Vaughan.

23. The Machens had moved to Soho Street in the meantime.

24. Arthur Machen, "The Great God Pan," in *Late Victorian Gothic Tales*, ed. Roger Luckhurst, 183–233 (Oxford: Oxford University Press, 2009), 189–90.

25. Tim Youngs, *Beastly Journeys: Travel and Transformation at the fin de siècle* (Liverpool: Liverpool University Press, 2013), 147.

26. As Elaine Showalter has noted, the final decades of the Victorian age witnessed the explosion of the discourses of feminists and homosexual apologists as well as the affirmation of the New Woman, all of which destabilized the patriarchal system that had hitherto reigned unchallenged. See Elaine Showalter, *Sexual Anarchy: Gender and Culture at the Fin de Siècle* (London: Virago, 2001).

27. Quoted in Gawsworth, *The Life of Arthur Machen*, 2340–43. According to the *Lady's Pictorial*, "This book is gruesome, ghastly, and dull. Mr. Machen has done his best with an impossible subject, but although men and women who are morbid and unhealthy in mind may find something that appeals to them in the description of Dr. Raymond's experiment and its results, the majority of readers will turn from it in utter disgust." Quoted in S.T. Joshi (ed.), "Introduction," in *The Three Impostors and Other Stories. The Best Weird Tales of Arthur Machen*, vol. 1, xi–xix (Hayward, CA: Chaosium, 2007), xiii. According to Joshi, the story is "extremely clumsy in construction and is written in a horribly florid and stilted style." Joshi, *The Weird Tale*, 22. Other critics generally praised Machen's 1894 novella. Starrett lauds the tale's "plausibility." Starrett, *Arthur Machen*, 15. Lovecraft affirms: "No one could begin to describe the cumulative suspense and ultimate horror with which every paragraph abounds without following fully the precise order in which Mr. Machen unfolds his gradual hints and revelations." Lovecraft, "Supernatural Horror in Literature." Reiter argues that the story is actually focused on the death of metaphysics and therefore it symbolizes the absence of spirituality (there is no Christian redemption at the end of the narrative, "only hell remains, and it is a materialistic hell") and the fear that materialism could be the only foundation of this world. Geoffrey Reiter, "'Man Is Made a Mystery': The Evolution of Arthur Machen's Religious Thought," PhD Dissertation (Baylor University, 2010), 48. Marco Pasi reads the novella as a reflection of "negative epistemology" (qtd. in Reiter, 42). Adrian Eckersley points out that Helen Vaughan has "a good pagan name" to contrast the "good Christian name" of her mother Mary (qtd. in Reiter, 49).

28. Gawsworth, *The Life of Arthur Machen*, 2157–65.
29. Genkle, *Arthur Machen*, 70.
30. Arthur Machen, "The Inmost Light," in *The House of Souls*, 245–86 (New York: Alfred A. Knopf, 1922), 254.
31. Ibid., 273.
32. Ibid., 284.
33. Arthur Machen, "The Shining Pyramid," in *The Shining Pyramid: Tales and Essays*, ed. Vincent Starrett, 1–35 (Chicago, IL: Covici-McGee, 1923), 26; Reiter, "Man Is Made a Mystery," 67.
34. Machen, "The Shining Pyramid," 21 and 24.
35. Reiter, "Man Is Made a Mystery," 71–72. According to Kelly Hurley, the impostors' tales "turn out to be brilliant formal exercises, produced sheerly for the pleasures of narrativization." Kelly Hurley, *The Gothic Body: Sexuality, Materialism, and degeneration at the fin de siècle* (Cambridge: Cambridge University Press, 2004), 166.
36. Lovecraft, "Supernatural Horror in Literature"; Reiter, "Man Is Made a Mystery," 6–7.
37. Arthur Machen, "The Red Hand" (Adelaide: The University of Adelaide, 2014), Ch. 3. Ebook.
38. Reiter, "Man Is Made a Mystery," 9.
39. Chic Cicero and Sandra Tabatha Cicero, *The Essential Golden Dawn: An Introduction to High Magic* (St. Paul, MN: Llewellyn, 2003), 88–93.
40. Machen admitted that the Order "shed no ray of any kind on my path." Quoted in R.A. Gilbert, Introduction, *The House of the Hidden Light*, 59–391 (Carlton-in-Coverdale: Tartarus, 2017), 211. Ebook. Regarding spiritualism, in a letter to Mr. Ireland dated Sept. 15, 1933, the Welsh writer affirmed: "I have known Spiritualists to be styled mystics—wherein they are most vilely miscalled. I have seen a good deal of them in my day, and also of people of a somewhat higher order, who would call themselves occultists; but they are all in utter darkness." Arthur Machen, *Complete Works of Arthur Machen* (Hastings: Delphi Classics, 2013), 93281–283. Ebook.
41. Arthur Machen, *Hieroglyphics* (London: Grant Richards, 1902), v.
42. Ibid., 11, 19, and 147.
43. Arthur Machen, "The White People," in *The House of Souls*, 111–66 (New York: Alfred A. Knopf, 1922), 141. According to Carl Van Vechten, there was not "a more malignantly depraved story written than *The White People* (which it might be profitable to compare with Henry James's *The Turn of the Screw*)." Quoted in Genkle, *Arthur Machen*, 183.
44. Joshi, *The Weird Tale*, 28–29.
45. Reiter argues that "The identification of Edward and Mary as legendary and their association with the Graal—a myth often believed to be pagan in origin—may indicate that Machen is merely superimposing a Christian structure over a more ancient Celtic belief system." Reiter, "Man Is Made a Mystery," 140.
46. Gilbert, Introduction, 333.
47. Arthur Machen and Arthur Edward Waite, *The House of the Hidden Light* (Carlton-in-Coverdale: Tartarus, 2017), 213–34.

48. The original edition of *The House of Souls* contains "The Great God Pan" (which was by then out of print), "The Inmost Light," *The Three Impostors*, "The Red Hand," "The White People," and *A Fragment of Life*.

49. See Gawsworth, *The Life of Arthur Machen*, 3364–69.

50. Arthur Machen, *Dr. Stiggins: His Views and Principles* (London: Francis Griffiths, 1906), 13.

51. *The Garden of Avallaunius* had been published in July 1904 in a serialized form in *Horlick's Magazine*.

52. Arthur Machen, *The Hill of Dreams* (Boston: Dana Esten & Company, 1907), 24.

53. Ibid., 54. In Machen's own words *The Hill of Dreams* "was . . . to represent loneliness not of the body on a desert island, but loneliness of the soul and mind and spirit in the midst of myriads and myriads of men." Quoted in Glenke, *Arthur Machen*, 78.

54. Douglas reviewed positively *The Secret Glory*, affirming: "It is like some dreadful liturgy of self-inflicted pain, set to measured music: and the cadence of that music becomes intolerable by its suave phrasing and perfect modulation. The last long chapter with its recurring themes is a masterpiece of prose, and in its way unique." Quoted in Gawsworth, *The Life of Arthur Machen*, 3542–44.

55. According to Joshi, Machen's articles in these journals adopted a discursive style that actually diminished the writer's literary style and inventiveness. See Joshi, *The Weird Tale*, 12 and 18.

56. The Machens' first son, Hilary, was born in February 1912.

57. Arthur Machen, Introduction, in *The Angels of Mons, The Bowmen and Other Legends of the War*, 5–27 (London: Simpkin, Marshall, Hamilton, Kent and Co., 1915), 13.

58. Arthur Machen, "The Great Return" (London: Faith Press, 1915), 20.

59. Ibid., 31.

60. Ibid., 33.

61. Arthur Machen, *The Terror: A Mystery* (New York: Robert M. McBride, 1917), 88.

62. Ibid., 131.

63. Ibid., 150. In this sense, the first part of *The Terror* could be compared to many episodes of the horror/science fiction television series *The X-Files* (1993–2002, 2016–18), whose apparently unexplainable and unrelated mysteries are often solved only near the end of the single episodes (or groups of episodes), after terror and fear have conquered over the characters (and, sometimes, the viewer).

64. *The Terror* can be read against the 1918 small volume *War and the Christian Faith*, especially those essays that examine religious matters such as God's lack of intervention against unjust wars and conquests as well as against misfortunes and the natural malevolence of human beings. Machen advocates therefore "a practical atheism, an elimination of God from all our considerations." Arthur Machen, "White Fires," in *War and the Christian Faith*, 12–19 (London: Skeffington and Son, 1918), 13. In "Conformity" Machen argues that animals can be considered as happy creatures, because they lead a single life (and not a double one as human

beings do) in conformity with "the rule and order of their being." For this reason, the writer affirms, animals "are still in paradise," whereas humans being are "distracted, and thus miserable" because they do not realize that their own business should be the immanent and transcendent God. Arthur Machen, "Conformity," in *War and the Christian Faith*, 23–36 (London: Skeffington and Son, 1918), respectively 33, 33, and 35.

    65. See Gawsworth, *The Life of Arthur Machen*, 4629–30.
    66. Genkle, *Arthur Machen*, 112.
    67. Arthur Machen, *The Secret Glory* (New York: Alfred A. Knopf, 1922), 209.
    68. Joshi, *The Weird Tale*, 31.
    69. Reiter, "Man Is Made a Mystery," 14.
    70. Arthur Machen, *Far Off Things* (London: Martin Secker, 1922), 20.
    71. Ibid., 63.
    72. The first two volumes were edited together in 1974 by Garnstone Press, with an introduction by Morchard Bishop, who was a personal friend with Machen. Bishop also published a sixteen-page chapbook in 1987, titled *Dreams and Visions: A Brief Journey into the Remarkable Imagination of* Arthur Machen.
    73. Arthur Machen, *Things Near and Far* (Carlton-in-Coverdale: Tartarus Press, 2017), 1967–68.
    74. Arthur Machen, *The London Adventure, or the Art of Wandering* (Carlton-in-Coverdale: Tartarus Press, 2017), 411.
    75. Ibid., 602.
    76. Quoted in Merlin Coverley, *Psychogeography* (Harpender: Pocket Essentials, 2006), 10. As Coverley explains, psychogeography consists primarily in the act of walking through the urban space, especially in those marginal areas that are overlooked by the city's inhabitants, an act defined by the spirit of political radicalism and by ironic humor whose aim is to reveal the true nature of the urban environment beyond the flux of the everyday. Prototype psychogeographers were, according to Coverley: Defoe, Blake, DeQuincey, Robert Louis Stevenson, Machen, and Alfred Watkins. A modern tradition of visionary walkers was then established in Paris, with *flâneur* writers such as Baudelaire, Walter Benjamin, Xavier de Maistre, and André Breton, whereas contemporary exponents of psychogeography are Iain Sinclair, Stewart Home, and Peter Ackroyd. In the specific case of the Welsh writer, Coverley argues, "as he frees himself from all geographical or historical markers, Machen remaps the city as he passes through it and, in establishing a trajectory away from the more well-trodden centre toward the overlooked suburban quarters of the city, Machen points the way for today's generation of psychogeographers as they explore London's anonymous outer limits" (50).
    77. Arthur Machen, *Strange Roads. With the Gods in Spring* (London: The Classic Press, 1923), 32.
    78. Arthur Machen, "Out of the Earth," in *The Shining Pyramid: Tales and Essays*, ed. Vincent Starrett, 37–46 (Chicago, IL: Covici-McGee, 1923), 38.
    79. Ibid., 43.
    80. In *Dog and Duck* Machen argues that fairies are "Skilled and scientific, they build up the molecules which compose the flowers" ("April Fool"), whereas, in "A

Midsummer Night's Dream," he explains conventional fairies as pre-Celtic inhabitants of the British isles, whose mysterious origins and habits led to the attribution of magical powers. Arthur Machen, "April Fool," in *Dock and Duck: A London Calendar Et Cætera*, 44–49 (London: Jonathan Cape: 1924), 47; Arthur Machen, "A Midsummer Night's Dream," in *Dock and Duck: A London Calendar Et Cætera*, 56–62 (London: Jonathan Cape: 1924).

81. "Psychology, or Fragments of Paper" and "The Ceremony," were written in 1897; "The Rose Garden" was written in 1908, but the rest of the poems were written in 1924.

82. Reiter, "Man Is Made a Mystery," 92.

83. Arthur Machen, "The Rose Garden," in *Complete Works of Arthur Machen*, 20495–528 (Hastings: Delphi Classics, 2013), 20524. Ebook.

84. Arthur Machen, "The Turanians," in *Complete Works of Arthur Machen*, 20684–730 (Hastings: Delphi Classics, 2013), 20723. Ebook. Reiter argues that the ecstasies described are almost pagan ("Man Is Made a Mystery," 93). The remaining story, "Torture," depicts a fifteen-year-old boy, who is not talented for school and for sports and returns home for the vacation, where he works at night on the construction of some instruments of torture.

85. Arthur Machen, *The Canning Wonder* (London: Chatto & Windus, 1925), v.

86. Ibid., 15.

87. Ibid., 249.

88. Arthur Machen, "Note," in *Complete Works of Arthur Machen*, 89589–641 (Hastings: Delphi Classics, 2013), 86620. Ebook.

89. Arthur Machen, "Opening the Door," in *Complete Works of Arthur Machen*, 21565–776 (Hastings: Delphi Classics, 2013), 21642. Ebook.

90. Gawsworth, *The Life of Arthur Machen*, 6076–77 and 6132–36. In the last two decades of the writer's life, several essays were published either privately or in limited editions, including the pamphlet "Parish of Amersham" (1931) and "A Note on Poetry" (written in 1943 and printed in 1959). See I.R. Willison (ed.), *The New Cambridge Bibliography of English Literature*, Vol. 4, 1900–50 (Cambridge: Cambridge University Press, 1972), 646–47. "A Note on Poetry" discusses the tradition of delivering in verse matter from Homer and Hesiod to European literature, its misappropriation in advertisement, and the fact that poetry derives from "an outburst of simple, sensuous, and passionate emotion." Arthur Machen, "A Note on Poetry," in *Complete Works of Arthur Machen*, 92585–839 (Hastings: Delphi Classics, 2013), 92747. Ebook.

91. Reiter, "Man Is Made a Mystery," 194.

92. Arthur Machen, "Change," in *Complete Works of Arthur Machen*, 22293–495 (Hastings: Delphi Classics, 2013), 22435. Ebook.

93. Arthur Machen, "Out of the Picture," in *Complete Works of Arthur Machen*, 23155–575 (Hastings: Delphi Classics, 2013), 23331. Ebook.

94. Arthur Machen, "The Exalted Omega," in *Complete Works of Arthur Machen*, 22499–852. (Hastings: Delphi Classics, 2013), 22602. Ebook.

95. Another short story written in this period by Machen is "The Dover Road," which was commissioned for the collection *Missing from Their Homes*. It was

inspired by announcements that the BBC used to make about missing people and was published by Hutchinson in 1936. "The Dover Road" is focused on the investigation of a haunted manor by a group of distinguished gentlemen and the inexplicable disappearance of one of them, antiquary Sir Halliday Stuart, whose physical appearance has been perceived differently by each member of the group. Once the real antiquary is found months later, he denies being involved in the events witnessed by the group of men. The fact is tentatively explained as an apparition of the "phantasm of the living." Noteworthy is the fact that, after initially dismissing a case of haunting and spiritualistic beliefs at the beginning of the story, Machen delves into an atmosphere of doubt and incredulity for the rest of the tale.

96. Arthur Machen, "The Cosy Room," in *Complete Works of Arthur Machen*, 21020–112 (Hastings: Delphi Classics, 2013), 21072. Ebook.

97. In 2017, the film *Holy Terrors* was broadcast on BBC. Co-directed and co-produced by Julian Butler and Mark Goodall, it is an anthology film containing the adaptation of six short stories by Machen.

98. Other collections of Machen's works published after the writer's death include *Tales of Horror and the Supernatural* (Knopf, 1948), *The Novel of the Black Seal* (Corgi, 1965), and *Guinevere and Lancelot & Others* (Purple Mouth, 1987)—which comprises rare essays such as "Local Color" (1898), "Gypsies" (1911), "The Grand Trouvaille: A Legend of Pentonville" (1923), "The Preface (from *Afterglow: Pastels of Greek Egypt 69 B.C.*)" (1924), "Art and Luck" (1933), and "Savages" (1936) alongside short stories such as the titular one and "Ritual." *The Collected Arthur Machen* (Duckworth Publishing, 1988) includes the assorted extracts "The Ars Magna of London: A Machen Miscellany" and the "Introduction to *A Handy Dickens*" (1941), but there are also *Ritual and Other Stories* (Tartarus Press, 1992)—which includes the rare short story "Johnny Double," on a young boy being telepathically linked to his own double—*The Islington Mystery and Other Stories* (Oxford City Press, 2011), *The White People and Other Weird Stories* (Penguin Modern Classics, 2011), and *Arthur Machen: Masters of the Weird Tale* (Centipede Press, 2012).

99. Susan Johnston Graf, *Talking to the Gods: Occultism in the Works of W.B. Yeats, Arthur Machen, Algernon Blackwood, and Dion Fortune* (Albany, NY: SUNY Press, 2015), 2.

REFERENCES

Aaron, Jane. *Welsh Gothic*. Cardiff: University of Wales Press, 2013.
Cicero, Chic and Sandra Tabatha Cicero. *The Essential Golden Dawn: An Introduction to High Magic*. St. Paul, MN: Llewellyn, 2003.
Coverley, Merlin. *Psychogeography*. Harpender: Pocket Essentials, 2006.
Gawsworth, John. *The Life of Arthur Machen*, edited by Roger Dobson. Carlton-in-Coverdale: Tartarus Press, 2017. Ebook.
Genkle, William Francis. *Arthur Machen: Weaver of Fantasy*. Millbrook, NY: Round Table Press, 1949.

Gilbert, R.A. Introduction. In Arthur Machen and E.A. Waite, *The House of the Hidden Light*, 58–391. Carlton-in-Coverdale: Tartarus, 2017. Ebook.

Graf, Susan Johnston. *Talking to the Gods: Occultism in the Works of W.B. Yeats, Arthur Machen, Algernon Blackwood, and Dion Fortune*. Albany, NY: SUNY Press, 2015.

Hurley, Kelly. *The Gothic Body: Sexuality, Materialism, and Degeneration at the fin de siècle*. Cambridge: Cambridge University Press, 2004.

Joshi, S.T. (ed.). Introduction. In *The Three Impostors and Other Stories. The Best Weird Tales of Arthur Machen, Volume 1*, xi–xix. Hayward, CA: Chaosium, 2007.

———. *The Weird Tale*. Holicong, PA: Wildside Press, 2003.

Lovecraft, H.P. "Supernatural Horror in Literature." http://www.hplovecraft.com/writings/texts/essays/shil.aspx.

Luckhurst, Roger. *The Invention of Telepathy, 1870-1901*. Oxford: Oxford University Press, 2002.

Machen, Arthur. "A Midsummer Night's Dream." In *Dock and Duck: A London Calendar Et Cætera*, 56–62. London: Jonathan Cape, 1924.

———. "A Note on Poetry." In *Complete Works of Arthur Machen*, 92585–839. Hastings: Delphi Classics, 2013. Ebook.

———. "April Fool." In *Dock and Duck: A London Calendar Et Cætera*, 44–49. London: Jonathan Cape, 1924.

———. *The Anatomy of Tobacco: or Smoking Methodised, Divided, and Considered After a New Fashion*. London: George Redway, 1884.

———. *The Canning Wonder*. London: Chatto & Windus, 1925.

———. "Change." In *Complete Works of Arthur Machen*, 22293–495. Hastings: Delphi Classics, 2013. Ebook.

———. *The Chronicle of Clemendy; or, The History of the IX Joyous Journeys*. Carbonnek: The Society of Pantagruelists, 1888.

———. "Conformity." In *War and the Christian Faith*, 23–36. London: Skeffington and Son, 1918.

———. "The Cosy Room." In *Complete Works of Arthur Machen*, 21020–112. Hastings: Delphi Classics, 2013. Ebook.

———. *Dr. Stiggins: His Views and Principles*. London: Francis Griffiths, 1906.

———. "Eleusinia." Hereford: Joseph Jones, 1881.

———. *The Enchanted Treasure; or, The Spagyric Quest of Beroaldus Cosmopolita, in which is sophically and mystagorically declared The First Matter of the Stone*. London: Thomas Marvell, 1923.

———. "The Exalted Omega." In *Complete Works of Arthur Machen*, 22499–852. Hastings: Delphi Classics, 2013. Ebook.

———. *Far Off Things*. London: Martin Secker, 1922.

———. "A Fragment of Life." In *The House of Souls*, 1–110. New York: Alfred A. Knopf, 1922.

———. "The Great God Pan." In *Late Victorian Gothic Tales*, edited by Roger Luckhurst, 183–233. Oxford: Oxford University Press, 2009.

———. "The Great Return." London: Faith Press, 1915.

———. *Hieroglyphics*. London: Grant Richards, 1902.

———. *The Hill of Dreams*. Boston: Dana Esten & Company, 1907.

———. "The Inmost Light." In *The House of Souls*, 245–86. New York: Alfred A. Knopf, 1922.

———. "Introduction." In *The Angels of Mons, The Bowmen and Other Legends of the War*, 5–27. London: Simpkin, Marshall, Hamilton, Kent and Co., 1915.

———. *The London Adventure, or the Art of Wandering*. Carlton-in-Coverdale: Tartarus Press, 2017.

———. "N." In *Complete Works of Arthur Machen*, 25848–26252. Hastings: Delphi Classics, 2013. Ebook.

———. "Note." In *Complete Works of Arthur Machen*, 89589–641. Hastings: Delphi Classics, 2013. Ebook.

———. *Notes and Queries*. London: Spurr & Swift, 1926.

———. "Opening the Door." In *Complete Works of Arthur Machen*, 21565–776. Hastings: Delphi Classics, 2013. Ebook.

———. "Out of the Earth." In *The Shining Pyramid: Tales and Essays*, edited by Vincent Starrett, 37–46. Chicago, IL: Covici-McGee, 1923.

———. "Out of the Picture." In *Complete Works of Arthur Machen*, 23155–575. Hastings: Delphi Classics, 2013. Ebook.

———. "The Red Hand." Adelaide: The University of Adelaide, 2014. Ebook.

———. "The Rose Garden." In *Complete Works of Arthur Machen*, 20495–528. Hastings: Delphi Classics, 2013. Ebook.

———. *The Secret Glory*. New York: Alfred A. Knopf, 1922.

———. "The Shining Pyramid." In *The Shining Pyramid: Tales and Essays*, edited by Vincent Starrett, 1–35. Chicago, IL: Covici-McGee, 1923.

———. *Strange Roads. With the Gods in Spring*. London: The Classic Press, 1923.

———. *The Terror: A Mystery*. New York: Robert M. McBride, 1917.

———. "The Three Impostors: or Transmutations." In *The Three Impostors and Other Stories. The Best Weird Tales of Arthur Machen, Volume 1*, 101–234. Hayward, CA: Chaosium, 2007.

———. *Things Near and Far*. Carlton-in-Coverdale: Tartarus Press, 2017.

———. "The Turanians." In *Complete Works of Arthur Machen*, 20684–730. Hastings: Delphi Classics, 2013. Ebook.

———. *Uncollected Tales*. Hastings: Delphi Classics, 2018.

———. "White Fires." In *War and the Christian Faith*, 12–19. London: Skeffington and Son, 1918.

———. "The White People." In *The House of Souls*, 111–66. New York: Alfred A. Knopf, 1922.

Machen, Arthur and Arthur Edward Waite. *The House of the Hidden Light*. Carlton-in-Coverdale: Tartarus, 2017.

McDonald, Keith and Roger Clark. *Guillermo del Toro: Film as Alchemic Art*. London: Bloomsbury, 2015.

Reiter, Geoffrey. "'Man Is Made a Mystery': The Evolution of Arthur Machen's Religious Thought." PhD Dissertation. Baylor University, 2010.

Showalter, Elaine. *Sexual Anarchy: Gender and Culture at the Fin de Siècle*. London: Virago, 2001.

Starrett, Vincent. *Arthur Machen: A Novelist of Ecstasy and Sin.* Chicago, IL: Walter M. Hill, 1918.
Youngs, Tim. *Beastly Journeys: Travel and Transformation at the fin de siècle.* Liverpool: Liverpool University Press, 2013.
Valentine, Mark. *Arthur Machen.* Bridgend: Seren, 1995.
Wagner, Corinna. *Gothic Evolutions: Poetry, Tales, Context, Theory.* Peterborough, Canada: Broadview, 2014.
Willison, I.R. (ed.). *The New Cambridge Bibliography of English Literature.* Vol. 4. 1900–50. Cambridge: Cambridge University Press, 1972.

Part I

HUMAN BEINGS AND THEIR ENVIRONMENTS

Chapter 1

"A London *cognita* and a London *incognita*"

Mapping London in Arthur Machen's The London Adventure, or the Art of Wandering[1]

Amanda M. Caleb

For Arthur Machen, there were multiple Londons: there was the London that called to him in Wales, the London that disgusted him when he lacked the money to enjoy it, and the Gothic London that haunted his autobiographical works and fictional stories. As Merlin Coverley notes:

> much of Machen's work can be viewed as . . . an attempt to gain mastery over London's streets by walking them, and through this knowledge a means of countering their menace . . . a gargantuan and never-ending project whose goal was to come to terms with a city whose perimeter was always out of sight and whose perpetual growth seemed always to outstrip the attempts of those who sought to capture it in its entirety.[2]

The limitations, however, were the essential of the mystery and adventure for Machen and formed the basis of his philosophy of the city itself, what he termed in his second autobiography, *Things Near and Far* (1923), "Ars Magna of London." In his words, "the Great Art of London has nothing to do with any map or guide-book or antiquarian knowledge, admirable as these are . . . For the essence of this art is that it must be an adventure into the unknown, and perhaps it may be found that this, at least, is the matter of all the arts."[3] This desire to explore the city for oneself is noted by several of his characters, including Edward Darnell in *A Fragment of Life* (1904) who, in recounting a walking tour of London, tells his wife, "I didn't buy a map; that would have spoilt it, somehow; to see everything plotted out, and named, and measured. What I wanted was to feel that I was going where nobody had been before."[4]

The very *flâneur*-like statement on wandering also introduces the framework for Machen's third autobiography *The London Adventure, or the Art of Wandering* (1924). The text is unlike a traditional autobiography, and even unlike Machen's previous installments: it is not linear, nor limited to his life, but is rather the story of how he experienced London and how literature offers that experience to readers. While Machen professes to be writing, or attempting to write, a book about wandering through London, he instead ambles through memories and stories linked to the city but without a sense of progression or purpose—like wandering itself. In its refusal to be a traditional autobiography, or travel guide, or literary essay, or any other recognizable genre, the text reflects Machen's argument that London is not just one thing or one experience: it is all the Londons, both real and imagined by others and ourselves. At the same time, Machen's narrative and style prevents the development of experience: his Londons are still and unchanging, existing in a single moment of space and time that does not develop through the act of remembering or revisiting. The narrative is challenged with the task of "mobiliz[ing] and organiz[ing] spaces and places" even as "all spaces and places are necessarily embedded with narratives."[5] The text must organize the stories of the spaces and places in a way that readers can reorganize in their own minds, telling the story of a London that becomes many Londons. Paradoxically, then, the work is about multiple Londons and a singular London, multiple experiences and a singular experience, understood through narrative.

The subtitle, *The Art of Wandering*, reveals the narrative structure and purpose of the book itself, which is to meander through London and through stories themselves, an embodiment of topophrenia: "thinking about place, which also means thinking about the relations among places, as well as those among subjects and places, in the broadest possible sense."[6] The act of association with a London-centric origin is a constant reminder of how place shapes experience, memories, and storytelling. As an act of both literal and cognitive mapping of London (and experiences of London), Machen's text produces simultaneous feelings of familiarity and unease that underpin topophrenia, the "subtle yet visceral feeling of spatial anxiety [that] subtends our thoughts and actions [. . . and function] as the fundamental impetus behind the desire for mapping, which is also the desire for narrative."[7] This unease is represented in the way in which Machen wanders through his own text: he repeatedly shares anecdotes that reveal the rejection of linear narrative and of a knowable or recognizable London, "originat[ing] in old rambles about London, rambles that began in 1890" and with the intention "utterly to shun the familiar."[8] He even makes a gesture toward rejecting traditional storytelling by recalling his news editor's words, "you must learn to recognize that sometimes there *is* no story."[9] Yet, like most of Machen's works, these comments are misdirection:

the text is not solely about his street wanderings, nor does the text rely only on the unfamiliar—and there is very much a story being told. The purpose of these misdirections is to engage the reader into experiencing London beyond its spatial dimension; Machen images the city to be something to write, to interpret and reinterpret, to read—in other words, a text.

To write the city is an act of knowing, interpreting, and communicating information to others, and here lies the challenge of Machen's work: if London is something that one must experience and know individually, what can an author offer that aids that experience without overpowering it? What story can the author tell that is both author-authentic and reader-centric? Robert T. Tally Jr. offers one way into understanding this relationship between place and narrative:

> On one hand . . . narratives are in some ways devices or methods used to map the real-and-imagined spaces of human experience. Narratives, are, in a sense, mapping machines. On the other hand, narratives—like maps, for that matter—never come before us in some pristine, original form. They are always and already formed by their interpretations or by the interpretative frameworks in which we, as readers, situate them.[10]

The overlap of physical map and literary map—and of author creation with reader interpretation—is a useful way of understanding Machen's claim of "a London *cognita* and a London *incognita*,"[11] in which London is not known by only its spatial dimensions, but also through temporal narrative experience, which is embedded with "chronotopic values."[12] Creating this doubled representation allows for "the formulation of distinctions between [Machen's] London and 'the' London that were convincingly beyond the common-sensical" and demonstrates the anxiety of two representations occupying a single space.[13] Examining *The London Adventure* as a textual depiction of a contested and contradictory London reveals how Machen challenges spatial boundaries of place to privilege an imaginative engagement that ultimately reveals the impossibility of knowing a place.

THRESHOLD CHRONOTOPES: THE CRISIS OF REPRESENTING LONDON

Machen begins *The London Adventure* by guiding the reader to a specific location at a specific time; paradoxically, his description lacks sufficient details and a single time by which to actually locate the setting. He begins:

> There is a certain tavern in the north-western parts of London which is so remote from the tracks of men and so securely hidden that few people have ever

> suspected its existence. For, in the first place, it is quite off the high roads of the leafy quarter once familiarly known as "the Wood," and then again, the byway in which it is situated does not suggest the presence of any house of public entertainment. Here are modest residences of stucco and grey brick, built for quiet people in the late 'thirties and early 'forties; their front gardens planted with trees of all sorts and varieties . . . Here and there in these gardens there survives an old gnarled thorn, a remnant, I suspect of the time when "the Wood" was really a wood or waste.[14]

The certainty of the tavern's existence is countered with the fact that so few people know of it; its specific location in northwestern London is undermined by its position off the high road and hidden among residences. In other words, it is a location that can be described but not easily located.

Moreover, the descriptions resist a single temporality or even two relational temporalities (as seen elsewhere in the text); rather, there are four related temporalities that are intricately tied to space: "the 'real' present which has somehow passed by this tavern; the 'remote' world in which the tavern exists; the period in which the surrounding neighbourhood was known as 'the Wood'; and the more distant past, when the area 'was really a wood or a waste'."[15] For Sam Wiseman, this temporal destabilization is indicative of Machen's belief that "by exploring suburbia . . . we engage in a kind of time travel, uncovering the persistence of an older world ... within the modern metropolis."[16] This act of time travel is emblematic of a chronotopic view of London, one that moves beyond the real-time chronotope of autobiography and the road chronotope of the adventure novel—what might be expected given the title and content—and instead adopts the threshold chronotope, which is "highly charged with emotion and value . . . it can be combined with the motif of encounter, but its most fundamental instance is as the chronotope of *crisis* and *break* in life."[17] The text details with the crisis of representation and unease of topophrenia: it is composed of breaks, slices of London adventures, that attempt at forming a whole view of London.

The threshold chronotope is both literal and metaphorical; "in Dostoevsky, for example, the threshold and related chronotopes—those of the staircase, the front hall and corridor, as well as the chronotopes of the street and square that extend those spaces into the open air—are the main places of action in his works, places where crisis events occur, the falls, resurrections, renewals, epiphanies, decisions that determine the whole life of man."[18] Similar chronotopes appear in Machen's works, in which adventures, and even the impetus to write, is framed within and around doorways and corridors which frame his effort to determine the wholeness of London. The indoor space spills to the extended outdoor space, but this relationship is more fluid than Bakhtin describes, by which the outdoor space extends into the indoor space by way of the threshold. The movement between inside and outside is also metaphorical in its meeting of the private and public, what is subjective and what is exposed to objectivity, and what is known and what is unknown—"a London *cognita* and a London *incognita*."

Returning to the opening passages, we can see how Machen shifts the outside to the inside, creating the sense of crisis and imperative in *The London Adventure*. He describes the solitary location of the tavern—both in terms of the natural and built environments—and then moves this space inside, describing how "in this pleasant and retired spot I was sitting more long ago, enjoying gin and that great luxury and blessing of idleness."[19] This isolated repose is interrupted through the same entryway that blended the outside with the inside space; a mysterious man with a threatening demeanor enters through this doorway and challenges Machen "in a very meaning tone: 'The leaves are beginning to come out.'"[20] The narrative becomes one of crisis: the temporal change the unnamed man describes echoes that which Machen uses to describe the tavern's location—thus bringing the outside in—and indicates a need for a second change within the narrative.

This presumed crisis is illustrated in Machen's response to this man, which is both physical and literary:

> I shuddered. I was very much in the condition of the Young Man in Spectacles—some of my readers may know whom I mean—when he was suddenly accosted in the public-house by the emissary of Lipsius.
>
> *At the first touch of the hand on his arm the unfortunate man had wheeled round as if spun on a pivot, and shrank back with a low, piteous cry, as if some beast were caught in the toils. The blood flew away from the wretch's face, etc. etc.*[21]

The parallel to *The Three Impostors* indicates initially a perilous turn for Machen, one that blurs the reality of his London with the literary London of his novel, creating an instability in space and even time. The reader soon learns the mysterious man is merely reminding Machen of his commitment to write a book about his London rambles once the season changed, which relocates Machen from character to author. The comparison, then, might be read as overdone; indeed, chapter two of *The London Adventure* acknowledges the inappropriateness of this parallel and his response: "I think I have described myself as shuddering, in the Young Man in Spectacles manner, when I received the message about the coming forth of the leaves. But, really, I do not know why I should have shuddered."[22] Machen's stated confusion about his involuntary shuddering—and voluntary literary allusion—is contradicted by another claim in his opening chapter: "thus I shuddered . . . always, or almost always, I have had the horror of beginning a new book. I have burnt my fingers to the bone again and again in the last forty years and I dread the fire of literature."[23] What Machen describes is the chronotope's function that "makes narrative events concrete, makes them take on flesh, causes blood to flow in their veins."[24] The crisis that evokes a visceral response is both the private utterance of writing a book that has become public with the unnamed stranger's return and the adventure of writing that new book, made concrete through the vocalization of its promised existence: the parallel to the Young Man in Spectacles, then, is fitting if we view the act of writing as an act of both revealing and concealing knowledge.

This crisis is even more pronounced when we consider Machen's subject of London, which he claims "has grown so vast that no man can know it, nay, nor even begin to know it!"[25] The impossibility of his task and the weight of this burden is the impetus for the work and is part of "paradoxical knot" of the threshold chronotope: "its temporality, so to speak, is at once open-ended and bound by the nature of the crisis. The threshold chronotope is consequently a moment simultaneously unique and ubiquitous."[26] Thus the crisis of representation is that he fears London may lack the distinction he seeks: "London, it was true, was unknowable, an unplumbed depth, but so was Caerleon-on-Usk, that you could see in its totality from the top of the hill; so was the pebble on the path."[27] As if to prove this claim wrong, Machen shares numerous unique experiences in London that speak to the temporality and distinctiveness of the city, situated, oftentimes, in literal thresholds. In describing the pleasure of viewing a doorstep near Gray's Inn Roads, Machen recounts the numerous people, "weary and hopeless, the glad and the exultant, the lustful and the pure" that have hollowed the doorstep.[28] He concludes:

> that doorstep is to me sacramental, if not a sacrament, even though the neighbourhood round about Mount Pleasant is a very poor one. For it seems to me that here you have the magic touch which redeems and exalts the dull mass of things, by tinging them with the soul of man . . . I see those worn and hollowed doorsteps round about Clerkenwell and the Gray's Inn Road and all the dim and desolate regions adjacent; I see them signed with tears and desires, agony and lamentation.[29]

Peter Ackroyd describes this passage as representing London as having "always been the abode of strange and solitary people who close their doors upon their own secrets in the middle of the populous city."[30] This contrast of isolation within a crowded location is paralleled to the secrets which a threshold both conceals and conveys: Machen alludes to the unknown and known of the threshold as emblematic of London itself. He embeds transcendent meaning into the doorstep itself: describing it as sacramental, or even a sacrament, both conveys an individual experience of place and connects all individuals, and not just Machen, who have crossed this threshold through the shared experience of place. Place, as distinguished from space, is defined by those who inhabit it and give it meaning; Machen embodies this geographical concept in how he describes the doorstep, blending past with the present and creating the crisis of the text: how does one map all of the unique stories of London that are also the universal stories of humankind?

MAPPING LONDON *COGNITA*

One way to begin addressing this crisis of representation is through physical orientation that allows the readers to situate themselves within the described place. Location and the act of storytelling and writing are intimately connected for Machen, as expressed throughout his autobiographies and even his fictional works, especially *The Three Imposters* (1895) and *The Hill of Dreams* (1907). In *Things Near and Far*, he writes that in 1885, "I resumed my old mooning walks out of London, going westward usually or always, sometimes Acton way and sometimes through Brentford—that curious, dirty, and most fascinating place—to Osterley Park, where in those days you could walk and wander anywhere you pleased . . . And then I fell to writing again."[31] The implication is that walking might help with his creative endeavors and, as evidenced in his published works, shape the trajectory of his stories, which are intricately tied to the city. Like Machen, Dyson, in *The Three Imposters*, describes wandering "rather aimlessly about the streets; my head was full of my tale, and I didn't much notice where I was going."[32] Dyson's recovery of the gold Tiberius coin leads to the storytelling of the novel itself—in other words, the art of wandering becomes the art of writing.

For all these obscure streets and locations in London, Machen counters his works with specific known locations, often as the origin of a jaunt into the unknown. In *Things Near and Far*, he recalls "that if you set out, without a map, from your house at 36 Great Russell Street and walk for an hour eastward or northward you are in fact in an unknown region, a new world."[33] Similarly, in "More About Back Streets," part of the "Wonderful London" series for *The Evening News*, he begins at Euston Square and then, in a section entitled "The Maze," describes the unfamiliarity and even uncertainty of the streets: "obscure streets, ways still more obscure branch off and wind and vanish into unconjectured territories."[34] In both examples, Machen concludes by describing that which cannot be described because it is both unknown and unimagined. The specific starting point is a reminder of how the unknown is grounded within and to the known; a starting point is real and required for any journey, even if the journey can devolve into the unknown. In other words, the act and art of wandering requires a real, tangible place to which all other experiences are anchored.

The known aspect of Machen's London is twofold: he presents detailed descriptions of specific locations in the city, to the point that a reader could likely find exact locations, and his tone in describing London is reminiscent of his descriptions in previous works. To this last point, Machen is blatant, even going as far as to reference his other works: "I was thinking of a sentence I had written in a book of mine called *Far Off Things* to the effect that no man has ever seen London."[35] The reference to *Far Off Things* (1922) in particular is fitting if we consider *The London Adventure* to be an extension of his existing autobiographical works and larger project that grapples with how one knows and describes a city.

For all of Machen's claims that he will write a book of the unfamiliar London, much of what he describes is only unfamiliar to a middle-class readership that does not wander through all parts of London. The issue of this specific unknown London is the same expressed in his other autobiographical works, notably *Things Near and Far*, which demonstrate his Gothic imaginations of Islington as an act of psychological distancing tied to "the contrast between middle-class streets and those of the working poor, a divide that is socio-temporal as well as spatial."[36] The same can be said of *The London Adventure*: his proposed approach at the onset of the work is very much grounded in a real London, one inhabited by real people and mapped onto a real location: "unknown, unvisited squares in Islington, dreary byways in Holloway, places traversed by railway arches and viaducts in the regions of Camden Town."[37] This claim of unknown spaces is not accurate in a literal sense—they appear on maps and certainly people lived and traversed through Islington, Holloway, and Camden Town. For Machen, they are unfamiliar because they are not where the typical middle-class visitor or even adventurer would visit, nor are they well documented in the guidebooks of London.[38] This classification of space by class is embedded in many of Machen's works, maybe none more so than "The Great God Pan." The horror of the novel is not just Helen Vaughan's physical threat to the London men but also her ability to alter her identity and ultimately her class, which is made possible by London's spatiality and anonymity: the city is composed of "obscure mazes and byways" and is defined by the "mysterious incidents and persons with which the streets of London teem in every quarter and at every hour."[39]

The notion of mapping the actual space is central to the stories that Machen tells throughout the work and reveals the mapping of the socio-temporal onto physical space. For instance, in recounting an experience on Greek Street that first inspired his "London science," Machen shares that:

instantly, without any reason that I could see, a crowd began to pour and buzz from all backways and hidden places and to gather in front of a house which looked as if it had been built for a Doctor of Divinity, c. 1720. Then people came down from the doorstep carrying queer objects with them which they bundled into a four-wheeler, and the crowd hummed with delight.

"Pore things," I heard a stout lady say to a stouter friend—both came straight out of Phiz's illustration of Kingsgate Street in *Martin Chuzzlewit*—"poor things: I daresay if the truth was known they only did it for the sake of their wives and families."[40]

At the heart of this interaction is the threshold chronotope, which serves as the physical location of the birth of Machen's London science and a metaphorical view of time and place. Machen speaks to both Greek Street's past grandeur and current disreputability: at the beginning of the eighteenth century, Greek Street, and more broadly Soho, housed a number of wealthy people, though by the end of the century; it was home to "people of modest social standing—artisans, shopkeepers and so forth."[41] The nineteenth century saw a further fall from respectability, with the influx of lodging houses, and by the early twentieth century, Greek Street was described by a police officer as "one of the very worst streets I have to deal with. In fact, it is the worst street in the West End of London. Crowds of people gather there nightly who are little better than a pest. I will go further and say that some of the vilest reptiles in London live there or frequent it."[42] Machen's allusions to both temporal representations of Greek street demonstrate how physical space can be stable in its existence (the road itself) and unstable in its meaning (class).

Machen maps another layer to this description, that of Phiz's illustration of Charles Dickens's *Martin Chuzzlewit* (1842–1844) and specifically the location of Kingsgate Street. While spatially separate from Greek Street by a half mile, Kingsgate becomes conflated with, and representative of, Greek Street through Machen's reference to Phiz's illustrations. Kingsgate Street has its own history that provides an additional spatiotemporal layer: while home to many shops and businesses in Victorian times, it was destroyed in 1902–1906 during a city rebuilding project, replaced with the much larger Southampton Row.[43] Rather than an unstable meaning, Kingsgate is an unstable place, one that requires an imaginative reach for Machen's reader, either as an act of remembrance or of creation. This marked shift between known and unknowable is representative of the two related Londons Machen depicts in his work.

MAPPING LONDON *INCOGNITA*

London *incognita* is, by definition, unstable; this instability includes the physical, temporal, social, and subjective and embodies Machen's claim that London "physically or intellectually is so vast and mighty a world, that the study of any one—of even the smallest and least considerable—of its aspects may well be the task of a lifetime."[44] The challenge of knowing or representing London is almost overwhelming, largely because of the different experiences of the city itself, whether that be poor vs. middle class, Victorian vs. Modern, or simply the individual experience. Yet everything about *The London Adventure* is an act of trying to express the experience of London, even as it protests the possibility of doing so. This contrast between wanting to do something and being unable to do it is the writer's threshold chronotope; for Machen, this is expressed in his desire to write, yet inability to do so: "I dig deep, I burrow, far under the ground, I hew out my laborious subterranean passages, I blast whole strata of unsuspected rocks which suddenly interpose themselves between me and my end, I dwell down in that stifling blackness of toil, month after month, year after year, scarcely emerging to see the light of the sun and the glow of the green world."[45] The metaphor Machen employs includes a passageway chronotope—related to the threshold—that alludes to the perception of time when he struggles to write and a physical space that exists beneath the world about which is trying to write.

Machen's view of writing echoes his view of London, not just in the seeming impossibility of doing or knowing, but also in the mysteries of what cannot be seen or easily grasped. His interest in mysticism and the occult is well-known and well-documented, and this interest is a main theme throughout *The London Adventure*—indeed, mysticism, whether written about, experienced when he was a journalist, or theorized, makes up about a third of the text. He aligns his interest in mysticism with the city itself, recounting the origins of his fiction, retelling stories of investigating a Poltergeist, and claiming about the city: "But the unknown world is, in truth, about us everywhere, everywhere near to our feet; the thinnest veil separates us from it, the door in the wall of the next street communicates with it."[46] Again, the threshold chronotope appears, this time in theorizing how he experiences London and emphasizing the connectivity of multiple worlds and multiple times that cannot be known, or known through typical means, such as vision.[47] Machen goes on to claim, "there are certain parts of Clapton from which it is possible, on sunny days, to see the pleasant hills of Beulah, though topographical experts might possibly assure you that it was only Epping Forest. But men of science are always wrong."[48] Machen positions the known space of London (Clapton) with the unknown and unknowable, the present with the past, and the actual with the mythical, acknowledging his previous criticisms about the limitations of the scientific vision because it only recognizes what can be seen or explained—in other words, the London *cognita*.[49] As he notes in his first installment of the three-part "The Joy of London" for *The Evening News*, "he who truly knows London will confess that he knows it not, and is most sure that he never will know it. It is mapped and charted, but only for the logical understanding, never for the imagination. London, in its essence, is an object of faith, not of science."[50] The cartography of London is limited and is limiting to the true experience of the city, which is embedded in imagined experiences.

The conceptualization of the city, then, is one informed by the experiences that resist a sole focus on definition or temporal-geographical grounding. In discussing his first trip to London in *Far Off Things*, Machen provides the impetus for this need to conceptualized space and time:

> My Strand is gone for ever; some of it is a wild rock-garden of purple flowers, some of it is imposing new buildings; but one way or another, the spirit is wholly departed. But on that June night in 1880 I walked up Surrey Street and stood on the Strand pavement and looked before me and to right and to left and gasped. No man has ever seen London; but at that moment I was very near to the vision—the *theoria* of London.[51]

Here, he reflects on the passage of time and physical change to the Strand that signals not only a different space, but also a different experience of that space, which is both clearly defined and indistinct: it is a combination of the natural and the industrial but without delineation between the two. However, through memory of a past Strand, Machen offers how the subjective experience of space, as divorced from outside influences, allows for a conceptualization of what that space could mean and signify. In other words, the description privileges the subjective experience of place as an attempt of knowing a space that cannot be known through maps and description alone.

Evident in Machen's lament for the loss of his Strand is the presence of psychogeography, which "was born with a sense of loss for the city," and which Alastair Bonnett associates with postwar Paris and "the perception that 'their' [the Situationists'] Paris—the street-based, intimate and organic Paris of the bohemian and working-class community—was under assault by the forces of banalization and modernization."[52] In many ways, Machen is dealing with this same sense of loss and same resistance to modernity, evident in his setting choice of the isolated and wooded tavern and his movement through his remembered London. As such, much of *The London Adventure* "is a journey through Machen's past," representing memories as a realm that "coexist[s] alongside the world of appearances."[53] We can liken him to a version of Nick Papadimitriou's imaginary civil engineer: "he is entrained in a world, a traveler in time as well as space. This place, and ideas, memories and emotions that he or others associate with it, shapes his experience of it and experiences in it."[54] Machen's past is linked to his literary works, which form the backbone of his London experience in all of his autobiographies. He reveals that he turned to a notebook filled with story ideas—some that came to fruition and others that did not—as inspiration for writing *The London Adventure*, but also as an act of delaying writing the work itself.[55] For Machen, the context for these written and unwritten works is London itself: his creative powers are tied to his time living in the city and can therefore serve as a source of writing about the city through this subjective, literary experience.

He extends this literary-city connection by representing his experience of being in London like being a character in his own works, offering an understanding of the city through both memory and imagination. These references include the opening comparison to the Young Man in Spectacles and a memory of how living in London in 1899–1900 was to be a character in his own books: "Publishers earnestly requested me to found secret societies; Miss Lally and the Young Man in Spectacles became my constant companions, uttering astounding things and involving themselves in the strangest adventures; I found, with something of a shock, that I was living more in *The Three Impostors* than in Verulam Buildings, Gray's Inn."[56] Machen relocates himself from the known Verulam Buildings to the unknown of the text, likening his past with London to his fictional characters' pasts, a means of understanding space as place through literary memory. This literary memory is also a personal memory of how he previously attempted to represent the city; his varying representations of London (always Gothic, but always situated differently within the work) and privileging of place "that exists at the level of the imagination suggests the difficulty of claiming that any one place exists in a stable form."[57] What the London *incognita* reveals, then, is an instability in representation and in knowledge of place, one that can be resolved individually but not collectively; in other words, Machen reveals the impossibility of an objective understanding of place.

This individuality of experience speaks to the decadence of Machen's early writing that is embedded with spatial insecurity, inspired by his own individual experience of the city. Near the end of *The London Adventure*, Machen recounts a time in 1896 when he was unable to orient himself in a familiar part of the city. The experience leads him to contemplate, "What about a tale of a man who 'lost his way'; who became so entangled in some maze of imagination and speculation that the common, material ways of the world became no significance to him?"[58] This speculative moment marks his decision to focus on spatial insecurities in *The Hill of Dreams*; the insignificance of the material world stems from an inability to find stability in that world, which Lucian experiences through his failure to separate the real London from his imagined one.[59] As Sam Wiseman notes, "this description could also apply to the narrative of *The London Adventure* itself, which ventures into increasingly imaginative metaphysical speculations as it progresses."[60] Machen persistently explains what the text will be about and the need to begin writing it but ultimately wanders off to another topic or story. On the one hand, this structure is fitting for a text about experiencing a city as knowing a city; on the other hand, if the city cannot be known, then the structure is one that disallows knowledge and completion.

THE THRESHOLD OF THE TEXT: READER AS WANDERER

We might view this contrast as the crisis of the chronotope itself, which "is a time-space in which the conscious mind frames and organizes the real, but it can also be the time-space where it disorganizes and re-presents the real."[61] The act of organizing and disorganizing, or presenting and representing, is the contrast between the London *cognita* and the London *incognita* that Machen fluctuates between throughout the text. Organized by reiterating what the text should be, it is simultaneously disorganized through the continued straying from the stated intention; the new presentation is one that represents London as only real within the realm of individual experience, in a time-space both defined by the depiction of London and by that of the reader's experience of the text itself, thereby existing in multiple times and multiple spaces and places.

Because Machen is self-referential of the text he is writing, *The London Adventure*, then, is itself a threshold, a space (pre)occupied with crisis and change, as evident in his concluding remark: "so here ends, without beginning, *The London Adventure*; and, indeed, I have been in London all this summer of 1923."[62] He represents a spatial-temporal threshold: beginnings and endings, as located both in a specific time and across a personal history of time. This final threshold chronotope is representative of the others that appear throughout the work: it demonstrates the inability to locate and represent a single and objective account of London. This sentiment is echoed in his other writings on London, notably those that appeared in the 1910s. In his third and final installment of "The Joy of London," Machen notes the embodiment of subjectivity within the very essence of the city itself, tied to an inability to experience all of London, "that to the most energetic and leisured explorer there must ever be myriads of streets that he will never enter."[63] He concludes the article: "Thus does London make for us a concrete image of the eternal things of space and time and thought."[64] His language reveals London as a product of senses, of experience, that transcend singular meaning and definition and at once both individual and collective: London, then, is an amalgamation of an individual's experience and imagination of it, derived from the personal, the communal, and the literary.

Thus, Machen ends *The London Adventure* leaving the reader to do the legwork to imagine London, a parallel to his use of his writer's notebook, which "absolves Machen from actually having to write the story . . . since the reader is compelled to exercise his own imagination in conceiving what the story might have been like; in effect, the reader writes the story."[65] *The London Adventure* certainly encourages the reader's own creation of London, mapped from the places he describes and imagines, leaving the reader "to explore the place *as* perceived or *as* experienced."[66] This individualized experience of the city is only possible through Machen's depictions, particularly for those unable to experience London directly: place, embedded with meaning, "is experienced as present within language and made present by language, if not also at times, making language possible at all." Intrinsically tied together, London's existence as a place is a product of how it is described, the language used to give it life, just as that language is given life through the existence of London itself.[67] However, the text also offers a final thought that perhaps the only one to know London is London itself: "*Londinia cognita Londiniensibus.*"[68] The solipsism reveals the impossibility of Machen's task and confirms that the adventure is, in fact, the act of trying to know and to imagine London rather than the knowledge itself.

NOTES

1. The writing of this chapter was supported by a faculty research grant from Misericordia University.

2. Merlin Coverley, *The Art of Wandering: The Writer as Walker* (Harpenden: Oldcastle Books, 2012), 49.

3. Arthur Machen, *Things Near and Far* (London: Martin Secker, 1923), 62, 63.

4. Arthur Machen, "A Fragment of Life," in *The White People and Other Weird Stories*, ed. S.T. Joshi, 148–222 (London: Penguin, 2011), 177.

5. Robert T. Tally, Jr., *Topophrenia: Place, Narrative, and the Spatial Imagination* (Bloomington: Indiana University Press, 2019), 31.

6. Ibid., 23.

7. Ibid.

8. Arthur Machen, *The London Adventure, Or the Art of Wandering* (London: Martin Seeker, 1924), 30, 49.

9. Ibid., 111.

10. Robert T. Tally, Jr., "Introduction: Mapping Narratives," in *Literary Cartographies: Spatiality, Representation, and Narrative*, ed. Robert T. Tally, Jr., 1–12 (New York: Palgrave, 2019), 3.

11. Machen, *The London Adventure*, 49.

12. "Chronotopic values" are the "temporal and spatial determinations [that] are inseparable from one another, and [are] always colored by emotions and values." Mikhail Bakhtin, "Forms of Time and of the Chronotope in the Novel," in *The Dialogic Imagination*, 9th ed., ed. Michael Holquist; trans. Caryl Emerson and Michael Holquist, 84–258 (Austin: University of Texas Press, 1994), 243.

13. Nicholas Freeman, *Conceiving the City: London, Literature, and Art, 1870–1914* (Oxford: Oxford University Press, 2007), 170.
14. Machen, *The London Adventure*, 5.
15. Sam Wiseman, "'Finding Infinity Round the Corner': Doublings, Dualities and Suburban Strangeness in Arthur Machen's *The London Adventure*," *The Irish Journal of Gothic and Horror Studies* 16 (Autumn 2017): 94–107, 96.
16. Wiseman, "'Finding Infinity'," 97.
17. Bakhtin, "Forms of Time," 248.
18. Ibid.
19. Machen, *The London Adventure*, 6.
20. Ibid., 10.
21. Ibid.
22. Ibid., 29.
23. Ibid., 12.
24. Mikhail Bakhtin, "Forms of Time," 250.
25. Machen, *The London Adventure*, 69.
26. Lene M. Johannessen, *Threshold Time: Passages of Crisis in Chicano Literature* (Amsterdam: Rodopi, 2008), 16.
27. Machen, *The London Adventure*, 71.
28. Ibid., 47.
29. Ibid., 47, 48.
30. Peter Ackroyd, *London: The Biography* (New York: Anchor Books, 2000), 496.
31. Machen, *Things Near and Far*, 27.
32. Arthur Machen, *The Three Imposters* (London: John Lane, 1895), 16.
33. Machen, *Things Near and Far*, 79.
34. Arthur Machen, "More About Back Streets," *The Evening News (London)*, May 3, 1912, 6, https://newspaperarchive.com/london-evening-news-may-03-1912-p-6/ (accessed July 25, 2020).
35. Machen, *The London Adventure*, 69.
36. Amanda Mordavsky Caleb, "'A City of Nightmares': Suburban Anxiety in Arthur Machen's London Gothic," in *London Gothic*, ed. Lawrence Phillips and Anne Witchard, 41–49 (London: Continuum, 2010), 42.
37. Machen, *The London Adventure*, 11.
38. See, for instance, *Black's Guide to London and its Environs*, 12th ed., ed. A.R. Hope Moncrieff (London: Adam and Charles Black, 1902). While this guide mentions Camden Town, Holloway, and Islington, the first two are only discussed as spaces to traverse to go elsewhere; Islington receives greater attention but is generally mentioned as a geographic reference to visiting other locations, such as Angel and Highbury.
39. Arthur Machen, *The Great God Pan* (London: John Lane, 1894), 31.
40. Machen, *The London Adventure*, 32.
41. Stephen Inwood, *Historic London: An Explorer's Companion* (London: Macmillan, 2008), 101.
42. Inspector McKay (1906), qtd. in Joseph McLaughlin, *Writing the Urban Jungle: Reading Empire in London from Doyle to Eliot* (Charlottesville: University of Virginia Press, 2000), 136.

43. For a brief history of Kingsgate Street (and a more detailed history of Bloomsbury), see Deborah Colville, "Kingsgate Street," *UCL Bloomsbury Project*, 2011. http://www.ucl.ac.uk/bloomsbury-project/streets/kingsgate_street.htm (accessed January 12, 2019).

44. Machen, *Far Off Things* (London: Martin Secker, 1922), 60.

45. Machen, *The London Adventure*, 92–93.

46. Ibid., 100.

47. Machen's description of the mysticism of London anticipates one of his last works of fiction, "N" (1934), a short story that imagines a mystical, primordial world that crosses into the real London suburb of Stoke Newington.

48. Ibid.

49. See Machen, *Far Off Things*, 124. Here, he offers the following criticism of science: "The bad people, or scientists as they are sometimes called, maintain that nothing is properly an object of awe or wonder as everything can be explained. They are duly punished."

50. Arthur Machen, "The Joy of London I," *The Evening News (London)*, January 27, 1914, 6, https://newspaperarchive.com/london-evening-news-jan-27-1914-p-6/ (accessed July 25, 2020).

51. Machen, *Far Off Things*, 70–71.

52. Alastair Bonnett, "Walking through Memory: Critical Nostalgia and the City," in *Walking Inside Out: Contemporary British Psychogeography*, ed. Tina Richardson, 75–88 (London: Rowman and Littlefield, 2015), 75.

53. Wiseman, "'Finding Infinity'," 102.

54. See Luke Bennett, "Incongruous Steps Towards a Legal Psychogeography," in *Walking Inside Out: Contemporary British Psychogeography*, ed. Tina Richardson, 59–72 (London: Rowman and Littlefield, 2015), 61. Bennett paraphrases Nick Papa Dimitriou's imaginary civil engineer visiting Suicide Corner in Middlesex to reveal how it aligns with concepts in phenomenology and "ordinary affects." We can read his paraphrase as encapsulating the layered subjective experiences of psychogeography.

55. Machen, *The London Adventure*, 72–91.

56. Ibid., 139.

57. Alex Murray, *Landscapes of Decadence: Literature and Place at the Fin de Siècle* (Cambridge: Cambridge University Press, 2016), 146.

58. Machen, *The London Adventure*, 141.

59. These blurred lines of real and imagined space are discussed at length in Caleb, "'A City of Nightmares.'"

60. Wiseman, "Finding Infinity," 100.

61. Paul Smethurst, *The Postmodern Chronotope: Reading Space and Time in Contemporary Fiction* (Amsterdam: Rodopi, 2000), 5.

62. Machen, *The London Adventure*, 142.

63. Arthur Machen, "Joys of London III," *The Evening News (London)*, April 15, 1914, 8, https://newspaperarchive.com/london-evening-news-apr-15-1914-p-8/ (accessed July 26, 2020).

64. Ibid.

65. S.T. Joshi, *The Weird Tale* (Holicong, PA: Wildside Press, 2003), 36.

66. Tally, Jr., *Topophrenia*, 20.
67. Sten Pultz Moslund, "The Presencing of Place in Literature: Toward an Embodied Topopoetic Mode of Reading," in *Geocritical Explorations: Space, Place, and Mapping in Literary and Cultural Studies*, ed. Robert T. Tally, Jr., 29–42 (New York: Palgrave Macmillan, 2011), 31.
68. Machen, *The London Adventure*, 135.

REFERENCES

Ackroyd, Peter. *London: The Biography*. New York: Anchor Books, 2000.
Bakhtin, Mikhail. "Forms of Time and of the Chronotope in the Novel." In *The Dialogic Imagination*, 9th ed., edited by Michael Holquist; translated by Caryl Emerson and Michael Holquist, 84–258. Austin: University of Texas Press, 1994.
Bennett, Luke. "Incongruous Steps Towards a Legal Psychogeography." In *Walking Inside Out: Contemporary British Psychogeography*, edited by Tina Richardson, 59–72. London: Rowman and Littlefield, 2015.
Bonnett, Alastair. "Walking through Memory: Critical Nostalgia and the City." In *Walking Inside Out: Contemporary British Psychogeography*, edited by Tina Richardson, 75–88. London: Rowman and Littlefield, 2015.
Caleb, Amanda Mordavsky. "'A City of Nightmares': Suburban Anxiety in Arthur Machen's London Gothic." In *London Gothic*, edited by Lawrence Phillips and Anne Witchard, 41–49. London: Continuum, 2010.
Colville, Deborah. "Kingsgate Street." *UCL Bloomsbury Project*, 2011. http://www.ucl.ac.uk/bloomsbury-project/streets/kingsgate_street.htm.
Coverley, Merlin. *The Art of Wandering: The Writer as Walker*. Harpenden: Oldcastle Books, 2012.
Freeman, Nicholas. *Conceiving the City: London, Literature, and Art, 1870-1914*. Oxford: Oxford University Press, 2007.
Inwood, Stephen. *Historic London: An Explorer's Companion*. London: Macmillan, 2008.
Johannessen, Lene M. *Threshold Time: Passages of Crisis in Chicano Literature*. Amsterdam: Rodopi, 2008.
Joshi, S.T. *The Weird Tale*. Holicong, PA: Wildside Press, 2003.
Machen, Arthur. *Far Off Things*. London: Martin Secker, 1922.
———. "A Fragment of Life." In *The White People and Other Weird Stories*, edited by S.T. Joshi, 148–222. London: Penguin, 2011.
———. *The Great God Pan*. London: John Lane, 1894.
———. "The Joy of London I." *The Evening News (London)*, January 27, 1914, 6. https://newspaperarchive.com/london-evening-news-jan-27-1914-p-6/.
———. "Joy of London III." *The Evening News (London)*, April 15, 1914, 8. https://newspaperarchive.com/london-evening-news-apr-15-1914-p-8/.
———. *The London Adventure, Or the Art of Wandering*. London: Martin Seeker, 1924.

———. "More About Back Streets." *The Evening News (London)*, May 3, 1912, 6. https://newspaperarchive.com/london-evening-news-may-03-1912-p-6/.
———. *Things Near and Far*. London: Martin Secker, 1923.
———. *The Three Imposters*. London: John Lane, 1895.
McLaughlin, Joseph. *Writing the Urban Jungle: Reading Empire in London from Doyle to Eliot*. Charlottesville: University of Virginia Press, 2000.
Moncrieff, A.R. Hope (ed.). *Black's Guide to London and its Environs*. 12th ed. London: Adam and Charles Black, 1902.
Moslund, Sten Pultz. "The Presencing of Place in Literature: Toward an Embodied Topopoetic Mode of Reading." In *Geocritical Explorations: Space, Place, and Mapping in Literary and Cultural Studies*, edited by Robert T. Tally, Jr., 29–42. New York: Palgrave Macmillan, 2011.
Murray, Alex. *Landscapes of Decadence: Literature and Place at the Fin de Siècle*. Cambridge: Cambridge University Press, 2016.
Smethurst, Paul. *The Postmodern Chronotope: Reading Space and Time in Contemporary Fiction*. Amsterdam: Rodopi, 2000.
Tally, Jr. Robert T. "Introduction: Mapping Narratives." In *Literary Cartographies: Spatiality, Representation, and Narrative*, edited by Robert T. Tally, Jr, 1–12. New York: Palgrave, 2019.
———. *Topophrenia: Place, Narrative, and the Spatial Imagination*. Bloomington: Indiana University Press, 2019.
Wiseman, Sam. "'Finding Infinity Round the Corner': Doublings, Dualities and Suburban Strangeness in Arthur Machen's *The London Adventure*." *The Irish Journal of Gothic and Horror Studies* 16 (Autumn 2017): 94–107.

Chapter 2

The Problem of Agency in Arthur Machen's *The Terror*

Francesco Corigliano

Arthur Machen's *The Terror* (1917) is one of the writer's most interesting works of supernatural fiction. The short novel focuses on a series of disturbing events in Britain's rural province. Its protagonist, a journalist interested in folkloristic stories (who is clearly modeled on Machen himself) starts to investigate the events, discovering many links between similar weird happenings all around Britain, during the years of the Great War. Many deaths, vanishings, and accidents occurring in busy factories or on peripheral streets are all led back to a single commune cause: the revolt of the animal species against human beings. However, framing *The Terror* in a greater literary tradition that describes the fights between humans and nature would be an oversimplification: the narrative should be considered as part of *weird fiction*, a type of narrative in which the paranormal manifests itself as a new order of reality, usually one where humankind has no relevant place. In *The Terror*, Machen's style and allusive narration is not only focused on the theme of the perils connected to the environment but rather focuses on the inability to fully understand the reality of the world around us. Starting from these premises, this chapter focuses on the representation of nature as a "willing agent" in the short novel. Using the aesthetic theories elaborated by Mark Fisher in *The Weird and the Eerie* (2016), it examines the importance of *eeriness* in *The Terror* by analyzing the transformation of the environment into a haunted location characterized by an ethereal and unconceivable malevolence.

In *The Weird and the Eerie*, Fisher establishes a difference between two aesthetics modes, the "weird" and the "eerie," both present in media as varied as films, novels, short tales, and music albums. According to Fisher, "weird" and "eerie" are not genres, but styles that can be used in specific sections of a text, and they are both intended to describe the particular feeling of ineffability proper to the encounter with the supernatural.[1] The "weird" involves a sensation of *wrongness*, whereas the "eerie" a sense of extraneousness:

> a weird entity or object is so strange that it makes us feel that it should not exist, or at least it should not exist in our reality. Yet if the entity or object *is* here, then the categories which we have up until now used to make sense of the world cannot be valid . . . the weird is constituted by a presence—the presence of *that which does not belong* . . . The eerie, by contrast, is constituted by a *failure of absence* or by a *failure of presence*.[2]

The "eerie" therefore conveys a sense of subtle extraneousness and provokes the feeling that something obscure and invisible is happening, such as a haunting where it is impossible to determine which is the haunted object and which is the phantom. Indeed, the "eerie" takes place "when there is something present where there should be nothing, or when is there nothing present when there should be something."[3] Fisher also indicates that the difference between the "weird" and the "eerie" is due to the influence of agency because in the latter the signs of a willing force are often evident. Such a force operates on the environment but simultaneously it is impossible to locate it precisely; it is akin to "the forces that govern our lives and the world."[4] As an example, Fisher specifically refers to the novel *The Birds* (1952) by Daphne du Maurier and examines the agency of the murderous birds, highlighting the importance of the animals' manifest will to cooperate against humans, even without a specific reason, in a deadly assault that threatens human individuals not only physically but also existentially, and therefore endangers "the very structures of explanation that had previously made sense of the world."[5] What *is there*—and should not be—is, in *The Birds*, the manifest and yet unintelligible malevolence of an animal breed.

Both *The Birds* and *The Terror* describe a seemingly coordinated attack conducted by animals against humans. Both texts also focus on the impossibility for the latter to understand the causes of such a sudden aggression by a species that were previously pacific toward human beings if not subjugated to them.[6] However, the two texts also differ in many aspects, the most important being the manifestation of the animals' agency. In du Maurier's novel, it is obvious from the beginning that the sense of latent anxiety experienced by the human characters is linked to the winged creatures, whereas in *The Terror* Machen depicts a particular type of "haunting" that concerns the entire landscape, revealing the animals' role in the massacre of the local inhabitants only at the end of the novel. Considering the style used by Machen, which is based on a *privation* of information for the reader and a continuous and misleading display of possible explanations for the strange events, this chapter will demonstrate that in *The Terror* the *eerie* aspect regards not only the animal breeds but the entire environment. It is for this reason that the titular emotion is defined as "a terror without shape, such as no man there had ever known."[7] The landscape portrayed in Machen's text is described from the beginning with an emphasis on its isolation, loneliness, and antiquity, which instills a sense of otherness in the reader, especially for the inhabitants of large cities and London:

> Here, then, one sees a wild and divided and scattered region, a land of outland hills and secret and hidden valleys. I know white farms on this coast which must be separated by two hours of hard, rough walking from any other habitation, which are invisible from any other house. And inland, again, the farms are often ringed about by thick groves of ash, planted by men of old days to shelter their roof-trees from rude winds of the mountain and stormy winds of the sea; so that these places, too, are hidden away, to be surmised only by the wood smoke that rises from the green surrounding leaves. A Londoner must see them to believe in them; and even then he can scarcely credit their utter isolation.[8]

In *The Terror*, these solitary places, where people live and work, manifest an additional sense of unfamiliarity when strange events begin interrupting their apparent tranquility. The episodes involving the deaths that occur on the rural streets contribute to build a sense of crawling danger, a suspense that summons old fears typical of primeval times, when human beings were more afraid of nature, and the woods and the fields were still dangerous places.[9] As the text specifies, several areas (mostly described with fictional names "for convenience,"[10] like the region of "Meirion," in the far west of Wales, the regions of Stratfordshire and Treff Loyne, and the cities of Midlingham and Porth) are filled with a sense of suspension, or, as we can see in the case of the events at the military camp, the sense of "the extraordinary and unheard of character of the dreadful agency that was at work."[11] At the same time, such locations are the setting for "incidents, quite as odd and incomprehensible"[12] such as the sudden horses' stampedes, rumbling sounds in the underground, inexplicable assaults in factories, and indescribable apparitions of trees. It appears that the only possible name for this diffused phenomenon, "some intolerable secret danger that must not be named," is "Terror."[13] Through this reticence to use other terms, Machen highlights the ineffability of the supernatural danger, characterizing it through its *effects* on the human mind and not through its own causes (and therefore implying that the causes are not intelligible).[14] Such a privation of precise information, as we mentioned before, is part of the text's narration and is essential for the *eerie* sense of the novel: the *failure of presence* and *failure of absence*, the two *eerie* modes theorized by Fisher, are therefore both present in *The Terror*.

For the *failure of presence*, in the novel we witness "some kind of intent at work," the latent sense of an active and impenetrable agency *that should not be* in nature.[15] The actions of the animals are described in their unjustified brutality, as in the case of the horses' stampede, the attack of the cows at Treff Loyne, and the aggressiveness of swarms of bees.[16] The narrator also hints at other "stories, hardly so clear or so credible, of sheep dogs, mild and trusted beasts, turning as savage as wolves and injuring the farm boys in a horrible manner—in one case, it is said, with fatal results."[17] All of these events are described with a specific focus on the effects of their frightening and abrupt violence as well as with a sensational approach that suits the journalistic style of the narration but that at the same time spreads a disturbing sense of vagueness. The sudden apparition of the strange tree in the garden,[18] for example, is also marked by the impalpability of its own shape:

> The mass of the tree—the tree that couldn't be there—stood out against the sky, but not so clearly, now that the clouds had rolled up. Its edges, the limits of its leafage, were not so distinct. Lewis thought that he could detect some sort of quivering movement in it.[19]

The text frequently (but implicitly) alludes to the possibility that all of these events that *should not* take place are somehow connected. Replying to the character of Remnant, who is suggesting a "link between all this and the horrible things that have been happening about here for the last month,"[20] Lewis, a doctor involved in the investigations on the "Terror," affirms:

> It is madness. Do you mean to tell me that you think there is some connection between a swarm or two of bees that have turned nasty, a cross dog, and a wicked old barn-door cock and these poor people that have been pitched over the cliffs and hammered to death on the road? There's no sense in it, you know.[21]

Nonetheless, at the same time, the attempts to find a credible common cause by both the story's narrator and the characters are fruitless. This leads us to the *failure of absence*, the inability to clearly identify what the characters are witnessing. Regarding the *eerie*, Fisher argues that "there must be also a sense of alterity, a feeling that the enigma might involve some forms of knowledge, subjectivity and sensation that lie beyond the common experience."[22] In *The Terror*, the human mind frequently fails to grasp the reasons for the creepy changes occurring in nature: it is unable to find an explanation, a reassuring overview *that should be there*. The characters attempting to justify the events and searching for a reasonable cause, all arrive at inconclusive statements that are dominated by a disturbing sense of fright:

> The tree that changed all its shape for an hour or two of the night, the growth of strange boughs, the apparition of secret fires among them, the sparkling of emerald and ruby lights: how could one fail to be afraid with great amazement at the thought of such a mystery?[23]

The mere allusion to the phenomena is characterized by a sense of evanescence and elusiveness. The alteration of a "shape," the apparition of "secret" glares, the vision of lights colored like precious stones, are depicted with a disarming vagueness that implies a void of human comprehension about the "Terror."

These strange manifestations' creepiness is amplified by the initial inability to link together all the events that the protagonists witness:

> But there was something else. It was scarcely a sound; it was as if the air itself trembled and fluttered, as the air trembles in a church when they open the great pedal pipes of the organ. The doctor listened intently. It was not an illusion, the sound was not in his own head, as he had suspected for a moment; but for the life of him he could not make out whence it came or what it was. He gazed down into the night over the terraces of his garden, now sweet with the scent of the flowers of the night; tried to peer over the tree-tops across the sea towards the Dragon's Head. It struck him suddenly that this strange fluttering vibration of the air might be the noise of a distant aeroplane or airship; there was not the usual droning hum, but this sound might be caused by a new type of engine. A new type of engine? Possibly it was an enemy airship; their range, it had been said, was getting longer; and Lewis was just going to call Remnant's attention to the sound, to its possible cause, and to the possible danger that might be hovering over them, when he saw something that caught his breath and his heart with wild amazement and a touch of terror.[24]

Even before seeing the apparition of a strange new tree in his garden, Lewis is overwhelmed by a sense of intangible danger which, in this case, does not only entail the sense of sight and the visual misperception of reality but also the sense of hearing and its fallacy. The impossibility to clearly identify the origins of "the Terror" (an impossibility that endures until the end of the novel, when the idea of the "animal revolt" is finally presented) transforms the land, the sea, and the air into hostile and unknown spaces.[25] The confusion about the changing environment is expressed through the hypothesis about the "strange fluttering vibration": since Lewis does not know what the source of the disturbing noise could be, he immediately relates it to some kind of new human-made machinery, a "new type of engine." Such an explanation would be reasonable and somehow reassuring. However, it is impossible for him to deny the perception of *danger* connected to the unknown sound—and, because of this, the newly created engine must then belong to an "enemy airship." Machen creates in the mind of the character of Lewis a compromise between the necessity to understand the sensation of incoming threat and the need to rationalize it.

This fragile mechanism fails later on in the text, when Lewis finally sees a tree that has apparently grown fully during the night and could possibly be the original source of the weird sound. The mutation of the space surrounding the characters destabilizes them, indicating the inappropriateness of the mental tools that they used to apply when relating to the world: nature is changing, in directions that they cannot possibly foresee. *The Terror* presents therefore a landscape that is more frightening and extreme than the environment depicted in nineteenth-century works belonging to fantastic literature such as the ancient castle in Edgar Allan Poe's "The Oval Portrait" (1842) or the Pyrenees mountains in "La Vénus d'Ille" by Mérimée (1834).[26] Indeed, according to critic Remo Ceserani, fantastic literature usually depicts a border that separates the space of normality from the space of the paranormal, whether it is the door of an abandoned house, the confines of an exotic country (or at least of a country *perceived* as exotic), or the entrance to old ruins.[27] In *The Terror*, instead, such a kind of boundary dissolves, and the abnormal, the strange permeates the entire natural environment. Even though the "Terror" is still thought to be an event linked to the war, and not a supernatural phenomenon, it is characterized by a perception of ubiquity, a pervasiveness that entrenches the danger in the land itself: "here were people ready, very likely, all over the country, who were prepared to murder and destroy everywhere as soon as they got the word."[28] In this passage, the dangers of war are seen mostly in their ability to strike everywhere (in accordance with the coeval perception of a conflict that was deeply felt as "total," because it involved all social classes), and the perception of the surrounding environment changes accordingly. There is an alteration in the perspective, an attempt to adapt to the slow but relentless mutation in the world, but this attempt misses the main point, and the characters do not understand that the mutation involves much more than the power balance between the European nations. Rather, it involves the paradigm of reality itself, what can be or cannot be considered as true.

Later on in the text, one of the inhabitants who is trapped inside Treff Loyne farm and is oppressed by famish and by the horror of the inexplicable danger threatening him writes:

> I have said of what I am writing, "if it ever gets into your hands," and I am not at all sure that it ever will. If what is happening here is happening everywhere else, then I suppose, the world is coming to an end. I cannot understand it, even now I can hardly believe it. I know that I dream such wild dreams and walk in

such mad fancies that I have to look out and look about me to make sure that I am not still dreaming.[29]

If the "Terror" "is happening everywhere else," then "the world is coming to an end": it is impossible, according to the character, to imagine a reality where such disturbances can exist in the ordinary mechanisms of life. There is no place for human beings in such a reality, where one "cannot understand" and "can hardly believe" what is happening in the surrounding space; it must be a dream, an oneiric projection mimicking reality. Indeed, in *The Terror*, the *eerie* landscape seems to possess also a hidden sense of will, a latent intention that somehow lies inside the hills, the trees, the rocks. The spaces haunted by "the Terror" become "governed by absence,"[30] whereas the desolate, solitary spaces seem on the verge of disclosing the presence of terrible enemies:

> And it seemed from that wonder of the burning tree, that the enemy mysteriously and terribly present at Midlingham, was present also in Meirion. Lewis, thinking of the country as he knew it, of its wild and desolate hillsides, its deep woods, its wastes and solitary places, could not but confess that no more fit region could be found for the deadly enterprise of secret men. Yet, he thought again, there was but little harm to be done in Meirion to the armies of England or to their munitionment. They were working for panic terror?[31]

The story's protagonists almost *desire* to see something that could be identified as the coherent, direct cause of the disturbing events, of the "panic" modeling the landscape into a frightful shape. Indeed, even facing the life-threatening emergencies and dangers of the warfront, with its perpetual violence, would be preferable to this strange and unidentifiable suspension: as Lewis admits, "It's more than extraordinary; it's an awful state of things. It's terror in the dark, and there's nothing worse than that. As that young fellow I was telling you about said, 'At the front you do know what you're up against'."[32]

The result of this lack of a tangible and visible cause is a historical—and cultural—contextualization which highlights the human tendency to find a causality in every situation. The story's characters attempt to reach an ordinary explanation of the "Terror" by rejecting every kind of supernatural element. Their assumptions involve enemy soldiers hiding on the Britannic soil and the use of new and imaginary weapons like the "Z ray." The inhabitants of Britain attempt to frame the disturbing facts according to the war context, wartime being a "mental space" that already involves the feelings of fear, suspension, and anxiety that they are experiencing in 1917, during World War I. In Machen's narration, the abnormal situation—the animal attacks, the changes in the environment—is allegedly explained through a "safer" perspective. The characters prefer to imagine a world filled only with prosaic dangers, even improbable secret weapons or concealed enemy invasions: "at the beginning of the terror men spoke of nothing else; now it had become all too awful for ingenious chatter or labored and grotesque theories."[33] They choose to believe in a peril that can be still attributed to human agency, and refuse a model of reality including phenomena that could not be attributed to any understandable cause (and could, therefore, be opposed to easily).

In the end, even the theory about German soldiers hiding underground is just a way to cope with and conceal the alienating sense of extraneousness stimulated by the changing nature. The natural environment has become more and more uncontrollable, it lacks a reassuring aspect that *should be there*, especially in the characters' homeland. According to the story, there is someone (or something) else that is modifying the landscape, someone who is moving the trees, digging caverns, changing the places, someone who exercises the same agency that once belonged only to humans. In *The Terror*, nature shows a will of its own, an astonishing impulse to act directly on reality and to persecute humanity, following schemes that are inconceivable to the characters' intellect. The usual boundaries between the actor (the person who uses *agency*) and the acted (the object exposed to *agency*) are broken and confused, and the characters doubt their own position in the world:

> we both wondered whether these contradictions that one can't avoid if one begins to think of time and space may not really be proofs that the whole of life is a dream, and the moon and the stars bits of nightmare. I have often thought over that lately. I kick at the walls as Dr. Johnson kicked at the stone, to make sure that the things about me are there. And then that other question gets into my mind—is the world really coming to an end, the world as we have always known it; and what on earth will this new world be like? I can't imagine it; it's a story like Noah's Ark and the Flood. People used to talk about the end of the world and fire, but no one ever thought of anything like this.[34]

As was the case with the episode of Treff Loyne, the difficulty to contextualize the "Terror" causes the characters to doubt reality itself and its concreteness. They need to verify that they are not living in a dream/nightmare, while the true origin of the present events seems somehow located outside, far from the grasp of the human mind. Maybe even the reference to the biblical story of Noah serves to shroud the "Terror" in a mystical aura, somehow linking it to that particular category of supernatural—divine manifestations—which imply an inevitable, superior, and potentially catastrophic will. Phenomena like the "Terror" should belong to the tales of ancient religions, stories set in distant eras and understandable only through metaphorical interpretations—excluded from any contact with the everyday life. As they perceive the sense of unbelievable yet undeniable reality of the "Terror," the characters in the tale think of themselves as the characters in the Old Testament, who witness in awe the sometimes inscrutable decisions of God.

The attribution of agency to the environment in Machen's text is then replicated in the story's depiction of the animal realm. Indeed, as it occurs in du Maurier's tale, in *The Terror* the animal species possess a will and malevolence of their own that is *eerie* because it *should not be there*. In *The Birds*, no explanation is provided about the ferocity of the winged animals and readers are left to wonder about the causes of their aggressive behavior. At the end of *The Terror*, instead, it is suggested that the animals have consciously (or almost) revolted against the human race. As the narrator suggests, the beasts possibly felt the "change" in modern humans and their fall from a spiritual leadership, thus revolting "because the king abdicated."[35] Such a resolution of the story partially eliminates the sense of mystery created throughout the text, but, from a literary perspective, it does not change the interpretation of *The Terror* as a manifestation of Fisher's *eerie* as a "mode" that can be performed in specific parts of a text, even if the text itself gives a final explanation about the lack of absence and lack of presence. This is confirmed by Fisher's definition of the *eerie*, which, he argues, "concerns the unknown. When knowledge is achieved, the eerie disappears."[36] Thus, as Fisher would affirm about the end of *The Terror*, "the questions and enigmas are resolved."[37] However, the ending of Machen's novel still presents some of the characteristics of the *eerie* mode in its suggestion that the animals possess a malevolence that they should not have, in a *failure of presence* that is typical of the *eerie* mode.

Furthermore, the explanation suggested by the narrator opens to somehow deeper *eerie* meanings. The "spiritual element" and the "tradition"[38] cited by the narrator at the end of the novel as important qualities that *should be* part of human nature, are dismissed at this point, and humankind thus negates its own agency as the ruler of the world, leaving its superior place to the beasts:

> But the beasts also have within them something which corresponds to the spiritual quality in men—we are content to call it instinct. They perceived that the throne was vacant—not even friendship was possible between them and the self-deposed monarch. If he were not king he was a sham, an imposter, a thing to be destroyed.[39]

The Terror therefore suggests the existence of a superior and supernatural order that rightfully punishes human attempts to deviate from a determined moral path—the renunciation of the "royal robe."[40] Such a moral discourse is specifically related to the Great War frequently alluded to in the short novel, especially in those passages in which human attitudes to destruction are made evident through the description of a country filled with military camps and factories where ammunitions and weapons are being produced.[41] In this work by Machen, a significant part of the human activities is indeed apparently devoted to warfare: thanks to the conflict, the workers employed in the fabrication of munitions can finally adopt a wealthy lifestyle, their salaries having been raised because of the dangers of working with explosive materials: "We're seeing money for the first time in our lives, and it's bright. And we work hard for it, and we risk our lives to get it."[42] Many factories have "guard of soldiers with drawn bayonets and loaded rifles day and night,"[43] as the act of working becomes entangled with a participation—direct or not—with the war effort. British life becomes somehow modeled on the conflict, it being implicitly and morally involved with the horrors of the battlefront. The supernatural phenomena of the "Terror" burst into this context, and may therefore resemble a sort of "superior" punishment for the belligerent attitude of human beings.

A moral and physical punishment enacted through supernatural means can surely be framed in the literary tradition of the Gothic and the fantastic, as is the case of Matthew Lewis' *The Monk* (1796), in which the evil Ambrose is killed at the end of the novel by the Devil because of the terrible actions he has committed (including the rape and murder of his own sister), or "La Morte amoureuse" (1840) by Théophile Gautier, in which a priest is punished for his attraction to a dead woman. However, while in nineteenth-century supernatural fiction the paranormal is always spatially and chronologically associated to an individual's guilt that has to be expiated or to a crime that needs to be avenged, in *The Terror*—through the *eerie* mode—the entire reality is altered.[44] Such a disruption of reality happens on two levels: the "natural" one—the beasts should not manifest an agency—and the "moral" one—humankind should not have refused its own assigned spiritual nature. However, the *eerie* impossibility to entirely understand human guilt and to decipher the rules of the superior system differentiate Machen's text from Gothic and fantastic literature.[45] In the ending, it is suggested that humankind has detached itself from its own spiritual nature, but the truth about the "Terror" is never clarified and the idea that humans left their precise path is somehow upsetting: who decided the path? How is it possible to understand it and its influence on the natural world? Characters (and readers) are unable to fully explain the nature of what actually happened (which is confirmed by the cautious tone used by the narrator at the end of the novel, before he explains his theory: "In my opinion, and it is only an opinion, the source of the great revolt of the beasts is to be sought in a much subtler region of inquiry").[46] Through these narrative expedients, Machen[47] writes a story that shows a reality orchestrated and directed by a someone else that cannot be identified.[48]

However, this "someone else" should not be hurriedly identified with a traditional Christian god. *The Terror* is not simply a symbolic representation of arrogant modern humans being punished by a superior deity for a sin (such as perpetrating the violence of the war).[49] Instead, *The Terror* shows that there is an equilibrium in the world that should not be altered, and when humans refuse to assume their role as spiritual and material beings at the same time, other parts of nature (the beasts in this case) rise to take their place, conquering the "throne" that has been abandoned:

> All that was in virtue of that singular spiritual element in man which the rational animals do not possess. Spiritual does not mean respectable, it does not even mean moral, it does not mean "good" in the ordinary acceptation of the word. It signifies the royal prerogative of man, differentiating him from the beasts. For long ages he has been putting off this royal robe, he has been wiping the balm of consecration from his own breast. He has declared, again and again, that he is not spiritual, but rational, that is, the equal of the beasts over whom he was once sovereign. He has vowed that he is not Orpheus but Caliban.[50]

When beasts attempt to destroy humanity, we witness then a breakdown in the worldview in which the agency shifts from an entity to another, destabilizing the normal order and, most importantly, showing that reality itself is not permanently centered on a human perspective. When we refuse our spiritual responsibility, a superior imperative—that cannot be fully comprehended—moves to threatens us; the animals' agency *should not be there*, whereas our spiritual supremacy *should be there*. Machen examines such an unsettling scenario by depicting a haunting and dehumanized landscape. Ultimately, the haunted landscape portrayed in *The Terror* is one governed by the presence of a force that we cannot recognize, and by an absence, *our* absence; it is an ominous vision of a world without us. In his 1917 short novel, Machen represents not only a series of animals manifesting a will that should not belong to them but also how the reassuring idea of an uncontested human superiority in the world can fade into a frightening scenario.

NOTES

1. The idea of a literary mode applied to supernatural fiction was debated by Remo Ceserani with reference to the "fantastic" or "fantastique"; see Remo Ceserani, *Il fantastico* (Bologna: Il Mulino, 1996).

2. Mark Fisher, *The Weird and the Eerie* (London: Repeater Books, 2016), 15.

3. Ibid.

4. Ibid., 64.

5. Ibid., 66.

6. The similarities between *The Birds* and *The Terror* are all the more relevant if we consider that du Maurier spent some time with relatives of Machen's family, but it is very difficult to prove that she ever read *The Terror*. Arculus, "Some of the greats who have enjoyed reading Machen's works," Caerleon.net, 2000, http://www.caerleon.net/history/machen/text/page4.html (accessed June 19, 2020).

7. Arthur Machen, *The Terror* (London: Martin Secker, 1928), 18.

8. Ibid.

9. According to Anna Maleska and Mateusz Maleska, "Machen made use of the Dionysian theme in his horror stories. . . . the world of his stories is haunted by the past—by the pagan remnants of the past, to be more specific." Anna Maleszka and Mateusz Maleszka, "Supernatural or Material: Haunted Places in H.P. Lovecraft's, M.R. James's, A. Machen's and A. Blackwood's Horror Fiction," in *Theoria et Historia Scientiarum* 14 (2017), 181–99, 193. Contrary to stories such as "The Great God Pan," *The Terror* demonstrates how not all the hauntings in Machen's fiction are directly linked to paganism.

10. Machen, *The Terror*, 16.

11. Ibid., 40.

12. Ibid., 41.

13. Ibid., 58.

14. In *The Terror* the act of naming objects and places (considering the displayed will by the narrator to use fictional toponyms) is presented as an ambiguous task, full of dangerous implications, as naming something would give it a more consistent reality.

15. Fisher, *The Weird and the Eerie*, 62.

16. Machen, *The Terror*, 40, 188, and 45.

17. Ibid., 41.

18. Ibid., 48.

19. Ibid., 52.

20. Ibid., 45.

21. Ibid., 45–46.

22. Fisher, *The Weird and the Eerie*, 62.

23. Machen, *The Terror*, 56.

24. Ibid., 49.

25. Ceserani, *Il fantastico*, 80–81. Such a characterization of the environment is not unique to *The Terror*. Machen's landscapes are often charged with an unsettling tension. In short stories such as "The Shining Pyramid" (1895), "The White People" (1904), and "Out of the Earth" (1915), for instance, the environment is characterized by a sense of potential danger which changes the human perspective of what can be perceived as "safe." In "The Shining Pyramid" the protagonist climbs a hill where a strange apparition supposedly occurs sometimes in the night: "As he went on, he seemed to mount ever higher above the world of human life and customary things . . . As he reached what seemed the summit of the hill, he realized for the first time the desolate loneliness and strangeness of the land; there was nothing but grey sky and grey hill, a high, vast plain that seemed to stretch on for ever and ever,

and a faint glimpse of a blue-peaked mountain far away and to the north." Arthur Machen, "The Shining Pyramid," in *Welsh Tales Of Terror*, ed. Ronald Chetwynd-Hayes, 46–69 (London: Fontana Books, 1973), 60. In "The White People," a young woman crosses a desolate landscape, where the inanimate objects inspire her with a sense of latent vitality: "I never saw such big ugly stones before; they came out of the earth some of them, and some looked as if they had been rolled to where they were, and they went on and on as far as I could see, a long, long way. I looked out from them and saw the country, but it was strange. It was winter time, and there were black terrible woods hanging from the hills all round; it was like seeing a large room hung with black curtains, and the shape of the trees seemed quite different from any I had ever seen before. I was afraid." Arthur Machen, "The White People," in *The House of Souls*, 111–66 (North Stratford: Ayer Company Publishers, 1999), 128. In "Out of the Earth," a coastal zone, rumored to be ruined by kids exhibiting a hostile behavior, inspires a natural majestic sense of respect that is all the more juxtaposed to the actions of the villainous children: "I felt that it could not be so, for the solemn rocks of Tremaen would have turned the liveliest Pierrot to stone. He would have frozen into a crag on the beach, and the seagulls would carry away his song and make it a lament by lonely, booming caverns that look on Avalon." Arthur Machen, "Out of the Earth," in *The Shining Pyramid*, 37–46 (Chicago: Covici-McGee, 1923), 40.

26. Ceserani, *Il fantastico*, 41 and 35.

27. According to Ceserani, "[fantastic literature] frequently sets the story in marginal geographical areas instead of those that belong to European countries and are influenced by the courses of modernity and scientific rationality. This is therefore the case of areas such as Poland, or Spain, or Southern Italy, or the extreme fringes of Scotland, where the comparison is evident between a dominant culture and another one pulling back—the former being based on rational knowledge and the latter on ancient and traditional creeds—where two cultures are struggling against each other or are forced to coexist." Ceserani, *Il fantastico*, 113. My translation.

28. Machen, *The Terror*, 36.

29. Ibid., 111–12.

30. Fisher, *The Weird and the Eerie*, 79. Something similar happens in the fictional works by M.R. James, which present haunted landscapes, silent and empty scenarios where both natural and supernatural apparitions (even the shape of a human figure walking in the distance) can acquire an ominous and terrible meaning. As Fisher notes, stories such as "Oh, Whistle and I'll Come For You, My Lad" (1904) or "A Warning to the Curious" (1925) depict landscapes that are full of *nothing*, scenes where the absence of something vivid or alive stimulates a feeling of creepiness and the uncanny.

31. Machen, *The Terror*, 70.

32. Ibid., 63.

33. Ibid., 95.

34. Ibid., 114.

35. Ibid., 144.

36. Fisher, *The Weird and the Eerie*, 62.
37. Ibid.
38. Machen, *The Terror*, 145.
39. Ibid., 146.
40. Ibid., 145.
41. In *The Terror* technology usually appears to be related to the war, since the narrator mentions industries involved in military production. The correlation between science and evil in supernatural fiction is examined in Jonas Prida, "Weird Modernism: Literary Modernism in the First Decade of Weird Tales," in *The Unique Legacy of Weird Tales: The Evolution of Modern Fantasy and Horror*, ed. Justin Everett and Jeffrey H. Shanks, 15–28 (Lanham, MD: Rowman & Littlefield, 2015), 20–21.
42. Machen, *The Terror*, 18.
43. Ibid., 57.
44. James Machin, *Weird Fiction in Britain* (Basingstoke: Palgrave Macmillan, 2018), 22–23.
45. Francesco Orlando argues: "the presence of the supernatural corresponds mainly with the presence of rules. In its forms and literary articulations, the supernatural . . . must be shaped, outlined, cut out by rules, up to the point of consisting in them . . . these rules' motivation may be unclear or latent, intuitive or evocative, in other words, arbitrary. They could also be the product of the writer's imagination, effective in his/her text and only inside of it, or they may derive from pre-existent codes, whether they are religious, folkloric or literary ones." Francesco Orlando, *Il soprannaturale letterario* (Turin: Einaudi, 2016), 17. My translation.
46. Machen, *The Terror*, 144.
47. Machen appeared to be perfectly aware of the inadequateness of old supernatural fiction topics for a late nineteenth-century audience: "His business acumen was at least enough to see that to sell a story to a late nineteenth-century audience, the old folkloric prototypes incommensurate with the modern age were no longer adequate, hence his use of science and pseudoscience to create the inciting incident of a narrative." Machin, *Weird Fiction in Britain*, 145. Subsequently Machen exhibited the intention to overcome the coeval supernatural fiction norms: Machin notes that in 1923 the Welsh writer admitted that he "had exhausted the Stevensonian experiments in horror" with "The Great God Pan," trying to pursue a "more consciously purist course." Machin, *Weird Fiction in Britain*, 137.
48. Something similar happens also in Lovecraft's fiction, as is the case of *The Call of Cthulhu* (1928), which contains the famous passage about human ignorance. The story concerning Cthulhu could be interpreted as *eerie* not only through a supernatural perspective, but also through a moral one, because the existence of the elder God destroys the lay and materialistic vision of the world held by the main character by hinting at a superior order that is impossible to understand.
49. The importance of symbolism in Machen's stories is clear, as S.T. Joshi suggested; see Joshi, *The Weird Tale*, 14–16. Joshi interprets the 1917 short novel by the Welsh writer through Christian culture and the idea of a transcendental truth.
50. Machen, *The Terror*, 145.

REFERENCES

Arculus. "Some of the greats who have enjoyed reading Machen's works." 2000, http://www.caerleon.net/history/machen/text/page4.html.

Ceserani, Remo. *Il fantastico*. Bologna: Il Mulino, 1996.

Chetwynd-Hayes, Ronald (ed.). *Welsh Tales of Terror*. London: Fontana Books, 1973.

Fisher, Mark. *The Weird and the Eerie*. London: Repeater Books, 2016.

Joshi, Sunand Tryambak. *The Weird Tale*. Holicong: Wildside Press, 1990.

Lovecraft, Howard Phillips. *The Complete Fiction Omnibus. The Prime Years 1926–1936*, edited by Finn J. D. John. Corvallis: Pulp-Lit Productions, 2016.

Machen, Arthur. "Out of the Earth." In *The Shining Pyramid*, 37–46. Chicago: Covici-McGee, 1923.

———. "The Shining Pyramid." In *Welsh Tales of Terror*, edited by Ronald Chetwynd-Hayes, 46–69. London: Fontana Books, 1973.

———. *The Terror*. London: Martin Secker, 1928.

———. "The White People." In *The House of Souls*, 111–66. North Stratford: Ayer Company Publishers, 1999.

Machin, James. *Weird Fiction in Britain*. Basingstoke: Palgrave Macmillan, 2018.

Maleszka, Anna and Mateusz Maleszka. "Supernatural or Material: Haunted Places in H.P. Lovecraft's, M.R. James's, A. Machen's and A. Blackwood's Horror Fiction." *Theoria et Historia Scientiarum* 14 (2017): 181–99.

Orlando, Francesco. *Il soprannaturale letterario*. Turin: Einaudi, 2016.

Prida, Jonas. "Weird Modernism: Literary Modernism in the First Decade of Weird Tales." In *The Unique Legacy of Weird Tales: The Evolution of Modern Fantasy and Horror*, edited by Justin Everett and Jeffrey H. Shanks, 15–28. Lanham, MD: Rowman & Littlefield, 2015.

Chapter 3

Heterotopic Spaces in Machen's Fiction

Antonio Sanna

In many of the stories published throughout his career, Machen represents a series of locations such as woods, hills, and even entire villages opening up to an alternative, supernatural reality. This chapter examines the natural and urban locations of Machen's fiction in which supernatural or extraordinary events occur through the concept of heterotopia, theorized by Michel Foucault (1926–1984). The various aspects of the French philosopher's theory will be applied to several stories by the Welsh writer, whether heterotopic spaces have a positive or a negative characterization. In the first case, the characters' encounters with the supernatural and the extraordinary are experienced as enriching, mystical, and beneficial, whereas negative heterotopias present a more sinister, alienating, and horrific encounter with the manifestations of the supernatural order that frightens and even threatens the lives of the characters.

Foucault first mentions the concept of heterotopia in the preface to his volume *The Order of Things* (1966), though, on such an occasion, he specifically refers to texts juxtaposing incongruous and inappropriate concepts and meanings with each other.[1] An in-depth elaboration of the concept was offered in a 1967 lecture that was posthumously published in the French journal *Architecture/Mouvement/Continuité* in 1984. The latter essay examines twentieth-century anxieties about space by investigating how "[external] space takes for us the form of relations among sites."[2] The French philosopher initially identifies heterotopias (as set against unreal spaces such as utopias and dystopias) as "something like counter-sites, a kind of effectively enacted utopia in which the real sites, all the other real sites that can be found within the culture, are simultaneously represented, contested, and inverted ... these places are absolutely different from all the sites that they reflect and speak about."[3] Heterotopias thus function as practically realized utopias that challenge or replace societal arrangements found elsewhere. Foucault gives the example of a mirror, ostensibly a utopia because a reflection comes from "a place without a place ... an unreal, virtual space that opens up behind the surface," but functioning simultaneously as a heterotopia because "it really exists and has a kind of come-back effect on the place that [it occupies]."[4] Mirrors allow a person to reflect on him/herself and the space he/she occupies in the environment; they allow individuals to both reflect (create a reflection of) their status, appearance, and position and reflect (induce a reflection) on them. Heterotopias at large have the same function: their otherness challenges other societal arrangements and they are set against "normal" spaces and locations. As the example of the mirror makes clear, heterotopias represent therefore a spatial otherness that nevertheless coincides physically with a real place in the world: they can be accessed in or have a point of contact with the real world (as is not the case with utopias instead, which are the product of human intellect and imagination).

Foucault then suggests a series of principles that govern heterotopias. The first tenet relates to the ubiquity of such sites, as "there is probably not a single culture in the world that fails to constitute heterotopias. That is a constant of every human group."[5] Heterotopic places can nevertheless take different forms. For instance, "crisis heterotopias," Foucault explains, "are privileged or sacred or forbidden places, reserved for individuals who are, in relation to society and to the human environment in which they live, in a state of crisis."[6] Residents of crisis heterotopias are, according to the French philosopher, adolescents, pregnant women, the elderly. Crisis heterotopias were identified with nineteenth-century boarding schools or the military service, places that have been disappearing during the twentieth century and have been replaced by "heterotopias of deviation," where "individuals whose behavior is deviant in relation to the required mean or norm are placed."[7] The latter are therefore places of confinement, such as rest homes, prisons, and psychiatric hospitals, whose function is to liberate society from inconvenient, troublesome people, who do not/cannot fit within the establishment.

Another principle governing heterotopias establishes that they are "most often linked to slices in time—which is to say that they open onto what might be termed, for the sake of symmetry, heterochronies. The heterotopia begins to function at full capacity when men arrive at a sort of absolute break with their traditional time."[8] Museums and libraries exemplify the perpetual accumulation and enclosure of time in a place that is thus constructed as inaccessible to its passage. In this sense, heterochronies are oriented toward the eternal. On the other hand, festivals and fairgrounds represent the most transitory and precarious aspect of time because they are "absolutely temporal."[9]

Foucault also argues that "heterotopias always presuppose a system of opening and closing that both isolates them and makes them penetrable. In general, the heterotopic site is not freely accessible like a public place. Either the entry is compulsory, as in the case of entering a barracks or a prison, or else the individual has to submit to rites and purifications. To get in one must have a certain permission and make certain gestures."[10] Finally, heterotopias can have a double role: either they "create a space of illusion that exposes every real space, all the sites inside of which human life is partitioned, as still more illusory . . . Or else, on the contrary, their role is to create a space that is other, another real space, as perfect, as meticulous, as well arranged as ours is messy, ill constructed, and jumbled. This latter type would be the heterotopia, not of illusion, but of compensation."[11]

According to Foucault, heterotopias, therefore, have the following defining characteristics: they are everywhere (each culture has its own heterotopias) and are connected to an entire community (cemeteries, for example, are the resting places for the relatives of all families in a community); they can take different forms and have different functions through time; they can either be transitory in time or oriented toward the eternal; entrance into them could be compulsory or could occur through ritual; and, finally, they can either expose reality as illusory or can create a perfect space. Many of these rules theorized by Foucault shall now be applied to pertinent locations in the works of Arthur Machen. In the literary production of the Welsh writer, such places are woods, hills, and even entire villages opening up to an alternative, supernatural reality where past and present coexist. This can alternatively induce happiness, mystical feelings, and fear in the characters or even threaten their lives. Each of these peculiar spaces has attributes entirely of its own: to use Foucault's words, "an unreal, virtual space . . . opens up behind the surface."[12] Heterotopic spaces can have positive connotations in the fiction by the Welsh writer, or can be characterized as dangerous spaces for those human beings who happen to encounter malevolent creatures (or are lured there by them).

Exemplary of a positive heterotopia is "The Great Return," the novella Machen published in 1915, in which the characters' encounters with the supernatural is experienced as enriching, mystical, and beneficial. The opening up of a world that is not usually or directly visible and accessible to all human beings functions as a window into the past, myth, and religion and therefore reflects the concept of "chronotopies" elaborated by the French philosopher when he argues that they represent the indefinite accumulation of time as set against the constant passing of it in the ordinary world. When entering a positive chronotopia, Machen's characters directly face a past that has favorable connotations and improves their lives, either spiritually or physically. "The Great Return" is introduced as the fictional study of a case of manifestations of the marvelous, of those events that "belong to the world on the other side of the dark curtain; and it is only by some queer mischance that a corner of that curtain is twitched aside for an instant."[13] The story, therefore, is presented as the encounter with a world that is not usually accessible to human beings in their ordinary lives. The protagonist (identifiable as a literary version of Machen himself) visits the village of Llantrisant near the Welsh coast and discovers a land experiencing peace and happiness, both in its magnificent landscapes and in its inhabitants' appearance and temperaments.[14] This is the result of a series of allegedly divine manifestations that have occurred for nine days: the church smells of incense and odors of paradise, a bright light shines from it at midnight, heavenly bells ring from the sea, a song "upon the water that was like heaven" is heard, and, finally, a vast rose of fire appears over the sea.[15]

A rational explanation for the occurrence of such remarkable, strange phenomena is attempted by the protagonist. He initially dismisses the mystical interpretation of them because he believes that they may consist in rumors and terrors due to the agency of the enemy during the "Great War." He then attempts to explain the sound of bells and the celestial song heard upon the water as "either a collective auditory hallucination or a manifestation of what is conveniently, if inaccurately, called the supernatural order."[16] Finally, the occurrences are tentatively connected to the old traditions on the Holy Grail, though the facts themselves are not explained away at the end of the work—its last words being "at the last, what do we know?"[17] Such a "visitation of great marvels" demonstrates therefore an opening from the world of beyond into our own, an entrance of the supernatural into the real world,[18] which creates a space that, as is the case of Foucauldian heterotopias, is connected to an entire community. Indeed, the contact of the people with the supernatural reality occurs all over Llantrisant and its surrounding areas. Moreover, the heterotopia manifesting in the Welsh town can be interpreted as oriented toward the eternal, because it connects the inhabitants of Llantrisant not only with a superior reality, but also with the ancient traditions (contemporary rituals in the church are not respected anymore, according to the tale, but ancient religious formulas and prayers are celebrated in their place) and the very origin of the town's name (the three saints are allegedly seen in a vision by many inhabitants).

The heterotopia in "The Great Return" also represents a perfect space, a heterotopia "of compensation," whose role, in Foucault's words, "is to create a space that is other, another real space, as perfect, as meticulous, as well arranged as ours is messy, ill constructed, and jumbled," especially when compared to the wretched reality of war affecting Great Britain (and the world) at the time in which the story is set. The perfection of such a space is evident from the fact that the people of the village appear to be younger and have brightening faces; they are filled with joy and wonder; some of them miraculously recover from incurable illnesses; and years-long feuds and quarrels are solved amicably. The heterotopia in "The Great Return," therefore, is experienced as a blissful, mystical encounter with the supernatural, with positive effects on both the people and the land, which is said to have become more fertile and prosperous after the blissful nine days.

Another ecstatic and peaceful heterotopia exemplifying a perfect place in Machen's fiction is depicted in "N" (1936). The narrative begins with three gentlemen recalling the appearance of the streets of London in earlier decades. One of the men mentions Canon's Park in Stoke Newington, an incredibly beautiful park once visited by a cousin of his, which is filled with lawns adorned by flowers, exotic trees, summer houses, and temples ("it was like finding yourself in another country").[19] None of the gentlemen knows of the existence of such a place, however, but one of them, Arnold, subsequently finds a reference to it in an 1853 book by Reverend Thomas Hampole. The latter recounts how he had been invited to take a view of the park from one of his parishioner's windows, and was able to admire "a panorama of unearthly, of astounding beauty."[20] The reverend affirms:

> my soul was ravished by the spectacle displayed before me. I was possessed by a degree of rapture and delight such as I had never experienced. A sense of beatitude pervaded my whole being; my bliss was such as cannot be expressed by words. I uttered an inarticulate cry of joy and wonder.[21]

Attempting to investigate on the reality of such a place and wondering whether its existence is actually the product of telepathy or hallucination, the protagonist visits Stoke Newington and learns that a madman who escaped from the lunatic asylum once rented a room in the area and told his landlady about such an enchanting view from his window. As is the case with "The Great Return," "N" represents a heterotopia of compensation, a perfect space apparently out of time that induces positive feelings in those few characters who witness its existence.

Other short stories by Machen depict a heterotopia where past and present coexist, though their beneficial effects on the local people are not evident or explicit. In the short story "The Happy Children" (1920), a reporter visits Banwick in the North-Eastern district the day after Christmas 1915. The seaside town is described as a fascinating place: the old houses, the quays, and the Norman church on the hill are briefly drawn in a realistic style and provide the reader with a very specific picture of a charming place inhabited by pleasant people. The reporter recounts his strolls in the dark winter evening before and after dinner and how he sees many children laughing, dancing, and singing wonderful, old melodies with happy voices in the village's courts and alleys. The unsuspecting reader cannot realize that the "extraordinary Banwick children"[22] are actually a manifestation of the supernatural, an intrusion from the otherworld, until the protagonist faces a long procession of them, all clad in white, leading to the abbey. The moment of discovery is experienced as marked by calm and composure ("Whether a faint moon now rose, or whether clouds passed from before the stars, I do not know; but the air lightened, and I could see the children plainly as they went by")[23] until the protagonist notices the seaweeds and bleeding wounds covering the children's bodies. Nevertheless, contrary to the inn's landlord (who explicitly expresses his discomfort after being told of the children's presence everywhere in the town), the narrator is never terrorized by such an apparition. A few weeks later, he learns from a book about the procession and mass of the innocents that used to be held during the Elizabethan age in Banwick and considers his experience as a repetition of the bygone age into his present. Banwick thus works as a chronotopia: the place is a real village, where past and present coexist for a brief lapse of time and allow for the simultaneous presence of the world beyond the veil and our own.[24]

Similarly, in "Munitions of War"—a short story originally published in Cynthia Asquith's *The Ghost-Book* (1926) and later included in the 1936 collection *The Cosy Room and Other Stories*—the encounter with the supernatural is related to the support given to the war effort at home during WW1. In this narrative, the first-person narrator (allegedly Machen himself) is sent to the town of Westpool to evaluate its prosperity and stress during the global conflict. He is astounded by finding the city and its center almost deserted, with no hurry or rush of war-business—a fact confirmed by the people he randomly interviews in the desolate streets (the protagonist, nevertheless, suspects that they are scared). Upon spending the night in a room, whose landlord is the only person acknowledging the intense activity being performed in the city, the protagonist discovers that the river's quays are swarming with ghost crews (one of them admits having died at Trafalgar) noisily rolling casks aboard ghost ships. He is therefore unexpectedly thrown into the world of the past and re-experiences events that are parallel to contemporary history. In "Munitions of War," the protagonist (who is neutral in his report of the facts and does not experience fear) witnesses a Foucauldian chronotopia, an actual physical place where the re-enactment of the past demonstrates the orientation of the place toward the eternal and the connection between the past and the present of an entire community (in this case, Great Britain as busy in its war effort against an enemy abroad).

As the aforementioned narratives demonstrate, the heterotopias represented in Machen's fiction are visible only to a few characters and access to them is not necessarily free to everyone. In his essay, Foucault specifies that one of the conditions for accessing some kinds of heterotopia can be the ceremonial performance of a ritual: "the individual has to submit to rites and purifications. To get in one must have a certain permission and make certain gestures."[25] In Machen's writings, the encounter with the supernatural also occurs by means of a ritualistic performance, as is the case of the prose poem "The Ceremony" from *Ornaments in Jade* (1924). The story, on a girl's remembrance of the rituals performed by her nurse on a grey stone in the middle of the woods in a hot afternoon when she was a child, focuses on the initial panic caused by the girl's discovery of the pillar and the sensations she experienced—along with her detailed auditory, visual, and even olfactory description of the surroundings (which emphasizes the importance of the location in all of its aspects). The narrator then focuses on the ritual performed by the nurse, who stains the grim stone with the red flowers she is carrying (though the text simultaneously seems to allude to blood being poured instead), only to abruptly interrupt the description: "the red color stained the grey stone, and there was nothing else."[26] Attempting to penetrate the layers of memory, the girl describes her experience with the following words:

> It was as if one gazed at a velvet curtain, heavy, mysterious, impenetrable blackness, and then, for the twinkling of an eye, one spied through a pin-hole a storeyed town that flamed, with fire about its walls and pinnacles. And then again the folding darkness, so that sight became illusion, almost in the seeing. So to her was that earliest, doubtful vision of the grey stone, of the red colour spilled upon it, with the incongruous episode of the nursemaid, who wept at night.[27]

"The Ceremony" presents the very dramatic image of an infernal city being consumed by flames, an image briefly registered in the mind of the girl as a brief glimpse on a supernatural reality. The very fact, however, that such a glimpse on an alternative reality after the performance of the ritual is only made through a simile ("It was as if") would not allow for an interpretation of the text as depicting the presence, though momentary, of a heterotopia, of the mysteries that lie beyond the veil of the material world actually being revealed in our reality. However, through a series of half-broken sentences reconstructing the girl's memories of her adolescence, the text further alludes to the continuing ritualistic use of the stone, from the puzzling conduct of the girl's parents to the dropping of flowers on the location by the passers-by and the constant presence of blossoms over the stone in all seasons of the year. At the end of the narrative, after witnessing a young girl's crowning of the stone with lilies, the protagonist finally performs herself "the antique immemorial rite."[28] The accumulation of the past typical of some Foucauldian heterotopias is here represented by the ritualistic performance enacted by the story's characters on the grey stone, which becomes a place beyond the ordinary conception of time, the ritual apparently being performed by different generations of people and throughout the seasons since immemorial time.

The performance of a ritual grants access to a heterotopia in *The White People* (1904). In this text, an adolescent girl's diary recalls the encounter with the titular "white people" coming out of the woods near a deep pool when she was five. The child, who was in the company of her nurse at the time, was not frightened at all, but rather fascinated by the ethereal figures singing and dancing around. She then recounts her "White Day," when she is nearly fourteen and, after walking a long, new way through dense woods and thorny thickets on the hills, she reaches a series of isolated (either bare or dark and enclosed) areas where she performs various rituals that had been taught to her by her nurse. The narrative alternates between the fear of the landscape by the young protagonist and her reverie in the practice of magical rituals.[29] Her description of the secretive valley she reaches, where she drinks from a little stream of water (whose nymph she invokes), however, reveals the exclusivity and otherness of the place, its distinctiveness in respect to the ordinary places she lives in:

> I felt I had come such a long, long way, just as if I were a hundred miles from home, or in some other country, or in one of those strange places I had read about in the "Tales of the Genie" and the "Arabian Nights," or as if I had found another world that nobody had ever seen or heard of before.[30]

After finding another dark, hidden place in the middle of the wood, the girl affirms she sees a most wonderful and strange sight. The girl's diary is very intimate, but it voluntarily omits any description of what actually occurs to her during her encounters with the supernatural. The girl returns home and, lying awake through the night, recounts her nurse's tales, including one on a ritualistic, secret encounter of a group of people on a hill where they drink wine, sing in an old language, dance, and model images from clay to worship. These tales, she affirms, have been handed down by her nurse's great-grandmother—which alludes to a feminine, secretive knowledge of the occult that is the exclusive dominion of generations of women. After realizing that her nurse's tales are true, the girl visits the secret wood beyond the hills for the second time and there she performs another series of ritualistic actions until another heterotopia is formed:

> and the story was all true, and I wished that the years were gone by, and that I had not so long a time to wait before I was happy forever and ever . . . I understood about the nymphs; how I might meet them in all kinds of places, and they would always help me, and I must always look for them, and find them in all sorts of strange shapes and appearances . . . And there were two kinds, the bright and the dark, and both were very lovely and very wonderful . . . so I went to the wood where the pool was, where I saw the white people, and I tried again [to call the nymphs]. The dark nymph, Alanna, came, and she turned the pool of water into a pool of fire.[31]

The girl, the epilogue reports, poisons herself by the pool described in her diary and her body is found near an Ancient Roman statue generally used for the Sabbath. Nature and illicit sex, especially on the part of women, therefore, are associated with paganism, which is explored here through the sacramental use of wine and the resurgence of a pre-Christian past that challenges the societal arrangements of the modern age.[32] Such a juxtaposition is further emphasized by means of the opposition between the sexual freedom and the happiness celebrated by the girl's narrative as set against the frame tale of the two male characters (Ambrose and Cotgrave) discussing the nature of evil and evaluating the veracity of the girl's story in the tale's preface and epilogue. A male perspective encloses a story about feminine liberty from constraints and social rules, liberty which she manages to achieve instead inside the dark woods, in what can therefore be interpreted as a Foucauldian heterotopia of crisis and/or deviance. Indeed, adolescents and pregnant women are the residents of crisis heterotopias, according to the French philosopher, whereas heterotopias of deviance are inhabited by inconvenient, troublesome people outside of the establishment. The very fact that the male narrator of the epilogue asserts that her death comes "on time,"[33] as both H.P. Lovecraft and S.T. Joshi have argued, alludes to the possibility that the girl might have been pregnant and her suicide has been motivated by the decision not to give birth to a horrific child.[34] The male narrator seems to be implying that her timely death is instrumental for the girl to avoid being (too) corrupted by her practice of magical rituals and her contact with the supernatural and thus reinscribes her narrative within the confines of the status quo.

The woods are the heterotopic locus of encounters with the supernatural in Machen's "The Great God Pan" (1894) as well, though the novella presents a more sinister and threatening encounter with the manifestations of the supernatural order. In the second chapter, Mr. Clarke receives news of extraordinary facts that have occurred in a village on the borders of Wales, where the adolescent Helen V. is provisionally staying at a well-to-do farmer's house. During a walk on the old Roman road in the middle of the woods, Helen is seen by the seven-year-old Trevor in the company of a "strange naked man."[35] The child, terrorized by the vision, subsequently recognizes such a creature in a Roman artifact depicting a faun, and becomes prey to fits of hysteria and a permanent weakness of intellect. A second encounter with the satyr-like creature is made years later by Helen's friend, Rachel M., who is then found "lying, half undressed, upon the bed, evidently in a state of great distress . . . [and] told a wild story."[36] Helen—whose birth from the titular Greek god and the seventeen-year-old Mary is the result of the experiment in transcendental medicine performed at the beginning of the tale by Dr. Raymond—subsequently seduces a series of respectable gentlemen and drives them to madness and despair (one of them declares he has been ruined "in body and soul").[37]

After an epidemic of suicides committed in London by those who have been revealed an arcane, forbidden knowledge by the maleficent woman, the male protagonists of the story force the evil trans-species being to kill herself. One of the fragments constituting the last chapter of the novella describes the visit of Austin to the woods where Trevor's and Rachel's encounters with Pan occurred many years earlier. Austin delays his walk on the ancient Roman road until the last day of his stay in the village and when he finally follows the steps of Helen Vaughan and poor Rachel he finds the "open space with a thick undergrowth around it"[38] where the misdeed occurred—readers are left to wonder whether it was a sexual assault or a ritualistic orgy (as in many passages throughout the tale, Machen refuses to provide detailed information about the horrific events and alludes to the forbidden nature of such a knowledge). Austin's discomfort and anxiety are expressed through his explicit, blunt, and short affirmation "I did not stay there long,"[39] which truncates the possibility for any actual description of the open space in the forest. However, in the last fragment of the novella, Dr. Raymond (who concludes the tale as a circular text narrated only by men, in which the character of Helen has no voice of her own) mentions the recent discovery of a pillar of white stone in the area containing an inscription alluding to unknown rites being practiced there. This further testifies to the place's characterization as a heterotopia where the encounter with the supernatural (in particular, the satyr god) has been occurring since the time of the Roman colonization of Wales. The heterotopia in the woods near Caermaen where Pan is invoked and encountered allows for a return of the pagan past, which is set against the enlightened, scientific, and industrial present of the late-Victorian age the characters live in.[40]

In this novella, paganism is also clearly associated with decadence and degeneration, as Sophie Mantrant suggests.[41] Significantly, the emphasis on the god Pan's and his daughter's sexual voraciousness, their practice of illicit sex, and their association with wild, unrestrained nature characterizes this natural space as Foucault's heterotopia of deviation, "in which individuals whose behavior is deviant in relation to the required mean or norm are placed."[42] Pan and Helen represent the deviation from the norms of decorum, decency, monogamy, and sexual restraint as much as the deviation from the idea of women as "angels of the house" and as dependent (economically and sexually) by men that were the foundation of Victorian morality and its patriarchal system.[43] Pan's and Helen's intrusion into the real world is confined to a secretive area of the woods that is the opposite of contemporary society and unwilling witnesses of the event are severely damaged by their discovery of such a mystery beyond the veil.[44]

In this sense, both *The White People* and "The Great God Pan" exemplify the interpretation of heterotopias offered by critic Fred Botting in his studies on Gothic novels. Botting argues:

Heterotopias are sites where subjects and behaviours that fit only partially within dominant norms can be both contained and excluded ... Heterotopias are thus necessary in the constitution and maintenance of social formations: their otherness enables the differentiation, ordering and policing of the limits of their own space as well as the boundaries of society.[45]

Precisely like castles, ruins, and labyrinths in the Gothic novels of the eighteenth century and their urban equivalents in the Gothic narratives of the late nineteenth century, these negative heterotopic sites present in Machen's fiction, as Botting would phrase it, "are constructed as antithetical locations in which selfish, criminal, and sexual passions are enacted."[46] Botting's definition of "Gothic landscapes [as] desolating, alienating and full of menace," identifies those attributes that can be easily applied to all of those heterotopic locations in which Machen's characters encounter some physical being that either threatens their lives or puts into crisis their system of belief.[47] The moral and rational structures on which contemporary society is founded are loosened in such areas.

The representation of the heterotopia of deviation is particularly evident in many of those stories that involve the "little people." In Machen's fiction, such creatures (also known in folklore as "fairies") are the descendants of the primeval races that inhabited Britain and, after being defeated by the Celts, allegedly found refuge inside caves until the present day. Descriptions of them are partial and rare throughout Machen's production, but the encounter with them in remote, isolated areas of the countryside is always a source of great fear or anxiety (if not lethal danger) for the characters.[48] These tales by Machen thus exemplify Foucault's argument (and Botting's interpretation of it) that some heterotopias can "hide curious exclusions," and provide a representation of heterotopic space that gives cover for secretive abuses.[49]

In his analysis of the stories by Machen on the little people, S.T. Joshi argues that they "are horrible and loathsome, to be sure, but they have at least one advantage over modern human beings: they have retained that primal sacrament (perverted, of course, by bestiality and violence) which links them with the Beyond."[50] In this sense, as remnants of the distant past of the human race itself and of a reality beyond the grasp of present-day human beings, the encounter with the little people perfectly epitomizes the definition of the hills and woods where they live and where horrible actions (such as assault on human beings, kidnapping, and human sacrifice) are still ignominiously committed as counter-sites that invert the values and culture of contemporary society. Exemplary is, in this sense, "The Shining Pyramid" (1895), in which Dyson (the man of letters who acts as Machen's detective in several tales published during the 1890s) and his friend Mr. Vaughan investigate on the changing arrangement of small, antique flint arrow-heads and several almond-shaped eyes painted in red on a small pillar near the cottage of the latter gentleman in Wales. The case, which is linked to the disappearance of a handsome girl from a track on the bare hillside, leads Dyson to the exploration of the hills.[51] The "desolate loneliness and strangeness of the land" particularly impress Dyson, who is astonished by the discovery of a circular depression circled by "ugly crags of limestone."[52] One of the following nights, the two men reach the spot where "the fantastic limestone rocks hinted horror through the darkness."[53] Vaughan specifies that such a place is feared by the local people, it being "supposed to be a fairies' castle."[54] Inside the circular depression, a group of dwarfish, loathsome, and deformed creatures venomously sibilating to each other and "with the almond eyes burning with evil and unspeakable lust," sacrifice the terrorized missing girl on a great pyramid of flames.[55] The tale presents the location where the extraordinary event occurs as a place that induces horror in Dyson and Vaughan (as much as in the reader), as an unwelcoming setting oriented toward the eternal (a barbarous, uncivilized past lives on through the little people), where unspeakable and violent acts are enacted and excessive passions (as it occurs in Gothic narratives) are experienced.

The characterization of space as heterotopic as due to the presence of the little people occurs also in "Strange Roads" (1923), which describes with a simple language a series of strange, beautiful pathways in the countryside. One of them, the first-person narrator reports, descends steeply from a silent hill near Marlborough to some ancient, twisted thorns. Such plants cause him and his companion to "think of the People—that is, the fairies ... And suddenly, quite instantly, without any preparation of a distant sound, soft at first, and growing louder by degrees, we both heard the sharp rattle of footfalls coming behind, and gaining on us."[56] The intrusion of the supernatural is sudden and immediate in this passage. As is the case of "The Shining Pyramid," the two protagonists step into a location that is not governed by present-day rules of conduct, where humans are not welcome and can become the victims of a race belonging to the past. When looking back, no one is visible by the two men in spite of the white road being clear before them and each time they turn and stop the sound ceases. The two protagonists are instantly frightened by the occurrence and decide to go back to the town. As the narrator reports, "The rattle of pursuing footsteps ceased as we saw the glimmer of the lamps in the darkness of the little town below. I do not explain."[57] The narrator thus refuses to offer an explanation of what has allegedly occurred: the actual experience of the two protagonists stands as a certain, incontrovertible evidence of a supernatural occurrence, but the evaluation of its veracity is left to the reader. The description of the two characters' fear as well as the editorial choice to include such a subject among the discussion of pleasant walks in the countryside sets this specific part of the narrative apart from the rest of the text. The presence of the supernatural, of bygone, invisible people/creatures characterizes the location represented in this passage from "Strange Roads" as a heterotopia, a place where the undead past represented by an ancient race of beings aggressively haunts the present as well as a space where the laws of physics apparently do not apply (the human characters hear the pursuing villains but cannot see them).

Another work by Machen that focuses on the little people is "The Strange Tale of Mount Nephin," from the collection *Bridles & Spurs* (1951). It is an essay on the "laws of the kingdom of the unseen" that examines a tale about the encounter with strange figures vanishing in the air by six climbers during an expedition on the titular mountain in Ireland in 1929.[58] After the separation of one of the members of the expedition from the rest of the group, the first woman returning to the cottage sees a figure that, once reached, has apparently disappeared, but she then hears a laughter in the air close to her. Later on, one of the men reports having being forced to fly away twice after seeing out of tail of his eyes a club whirling down at him though no aggressor was visible. Near the end of the story, the lost woman's account is reported by the narrator in indirect speech:

> She does not know, she cannot possibly imagine what happened to her. She can only say that it was as though she had lapsed into complete unconsciousness, and all the while thought she was walking beside us. She was in reality walking straight away from us. She does not know what it was that "took" her suddenly; she said it was as though there were no time for a moment, and some strange force were pulling her away. Then she realised that we were not there, and heard the crying of voices.[59]

The woman follows the voices and sees some child-like beings from afar but is not able to reach them, and thus heads toward a country road at the bottom of the mountain. In spite of her unconsciousness on the direction of her march, her description of the surrounding space, the mountainside, and a ravine is, though not detailed, always lucid, as if she were unmistakably aware of and clear about the landscape. It is the presence of the supernatural in it that transforms the mountainside into a heterotopic space, a heterochronia where, as she affirms, there is no time and the past still lives in the present through the little people, who haunt and even physically threaten the characters. An explanation is indeed attempted about the possible presence of the unknown race by the narrator near the end of the essay, though it is inconclusive:

> I am convinced that the persons of the tale really experienced the impressions and sensations which they say that they experienced. And what, or who, caused

these impressions and sensations? . . . I dare not say that the people who climbed Mount Nephin in July, 1929, were beset by fairies; but I think we may say that experiences such as theirs were the foundation of the older fairy lore.[60]

Whether fairies exist or not, the narrator testifies to an experience of space as a negative heterotopia.

A similar representation of a heterotopic space occurs in "The Children of the Pool" (1936), though the story does not directly involve the presence of the little people, but rather presents another, unidentified creature that in this case attempts to ruin the mind of the male victim. The narrative concerns two friends, Meyrick and Roberts, spending a summer vacation in Wales. The two men meet by chance in a remote grey cottage in the countryside, in the middle of a land described as thriving with trees and shining flowers. Roberts is a round, good-natured, cheery, and cordial man and the time spent by the two men together is defined by friendliness and pleasantries such as good food, drinks, and pipe smoking. However, on a following meeting, Roberts has turned into a grave, frightened, and wretched individual after a night stroll to the titular swampy pool, where muddy water is surrounded by ghastly dead trees whose bare trunks look like leprous limbs. The latter location is intentionally set against the scenery praised at the beginning of the tale: the area near the black pool, Roberts affirms, "was the most strange place. I thought, hidden away under the hills as if it were a secret."[61] During his walk and after he returns to the cottage, Roberts hears his name called out in the darkness by a girl's voice that reminds him of some grave and shameful sins he committed when he was young. The voice, an excellent allegory of a man's conscience as much as of the Freudian's unconscious (psychoanalysis itself is mentioned in the text, though it is derisively dismissed as nonsensical),[62] even reminds Roberts of facts he had himself forgotten. Meyrick explains away such a narrative as the product of a guilty conscience, and quotes Professor Koffka's argument that the landscape can affect human beings as much as wine and opium do. Meyrick does not believe in the reality of the apparition of what the landlady of the cottage calls "the children of the pool," but argues that the black waters of the isolated area have evoked the darker part of his friend's psyche. The text nevertheless legitimizes an interpretation of the space near the pool as an heterotopic location acting as a character's reflection of his own guilt. In this case, it is not the past represented by Pan or the little people that haunts one of the characters, but the past of the character himself is revived in the remote location, which has, in Foucault's words, a "come-back effect" on the character. On the other hand, if we accept the existence of the female child of the pool, the latter place is represented as a heterotopia of deviance where an unacceptable act of outrage is committed and the extraordinary interferes menacingly on the present.

Several texts by Arthur Machen thus represent a series of locations that lie outside all spaces and yet are actually localizable (heterotopias are by definition rooted in reality). In such places, an unreal space opens up potentially beyond its surface and the past emerges and coexist with the present, either in the repetition of rituals that belong to the past or in the apparition of people (or other beings) that do not fit with the values and the status quo of the present. Heterochronies and heterotopias at large in Machen can be either positive, granting access to a beneficial return of the past and the opening up of the world beyond the veil (a world that can be perfect, as set against the present reality of the characters), or they can be dangerous places where the moral guidelines and even the material lives of the characters are threatened.

NOTES

1. See Michel Foucault, *The Order of Things: An Archaeology of the Human Sciences*, trans. Tavistock/Routledge (London: Routledge, 2005), xix.

2. Michel Foucault, "Of Other Spaces: Utopias and Heterotopias," trans. Jay Miskowiec *Architecture/Mouvement/Continuité* 5 (October, 1984): 1–9, 2. https://web.mit.edu/allanmc/www/foucault1.pdf (accessed November 12, 2020).

3. Ibid., 3–4.
4. Ibid., 4.
5. Ibid.
6. Ibid.
7. Ibid., 5.
8. Ibid.
9. Ibid., 7.
10. Ibid.
11. Ibid., 8. Examples of heterotopias of compensation, according to Foucault, were certain colonies founded in America during the first wave of colonization in the seventeenth century.
12. Ibid., 4.
13. Arthur Machen, "The Great Return" (London: Faith Press, 1915), 12.
14. The blissful joy experienced in Llantrisant is all the more exalted by being juxtaposed to the weather in London and the feelings of the metropolis' inhabitants. In the narrator's words, the London weather seems to encompass all "the horror and fury of the war [and] . . . the torment of the world. The city wore a terrible vesture; within our hearts was dread; without we were clothed in black clouds and angry fire." Machen, "The Great Return," 19.
15. Ibid., 45.
16. Ibid., 46.
17. Ibid., 79.
18. Ibid., 46 and 50.

19. Arthur Machen, "N," in *Complete Works of Arthur Machen*, 25848–26252 (Hastings: Delphi Classics, 2013), 25970. Ebook.
20. Ibid., 26081.
21. Ibid., 26085–89.
22. Arthur Machen, "The Happy Children," in *Uncollected Tales. Complete Works of Arthur Machen*, 26256–340 (Hastings: Delphi Classics, 2013), 26309. Ebook.
23. Ibid., 26318.
24. The coexistence of past and present requires no further explanation from the narrator of "The Happy Children": he does not doubt about his experience nor he attempts any rationalization of the event.
25. Foucault, "Of Other Spaces," 7.
26. Machen, "The Ceremony," in *Ornaments in Jade, Complete Works of Arthur Machen*, 20853–93 (Hastings: Delphi Classics, 2013), 20867–71. Ebook.
27. Ibid., 20871–75.
28. Ibid., 20894.
29. As Emily Foster points out, "*The White People* closely draws on the idea that the landscape around us can act as a portal into another mystical realm." Foster then applies Max Nordau's theory of mysticism and degeneration to Machen's story and argues that the protagonist could be read as suffering from a weakness of mind distorting her perception of reality. Emily Foster, "Beyond the Veil of Reality: Mysticism in Arthur Machen's *The White People*," in *The Secret Ceremonies: Critical Essays on Arthur Machen*, ed. Mark Valentine, 238–48 (New York: Hippocampus Press, 2019), 243 and 246.
30. Arthur Machen, "The White People," in *The House of Souls*, 111–66 (New York: Alfred A. Knopf, 1922), 128–29.
31. Ibid., 161–63.
32. As Sophie Mantrant has noted, interest in paganism was common to several writers in the final decades of the nineteenth century, including Walter Pater (in "Denys l'Auxerrois," 1886) and Vernon Lee (in "Dionea," 1890). According to Mantrant, in *The White People* "The choice of a child's point of view may be seen as a way of returning to a more 'primitive' vision of the Dionysian mysteries, one that has not yet turned them into diabolic rituals." See Sophie Mantrant, "Pagan Revenants in Arthur Machen's Supernatural Tales of the Nineties," *Cahiers victoriens et édouardiens* 80 (Autumn 2014). http://journals. Openedition.org/cve/1466 (accessed on November 26, 2020).
33. Machen, *The White People*, 165.
34. See S.T. Joshi, "Arthur Machen: The Evils of Materialism," in *The Secret Ceremonies: Critical Essays on Arthur Machen*, ed. Mark Valentine, 17–31 (New York: Hippocampus Press, 2019), 26.
35. Arthur Machen, "The Great God Pan," in *The Great God Pan and the Inmost Light*, 7–156 (London: John Lane, 1894), 38.
36. Ibid., 44.
37. Ibid., 55.
38. Ibid., 151.
39. Ibid.

40. S.T. Joshi argues: "If there is any dominant theme that unites [Machen's tales], it is the constant contrast between mundane modernity and the hoary past—a past that is simultaneously terrifying in its primitivism and awesome in its suggestions of intimate, symbolic connexions with the essence of life and Nature." Joshi, "Arthur Machen," 25.

41. Mantrant, "Pagan Revenants."

42. Foucault, "Of Other Spaces," 5.

43. As Trevor Fisher points out, "By the 1890s . . . respectability had powerfully tightened its grip on Victorian society . . . there is certainly abundant evidence that many Victorians, especially men, fell short of the ideal, prompting the charge of hypocrisy. But there is also abundant evidence that many did live their lives informed by 'respectable values'." Trevor Fisher, *Scandal: The Sexual Politics of Late Victorian Britain* (Stroud, UK: Alan Sutton, 1995), 164–65.

44. Pan's first victim is Mary, who becomes a "hopeless idiot" after seeing the faun-like god after Dr. Raymond's experiment. Subsequent victims are the men Helen Vaughan encounters and exploits: they are terrorized by something they are told or shown by the malevolent woman. Whether the encounter with the supernatural actually occurs in front of these men is never spelled out explicitly by the text, which does not allow us therefore to read for the formation of further heterotopias in the other locations where the story is set (including several houses in London).

45. Fred Botting, "Power in the Darkness: Heterotopias, Literature and Gothic Labyrinths," in *Gothic: Critical Concepts in Literary and Cultural Studies*, Vol. 1, ed. Fred Botting and Dale Townshend, 243–68 (London: Routledge, 2004), 243.

46. Ibid., 260.

47. Fred Botting, *Gothic* (London: Routledge, 1996), 2.

48. Peter Bell notes that "the power of Machen's horror lies in his restriction of information, allowing the reader's imagination full rein. The peril of the little folk is the greater for being indirect, understated, conveyed by subtle glimpses." Peter Bell, "Of Sacred Groves and Ancient Mysteries: Parallel Themes in the Writings of Arthur Machen and John Buchan," in *The Secret Ceremonies: Critical Essays on Arthur Machen*, ed. Mark Valentine, 217–37 (New York: Hippocampus Press, 2019), 234.

49. Foucault, "Of Other Spaces," 7.

50. Joshi, "Arthur Machen," 20.

51. Arthur Machen, "The Shining Pyramid," in *The Shining Pyramid: Tales and Essays*, edited by Vincent Starrett, 1–35 (Chicago, IL: Covici-McGee, 1923), 21.

52. Ibid.

53. Ibid., 24.

54. Ibid.

55. Ibid., 27.

56. Arthur Machen, *Strange Roads. With the Gods in Spring* (London: The Classic Press, 1923), 18–19.

57. Ibid., 20.

58. Arthur Machen, "The Strange Tale of Mount Nephin," in *Bridles and Spurs. Complete Works of Arthur Machen*, 89871–934 (Hastings: Delphi Classics, Series Four, 2013), 89876. Ebook.

59. Ibid., 89918.
60. Ibid., 89925–29 and 89934.
61. Arthur Machen, "The Children of the Pool," in *The Children of the Pool, and Other Stories. Complete Works of Arthur Machen*, 21848–22172 (Hastings: Delphi Classics, Series Four, 2013), 21914. Ebook.
62. The narrator affirms: "Now, everybody, I suppose, is aware that in recent years the silly business of divination by dreams has ceased to be a joke and has become a very serious science. It is called 'Psycho-analysis'; and is compounded, I would say, by mingling one grain of sense with a hundred of pure nonsense. From the simplest and most obvious dreams, the psycho-analyst deduces the most incongruous and extravagant results." Machen, "The Children of the Pool," 22124.

REFERENCES

Bell, Peter. "Of Sacred Groves and Ancient Mysteries: Parallel Themes in the Writings of Arthur Machen and John Buchan." In *The Secret Ceremonies: Critical Essays on Arthur Machen*, edited by Mark Valentine, 217–37. New York: Hippocampus Press, 2019.

Botting, Fred. *Gothic*. London: Routledge, 1996.

———. "Power in the Darkness: Heterotopias, Literature and Gothic Labyrinths." In *Gothic: Critical Concepts in Literary and Cultural Studies*, Vol. 1, edited by Fred Botting and Dale Townshend, 243–68. London: Routledge, 2004.

Fisher, Trevor. *Scandal: The Sexual Politics of Late Victorian Britain*. Stroud, UK: Alan Sutton, 1995.

Foster, Emily. "Beyond the Veil of Reality: Mysticism in Arthur Machen's *The White People*." In *The Secret Ceremonies: Critical Essays on Arthur Machen*, edited by Mark Valentine, 238–48. New York: Hippocampus Press, 2019.

Foucault, Michel. "Of Other Spaces: Utopias and Heterotopias." Translated by Jay Miskowiec *Architecture/Mouvement/Continuité* 5 (October 1984): 1–9. https://web.mit.edu/allanmc/www/foucault1.pdf.

———. *The Order of Things: An Archaeology of the Human Sciences*. Translated by Tavistock/Routledge. London: Routledge, 2005.

Joshi, S.T. "Arthur Machen: The Evils of Materialism." In *The Secret Ceremonies: Critical Essays on Arthur Machen*, edited by Mark Valentine, 17–31. New York: Hippocampus Press, 2019.

Machen, Arthur. "The Ceremony." In *Ornaments in Jade. Complete Works of Arthur Machen*, 20853–94. Hastings: Delphi Classics, 2013. Ebook.

———. "The Children of the Pool." In *The Children of the Pool, and Other Stories. Complete Works of Arthur Machen*, 21848–22172. Hastings: Delphi Classics, 2013. Ebook.

———. "The Great God Pan." In *The Great God Pan and the Inmost Light*, 7–156. London: John Lane, 1894.

———. "The Great Return." London: Faith Press, 1915.

———. "The Happy Children." In *Uncollected Tales. Complete Works of Arthur Machen*, 26256–340. Hastings: Delphi Classics, 2013.

———. "N." In *Complete Works of Arthur Machen*, 25848–26252. Hastings: Delphi Classics, 2013. Ebook.

———. "The Shining Pyramid." In *The Shining Pyramid: Tales and Essays*, edited by Vincent Starrett, 1–35. Chicago, IL: Covici-McGee, 1923.

———. *Strange Roads. With the Gods in Spring*. London: The Classic Press, 1923.

———. "The White People." In *The House of Souls*, 111–66. New York: Alfred A. Knopf, 1922.

Mantrant, Sophie. "Pagan Revenants in Arthur Machen's Supernatural Tales of the Nineties." *Cahiers victoriens et édouardiens* 80 (Autumn 2014). http://journals.openedition.org/cve/1466.

Chapter 4

Dead Matter

Posthumanism and Stones

Fernando Gabriel Pagnoni Berns and Emiliano Aguilar

In many stories by Machen, the sense of wonder comes from the realization that vibes of the past still shape our contemporary lives. The threat of human devolution is illustrated through narratives populated by horrifying fairies and snail-like creatures, all of them survivors from an ancient past. Humankind, in this scenario, is just another species. This decentering of the humanist paradigm predates the new examinations on posthumanism, a discipline investigating "the end of a 'man-centred' universe or, put less phallocentrically, a 'human-centred' universe."[1] According to Alan and Josephine Smart, being human involves "our intimate interaction with more-than-human elements."[2] The historical relationships between humans and machines and humans and animals, rife with tensions, are now discussed through the posthuman lens. Critical examination of minerals as objects of posthuman study, however, is still lacking. The ontology of stones, after all, is inextricably linked to both, the most humble form of materialism and the dawn of humanity; the "crude" Stone Age, a far cry from the process of dematerialization favored by theology and posthumanism alike. The concept of the soul or the virtual posthuman is opposed to the merely embodied and the organic. Materiality, thus, becomes somehow "inferior" to transcendence.

Against the absolute identification of idealism and transcendence with immateriality, some posthumanists try to recuperate the material in the most modest of forms: mud, clay, minerals, and stones. Scholars such as Jeffrey Jerome Cohen[3] and Argyro Loukaki[4] and the 2016 collection edited by Paul Kingsbury and Steve Pile *Psychoanalytic Geographies*[5] argue for a posthuman materialism that recuperates the dirt and the filthy in connection with the human. The hardness and radical difference of stones seems to reject the human ethos: the stone is a figure that flees from meaning and narratology. As Cohen argues, nature is "a scale innate to being, with rocks at the bottom and divinity atop."[6] Even the vegetal realm is closer to humankind. As Cohen further affirms, however, "nature's discrepant intricacies are amply evident within its frequent metonym, stone."[7] Stones are markers of something beyond the human and, at the same time, deeply connected with humanity.

In Machen's works, stones are markers of posthumanism in a double way: first, because minerals are material embodiments of the sacred and the (most likely, pagan) past. Unlike human beings, stones are capable of retaining, within, entire cosmogonies, time strata, and the human soul. Second, the stones scattered through Machen's works are traces of posthuman races (meaning, life beyond the merely human, such as fairies) and long-lost languages. Stones, thus, decenter the exceptionalism of humankind as the main provider of meaning in our world. As such, the many stones strewn through Machen's fiction navigate between being portals to the sacred and radical signposts of alterity.

Humanism was constructed from the Latin, *humanus*. This "being human," however, was not subscribed to all humans but only to the civilized ones, who were therefore distinctly separated from "nonhuman" beings such as animals and barbarians. Thus, from its very inception, the human was "predicated upon that which it excludes,"[8] not only the vegetal and the animal, but other humans as well. Further, humanism has been constructed through the opposition, rejection of and abjection for the object which does not fall into the totalizing category of "man," the latter solely understood in terms of white Western man.[9] The animal/vegetal world has been, historically, subjected to domination, exploitation, and extermination sustained on the premise that both the animal and the vegetal are objects and, as such, beings without rights.

Only with the coming of the posthuman in the humanities, together with animal/ecological studies, the logics of exploitation and degradation taking place between the human and the nonhuman started to be revealed. In his groundbreaking essay "What is Posthumanism?" (2010), Cary Wolfe refers to the humanity/animality dichotomy, namely, that the concept of the human is "achieved by escaping or repressing not just its animal origins in nature, the biological, and the evolutionary, but more generally by transcending the bonds of materiality and embodiment altogether."[10] In fact, as Jane Bennett argues, notions of material embodiment are insufficient: "we are, through and through, an array of bodies, many different kinds of them in nested sets."[11] We, humans, are a complex composite of cells, atoms, minerals. That is why Bennett calls for an "inorganic sympathy."[12] After all, humans "walk upright over earth because the mineral long ago infiltrated animal life to become a partner in mobility."[13] Still, if the human is our standard for any experience, then all other things should be measured against it. Anything nonhuman, then, holds less value. Rocks, stones, and minerals in general were "condemned to silent roles in human dramas,"[14] their passivity favoring human mastery and exploitation. Their lack of any visible sign of life, together with their hardness and passivity render minerals as the complete opposite of humanity.

Nevertheless, stones never fully escaped the humanizing effect that filters all things. The image of stones, for example, navigates between radical difference with the human and a deep historical engagement with the anthropocene. The registers of the discourse of minerals radically reconfigures the meaning of stones through an engagement with human figuration: simple phrases such as "heart of stone" or "heart of gold" show that minerals were unable to escape the totalizing effects of humanity. To say "dumber than a box of rocks" is "to give insult by degrading the dynamic into the inert,"[15] the latter historically coded in negative ways. Still, it is undeniable that minerals are harder to include within humanism than, say, animals or plants.

Even so, in his *Formproblem der Gotik* (1911),[16] Wilhelm Worringer stipulates that the stones which mounted the gothic cathedrals were filled with a sense of vitality that manifests a higher transcendent spirituality. The gothic architectural structure becomes a "breathing body"[17] where stones, their forms irregular rather than normative, seem to grow and reproduce as living beings. Megalithic tomb-shrines scattered through Britain connects the contemporary world with the pagan roots, as classic dolmens, consisting of a capstone supported by uprights worked as burial sites, places for contemplation or ceremonial meeting points. These were "stones that float to the sky,"[18] uniting the humble materiality of stones with the sacred. Kellie Robertson argues that "medieval stones were irrepressibly vital," with human-like virtues bestowing quasi-animate qualities of motion and action on them.[19]

Further, stones are keepers of the memory of the world. Unlike animals and plants, stones can live for centuries. We can touch stones through which Romans walked on. Greek or Roman amphitheaters saw the representations of Greek and Roman tragedies, and we can sit in the same place where people who died centuries ago sat. Stones are keepers of history, containers of past happenings. Paranormal abilities such as psychometry, the paranormal reading of the vibrations of an object and the people who previously touched it, engage with this capacity of the immaterial to refer to past happenings. In 1863, William and Elizabeth Denton published a treatise on psychometry where they stated that this discipline could read the "soul" of inanimate objects, including rocks. According to them, prehistoric objects are "photographs" of past moments.[20] Rocks were especially interesting objects of study: "why could not rocks receive impressions of surrounding objects, some of which they have been in the immediate neighborhood of for years."[21] Further, stones could communicate the past to "sensitive persons," thus "giving us the clue to the conditions of the earth and its inhabitants during the vast eras of the past."[22]

We are not here arguing that Machen was a follower of psychometry or a believer in the psychic possibilities embedded in the landscapes. The Welsh writer, however, gives expression to a kind of posthuman materialism, a writing describing our relationships with the sacred without reverting to worn-out conceptions of the supreme human. In Machen's language and writing, stones are "precious,"[23] "white with the leprosy of age,"[24] engraved with "delicate and wonderful imagery,"[25] "shining,"[26] "immortal,"[27] "sculptured,"[28] "translucent,"[29] or "ugly."[30] The Welsh writer was not indifferent to the dethroning of the Western man, as many of his stories revolve around the return of the pre-apollonian man ("The Great God Pan" [1894]), posthuman entities living within the bowels of earth ("The Shining Pyramid" [1895]) and human degeneration ("The Novel of the White Powder" [1895]). His celebration of a posthuman ethos, however, can be traced also to his interest in the capacity of stones to be alive, sacred, connected with life and the beyond. In Machen's stories, stones can be literally more important than humans.

Psychometry speaks about the "soul" of objects, thus making the boundaries separating the human from the nonhuman flexible. Arguably, this tracing of the past embedded in inanimate objects can be read as a search for the soul but, also, for the unconscious, what lies deep within. One of the darkest aspects of the modern project was the rise of Sigmund Freud's theories on the subconscious, which revealed the nature of the human being as driven by basic instincts. The subconscious establishes that there is something darker, powerful, and unreachable pulsating behind the surface of everyday reality. The revelation of an ulterior reality given substance to our daily behaviors disrupts our securities and turns reality into an ephemeral thing. Argyro Loukaki takes the Freudian notion of the unconscious as a "dark, archetypal, sacred power"[31] to the geographical and the material spatiality. The past, "hidden, but never completely erased,"[32] produces a connectedness with past long archaisms in space, thus rupturing both the present and modernity. One of the most urgent needs of modernity, according to Loukaki, was that of stripping the world of divine presence and turning the landscapes into passive matter for humans to exploit. Rather than being the reservoir of divinity, landscapes were just dead matter to serve humanity (i.e., men).

In many of his writings, Machen predates Argyro Loukaki's thesis about the "geographical unconscious" through which modern Britain still keeps, within the materiality of stone, the pagan era alive. For it is not a rare occurrence for archaic architectures, and other artifacts from long time past, to come to light and constantly revive the pagan era. As a native of Caerleon-on-Usk, Machen was probably familiar with the Roman architectures found in that location[33] and, as a British, he was well aware of the significance of stones, in the forms of dolmens or burial sites, as evocative of old forgotten religions. In the novel *The Hill of Dreams* (1907), for example, the main narrator, Lucian Taylor, the introvert son of a poor Welsh minister, experiences the uncanny within the ruins of a Roman fort. Resting among the ruins, Lucian experiences a sexual and mystical encounter with a fairy that will change his life. Circled by old stones marked by age and "the work of the [Roman] axe,"[34] Lucian engages with a past long deceased. Britain is widely known for being haunted by its pagan history; in this scenario, Machen carefully chooses to stage the survival of the ancient mind within Roman ruins, the old stones containing the "geographical unconscious" examined by Loukaki. Lucian experiences a psychometric reading of the rocks, as traces of the past manifest themselves as a recuperation of the pagan unconscious. The fort itself seems to be master of some uncanny quality: within it, the walls "seemed higher than without," transforming the fort into a "green vault."[35] Even the humble earth is sketched with fascinating unnatural hues: "the earth was black and unctuous, and bubbling under the feet, left no track behind."[36]

There, in the ruins, Lucian sits to get some rest after climbing to the fort. Suddenly, he "felt as if he were growing hotter and hotter"[37] and sleepy. Soon, he sees human forms in the trees surrounding him while his body is overcome by "quick flames" which hint to "unknown desires."[38] The reference to "unknown desires" ties Lucian's sexual desire with the unconscious of his surroundings; he only gets glimpses of his visitor during his sleep state; when he wakes up, everything returns to a common-quality. Lucian, however, vividly remembers "dark eyes that had shone over him" and "scarlet lips that had kissed him."[39] After this encounter, Lucian will be forever trapped in this hierophantic instant of connection (his own unconscious and that of the landscape). His subsequent life in grey, horrid London (where he struggles with poverty and opium) becomes an incessant search for the recuperation of this moment of delirium and is haunted by the memories of his brief encounter amidst the "flaming fort."[40] While the materiality of modern London's architecture is described in bitter tones ("and beyond, he knew, stretched the labyrinth of streets more or less squalid, but all grey and dull, and behind were the mud pits and the steaming heaps of yellowish bricks"),[41] the Roman fort is evoked as bathed in "moonfire" and terrible beauty: "the old Roman fort was invested with fire; flames from heaven were smitten about its walls, and above there was a dark floating cloud, like fume of smoke."[42]

The "geographical unconscious," however, does not need a whole construction as in *The Hill of Dreams*. Sometimes the pagan past survives in a piece of stone such as an altar that evokes a lost sacredness. In "The Ceremony" (1924) Machen sketches a very brief story about a forest, a girl, and a mysterious grey stone. There is little information about what really occurs in the story. A female anonymous narrator evokes her childhood and, amidst her memories, a grey stone resting within the forest which she has a deep fear of. Readers know the stone is sacred and, also, a site for sacrifice: "and the red colour stained the grim stone, and there was nothing else."[43] Already as an adult, the narrator spies a little girl leaving flowers near the grey stone; months later, she leaves flowers as well, having now turned into another participant of this "antique immemorial rite."[44] The tale lacks any clear explanation on the nature of the stone; neither Machen needs to provide one. Sacrifices of blood and flowers are made to the stone, which transfigures materiality into an uncanny medium to other times, a material form of connection with the beyond and the past. Like the "flaming fort," the stone is a medium that connects the contemporary with a past of fauns[45] and hieroglyphic rites that the modern mind cannot decipher. This sacred generality rouses emotional responses which communicate participants to the divine rooted in the stones.

This kind of material fetish, which replaces the "original" (the beyond and the past) is analogous to what Mircea Eliade defines in his *The Sacred and the Profane* (1987) as "hierophanies," meaning, "the act of manifestation of the sacred."[46] Eliade argues:

> by manifesting the sacred, any object becomes something else, yet it continues to remain itself . . . A sacred stone remains a stone; apparently (or, more precisely, from the profane point of view), nothing distinguishes it from all other stones. But for those to whom a stone reveals itself as sacred, its immediate reality is transmuted into a supernatural reality.[47]

Indeed, the stone is material, but it exceeds the human in value since it is a manifestation of the sacred. Humans bend their knees before the altar. Stones, thus, work as veils that connect one world, one reality (ours) with divine spatialities that shape a second geographical field, that of the past trapped within natural formations of rocks turned into places of worship ("The Ceremony") or pagan lovemaking (*The Hills of Dreams*). As Loukaki argues, these uncanny geographies and materiality can be read as "repeated instances when divine and human spatialities are mingled during moments of epiphany. These spatialities coexisted with Euclidean space (gods were celebrated in temples and altars)."[48]

The inaccessibility of the beyond and the past finds expression through the profane materiality of stones and rocks. There is ecstasy to be found exploring the comforting solidity of stones. In Machen's full-length work of literary criticism, *Hieroglyphics* (1902), the author attempts to provoke "ecstasy" in the readers. Fine literature should actively work to produce ecstasy which, if present, "then I say there is fine literature."[49] Next, Machen admits that "ecstasy" can be replaced "with rapture, beauty, adoration, wonder, awe, mystery, sense of the unknown, desire for the unknown."⁵⁰ Machen basically advocates literature as an escape from profane time and as a way to experience the sacred and the numinous. Fine literature parallels the effect produced by getting into contact with the grey stone of "The Ceremony": a hierophany. The stone of the short tale has become for Machen what literature should be: a sacred object, a material manifestation of divinity. There is an ulterior reality beyond our senses (senses which can deceive us), but this reality is of hieroglyphic content: it hardly can be deciphered. This numinous reality is covered by the veil of "common life and the common consciousness;"⁵¹ and people such as Lucian can only get brief glimpses of said beyond.

Such an interest for occult realities was not only related to the supernatural, but also to the scientific mind. Machen wrote in an era in which scientific developments—like the investigations on the unconscious—cohabited with a strong resurgence of occultism. Occultism and rational scientific thinking were not considered as mutually exclusive spheres at the time of Machen's writing. Both people of science and occultists strongly believed in the existence of invisible worlds co-existing with the daily reality perceived by the common senses. For example, the world of atoms and magnetism blended together the scientific and the occultist mind. Atoms exhibited "occult" characteristics⁵² while the powers of the magnetic stones were akin to those exhibited by the human mind: the capacity to influence objects and humans at distance.⁵³ The magnetism produced by stones was replicated by the magnetic powers dormant within humans. Thus, the pure materiality of stones could hold human-like properties: for example, Helena Petrovna Blavatsky, who co-founded the Theosophical Society in 1875, argued that "statues, if properly prepared, might, without any accusation of superstition, be allowed to have the property of imparting health and disease by contact."⁵⁴

In this scenario, the idea of "mineral life" was not extraordinary as believed in more recent times. In their book *The Origin of Creation: The Science of Matter and Force. A New System of Natural Philosophy* (1874), Thomas Roderick Fraser and Andrew Dewar dedicated a whole chapter to "mineral life." They acknowledged that "mineral life" seems a contradiction at first. For Fraser and Dewar, however, mineral life is "a low form of vegetable and mineral life."⁵⁵ Their views are close to the posthumanist ethos: "minerals have been locked upon as dead matter, but . . . every atom in this universe has the element of life."⁵⁶ They continue: "Mineral life is indeed the lowest form of life."⁵⁷ Two years later, Robert H. Armit wrote a book on the powers of light and energy, stating that earth and life as we know them derive from mineral life: "It is in the mineral life of the earth that the rocks, the soil, the lakes, the rivers, the streams, the forests, the plants, the animals and the human beings, all take their existence."⁵⁸ Decades earlier, in 1859, an article in *The New Jerusalem Magazine* also predicated on the idea that all life (including human life) derives from mineral life, the latter making "all the varied forms and combinations of the earth."[59] The distance between humans and stones, thus, is slightly abolished.

Machen's "The Inmost Light" (1894) takes this posthuman momentum even farther. The tale revolves around a man who succeeds in trapping his wife's soul inside a precious stone. Dyson, an occult detective, investigates on Steven Black, a doctor whose wife mysteriously disappeared for a large period of time. Dyson, however, suddenly finds her staring out, with a face filled with "a lust that cannot be satiated" and "a fire that is unquenchable,"[60] from a window of her house. Later he learns that Mrs. Black's soul was extracted and enclosed into the boundaries of a precious stone, while her body was possessed by a demon. After Dr. Black's death, the detective finds the opal, a stone that produces "awe" and with a "wonderful flame that shone and sparkled in its centre."[61] The material qualities of the stone are strong enough to trap a human soul within; still, the jewel itself can be killed. After Dyson shatters the stone to free the woman's soul, the rock crumbles down like cinder,[62] revealing an organic nature which can die. A stone with an active human soul evokes animistic thinking, depicting a scenario in which nonhuman materials must be understood in terms of persons or, at least, person-like.

Embedded with life and human-like attributes, stones are not passive material to control and exploit to specific uses but powerful elements with transformative capacities. The qualities of minerals "are inherent, always emanating, always seeking" the connections that will allow the rock to become a "powerful" agent.[63] In "The Novel of the White Powder," a medicinal salt given to the young law student Francis Leicester to calm his fatigue after straining his nerves too hard with study ends up producing horrifying consequences. After days of ingestion, the titular white powder turns the young man into an amoeba-like creature:

> There upon the floor was a dark and putrid mass, seething with corruption and hideous rottenness, neither liquid nor solid, but melting and changing before our eyes, and bubbling with unctuous oily bubbles like boiling pitch. And out of the midst of it shone two burning points like eyes, and I saw a writhing and stirring as of limbs, and something moved and lifted up that might have been an arm.[64]

"The Novel of the White Powder" destabilizes the narrative of Darwinian evolution. Kelly Hurley calls Darwinian evolution "supernaturalist or Gothic"[65] as she astutely observes that evolution theory described the body as containing within the "mark of the beast" as humans, derived from beasts and minerals, "might still be abhuman entities."[66] Still worse, "the evolutionary process might be reversible: the human race might ultimately retrogress into a sordid animalism rather than progress"[67] to ultimate perfection. The body becomes a site of Gothic tensions, as it is rendered unstable, regressing to a previous state that is even inferior to other life forms.

What is remarkable about the white powder that produces the hideous regression to an abhuman state is its mineral qualities. It is stated by Doctor Chambers, the man in charge of investigating the nature of the salts, that the powders resemble those which were used to make the wine poured down in the Sabbath and the black masses performed by witches in past eras. The salts ingested by Francis, however, are not magical. The uncanny qualities of the transformation are a consequence of the minerals' expositions "to recurring variations of temperature, variations probably ranging from 40° to 80°."[68] These changes stimulate a process that turned medical salts into powders like those used by witchcraft. Rather than inert, the minerals devolved into something primitive, something that will, eventually, affect human embodiment. The powers within the salts are awakened by the temperatures, becoming magical, becoming alive. In brief, the medicines, like Francis, suffer the same regression to a primitive, magical, pre-cultural state. Both the minerals and Francis share co-devolution to previous, pre-cultural states.

Such a return to a time before Western men have considered themselves superior to any other form of life is accompanied with the evocation of previous races: "The secrets of the true Sabbath were the secrets of remote times surviving into the Middle Ages, secrets of an evil science which existed long before Aryan man entered Europe."[69] If, as R. L. Rutsky argues, "instrumental technology and rationality"[70] have long been the basis on which humanism was historically sustained, these long-lost races utilize their pre-technological fabrications on stone not in instrumental ways but as sacred, magical materialism. Silvia Battista, following philosophers Drew Dalton and Rudolf Otto, provides further thoughts into the characteristics of the hierophantic experience "with particular interest in the relationship between the self and the numinous object."[71] She argues that "it is the self who conceives an object of this world as something 'wholly other' and transcendental."[72] However, the nonhuman object is also the carrier of an "overplus" of meaning or excess of value, "and is thus the initiator of the numinous experience."[73] This overplus of meaning, however, is cultural:[74] humans are those who charge objects with a utilitarian end—as the modern mind does—or with the numinous, posthuman qualities.

According to Kelly Robertson, stones suggest "something about the human relationship to the world that a human being cannot, unprompted, comprehend by itself. In this way, stones are both marvelous and monstrous."[75] Our relationships with stones scenify, in part, our sense of meaning-making. World-making and meaning-making heavily depends, in the humanist ethos, on language. In some of Machen's works, human language is replaced with rocks, the elements more alien to the human. This opens the path to alternative conceptions of existence where the anthropocene is recurrently downplayed. In the tale that works as prologue to "The Novel of the Black Seal" (1895) ("Adventure of the Missing Brother"). Miss Lally, the young narrator, affirms that she knows the whereabouts of a certain professor Gregg, an expert in ethnology, who has allegedly fallen into a river and disappeared in one of his excursions. The young woman says she does not know where he is but points out that he may be alive, since his belongings have been found "beside a limestone rock of fantastic form."[76]

The professor, a passionate researcher of the occult, had previously told Miss Lally that he was following a clue, which consists of "a lump of black stone, rudely annotated with queer marks and scratches."[77] This rock contains writing marks probably made fifteen years ago, but it coincides with a script found in an old seal whose antiquity dates from "four thousand years old at least. Perhaps much more."[78] Professor Gregg was searching the whereabouts of a lost race with the help of these clues engraved in stone. On the one hand, Machen therefore highlights the validity of rocks as the repository of a culture or a presence of a race (supposedly) extinct thousands of years ago but still alive. On the other hand, this race has nothing in common with human beings. The creatures, it is explained, give base to the fair folk, which will be later reconceptualized as pretty, inoffensive beings. As Jessica George explains, the fairies "provided a focal point for Victorian anxieties about other boundaries; national, 'racial,' and 'human'." The traditional fairylore "constituted a folk memory of aboriginal Britons who had been driven underground by the invading Celts. And as evidence of humanity's distant past, the fairies came to represent the blurring of boundaries between the 'human' and the pre-human."[79] Or between the human and the posthuman, the prefix "post," meaning here "beyond," and not so much as "after" the human, predicating new relationships of the human with the environment and other life forms; in brief, a complete new system of values, as those sustained by the fairies with the stones. The fairies depicted by Machen disrupt the evolutionary chain through a posthuman monstrosity: rather than being complete Otherness, they represent a forgotten step in our (or, at least, Welsh) human evolution, including a language fabricated with stones which prefigures ours by centuries, the materiality of stones replacing the complete abstractness of human words and orality.

After finding a strange book written in Latin, Miss Lally observes that the text speaks of people who live far from humanity, who have different customs and speak another language. The text refers to a stone called "sixty stone" that shows sixty characters and also "has a secret unspeakable name; which is Ixaxar."[80] The inscriptions made in the rock evoke the existence of other races who possess a system of thought completely foreign to the Western man but which can hardly be described as "primitive." It is interesting how

Machen gives value to the material: "matter is as really awful and unknown as spirit"[81] linking two seemingly disparate spheres: the materialism of stones and the existence of nonhuman races capable of creating highly complicated systems of thought. Like the sacred stones of "The Ceremony" or *The Hill of Dreams*, the mysterious engraved rocks are veils to "awful things done long ago, and forgotten before the hills were moulded into form."[82]

Western cultures perceive these lost races in terms of irrationality and primitiveness. A stone ax that the professor found, however, is "utterly unmanageable," thus revealing some superiority inscribed within the technology of this forgotten race; even an expert lumberjack when trying the stone ax "missed every stroke most ludicrously."[83] Gregg's conclusion is shocking, because it suggests that for four thousand years no one on earth could have struck an effective blow with this particular stone tool, suggesting a completely alien form of ability and relationship with stones and technology. The tale ends with the revelation that this other race is what is now called "fairies," "little people" which, still living within the subterranean caves of the Welsh landscapes, hold a closer relationship with the materiality of stones.

Interestingly, these obscure races are not defeated at the tale's climax: Professor Greg is killed and Miss Lally abandons the place never to return. The fairy races are left in peace rather than exterminated. In Machen's tales, the posthuman races are evocations of some obliterated past, a disruption on the evolutionary chain, not creatures to be annihilated. "The Shining Pyramid" is a rewriting of sorts of the themes framing "The Novel of the Black Seal" and, like that story, narrates the discovery of a posthuman race of fairies which is left alone, rather than exterminated, at the tale's climax. Two friends, Vaughan and Dyson, talk about a curious fact; while walking the countryside, the former has found twelve little pointed stones resting on the grass in neatly arranged lines pointing toward the same place. This disposition lays the foundations for the mystery. The meticulous arrangement must respond to human activity (or to a certain intelligence). This assumption is further confirmed by the appearance of another construction made with stones, in this case placed "like the spokes of a wheel, all meeting at a common center, and this center formed by a device which looked like a bowl."[84] A day later, a new configuration resembles a pyramid and, days later, a half moon. This series of configurations made with stones denotes a pattern, a language that predates words and human speech, stones becoming the central net of symbolic constructions. Unlike human language, which emanates from the human (hands to write, mouth to speak), a language made with found stones pushes the human to the margins privileging, rather, the primal nature of earth.

Searching for a lost girl, Dyson meets "the great limestone rocks that cropped out of the turf, grim and hideous, and of an aspect as forbidding as idol of the South Seas."[85] In addition, when encountering a circular depression similar to a Roman amphitheater, he notices how the limestone rocks rest around him like a broken wall. The appearance of the "queer" limestone rock, he says later, "hinted horror through the darkness."[86] Later, on a stone wall, he notices that someone has drawn a human eye, even if a little distorted one. More drawings appear on the wall in the following days, while further arrangements of rocks indicate that someone or something is communicating through stones. The "little people," the horrible abhuman race of fairies, are responsible for the disturbances. At the climax of "The Shining Pyramid," Machen returns to the "geographical unconscious" of *The Hill of Dreams*. It is within the natural formations of a "Roman amphitheatre, and the ugly crags of limestone rimmed it round"[87] that Dyson gets a glimpse of the abominable creatures still living within the subterranean bowels of the earth. Their vocal language consisting in just a series of hissings, they communicate using images made with stones. The tale ends with a new revelation: a "queer, old limestone pillar by your [Vaughn's] garden wall was a place of meeting before the Celt set foot in Britain,"[88] thus returning to the sacred nature of stones as observed in "The Ceremony."

Much of this sense of an increased fetishism of minerals parallels a posthuman conception that shifts away from a purely instrumental conception of stones. On the one hand, stones shape complex signifying systems, prosthetic processes which replace the "properly" human: since the dwarfish beings are unable to speak, they communicate through the use of stones as replacement of words ("The Shining Pyramid") or as containers of uncanny enchantments ("The Novel of the Black Seal"). On the other hand, stones are embedded with the sacred ("The Ceremony"), life ("The Inmost Light" and "The Novel of the White Powder"), or the survival of the past (*The Hill of Dreams*). Stones, then, are inextricably connected with life or are explicitly represented as living things. Mineral life, rather than dead matter. This is evident also in the autobiographical volume *Far Off Things* (1922), in which Machen evokes his early life, up to the mid-1880s, together with his appreciation of the Welsh countryside. In the book, he mentions the names of people who lived and died and how their houses, even in their humility, had become "memorials": "The pride of race that belonged to the Morgans, Herberts, Meyricks that once lived in them has passed into their stones, and still shines there."[89] This is a clear indication that stones can contain the spirits and the memories of people, the soul of the land, the history of Britain.

At the intersection between stones as mere materiality and literary intervention, Arthur Machen's fiction molds the original substance of stones into themselves and at the same time into something new. In other words, through Machen's intervention, stones reveal the memories of humanity's past while opening up to produce something completely other than themselves;

transcendence to another reality. The dead matter of stones, then, is revealed as a container of vibes of human existence, sacrality, organicity, and human-like features such as a soul. This cultural reference to humanity in stones activates its narrative qualities that disrupt the anthropocentric nature of humanism and its positioning of the human as the most important being in the world.

NOTES

1. Robert Pepeperell, *The Posthuman Condition: Consciousness beyond the Brain* (Bristol: Intellect, 2003), 171.
2. Alan Smart and Josephine Smart, *Posthumanism: Anthropological Insights* (Toronto: University of Toronto Press), 2.
3. Jeffrey Jerome Cohen, *Stone: An Ecology of the Inhuman* (Minneapolis, MN: University of Minnesota Press, 2015).
4. Argyro Loukaki, *The Geographical Unconscious* (New York: Routledge, 2016).
5. Paul Kingsbury and Steve Pile (eds.), *Psychoanalytic Geographies* (New York: Routledge, 2016).
6. Cohen, *Stone*, 28.
7. Ibid., 29.
8. Neni Panourgiá, "Anthropism/Immanent Humanism," in *Posthuman Glossary*, ed. Rosi Braidotti and Maria Hlavajova, 44–45 (London: Bloomsbury, 2018), 44.
9. Juliana Schiesari, *Beasts and Beauties: Animals, Gender, and Domestication in the Italian Renaissance* (Toronto: University of Toronto Press, 2010), 11.
10. Cary Wolfe, *What Is Posthumanism?* (Minneapolis, MN: University of Minnesota Press, 2010), xv.
11. Jane Bennett, "Powers of the Hoard: Further Notes on Material Agency," in *Animal, Mineral, Vegetable: Ethics and Objects*, ed. Jeffrey Jerome Cohen, 237–69 (Washington, DC: Oliphaunt Books, 2012), 258.
12. Ibid.
13. Cohen, *Stone*, 20.
14. Jeffrey Jerome Cohen (ed.), "Introduction: All Things," in *Animal, Mineral, Vegetable: Ethics and Objects*, 1–8 (Washington, DC: Oliphaunt Books, 2012), 6.
15. Kellie Robertson, "Exemplary Rocks," in *Animal, Mineral, Vegetable: Ethics and Objects*, ed. Jeffrey Jerome Cohen, 91–121 (Washington, DC: Oliphaunt Books, 2012), 91.
16. Wilhelm Worringer, *Formproblem der Gotik* (München: Piper Verlag, 1911).
17. David Nielsen, *Bruno Taut's Design Inspiration for the Glashaus* (New York: Routledge, 2015), 137.
18. Ronald Hutton, *Pagan Britain* (New Haven: Yale University Press, 2013), 51.
19. Robertson, "Exemplary Stones," 92–93.
20. William and Elizabeth Denton, *The Soul of Things, or Psychometry. Researches and Discoveries* (Boston: Walker, Wise and Company, 1863), 31.

21. Denton, *The Soul of Things*, 36.
22. Ibid.
23. Arthur Machen, *The Hill of Dreams* (East Sussex: Delphi Classics, 2013), 159.
24. Ibid., 22.
25. Machen, *The Secret Glory* (East Sussex: Delphi Classics, 2013), 309.
26. Ibid., 323.
27. Ibid., 361.
28. Machen, *The Great God Pan* (East Sussex: Delphi Classics, 2013), 824.
29. Machen, *The House of Souls* (East Sussex: Delphi Classics, 2013), 1.085.
30. Ibid., 1.099.
31. Loukaki, *The Geographical Unconscious*, 9.
32. Ibid., 3.
33. Ronald Hutton, *The Pagan Religions of the Ancient British Isles: Their Nature and Legacy* (Oxford: Blackwell, 1998), 317.
34. Machen, *The Hill of Dreams*, 22.
35. Ibid.
36. Ibid.
37. Ibid., 23.
38. Ibid.
39. Ibid., 24.
40. Ibid., 18.
41. Ibid., 108.
42. Ibid., 16.
43. Arthur Machen. "The Ceremony," in *The Great God Pan and Other Horror Stories*, 252–54 (Oxford: Oxford University Press, 2018), 252.
44. Ibid., 254.
45. Machen, *The Hill of Dreams*, 24.
46. Mircea Eliade, *The Sacred and the Profane: The Nature of Religion* (London: Harcourt, 1987), 11.
47. Ibid., 12.
48. Loukaki, *The Geographical Unconscious*, 49.
49. Arthur Machen, *Hieroglyphics*, 4628.
50. Ibid.
51. Ibid.
52. Philip Ball, *Invisible: The Dangerous Allure of the Unseen* (Chicago, IL: The University of Chicago Press, 2015), 123.
53. Helena Petrovna Blavatsky, *Studies in Occultism* (Point Loma, CA: The Aryan Theosophical Press, 1910), 42.
54. Helena Petrovna Blavatsky, *Isis Unveiled: A Master-Key to the Mysteries of Ancient and Modern Science and Theology*, Vol. I (New York: J. W. Bouton, 1877), 283.
55. Fraser, Thomas Roderick and Andrew Dewar, *The Origin of Creation: The Science of Matter and Force. A New System of Natural Philosophy* (London: Longmans, Green, Reader and Dyer, 1874), 11.

56. Ibid.
57. Ibid.
58. Robert Armit, *Light as a Motive Power* (London: Trübner and Co., 1876), 227.
59. Louis Agassiz, "Notice of an Essay on Classification," in *The New Jerusalem Magazine*, 30, no. 5 (November 1957), 238–46, 245.
60. Arthur Machen, *The Inmost Light* (East Sussex: Delphi Classics, 2013), 832.
61. Ibid., 855.
62. Ibid., 859.
63. Cohen, *Stone*, 220.
64. Arthur Machen, "The Novel of the White Powder" (East Sussex: Delphi Classics, 2013), 981.
65. Kelly Hurley, *The Gothic Body: sSexuality, Materialism, and Degeneration at the fin de siècle* (Cambridge: Cambridge University Press, 2004), 56.
66. Ibid.
67. Ibid.
68. Machen, "The Novel of the White Powder," 983.
69. Ibid.
70. R. L. Rutsky, *High Techne: Art and Technology from the Machine Aesthetic to the Posthuman* (Minneapolis, MN: University of Minnesota Press), 3.
71. Silvia Battista, *Posthuman Spiritualities in Contemporary Performance: Politics, Ecologies and Perceptions* (New York: Palgrave Macmillan, 2018), 19.
72. Ibid.
73. Ibid.
74. Ibid.
75. Robertson, "Exemplary Rocks," 111.
76. Arthur Machen, "The Novel of the Black Seal" (East Sussex: Delphi Classics, 2013), 906.
77. Ibid., 912.
78. Ibid., 913.
79. Jessica George, "Impossible Spaces: Finding Their Way to the Queen of Fairyland," *TheGothicImagination.com*, October 27, 2013, http://www.gothic.stir.ac.uk/guestblog/impossible-spaces-finding-their-way-to-the-queen-of-fairyland/ (accessed July 2, 2020).
80. Machen, "The Novel of the Black Seal," 918.
81. Ibid., 923.
82. Ibid., 926.
83. Ibid., 937.
84. Arthur Machen, "The Shining Pyramid" (East Sussex: Delphi Classics, 2013), 1276.
85. Ibid., 1288.
86. Ibid., 1290.
87. Ibid., 1288.
88. Ibid., 1298.
89. Arthur Machen, *Far Off Things* (East Sussex: Delphi Classics, 2013), 4988.

REFERENCES

Agassiz, Louis. "Notice of an Essay on Classification." *The New Jerusalem Magazine* 30, no. 5 (November 1957): 238–46.
Armit, Robert. *Light as a Motive Power*. London: Trübner and Co., 1876.
Ball, Philip. *Invisible: The Dangerous Allure of the Unseen*. Chicago, IL: The University of Chicago Press, 2015.
Battista, Silvia. *Posthuman Spiritualities in Contemporary Performance: Politics, Ecologies and Perceptions*. New York: Palgrave Macmillan, 2018.
Bennett, Jane. "Powers of the Hoard: Further Notes on Material Agency." In *Animal, Mineral, Vegetable: Ethics and Objects*, edited by Jeffrey Jerome Cohen, 237–69. Washington, DC: Oliphaunt Books, 2012.
Blavatsky, Helena. *Isis Unveiled: A Master-Key to the Mysteries of Ancient and Modern Science and Theology*, Vol. I. New York: J. W. Bouton, 1877.
———. *Studies in Occultism*. Point Loma, CA: The Aryan Theosophical Press, 1910.
Cohen, Jeffrey Jerome. "Introduction: All Things." In *Animal, Mineral, Vegetable: Ethics and Objects*, edited by Jeffrey Jerome Cohen, 1–8. Washington, DC: Oliphaunt Books, 2012.
———. *Stone: An Ecology of the Inhuman*. Minneapolis, MN: University of Minnesota Press, 2015.
Denton, William and Elizabeth. *The Soul of Things, or Psychometry. Researches and Discoveries*. Boston, MA: Walker, Wise and Company, 1863.
Eliade, Mircea. *The Sacred and the Profane: The Nature of Religion*. London: Harcourt, 1987.
Fraser, Roderick and Andrew Dewar. *The Origin of Creation: The Science of Matter and Force. A New System of Natural Philosophy*. London: Longmans, Green, Reader and Dyer, 1874.
George, Jessica. "Impossible Spaces: Finding Their Way to the Queen of Fairyland." In *TheGothicImagination.com*. October 27, 2013. http://www.gothic.stir.ac.uk/guestblog/impossible-spaces-finding-their-way-to-the-queen-of-fairyland/.
Hurley, Kelly. *The Gothic Body: Sexuality, Materialism, and Degeneration at the fin de siècle*. Cambridge: Cambridge University Press, 2004.
Hutton, Ronald. *Pagan Britain*. New Haven: Yale University Press, 2013.
———. *The Pagan Religions of the Ancient British Isles: Their Nature and Legacy*. Oxford: Blackwell, 1998.
Loukaki, Argyro. *The Geographical Unconscious*. New York: Routledge, 2016.
Machen, Arthur. "The Ceremony." In *The Great God Pan and Other Horror Stories*, 252–54. Oxford: Oxford University Press, 2018.
———. *Far Off Things*. East Sussex: Delphi Classics, 2013.
———. *Hieroglyphics*. East Sussex: Delphi Classics, 2013.
———. *The Great God Pan*. East Sussex: Delphi Classics, 2013.
———. *The Inmost Light*. East Sussex: Delphi Classics, 2013.
———. *The Hill of Dreams*. East Sussex: Delphi Classics, 2013.
———. "The Novel of the Black Seal." East Sussex: Delphi Classics, 2013.

———. "The Novel of the White Powder." East Sussex: Delphi Classics, 2013.
———. *The Secret Glory*. East Sussex: Delphi Classics, 2013.
———. "The Shining Pyramid." East Sussex: Delphi Classics, 2013.
Nielsen, David. *Bruno Taut's Design Inspiration for the Glashaus*. New York: Routledge, 2015.
Panourgiá, Neni. "Anthropism/Immanent Humanism." In *Posthuman Glossary*, edited by Rosi Braidotti and Maria Hlavajova, 44–45. London: Bloomsbury, 2018.
Pepeperell, Robert. *The Posthuman Condition: Consciousness beyond the Brain*. Bristol: Intellect, 2003.
Robertson, Kellie. "Exemplary Rocks." In *Animal, Mineral, Vegetable: Ethics and Objects*, edited by Jeffrey Jerome Cohen, 91–121. Washington, DC: Oliphaunt Books, 2012.
Rutsky, R. L. *High Techne: Art and Technology from the Machine Aesthetic to the Posthuman*. Minneapolis, MN: University of Minnesota Press, 1999.
Schiesari, Juliana. *Beasts and Beauties: Animals, Gender, and Domestication in the Italian Renaissance*. Toronto: University of Toronto Press, 2010.
Smart, Alan and Josephine Smart. *Posthumanism: Anthropological Insights*. Toronto: University of Toronto Press, 2017.
Wolfe, Cary. *What is Posthumanism?* Minneapolis, MN: University of Minnesota Press, 2010.
Worringer, Wilhelm. *Formproblem der Gotik*. München: Piper Verlag, 1911.

Part II

DARWINISM AND DEGENERATION

Chapter 5

Fear, Fairies, and Fossils
The Legacy of Arthur Machen's "Little People" Stories

Justin Mullis

The popular folkloric figure of the fairy is not one typically associated with the horror genre. However, for Arthur Machen, the use of fairies as figures of horror can be most clearly seen in his cycle of "little people" tales, which includes "The Shining Pyramid" (1895), "The Novel of the Black Seal" (1895), and "Out of the Earth" (1920). These short stories build upon the foundation of popular European folk-beliefs in not only fairies but elves, trolls, and other related fantastic beings but with the science-fiction-style twist that such entities are not magical creatures of fantasy but rather the prehistoric remnants of a loathsome dwarf race which once inhabited the British Isles. Furthermore, in Machen's tales, this race has not entirely vanished but rather merely retreated underground to be later discovered by scientists who ultimately pay a terrible price for their desire to unearth the past.

While such a premise may make for good horror fiction, what many modern readers would probably never guess is that such conjectures were actually based on what was, in Machen's time, legitimate anthropological speculation about the existence of a prehistoric race of diminutive subhumans. This ancient race had once inhabited the British Isles and European continent before dying out, but their memory gave rise to the widespread belief in fairies, elves, dwarves, and other similar entities. This chapter will examine this belief—dubbed fairy euhemerism—in both Machen's "little people" tales as well as the then-emerging sciences of archeology, paleontology, and anthropology. Though seen as commonplace today, many of the scientific revelations unveiled by these new fields proved to be a major source of anxiety when they first burst onto the scene in the nineteenth century with such disquieting disclosures as an earth which was millions of years older than previously supposed by Christian theologians and once dominated not by the children of Adam but rather by monstrous beasts which even their discoverers likened to fairies, dragons, and demons.[1] Further exacerbating these apprehensions were the controversial theories of biological evolution being put forth in works such as *Vestiges of the Natural History of Creation* (1844) by writer Robert Chamber and naturalist Charles Darwin's *On the Origin of Species* (1859). Such theories proposed a worldview in which even human beings themselves were but a product of nature and whose ancestors had been subhuman ape-like creatures prior to becoming noble patriarchs. Confirmation of such conjectures arrived in 1856 when the bones of the first Neanderthal man were unearthed in the Neander Valley in Germany. Embroiled in controversy at first, the Victorian scientific community eventually reached the consensus that Neanderthals were in fact our prehistoric cousins. However, because the earliest fossil material came from an aged and diseased individual, and thus provided a distorted view of Neanderthal physiology, the first reconstructions tended to appear more ape than man. Artist Frantisek Kupka's 1909 drawing of a Neanderthal, printed in the *Illustrated London News* where it received wide exposure, showed a club wielding brute that looked more like an erect gorilla than an ancient human.[2]

The following will first summarize Machen's "little people" stories before proceeding with a detailed examination of their scientific influences, literary legacy, and larger cultural implications. And while it is true that the scientific theories which influenced Machen are no longer deemed credible by the academic mainstream, they have nevertheless survived in the form of fictions: fictions that affect how contemporary science is done and how future discoveries are perceived and received by the public. Hopefully, such an examination not only works to enrich Machen's stories by providing historical context but also to help us think critically about the complex and interwoven role played by both science and fiction in the popular imagination.

Machen wrote multiple stories throughout his career dealing with the themes of fairy lore and "little people." However, his two most famous and influential remain the short-stories "The Shining Pyramid" and "The Novel of the Black Seal," both published in 1895. "The Shining Pyramid" is a Sherlock Holmes-style detective story in which a writer named Dyson is called upon to investigate the mysterious goings-on at a friend's country estate, including the disappearance of a local girl. Dyson examines a number of clues including mysterious flint arrowheads found on his friend's property and cryptic graffiti on an ancient stone wall showing slanted Asiatic eyes. Ultimately, Dyson concludes that it is the "little people," who live in the hills of the surrounding countryside, who are responsible for the strange happenings including the kidnapping of the girl for the purpose of ritual sacrifice. Dyson and his friend journey to the site of the sacrifice and watch in horror as the poor girl is burned alive by the diminutive sub-humans.[3]

Machen, reportedly, did not think very highly of "The Shining Pyramid."[4] A far superior take on the same theme is found in "The Novel of the Black Seal" (1895), originally published as part of *The Three Imposters*, an anthology of short-stories connected via a shared framing device. In "The Novel of the Black Seal," Miss Lally, a housekeeper, relates to a man the story of her former employer's disappearance. Her employer was Prof. William Gregg, an ethnologist of some repute, who had discovered a strange seal made of black stone covered in ancient writing. Prof. Gregg subsequently became obsessed with solving the mystery of the stone's origin going so far as to uproot his family from their life in the city and move them out to the English countryside. The professor's investigations involve a local boy who seems only half-human (he is eventually revealed to be a human-fairy hybrid or Changeling) and leads to the revelation that the mysterious seal was forged by the "little people." Ultimately, Prof. Gregg's search for the truth brings him into direct contact with the "little people" with tragic results.[5]

A much later "little people" story by Machen is "Out of the Earth" (1920) and, unlike the other two, it is presented as autobiographic. Machen recounts how one summer rumors began circulating that a small seaside town in Wales, which he and his family frequently liked to vacation at, had been overrun by rambunctious and dangerous children who were roaming the area in gangs and assaulting tourists. Machen is skeptical of the rumors and dismisses them after a London newspaper runs an article declaring them groundless. The Machen family makes their regular holiday sojourn to the village and has a lovely time; though Machen recalls a strange incident in which his son, while exploring some dunes on the beach, claims to have encountered a group of "funny [looking] children" who badly frightened him.[6] Machen ends the story by recounting how his friend Morgan, who lives in the area, subsequently solved the mystery when, while on a picnic, he spied "a swarm of noisome children, horrible little stunted creatures with old men's faces, with bloated faces, with little sunken eyes, with leering eyes" uttering cries that "were to the ear what slime is to the touch."[7] When Morgan inquires of the village postmaster as to whom these odd children may have been, he is told that he has not seen human children but rather the "little people of the earth" who "[hide] in the deep bracken" up in the hills.[8]

Despite the fantastic nature of these stories, they were not merely the "monstrous creations" of Machen's "diseased brain" as his critics would have it.[9] While fairies are most commonly thought of today as the subject of juvenile fantasy, the belief in the literal reality of such entities was quite common throughout much of Europe until as recently as the early twentieth century.[10] However, as noted above, Machen's "Little People" were not supernatural maidens with gossamer wings but rather a savage diminutive prehistoric race of sub-humans whose hypothetical existence was rooted in what was, at the time, legitimate scientific speculation about the original inhabitants of the British Isles and European continent.[11] Machen was quite aware of such speculation and even contributed to it himself via his essay "The Little People," published in 1926 as part of his collection *Dreads and Drolls*. After expounding at length about the late nineteenth-century discovery of African pygmies, Machen writes that

> The fact is that here, in all likelihood, we have a pretty exact parallel to the Little People of our own folk-lore: the Daione Sidhe of Ireland, the Tylwyth Teg of Wales. The substratum in both cases is the same: an aboriginal people of small stature overcome and sent into the dark by invaders. In Britain and Ireland the dark meant subterranean dwellings made under the hills in the wildest and most remote parts of the country; they will point you out the place of these dwellings in Antrim to this day, and tell you that they are Fairy Raths. And in nine cases out of ten you may accept the statement with entire confidence; so long as you define "fairies" or "the People" as small, dark aborigines who hid from the invading Celt somewhere about 1500-1000 B.C.[12]

Furthermore, the connection between fairies and the new and important scientific fields of archeology and paleontology had already been well established in European folklore. Neolithic burial mounds were commonly referred to as "elf barrows" or "goblin hills," while megalithic standing stones—typified by the famous Stonehenge—were said to be trolls who had been turned to stone after being exposed to sunlight.[13] Likewise, Mesolithic and Neolithic arrowheads were popularly known as "elf shot" or "elf missiles" and believed to harbor magical properties and thus sometimes made into jewelry and worn as protective charms.[14] Fossils were also subject to the same kind of folk-beliefs. It is therefore not at all surprising to find the following anecdote in pioneering paleontologist and famed medical practitioner James Parkinson's *Organic Remains of a Former World* (1804) in which he recalls a fossil-hunting expedition undertaken with two companions near Oxford. According to Parkinson upon retiring to a nearby inn the party was greeted by the landlady who, learning of their pursuit, offered to show off her own collection of fossils which she said included

> "a petrified snake, with which this part of the country abounds. These were," continued she, "fairies, and once the inhabitants of these parts, who for their crimes were changed, first into snakes, and then into stones. Here," said she, showing us a stone of a conical form, "is one of the fairies night-caps, now also become stone. Do, madam," said she, addressing Emma, "pray observe;

is it possible that lace-work, so beautiful as this, should ever be worked by human hands? This," said she, "and this, are pieces of the bones of giants; who came to live here, when the race of fairies was destroyed." These bones, she informed us, were frequently dug up in several parts of the county; as well as innumerable thunderbolts: some of which she also showed us; stating, that these were the very thunderbolts, with which these people were, in their turn, also exterminated.[15]

The fossils displayed by the landlady were most likely spiral shelled ammonites (the fairies turned to snakes turned to stones), Echinocory sea urchins (the fairies night-cap), possible dinosaur bones (giant's bones), and belemnites; a type of extinct cephalopod (the thunderbolts).[16] The result of identifying actual archeological and paleontological objects with fairies was that the subsequent identification of the fairies themselves as the creators of such objects was not an incredible leap in the minds of many nineteenth-century scholars or writers like Machen. Euhemeristic explanations for myths and legends were in vogue at this time; euhemerism being the notion that fantastic stories inevitably have a naturalistic explanation behind them. Under this hermeneutic, pagan gods became ancient kings and fearsome monsters misidentified animals.[17] Fairies then, as seen in Machen's short-stories, were remnants of a prehistoric aboriginal race which had inhabited both the British Isles and the continental mainland before the advent of modern Europeans. A comprehensive overview of the history of this idea is outside the scope of this present chapter, but readers are directed to seek out Carole G. Silver's authoritative *Strange and Secret Peoples* (1999) for such an overview. Nevertheless, a cursory recapitulation of this school of thought is still helpful for the intended purpose of fleshing out the sources for Machen's "little people" stories.

The first major figure to put forth a euhemeristic explanation for the belief in fairies was the celebrated Scottish novelist and poet Sir Walter Scott (1771–1832) whose longstanding interest in the occult eventually produced his 1830 study *Letters on Demonology and Witchcraft*. Scott writes that the oldest kind of fairies to be believed in were "the duergar, or dwarfs" who were admittedly "spirits of a coarser sort, [of] more laborious vocation, and more malignant temper, and in all respects less propitious to humanity, than the fairies, properly so called, which were the invention of the Celtic people."[18] The novelist then goes on to espouse that

> there seems reason to conclude that these duergar were originally nothing else than the diminutive natives of the Lappish, Lettish, and Finnish nations, who, flying before the conquering weapons of the Asæ [i.e. Asiatic], sought the most retired regions of the north, and there endeavored to hide themselves from their

Eastern invaders. They were a little, diminutive race, but possessed of some skill probably in mining or smelting minerals, with which the country abounds. Perhaps also they might, from their acquaintance with the changes of the clouds, or meteorological phenomena, be judges of weather, and so enjoy another title to supernatural skill.[19]

For Scott, there is nothing preternatural about these fairies. Rather it was only their proficiency with metallurgy and possible skills at meteorology, coupled with their diminutive stature, which made these indigenous people appear supernatural to the first Europeans.

Following Scott was John Francis Campbell of Islay (1821–1885) whose *Popular Tales of the West Highlands* (Vol. 1, 1860) proclaims that "Men do believe in fairies, though they will not readily confess the fact. And though I do not myself believe that fairies *are*, in spite of the strong evidence offered, I believe there once was a small race of people in these islands, who are remembered as fairies."[20] Campbell goes on to describe fairies as "living in green mounds. They pop up their heads when disturbed by people treading on their houses. They steal children. They seem to live on familiar terms with the people about them when they treat them well, to punish them when they ill treat them." Campbell then rhetorically asks if "there are such people now [?]" before answering his own question by declaring that "a Lapp is such a man—he is a little, flesh-eating mortal—having control over the beasts, and living in a green mound—when he is not living in a tent, or sleeping out of doors, wrapped in his deer-skin shirt."[21] Like Scott, Campbell exocitizes the indigenous Sámi people transforming them into ideal candidates for the source of fairy lore.

Not all advocates of this view were Scottish, however. Swedish folklorist Gunnar Olof Hyltén-Cavallius (1818–1889) advocated in his ethnological study *Wärendoch Wirdarne* (Vol. II, 1868) that Scandinavian tales of trolls were based on real encounters with a dark-skinned, hairy aboriginal race which had survived in various regions of Sweden, Denmark, and Iceland until as recently as the mid-eighteenth century.[22] Evidence for the corporal reality of trolls, according to Hyltén-Cavallius, included a 1691 court case in which a Swedish laborer had been tried and found guilty of engaging in "illicit intercourse" with such an entity.[23]

Another supporter of fairy euhemerism was English anthropologist Sir Edward Burnett Tylor (1832–1917), who was heavily influenced by the evolutionary theories of Charles Darwin's *On the Origin of Species*. Taylor's own groundbreaking study of cultural evolution, *Primitive Culture* (1871), debuted the same year as Darwin's even more controversial follow-up *The Descent of Man*, and argued that "myths of giants and dwarfs" were "connected with traditions of indigenous or hostile tribes" and observed that "in

European folk-lore iron drives away fairies and elves, and destroys their power."[24] From this Tylor inferred that fairies had been "creatures belonging to the ancient Stone Age" and so "the new metal" of iron "is hateful and hurtful to them."[25] By this Tylor meant that the apotropaic use of iron against fairies was a tradition derived from the fact that the primitive race which had been their basis had been limited to stone tools and so had been technologically outclassed by European colonizers wielding iron weapons. In a similar vein, folklorist John Stuart Stuart-Glennie (1841–1910) also felt that fairy tales such as "The Swan Maiden"—a variation on the classic Beauty and the Beast trope—were based on historical events. However, Stuart-Glennie's interpretation took on a more pronounced and troubling racialized aspect when he argued that in times past white European women had been abducted, raped, and forced to marry bestial black or brown-skinned men.[26] These women in turn had birthed hybrid-children who were the basis for the folklore of fairy-human Changelings like the one featured in Machen's "The Novel of the Black Seal."

The most vocal proponent of fairy euhemerism however was Scottish-born folklorist and antiquarian David MacRitchie (1851–1925). MacRitchie wrote several books throughout his life championing the euhemerist view of fairies but his two most important were *The Testimony of Tradition* (1890) and *Fians, Fairies and Picts* (1893), in which he advanced the claim that the "little people" had really been a race of Turanian or Mongoloid pygmies that had inhabited the British Isles and continental mainland until at least the eleventh century when they were wiped out by modern white Europeans.[27] This is the exact same scenario we find being advanced by Machen in his essays as well as via his fictional characters like Prof. Gregg in "The Novel of the Black Seal" and Dyson in "The Shining Pyramid."

The identification of this prehistoric race as "pygmies" by MacRitchie deserves some unpacking as it precedes the discovery of African pygmies. In 1698, English physician Edward Tyson (1651–1708) was presented with the diminutive body of a recently deceased man-like creature. Tyson sketched and dissected the corpse then wrote up his findings in a 1699 report titled *The Anatomy of a Pygmie* in which he declared that the "Pygmie is no man, nor yet the common ape; but a sort of animal between both."[28] Tyson speculated that his half-man half-ape pygmy was the source of the mythical satyr as well as the hirsute European "wild man of the woods."[29] His sketch shows an ape-like creature standing erect with the aid of a walking stick (an obvious artistic embellishment), and while it is clear today that what Tyson's drawing actually shows is a juvenile chimpanzee it is worth noting that popular reproductions of the image, such as one found on the cover of *Bickerstaff's Boston Almanac* (1785), show a creature more closely resembling our present-day conception of a Sasquatch.[30] Like Tyson, MacRitchie's pygmies were also not entirely human. Though he likened them to the Sámi—as his precursors had—as well as Celtic Picts, American Eskimos, and Japanese Ainu, MacRitchie also characterized his hypothetical fairy-pygmies as being agile, covered in hair, eating raw flesh, and having the ability to see in the dark like nocturnal animals on account of having lived for so many generations in underground caves.[31] MacRitchie also held that when white Europeans arrived they decimated this Turanian dwarf race, or else enslaved them; this latter fact explaining the folklore surrounding helpful domestic fairies like brownies.[32]

Like MacRitchie, the majority of scholars held that these diminutive subhumans had long ago died out, at least in the British Isles and Europe as the discovery of actual pygmies living in Africa in the 1870s was taken as confirmation that some remnants of this race still survived as observed by Machen in his *Dreads and Drolls* essay.[33] Nevertheless, advocates for the existence of a relic population inhabiting the backwoods of Scotland and Ireland did occasionally appear. One of these was Henry Jenner, Local Secretary for the Society Antiquarians in Cornwall, who was certain that "a strange and separate people of Mongol type" still dwelled in the English countryside unseen, though not unseen by all.[34] The celebrated English folklorist Rev. Sabine Baring-Gould (1834–1924) for one claimed to have seen "a crowd of little imps or dwarfs" which had come out of the woods and surrounded his carriage while traveling to Montpellier. The Reverend's wife and young son also had their own sightings of "creatures they identified as elves or gnomes."[35]

Another subscriber to the relic population idea was the notorious American eugenicist Madison Grant (1865–1937) whose highly xenophobic *The Passing of the Great Race* (1916)—a book beloved by the Nazi Party—alleged that "In the old black breed of Scotland . . . ferocious gorilla-like living specimens of Paleolithic man are found not infrequently on the west coast of Ireland and are easily recognized by the great upper lip, bridgeless nose, beetling brow with low growing hair and wild and savage aspect. The proportions of the skull which give rise to this large upper lip, the low forehead and the superorbital ridges are certainly Neanderthal characters" and if not Neanderthal then certainly "derived from some very ancient and primitive race as yet undescribed."[36] As discussed above, early reconstructions of Neanderthals—like Tyson's pygmy—depicted a creature appearing at least as much ape as man if not more so.

Grant's blatantly racist remarks also recall another of Machen's tales, "The Red Hand" (1895), a murder mystery in which a man is slain in the London suburbs with a prehistoric stone ax. Dyson, the protagonist of "The Shinning Pyramid," returns in this story, at once theorizing that the presence of the weapon may indicate that the perpetrator is a "troglodyte," or caveman, having survived into the present day.[37] Dyson's friend, an ethnologist named

Phillips, dismisses this possibility as a fantasy and, in this instance, is proven correct when Dyson manages to locate the murderer who turns out to be a perfectly modern person who had pilfered the ax from a Neolithic burial site.[38]

Machen was not the only writer to exploit the interest and anxiety provoked by contemporary theories concerning prehistoric subhuman dwarves. Many writers, some far more famous than Machen, also wrote stories featuring such dreadful monsters. Sir Arthur Conan Doyle's second Sherlock Holmes novel, *The Sign of the Four* (1890), has the Great Detective pursue an assassin who turns out to be "a little black man—the smallest I have ever seen—with a great, misshapen head and a shock of tangled, disheveled hair" and a "face [that] was enough to give a man a sleepless night" on account of its "small eyes [which] glowed and burned with a sombre light" and "thick lips" which when pulled back revealed "his teeth, which grinned and chattered at us with a half animal fury."[39] Likewise, in Robert Louis Stevenson's *The Strange Case of Dr. Jekyll and Mr. Hyde* (1886), the esteemed Dr. Jekyll invents a serum which causes him to de-evolve into the bestial Mr. Hyde who is described as "pale and dwarfish," covered in "a swart growth of hair," and possessing an "ape-like fury."[40] Ultimately, Hyde is characterized as being "hardly human!" but rather "something troglodytic."[41]

The legacy of Machen's "little people" stories is also evident in the affect it exerted on several early twentieth-century American horror authors, most noticeably Texan Robert E. Howard (1906–1936), best remembered today as the creator of Conan the Barbarian. Howard regarded Machen's "The Novel of the Black Seal" as one of the three greatest horror stories ever conceived and wrote several "little people" short-stories of his own, including "The Children of the Night" (1931) and "People of the Dark" (1932), which should be regarded as pastiches of Machen.[42] "People of the Dark" provides a perfectly concise summation of the theory of fairy euhemerism explaining that "The Little People" were

> a squat Mongoloid aboriginal race, so low in the scale of evolution as to be scarcely human, yet possessing a distinct, though repulsive, culture of their own. They had vanished before the invading races, theory said, forming the base of all Aryan legends of trolls, elves, dwarfs and witches. Living in caves from the start, these aborigines had retreated farther and farther into the caverns of the hills, before the conquerors, vanishing at last entirely, though folklore fancy pictures their descendants still dwelling in the lost chasms far beneath the hills, loathsome survivors of an outworn age.[43]

This demonstrates that Howard, like Machen, was well versed in the scientific literature upon which such fantastic conjectures were based. "The Children of the Night" then is a racially charged horror story in which a scholar named

John O'Donnel is attending a small gathering of academics engaged in friendly anthropological debate and speculation. Though O'Donnel observes that all in attendance are of "pure Anglo-Saxon descent," he notes that one member, a man named Ketrick, possesses some unusual physical features including "amber, almost yellow" eyes which "seemed to slant like a Chinaman's."[44] When the subject of which race originally inhabited the British Isles and European continent is broached, their host suggests that the first were "an extremely inhuman" "Mongoloid type" with another man chiming in that such inhabitants were surely the basis of the "troll and dwarf legends [found] all over the Continent."[45] Their host then produces a Neolithic stone ax, but one so small it might be mistaken for a child's toy. The ax is passed around the room and Ketrick accidentally strikes O'Donnell with it while swinging it about. The blow awakens latent race memories in O'Donnell of how centuries ago his ancestors had arrived in Britain and driven out "the Children of the Night" who are described as being "short and stocky, with broad heads too large for their scrawny bodies. Their hair was snaky and stringy, their faces broad and square, with flat noses, hideously slanted eyes, a thin gash for a mouth, and pointed ears."[46] Drawing on Machen's suggestion in "Out of the Earth" that the "little people" converse in an inhuman tongue, Howard has O'Donnell note that the language of the Children of the Night "sounded much like the repeated hissing of many great snakes."[47] The resurgence of these memories drives O'Donnell into a murderous frenzy as he now believes that Ketrick, with his strange Asiatic eyes, is a descendant of the Children of the Night and must be exterminated in the interest of racial purity.

Another of Howard's Machen-influenced stories is "The Little People," which was written sometime around 1932 but never published until decades after the author's death. Today, it exists only in fragments and concerns an American brother and sister's trip to England. The sister reads Machen's "The Shining Pyramid" which she dismisses as "fairy-tales" and "rot!"[48] Her brother chides her for not recognizing the truth behind the story and relates a concise lesson on fairy euhemerism. He then dares her to spend the night in a nearby ring of standing stones, which the headstrong and foolish girl accepts without hesitation. Fearing for his sister's safety the brother retracts the challenge but later that night discovers that his sibling has slipped from her room. Though he moves to save her, the end results are predictably tragic.

Another American horror author with a great admiration for Machen was H.P. Lovecraft (1890–1937) who praised "The Novel of the Black Seal" in his pioneering study "Supernatural Horror in Literature." Despite his obvious veneration of Machen's writing, Lovecraft never attempted a direct pastiche in the style that Howard did, with the possible exception of his epistolary narrative "The Very Old Folk" (1927). This 2,712-word short story, allegedly based on a recurring dream, is set in ancient Rome and concerns a military excursion into the hills of the "tiny provincial town of Pompelo, at the foot of the Pyrenees in Hispania Citerior."[49] The residents of this community are being terrorized by an ancient race of "little yellow, squint-eyed" hill-people who biannually make-off with several citizens for the purpose of ritual sacrifice—just like the poor peasant girl in Machen's "The Shining Pyramid."[50] Lovecraft never attempted to publish or expand upon this story but rather included it in a letter to friend and acclaimed sci-fi editor Donald Wandrei. Wandrei was also an admirer of Machen and had exchanged letters with the British writer as a teenager. Eventually, the story came to the attention of Lovecraft's friend and fellow horror author Frank Belknap Long who, with Lovecraft's permission, incorporated it verbatim into his 110-page novella *The Horror from the Hills* (1931). Long, like Howard, Lovecraft, and Wandrei, was also a fan of Machen and his celebratory poem, "On Reading Arthur Machen," was republished as part of Lovecraft's "Supernatural Horror in Literature."

Also worth mentioning is Lovecraft's "The Whisperer in Darkness" (1931), which concerns a folklorist's doomed trip to Vermont to investigate a local legend about strange creatures lurking in the state's hills and backwoods. Here, Lovecraft explicitly references "the fantastic lore of lurking 'little people' made popular by the magnificent horror fiction of Arthur Machen," though it is ultimately revealed that the monsters in question are extraterrestrial arthropods rather than prehistoric anthropoids.[51] Nevertheless, Lovecraft scholar Robert M. Price has argued that "The Whisperer in Darkness" so closely parallels Machen's "The Novel of the Black Seal" not only in regard to plot but even down to the level of sentence structure, that the later should be regarded as a rewrite of the former.[52]

The subject of Machen's influence on the sub-genre of dark fantasy films is also, regrettably, outside the scope of this present chapter, but several films including Neil Marshall's *The Descent* (2005), André Øvredal's *Trollhunter* (2010), and Corin Hardy's *The Hallow* (2015) deserve to at least be mentioned. One film which deserves more than just a mention is Troy Nixey's *Don't Be Afraid of the Dark* (2010) written by Guillermo del Toro (*Pan's Labyrinth*, *The Shape of Water*) and Matthew Robbins (*Dragonslayer*). Though ostensibly based on the 1973 made-for-TV movie of the same name about a woman who moves into an old Victorian house and subsequently discovers she is being stalked by strange dwarf-like creatures, del Toro and Robbins' version takes this basic premise and greatly expands upon it by explicitly using Machen's "little people" stories as a foundation. Here, the Muppet-like dwarves of the 1970s incarnation are reimagined as rat-like "tooth-fairies" and the old Victorian house is the former domicile of a nineteenth-century scholar named Lord Blackwood who harbored a dangerous interest in fairies and is clearly modeled after characters like Machen's Prof.

Gregg and real-life individuals such as David MacRitchie. A prequel novel to the film, *Blackwood's Guide to Dangerous Fairies* (2011), written by Christopher Golden and del Toro, with illustrations by the movie's director, reads like a euhemerist's field guide to fairy lore.

However, the single greatest contemporary conveyor of fairy euhemerism is undoubtedly fantasy writer George R.R. Martin whose novel series *A Song of Ice and Fire*, served as the basis for the hit HBO television series *Game of Thrones* (2011–2019). Set in the faux-European world of Westeros, readers and viewers learn that this land was once inhabited by the fairy-like "Children of the Forest."[53] Possessing only stone-age technology, the children were subsequently wiped out by the "First Men" who "killed half of them with bronze blades, and . . . finished the job with iron."[54]

Though it may be tempting to imagine that such seemingly outlandish speculation as that exposited by the fairy euhemerists and embodied in the horror fiction of Machen is merely a product of decadent Victorian imaginations, recent examples show that we have not moved all that far from the nineteenth century. In 2003, paleoanthropologists Mike Moorwood, Thomas Sutikna, Richard Roberts, Peter Brown, and a team of seven other scientists were digging for fossils on the island of Flores in Indonesia when they made a remarkable discovery: a new species of hominid, another type of prehistoric human-like Neanderthal, but one which was only three-feet-tall with a brain cavity smaller than that of a chimp. The official scientific name for this group is *Homo floresiensis*, but Moorwood, realizing the find would need a catchy nickname to grab the attention of the media and thus secure the expedition additional funding, decided to call the diminutive humans "hobbits" after the similarly small and hairy race which appears alongside dwarves, elves, and goblins in J.R.R. Tolkien's beloved fantasy novel *The Hobbit* (1937) and its continuation *The Lord of the Rings* trilogy (1954–1955).

The excitement and controversy surrounding the discovery of *Homo floresiensis* was compounded by the fact that the scientists initially had difficulty dating the fossils leaving open the possibility that the hobbits may have inhabited the island of Flores at the same time as modern humans which first arrived there around 11,000 years ago. Such speculation was most exciting to those engaged in the practice of cryptozoology, or "the study of hidden animals," a term that colloquially denotes the vocation of "monster hunter." The most talked-about game in cryptozoology—known as "cryptids"—includes such legendary beasts as Bigfoot and the Yeti as well as various "living dinosaurs" such as the Loch Ness Monster. Scholars who look at cryptozoology from a historical perspective tend to trace the beginnings of the field to the mid-twentieth-century activities of two men: Scottish-born naturalist Ivan T. Sanderson (1911–1973) and French-Belgian zoologist Bernard Heuvelmans (1916–2001).[55] But, as archeologist Jeb Card observes, the nineteenth-century theories regarding the reality of fairies are remarkably similar to contemporary cryptozoological speculations about Bigfoot and other "mystery anthropoids."[56] In fact, Heuvelmans could very well be considered a latter-day fairy euhemerist. In his landmark book *On the Track of Unknown Animals*, first published in 1955 and widely credited as the cryptozoologist's bible, Heuvelmans discusses what he calls the "disturbing" East African legend of the *agogwe*, or "little hairy men," which he notes are virtually indistinguishable from "those elves called leprechauns in Ireland, brownies in Scotland and *nutons* in Scandinavia."[57] Like his Victorian precursors Heuvelmans speculated that these legends are based in truth and pegs the *agogwe* as a relic population of Australopithecus; an extinct species of anthropoid which had been discovered by a paleontologist in Taung, South Africa in the 1920s.[58]

Indeed, the specter of cryptozoology has been with us throughout this entire chapter. From the Sasquatch-like popular reconstructions of Tyson's pygmy to Kupka's Neanderthal which looks so much like a yeti that it has occasionally been used as an illustration of one in subsequent publications.[59] Likewise, Machen's Prof. Gregg is something of a proto-cryptozoologist not only due to his wild conjectures about the reality of fairies but also because he suggests that living dinosaurs could be the basis for medieval dragon legends: a proposition that was supported, in real-life, by both Sir Walter Scott and Gunnar Olof Hyltén-Cavallius.[60] Additionally, Gregg's drive to discover the "little people" is based on his conviction that there are still "undiscovered countries and continents of strange extent" which is a common cryptozoological conceit.[61] Finally, Lovecraft likens his forest-dwelling extraterrestrials from "The Whisperer in Darkness" not only to Machen's "little people" but also to the "Abominable Snow-Men who lurk hideously amidst the ice and rock pinnacles of the Himalayan summits."[62]

But while cryptozoology has been largely regarded as a pseudoscience by those involved in the scientific mainstream, the discovery of *Homo floresiensis* seemed to cause a reversal of those opinions among some. Paleontologist Henry Gee, a senior editor at the highly respected scientific journal *Nature*, penned an editorial inspired by the discovery in which he boldly proclaimed that "cryptozoology . . . can come in from the cold" as the discovery of the hobbits now made "stories of other mythical, humanlike creatures such as yetis" more plausible.[63] Gregory Forth, Professor in the Department of Anthropology at the University of Alberta, writing for *Anthropology Today*, went a step further drawing a connection between the hobbits and folktales concerning the *ebugogo*; the Indonesian version of fairies. Like his nineteenth-century counterparts, Forth suggested that stories of the *ebugogo* were based in reality and that that reality was *Homo floresiensis*.[64]

This blurring of paleontological fact with euhemerist speculation about the possible link between *Homo florensiensis* and Indonesian folklore plus the apparent endorsement of cryptozoological conjectures inevitably led to a whirlwind of sensationalized media coverage and public attention, much of it taking forms which Moorwood and his colleagues never anticipated or desired. In a subsequent 2014 interview with *Nature*, *Homo floresiensis* co-discoverer Peter Brown lamented the hobbit nickname saying that it had both "trivialized" the fossil find and led to him receiving "endless bizarre telephone calls from people who had seen some small hairy person in their backyard."[65] Even otherwise reputable media outlets dedicated to science news, such as National Geographic, seemed intent on playing up the fantastic angle of the discovery with their April 2005 issue featuring a story on "The Lost World of the Little People"; a title which invokes both Sir Arthur Conan Doyle and Arthur Machen. Inside that same issue was an article on *Homo floresiensis* titled "The People Time Forgot," which is exactly one word away from Edgar Rice Burroughs' novel *The People that Time Forgot* (1924) about a team of explorers trapped on an island filled with relic dinosaurs and cavemen; an impression which was only enhanced by National Geographic's choice of accompanying art which showed a hobbit confronting a gigantic komodo dragon in a scene straight out of a 1950s B-movie.

But the most sensationalized take of all would have to be Animal Planet's faux-documentary *The Cannibal in the Jungle* (2015, directed by Simon George) which is nothing less than a pastiche of one of Machen's "little people" stories updated for the age of found-footage horror movies. Though a complete work of fiction, *The Cannibal in the Jungle* purports to be the true story of a 1977 expedition into the Indonesian jungle in which only one of the members, an American ornithologist named Timothy Darrow, came out alive. Darrow claims that he and his colleagues were attacked by an unknown tribe of diminutive ape-like cannibals, but the Indonesian authorities suspect Darrow of murdering his fellow explorers and throw him in prison. The fictional protagonist of the film is anthropologist Dr. Richard Hoernbeck, who is determined to prove Darrow's innocence by returning to the jungle and finding proof of the tribe which attacked Darrow and killed his companions. Along the way, Hoernbeck marshals everything from the discovery of *Homo floresiensis*, the folklore of the *ebugogo*, and a cryptid known as the Orang Pendek (Indonesian for "short person") as evidence for Darrow's claims.[66] Unlike some found-footage films, *The Cannibal in the Jungle* does eventually show viewers the monsters, depicted via practical makeup effects, which appear as feral-looking hirsute dwarves.[67] The scenes involving them are genuinely chilling in large part due to the authenticity of the faux-documentary footage.

The treatment of new paleoanthropological discoveries like *Homo floresiensis* as sites for horror-tinged cryptozoological speculation demonstrates the continued relevance of Machen's "little people" stories today. Such tales, despite being avowed works of horror fiction, serve as a time capsule tapping into very real nineteenth-century scientific ideas and the deep-seated anxieties brought about by such speculations. These fears found expression in old folk traditions about the mischievous and often dangerous figures of fairies, elves, and trolls who already populated the western imagination since often when we go looking for modern monsters we simply find the ones we already know dressed up for a new century. And while ideas about a lost dwarf race being the origin of fairy lore were eventually discarded by mainstream academics, they remained active in the realm of fantastic-fiction beginning with the "little people" tales of Machen and continuing on through later writers, such as Robert E. Howard and H.P. Lovecraft, who in turn would inspire filmmakers like Guillermo del Toro. And, as the public reception of *Homo floresiensis* demonstrates, Arthur Machen's "little people" continue to haunt us to this day.

NOTES

1. For an exploration of how Machen's stories utilize the horror of ancient history see Aaron Worth, "Arthur Machen and the Horrors of Deep History," *Victorian Literature and Culture* 40 (2012), 215–27. For a discussion of how early paleontologists frequently described their fossil discoveries in overtly monstrous terms see Ralph O'Connor, *The Earth on Show: Fossils and the Poetics of Popular Science, 1802-1856* (Chicago, IL: University of Chicago Press, 2007), 53.

2. Lydia Pyne, *Seven Skeletons: The Evolution of the World's Most Famous Human Fossils* (New York: Viking 2016), 31–32.

3. Arthur Machen, *The Great God Pan and Other Horror Stories* (New York: Oxford University Press, 2018), 222–41.

4. Ibid., 373–74.

5. Ibid., 111–44.

6. Arthur Machen, "Out of the Earth," https://tinyurl.com/ybsqlq5b (accessed Febr. 19, 2019).

7. Ibid.

8. Ibid.

9. James Machin, *Weird Fiction in Britain 1880–1939* (New York: Palgrave Macmillan, 2018), 142.

10. There is anecdotal evidence suggesting that the belief in fairies is still quite prevalent in some parts of the British Isles and Europe. See Ryan Jacobs, "Why So Many Icelanders Still Believe in Invisible Elves," *The Atlantic*, Oct. 29, 2013, https://tinyurl.com/y8b6vne4, and Manchan Magan, "Away with the faeries," *Irish Times*, Mar. 15, 2014, https://tinyurl.com/y9wtokjr (both accessed Feb. 19, 2019).

11. The image of fairies as winged entities is a fairly recent creation. For a concise history of this visual see Simon Young, "When Did Fairies Get Wings?" in

The Paranormal and Popular Culture, ed. Darryl Caterine and John W. Morehead, 253–74 (New York: Routledge, 2019).

12. Arthur Machen, "The Little People," in *Dreads and Drolls*, https://tinyurl.com/y99qjy9n (accessed Feb. 19, 2019).

13. Jeb Card, *Spooky Archeology: Myth and the Science of the Past* (Albuquerque, NM: University of New Mexico Press, 2018), 23–23.

14. Ibid.

15. James Parkinson, *Organic Remains of a Former World* (London: M.A. Nattali, 1804), 4.

16. Kenneth Oakle, "Folklore of Fossils Part 2," *Antiquity* 39, no. 153 (Mar. 1, 1965): 117–19.

17. For a brief discussion of the popularity of euhemerism among the Victorians see Robert A. Segal, *Myth: A Very Short Introduction* (Oxford: Oxford University Press, 2004), 19–20.

18. Walter Scott, *Letters on Demonology and Witchcraft* (London: John Murray, 1830), 120–21.

19. Ibid.

20. John Francis Campbell, *Popular Tales of the West Highlands*, Vol. 1 (Edinburgh: Edmonston and Douglas, 1860), 95.

21. Ibid.

22. George M. Eberhart, *Mysterious Creatures: A Guide to Cryptozoology* (Santa Barbara, CA: ABC CLIO, 2002), 558–59.

23. Michael Meurger and Claude Gagnon, *Lake Monsters Traditions: A Cross-Cultural Analysis* (London: Fortean Tomes, 1988), 31.

24. Edward B. Tylor, *Primitive Culture* (London: John Murray, 1871), 385 and 140.

25. Ibid.

26. Carol G. Silver, *Strange and Secret Peoples: Fairies and Victorian Consciousness* (Oxford: Oxford University Press, 1999), 46 and 97–98.

27. Katharine Briggs, *The Vanishing People: Fairy Lore and Legends* (New York: Pantheon Books, 1978), 33–35.

28. Brian Switek, *Written in Stone: Evolution, the Fossil Record, and Our Place in Nature* (New York: Bellevue Literary Press, 2010), 227–28. See also Brian Regal, *Searching for Sasquatch: Crackpots, Eggheads and Cryptozoology* (New York: Palgrave Macmillan, 2011), 78.

29. Ibid. The satyr, of course, is linked to the Greco-Roman Pan who is the subject of Machen's most celebrated horror text, "The Great God Pan" (1894).

30. Regal, *Searching for Sasquatch*. For another similar image see also Herbert Wendt, *Out of Noah's Ark: The Story of Man's Discovery of the Animal Kingdom* (Cambridge, MA: The Riverside Press, 1959), 23.

31. David MacRitchie, *The Testimony of Tradition* (London: Kegan Paul, Trench, Trübner & Co., 1890), 158–59; and David MacRitchie, *Fians, Fairies and Picts* (London: Kegan Paul, Trench, Trübner & Co., 1893), 43–44.

32. Card, *Spooky Archeology*, 27.

33. Silver, *Strange and Secret Peoples*, 50.

34. Carol G. Silver, "On the Origin of Fairies: Victorians, Romantics, and Folk Belief," *Browning Institute Studies* 14 (1986), 152.

35. Ibid., 146.

36. Madison Grant, *The Passing of the Great Race: Or, The Racial Basis of European History* (New York: Charles Scribner's Sons, 1916), 107–08.

37. Machen, *The Great God Pan*, 197–98.

38. Ibid., 197–221.

39. Arthur Conan Doyle, *The Complete Sherlock Holmes*, Vol. 1 (New York: Barnes & Nobels Classics, 2003), 161–62.

40. Robert Louis Stevenson, *The Strange Case of Dr. Jekyll and Mr. Hyde: And Other Tales of Terror* (London: Penguin Classics, 2003), 16 and 22.

41. Ibid., 16. The interpretation of Hyde as Jekyll's prehistoric past-self has resulted in a number of sci-fi films and TV shows which have directly played with this idea. These films include E.A. Dupont's *The Neanderthal Man* (1953), Jack Arnold's *Monster on Campus* (1958), and Ken Russell's *Alter States* (1980). TV series presenting the same topic include *Buffy the Vampire Slayer*, Season 4, Episode 5, and *Freaky Links*, Season 1 Episode 12.

42. Robert E. Howard, *The Horror Stories of Robert E. Howard* (New York: Del Rey, 2008), 145. Howard's other two favorite horror stories were Poe's "Fall of the House of Usher" and Lovecraft's "The Call of Cthulhu."

43. Ibid., 203.

44. Ibid., 144.

45. Ibid., 147.

46. Ibid., 148.

47. Ibid.

48. Ibid., 43.

49. H.P. Lovecraft, "The Very Old Folk," https://tinyurl.com/y6vdurba (accessed Feb. 19, 2019).

50. Ibid.

51. H.P. Lovecraft, "The Whisperer in Darkness," in *The Hastur Cycle*, 2nd edn., edited by Robert M. Price, 146–98 (Oakland, CA: Chaosium, 2006), 151.

52. Robert M. Price (ed.), "The Mythology of Hastur," in *The Hastur Cycle,* 2nd edn., vii–xiv (Oakland, CA: Chaosium, 2006), xi–xiii.

53. George R.R. Martin, *A Game of Thrones* (New York: Bantam Books Reprint Edition, 2011), 616–18.

54. George R.R. Martin, *A Storm of Swords* (New York: Bantam Books Trade Paperback Edition, 2011), 373.

55. W. Scott Poole, *American Monsters: Our Historical Obsession with the Hideous and the Haunting* (Waco, TX: Baylor University Press, 2011), 134; and Regal, *Searching for Sasquatch*, 18–19. Although Sanderson and Heuvelmans are also usually credited with having coined the term "cryptozoology," there is some debate over this. See Daniel Loxton and Stephen Prothero, *Abominable Science! Origins of the Yeti, Nessie, and Other Famous Cryptids* (New York: Columbia University Press, 2013), 16–17.

56. Card, *Spooky Archeology*, 27.

57. Bernard Heuvelmans, *On the Track of Unknown Animals*, 3rd ed. (New York: Routledge, 1995), 504.

58. Ibid., 513–19.

59. Robert Deis, David Coleman and Wyatt Doyle (ed.), *Cryptozoology Anthology: Strange and Mysterious Creatures in Men's Adventure Magazines* (n.p.: New Texture, 2015), 24–25.

60. Machen, *The Great God Pan*, 137. For Hyltén-Cavallius' dragon hunts see Meurger and Gagnon, *Lake Monsters Traditions*, 31–36. For Scott's thoughts on English dragon legends see Justin Mullis, "Dragon, legend, or cryptid? The legacy of the Lambton Worm: A case study in folklore development," *AIPT* May 1, 2020, https://tinyurl.com/y7o56f9u (accessed Jun. 12, 2020).

61. Machen, *The Great God Pan*, 116. For an example of this kind of declaration see Heuvelmans, *On the Track of Unknown Animals*, 3–17.

62. Lovecraft, "The Whisperer in Darkness," 150–51.

63. Henry Gee, "Flores, God and Cryptozoology," *Nature*, Oct. 27, 2004, https://tinyurl.com/ybcsme36 (accessed Feb. 19, 2019).

64. Gregory Forth, "Hominids, Hairy Hominoids and the Science of Humanity," *Anthropology Today* 21, no. 3 (Jun., 2005), 13–17.

65. Ewen Callaway, "The Discovery of *Homo Floresiensis*: Tales of the Hobbit," *Nature* 514, no. 7523 (Oct. 23, 2014), 424.

66. For more on the Orang Pendek see Heuvelmans, *On the Track of Unknown Animals*, 119–42, and Wendt, *Out of Noah's Ark*, 322–32.

67. In fact, they look almost exactly like Greg Staple's illustration of the same sort of creatures featured in Robert E. Howard's "Children of the Night." Howard, *The Horror Stories of Robert E. Howard*, 149.

REFERENCES

Briggs, Katharine. *The Vanishing People: Fairy Lore and Legends*. New York: Pantheon Books, 1978.

Callaway, Ewen. "The Discovery of Homo Floresiensis: Tales of the Hobbit." *Nature* 514, no. 7523 (Oct. 23, 2014): 422–26.

Campbell, John Francis. *Popular Tales of the West Highlands*. Vol. 1. Edinburgh: Edmonston and Douglas, 1860.

Card, Jeb. *Spooky Archeology: Myth and the Science of the Past*. Albuquerque, NM: University of New Mexico Press, 2018.

Deis, Robert, David Coleman and Wyatt Doyle (ed.). *Cryptozoology Anthology: Strange and Mysterious Creatures in Men's Adventure Magazines*. n.p.: New Texture, 2015.

Doyle, Arthur Conan. *The Complete Sherlock Holmes*. Vol. 1. New York: Barnes & Noble Classics, 2003.

Eberhart, George M. *Mysterious Creatures: A Guide to Cryptozoology*. Santa Barbara, CA: ABC CLIO, 2002.

Forth, Gregory. "Hominids, Hairy Hominoids and the Science of Humanity." *Anthropology Today* 21, no. 3 (Jun. 2005): 13–17.
Gee, Henry. "Flores, God and Cryptozoology." *Nature*, Oct. 27, 2004: https://www.nature.com/articles/news041025-2.
Grant, Madison. *The Passing of the Great Race: Or, The Racial Basis of European History*. New York: Charles Scribner's Sons, 1916.
Heuvelmans, Bernard. *On the Track of Unknown Animals*. 3rd edn. New York: Routledge, 1995.
Howard, Robert E. *The Horror Stories of Robert E. Howard*. New York: Del Rey, 2008.
Jacobs, Ryan. "Why So Many Icelanders Still Believe in Invisible Elves." *The Atlantic*, Oct. 29, 2013, https://www.theatlantic.com/international/archive/2013/10/why-so-many-icelanders-still-believe-in-invisible-elves/280783/.
Lovecraft, H.P. "The Whisperer in Darkness." In *The Hastur Cycle*. 2nd edn., edited by Robert M. Price, 146–98. Oakland, CA: Chaosium, 2006.
———. *Supernatural Horror in Literature*. http://www.hplovecraft.com/writings/texts/essays/shil.aspx.
———. "The Very Old Folk." http://www.hplovecraft.com/writings/texts/fiction/vof.aspx.
Loxton, Daniel and Stephen Prothero. *Abominable Science! Origins of the Yeti, Nessie, and Other Famous Cryptids*. New York: Columbia University Press, 2013.
MacRitchie, David. *The Testimony of Tradition*. London: Kegan Paul, Trench, Trübner & Co., 1890.
———. *Fians, Fairies and Picts*. London: Kegan Paul, Trench, Trübner & Co., 1893.
Machen, Arthur. *The Great God Pan and Other Horror Stories*. New York: Oxford University Press, 2018.
———. "Out of the Earth." http://gutenberg.net.au/ebooks07/0700381h.html.
———. "The Little People." in *Dreads and Drolls*. https://ebooks.adelaide.edu.au/m/machen/arthur/dreads-and-drolls/chapter6.html.
Machin, James. *Weird Fiction in Britain 1880–1939*. New York: Palgrave Macmillan, 2018.
Magan, Manchan. "Away with the faeries." *Irish Times*, Mar. 15, 2014, https://www.irishtimes.com/culture/heritage/away-with-the-faeries-1.172537.
Martin, George R. R. *A Game of Thrones*. New York: Bantam Books Reprint Edition, 2011.
———. *A Storm of Swords*. New York: Bantam Books Trade Paperback Edition, 2011.
Meurger, Michael and Claude Gagnon. *Lake Monsters Traditions: A Cross-Cultural Analysis*. London: Fortean Tomes, 1988.
Mullis, Justin. "Dragon, legend, or cryptid? The legacy of the Lambton Worm: A case study in folklore development." *AIPT*, May 1, 2020. https://aiptcomics.com/2020/05/01/dragon-legend-or-cryptid-the-legacy-of-the-lambton-worm/.
Oakle, Kenneth. "Folklore of Fossils Part 2." *Antiquity* 39, no. 153 (Mar. 1, 1965): 117–19.

O'Connor, Ralph. *The Earth on Show: Fossils and the Poetics of Popular Science, 1802–1856*. Chicago, IL: University of Chicago Press, 2007.

Parkinson, James. *Organic Remains of a Former World: An Examination of the Mineralized Remains of the Vegetables and Animals of the Antediluvian World*. London: M.A. Nattali, 1804.

Poole, W. Scott. *American Monsters: Our Historical Obsession with the Hideous and the Haunting*. Waco, TX: Baylor University Press, 2011.

Price, Robert M. "The Mythology of Hastur." In *The Hastur Cycle*. 2nd edn., edited by Robert M. Price, vii–xiv. Oakland, CA: 2006.

Pyne, Lydia. *Seven Skeletons: The Evolution of the World's Most Famous Human Fossils*. New York: Viking, 2016.

Regal, Brian. *Searching for Sasquatch: Crackpots, Eggheads and Cryptozoology*. New York: Palgrave Macmillan, 2011.

Scott, Walter. *Letters on Demonology and Witchcraft*. London: John Murray, 1830.

Segal, Robert A. *Myth: A Very Short Introduction*. Oxford: Oxford University Press, 2004.

Silver, Carol G. *Strange and Secret Peoples: Fairies and Victorian Consciousness*. Oxford: Oxford University Press, 1999.

———. "On the Origin of Fairies: Victorians, Romantics, and Folk Belief." *Browning Institute Studies* 14 (1986): 141–56.

Stevenson, Robert Louis. *The Strange Case of Dr. Jekyll and Mr. Hyde: And Other Tales of Terror*. London: Penguin Classics, 2003.

Switek, Brian. *Written in Stone: Evolution, the Fossil Record, and Our Place in Nature*. New York: Bellevue Literary Press, 2010.

Tylor, Edward B. *Primitive Culture: Researches into the Development of Mythology, Philosophy, Religion, Language, Art and Custom*. London: John Murray, 1871.

Wendt, Herbert. *Out of Noah's Ark: The Story of Man's Discovery of the Animal Kingdom*. Cambridge, MA: The Riverside Press, 1959.

Worth, Aaron. "Arthur Machen and the Horrors of Deep History." *Victorian Literature and Culture* 40 (2012): 215–27.

Young, Simon. "When did fairies get wings?" In *The Paranormal and Popular Culture*, edited by Darryl Caterine and John W. Morehead, 253–74. New York: Routledge, 2019.

Chapter 6

"Dissolution and Change"
Reading The Great God Pan *as Monstrous Adaptation*

Jessica George

The climactic moment of Arthur Machen's 1894 novella *The Great God Pan* centers on the physical dissolution of Helen Vaughan, the tale's villainess and daughter of the titular deity. The story comes full circle here, her death being brought about by one of the two men who presided over her supernatural conception at the beginning, but it is the manner of her destruction that stands out the most, providing some of the tale's most striking imagery. In her death throes, Helen shifts between shapes, wavering "from sex to sex" and "[descending] to the beasts," deliquescing into "a substance like to jelly," a kind of primordial slime, and finally ascending "the ladder" once more, taking on a form that is "neither man nor beast" and about which the observing narrator, Dr. Matheson, can only say that he "will not further describe" it.[1] This moment clearly draws on the narratives of evolutionary degeneration that enjoyed wide currency at the *fin de siècle*, Max Nordau's gloomy treatise, *Degeneration*, having been published only two years before "The Great God Pan." The novella has been read as expressing evolutionary, racial, and imperial anxieties, all of which became entangled in the contemporary Gothic discourses around degeneration theory. Helen's ascent of the evolutionary ladder at the end of her transformation, however—implicitly assuming a form close to that of her divine progenitor—complicates the degenerative interpretation, invoking the possibility of evolutionary ascent through adaptation.

"Adaptation" refers, of course, not only to an evolutionary process but to a literary practice. The former—as in Linda Hutcheon's *A Theory of Adaptation* (2006)—may provide a useful metaphor for thinking through the latter.[2] Engaging this notion of literary adaptation as evolutionary metaphor, this chapter will explore "The Great God Pan" as a monstrous adaptation, stitching together mythic, literary, and scientific discourses to form a whole in which the tension between the evolutionary and the transcendent threatens at all times to pull the narrative apart.

Darwin's popularization of evolutionary theory in the latter part of the nineteenth century challenged a traditional Christian worldview in which human beings had always existed, unchanging, in their present form, and had always been civilized. That humans were fundamentally different from animals was taken for granted. Even when eighteenth-century naturalists began to take an interest in the transformation of species and to note the similarity of the great apes to humans, most, in the words of Peter Bowler, "agreed to follow the conventional view that humans' mental and moral powers lifted them above the brutes" and held humans to be "quite distinct from the rest of the animal kingdom."[3] By the end of the eighteenth century, discoveries in geology had made it clear that the historical timescale of the earth was not concurrent with human history: it had not, in other words, been formed for us by a kindly creator.[4] The publication of the *Origin of Species* in 1859 further challenged traditional values, implicitly proposing that "humans were merely improved apes, and nature only a senseless round of struggle and death," and thereby challenging both "the divine source of moral values" and the authority of the church.[5]

Evolution was a never-ending process, and this notion of constant change called into question both the stability of the human form and the continued supremacy of human beings on the planet. Human beings might revert to earlier forms, losing their dominance on earth. The human relationship to animals raised the specter of monstrous hybrid forms. There even remained the possibility that some other species might outstrip the human in the struggle for survival. These evolutionary anxieties were entangled with the racial, national, and imperial anxieties of a white European and American culture that felt its supremacy threatened. The humanity of other races, the poor, and the disabled was called into question, and they came to be seen as threats to racial and national "fitness." E. Ray Lankester, in his *Degeneration: A Chapter in Darwinism* (1880), employed the image of imperial collapse as a biological metaphor, arguing that animals and humans whose lives became too easy might well degenerate physically, "as Rome degenerated when possessed of the riches of the ancient world."[6] The first chapter of Nordau's *Degeneration*, portentously titled, "The Dusk of the Nations," claims that the degenerate "*fin-de-siècle* state of mind is to-day everywhere to be met with," casting this enervated and "curiously confused" mental state as an unwelcome invader threatening to enter and destroy all "civilised" nations.[7] Degeneration here is a social contagion, one which threatens to destroy the superiority of Western nations. Darwin himself, in *The Descent of Man* (1871), warns that unless "the reckless, the vicious and otherwise inferior members of society" are prevented from "increasing at a quicker rate than the better class of men," then "the nation will retrograde."[8] The development of the eugenics movement in the late nineteenth century aimed to counteract such possibilities: nations were exhorted to see to their national and racial "fitness" by ensuring that their most desirable members reproduced.[9]

In this context, and with reference to Machen's status as a Welsh writer in London, Machen's fiction has been read by Kirsti Bohata as expressing "the fears of a 'border' identity, who wants to be 'English' (the superior race) but fears he is contaminated by 'undesirable' Welshness," here stereotyped as atavistic and biologically inferior.[10] It is the tension between these identities which drives much of Machen's horror. In the words of Jane Aaron, "it is not always clear where his allegiances lie."[11] As James Machin has pointed out, however, Machen made no secret of his hostility to scientific materialism, at times expressing "exasperation with a (to his mind) misplaced emphasis on the represented rather than the ineffable 'mystery' and 'ecstasy' accessible only through art and religion, sometimes expressed in terms explicitly disdainful of Huxley and Darwin."[12] With this in mind, it is possible to read both the narrative of "The Great God Pan" and its treatment of its mythic and literary intertexts as illustrating the tension between the mystic and the material, with the Godless, life-driven universe of evolutionary theory threatening to drag divine "mystery" and "ecstasy" into the brute physical realm.

Literary theories of adaptation may be read as straining in similarly disparate directions, some employing the scientific metaphor of evolution, others the anthropological and sometimes religious metaphor of myth. In *In Frankenstein's Shadow* (1987), his study of the wide-ranging influence of Mary Shelley's 1818 novel, Chris Baldick attributes the proliferation of adaptations of and borrowings from *Frankenstein* to its status as a modern myth. Far from being confined to a prelapsarian past, as literary critics have been prone to assume, the process of myth-making is ongoing and allows for the production of many and varied "new narrative or interpretive elaborations."[13] Baldick makes a distinction between myth—a simplified or shortened version of the story, which may be repeated with numerous variations—and the specificity of the literary text. The myth of Frankenstein, distinct from the literary text *Frankenstein*, is therefore a radically foreshortened version of its plot which retains its "basic unity of meaning" but accrues new versions over time—unlike the literary text, whose substance may lie as much in style as in story.[14] The *Oxford English Dictionary* defines a myth as "A traditional story, typically involving supernatural beings or forces, which embodies and provides an explanation, aetiology, or justification for something such as the early history of a society, a religious belief or ritual, or a natural phenomenon."[15] The Christian creation myth undermined by Darwinism clearly fits into this category, while in Baldick's analysis, the dark counter-creation myth of the Frankenstein story, boiled down to its simplest elements, allows itself to be used by authors and filmmakers for a variety of purposes. The idea of myth, central to Baldick's ideas on adaptation, has religious and supernatural resonances.

For Linda Hutcheon, in contrast, adaptation is best understood via scientific metaphors. She writes, "biology thinks about adaptation . . . in terms of successful replication and change. Perhaps cultural adaptation can be seen to work in similar ways."[16] In evolution, adaptation is the process by which a species becomes fitted to its environment, and something similar may be said of narratives and their cultural environments. Stories "evolve by adaptation," undergoing a "process of mutation or adjustment" as they encounter new environments.[17] Hutcheon notes that theories of intertextuality—obviously central to adapted texts—challenged "dominant post-Romantic notions of originality, uniqueness, and autonomy" in which works were held to be created, discrete and entire, by an individual, Godlike author.[18] Instead, they became, in the words of Roland Barthes, "tissue[s] of quotations" which could no longer be read to impart any "single 'theological' meaning (the 'message' of the Author-God)."[19] Read in conjunction with Hutcheon's evolutionary metaphor, this challenge to the myth of literary creation irresistibly echoes evolution's challenge to the myth of Biblical creation. The fragmented "tissue" of the text, divorced from its single autonomous creator and comprised of disparate parts, echoes the monstrous bodies of the evolutionary Gothic, no longer created in God's image, but continuous with the rest of the animal kingdom, and liable to display any number of animal features. As Kelly Hurley notes, the evolutionary horrors of the *fin-de-siècle* Gothic imagined "a randomly working Nature . . . as *too* imaginative, *too* prolific. Any admixture of diverse morphic traits is possible, so that even highly complex bodies, ingeniously specialized for their environment . . . are abominable."[20] Though superbly adapted to their environments, these bodies are rendered monstrous in much the same way as Helen Vaughan at the moment of her climactic breakdown: by the diversity of features they exhibit.

This diversity of features, the impossibility of reconciling them into a single, classifiable whole, is integral to monstrosity. The monster as theorized by Jeffrey Jerome Cohen in his influential essay "Monster Culture (Seven Theses)" (1996) is defined by its hybrid resistance to categorization, its "polyphony, mixed response . . . and resistance to integration."[21] The adapted text and the text which wears its intertextual relations on its sleeve similarly resist unification and classification. We might read them as monstrous. Hutcheon, arguing that adaptation is not necessarily an act of faithful homage, suggests that the adapter may well wish to challenge the vision and authority of the original author.[22] With the advent of evolutionary theory, as Stephen T.

Asma has argued, monstrous bodies came to be interpreted as a challenge to the authority of God and the notion of a "perfect, purposeful nature," divinely ordained.[23] Resemblances between the form of the adapted text and the evolutionary monsters of its narrative begin to suggest themselves. Indeed, Richard J. Hand and Jay McRoy have noted the frequency with which adapted horror films "frequently abound with adaptation on a thematic level," and the title of their edited collection, *Monstrous Adaptations* (2007), is highly suggestive, again hinting at the monstrous nature of the texts themselves, as well as their denizens.[24] The process of adaptation becomes a kind of literary monster-making. By identifying the mythic, scientific, and literary sources of "The Great God Pan," and examining the uses Machen makes of them, it is possible to read the novella as a monstrous adaptation, a collection of mythic, Gothic, and scientific parts that themselves resist integration.

Machen's 1894 novella is not an adaptation in the sense Hutcheon uses the term, not being tied to a single, identifiable previous text. Hutcheon, however, is clear that her relatively restricted definition of adaptation is pragmatic: to theorize adaptation, one has to draw the line somewhere.[25] Viewed more widely, there is continuity between straightforward adaptation and a more general process of cultural and intertextual recycling, challenging, and recreation. This is a process in which Machen's novella quite consciously takes part, both explicitly and more subtly invoking a range of classical and nineteenth-century intertexts. Its writing also seems to have involved a species of adaptation. In his introduction, Machen notes that the first chapter was initially conceived and sold as a standalone story, with "no notion that there would be anything to follow" it.[26] The third chapter (in which Villiers encounters Herbert and learns about his wife) also began life as a separate short story, but, finding it unsuccessful in its own right, Machen decided to connect it to the previous story, constructing a wider narrative around both and perhaps, in the process, creating a Frankenstein "tissue" of fragments.

"The Great God Pan" begins with a scientific experiment observed by Clarke, a London gentleman with occult fascinations. The experimenter is Clarke's friend, Raymond; the subject, Raymond's ward, Mary, with whom he seems to be carrying on a romantic relationship. An operation is carried out on Mary's brain, causing her, in Raymond's words, to "see the god Pan."[27] The experiment leaves her "a hopeless idiot," and she never regains her reason, but nine months later gives birth to Helen.[28] Years later, Clarke, who does not know of her birth, hears the tale of a young girl called Helen who is fostered by a farming family and befriends their daughter. She is fond of taking walks in the woods, and is seen in strange situations, accompanied by a being who looks like a naked man. A young boy who sees her on one of her rambles suffers a fit of terror, while the daughter of the foster family goes missing after accompanying her into the woods and seeing an unspecified scene. Later, Clarke is told a bizarre tale by his friend Villiers, who has encountered an old college friend, Herbert, begging for money in the street. Herbert claims to have been ruined "body and soul" by his former wife, who induced him to participate in disturbing scenes—unspecified but, since this began on their wedding night, perhaps sexual—and then absconded with all his money.[29] When Villiers investigates their now-vacant house, he is stricken with a mysterious illness which leaves him bed-bound for a week.[30] At the house, he also finds a sketch of Mrs. Herbert, whom Clarke believes he recognizes as Mary. Villiers' friend Austin receives a packet of papers belonging to a deceased acquaintance, a painter who died in South America after a mysterious illness. Among the papers is a portrait of Mrs. Herbert. Villiers learns of the growing popularity in society of a woman called Mrs. Beaumont, whose parties are attended by London's well-to-do and fashionable. A number of wealthy gentlemen commit suicide after visiting her home, and after piecing together the various stories, he comes to the conclusion that Mrs. Herbert, Mrs. Beaumont, and Helen Vaughan are the same person. Clarke and Villiers, witnessed by a doctor named Matheson, succeed in destroying her, resulting in the shapeshifting physical dissolution described earlier. After being told the story by Clarke, Raymond writes back to him confirming Helen's identity. She is the hybrid offspring of Mary and the god Pan, born nine months after the experiment.

The novella clearly signposts its religious and mythical sources in both its title and the names it uses for its characters. "Mary" suggests an ironic spin on Christian mythology, with Helen functioning as a kind of dark messiah who damns human beings instead of saving them. The mention of Mary in the context of divinity also brings to mind the pagan roots of Christianity, a theory with which Machen was certainly familiar through his reading of James Frazer's *The Golden Bough* (1890) (though, as Machin has noted, he was scathing about the materialist explanations Frazer offered for some religious motifs).[31] Stephen Benko has argued that "there is a direct line, unbroken and clearly discernible, from the goddess-cults of the ancients to the reverence paid and eventually the cult accorded to the Virgin Mary," and that "Mariology . . . is paganism baptized, pure and simple."[32] Goddesses such as the Egyptian Isis and the Phrygian Cybele influenced or were incorporated into the worship of Mary.[33]

As the daughter of Pan, Helen may also be read as analogous to the Roman goddess Bona Dea, who was portrayed sometimes as the sister and wife of Faunus—a deity equivalent to Pan—and sometimes as the daughter for whom he harbors incestuous desires.[34] The worship of Bona Dea seems to have been the focus of some anxiety regarding female autonomy. The December festival dedicated to the goddess was forbidden to men, and the 62 BCE festival became the center of a scandal when the rites were infiltrated by the politician

Clodius disguised as a woman.[35] The satirist Juvenal depicted the festival as a drunken orgy, though Ariadne Staples has argued that this is likely spurious.[36] The crossing of boundaries and witnessing of forbidden mysteries enacted by Clodius becomes, in Machen's story, an experience into which unwitting men are drawn by Helen herself. The mythology surrounding Bona Dea has her being sexually approached by her father Faunus, rejecting him, and finally being seduced when he disguises himself as a snake,[37] an animal which was also sacred to her.[38] Machen's Helen exists at a crossroads between this story and that of the Biblical fall of man. She is Pan's daughter, but far from the reluctant Bona Dea, whose chastity causes her to shun even the gaze of men.[39] Rather, she is an active and willing participant, midwifing Pan and others like him into the human world and seducing her male victims into sharing her forbidden knowledge.

The figure of Pan or Faunus is, of course, the story's most obvious mythological allusion. Staples argues that the significance of Faunus was as a mutable, morphic figure able to "slide unceremoniously across boundaries" and to be "every thing at once—beneficent and maleficent, singular and plural, man and god."[40] This description echoes the final breakdown of Helen in Machen's novella, as does the "sexual confusion" evidenced by Faunus in a story where he attempts to seduce Omphale but finds himself making advances upon her husband, Hercules, instead.[41] Faunus is associated not only with the crossing of boundaries but also with a "vague, amorphous" mythic past whose impenetrability was, when Machen was writing, being threatened by the deep timescales of evolution.[42] Bona Dea, too, is associated with a mythical past, her cult predating the establishment of Rome.[43] There is also an obvious Christian analog for the horned figure of Pan, and one that reinforces the image of Helen as Antichrist mentioned above. Ronald Hutton has argued that "the standard modern conception of the Devil as a being with cloven hoofs, goat's horns and pointed beard is a nineteenth-century creation, representing a Christian reaction to the growing importance of Pan as an alternative focus for the literary imagination."[44] The Romantic image of Pan as "symbol of creative imagination,"[45] coupled with this Satanic association, invokes the monstrous as an attribute not only of Pan or of Helen, but of the text itself.

The name "Helen" evokes another figure from classical mythology, Helen of Argos or Helen of Troy. The mythological Helen is also the daughter of a god, in this case Zeus. Mihoko Suzuki has argued that Helen is defined by her "liminality, her crossing of various boundaries," which makes her "a perfectly ambiguous sign."[46] The Helen of "The Great God Pan" is certainly a liminal figure: part human, part divinity; at once beautiful and repulsive; apparently possessed of the ability to breach the boundaries between human and divine worlds and to help others cross over. Helen of Troy is described in terms of the "terror of her goddesslike beauty," as Suzuki puts it.[47] This is certainly echoed in the portrayal of Machen's Helen, who is described by onlookers as "at once the most beautiful woman and the most repulsive they had ever set eyes on"[48] and whose portrait causes Clarke to "[shudder] before it in his inmost soul."[49] Like Machen's Helen, the mythological Helen is sometimes depicted as having a sinister side, rejoicing over the Greeks' victory in the midst of mourning Trojan women, or demonstrating an "almost supernatural ability to enchant and beguile" when she taunts the concealed Greek warriors by imitating the voices of their wives.[50] Also like Machen's Helen, she often lacks a voice of her own. In the *Aeneid*, for example, she is always "the subject of stories told about her; no longer a character in the poem, she has become a myth."[51] Something similar happens to Helen Vaughan, whom the reader never encounters directly, as it were. She is always mediated through stories related at one or even several removes, and does not speak for herself.

Finally, and more obliquely, Machen's Helen also recalls a figure from Welsh mythology: Blodeuwedd, the woman created as a wife for Llew Llaw Gyffes in the Fourth Branch of the *Mabinogi*. The Fourth Branch shares with Shelley's *Frankenstein* a concern with masculine usurping of a generative power regarded as properly and uniquely feminine. As well as symbolically birthing his nephew, Llew, the magician Gwydion also takes it upon himself to create a woman out of flowers to provide him with a wife, since a magical prohibition keeps Llew from marrying a human woman. The creation of Blodeuwedd by Gwydion and his own uncle, Math, has echoes in the creation of Helen by Raymond, for whom Mary seems to function as a conduit or vessel rather than an active participant. Blodeuwedd is also destructive toward men, persuading Llew to reveal the means by which her lover, Gronw Pebr, may kill him, and is forced into a shapeshifting transformation as punishment. For her transgressions, Gwydion turns her into an owl. He himself is punished earlier in the story by being transformed into a series of animals, some of them female. Roberta Valente has argued that the tragic narrative of the Fourth Branch represents the breakdown of social fabric that occurs when men and women fail to fulfill their social roles, and the crossing of gender and species boundaries is once again brought to the fore.[52] The crossing of social and gender boundaries here threatens the stable boundaries of the human form, something we see clearly in nineteenth-century portrayals of degeneration, and in the social havoc wreaked by Helen and her eventual transformations.

We cannot read "The Great God Pan" simply as a patchwork of mythological sources, however. As mentioned above, the novella was published at a period when anxieties about evolutionary and moral degeneration, about the integrity of the human self, and about the relationship of human beings to a Godless cosmos, abounded in scientific and literary discourse. "The Great

God Pan" participates in the Gothic literary discourse of its day, evoking other works of nineteenth-century fiction with similar themes in the context of its struggle between mysticism and materiality.

Though Mary Shelley's *Frankenstein* was first published in 1818, well before Darwinian evolution came to the forefront of public consciousness, one of the most striking aspects of the novel is what Baldick calls its "starkly secular nature."[53] Though its narrative bears resemblances to stories of Faustian overreaching, in which human beings are punished for seeking entry into realms reserved for God, Frankenstein lacks a Mephistopheles, and no divine wrath is visited upon his head. For Baldick, this dissolves "the moral framework of the novel . . . into an open contest or debate between Victor and the monster, in which the reassuring categories of Good, Evil, Guilt and Justice can never be allotted a settled place."[54] Without divine moral guidance, the relationship of humans and other creatures to the world is up for debate, just as was implied in the evolutionary account of human origins. The other major theme of Shelley's novel, which has echoed through mad scientist stories ever since, is "the remaking of people in the modern world," which finds its scientific echo in the discourses of degeneration and eugenics in the latter part of the nineteenth century.[55] Frankenstein's creature is made not only by Frankenstein himself, in the literal sense, but by the rejection he experiences from the world around him. Human beings, according to degeneration theory, might be unmade, or made worse, by the conditions of life at the end of the nineteenth century; or, according to the theory of eugenics put forward by Francis Galton (1868), human beings might be made better by selective breeding. The former possibility always haunted the latter.

Robert Louis Stevenson's *Strange Case of Dr Jekyll and Mr Hyde*, published in 1886, also gives us a malevolent being brought into existence through scientific experiment, though Hyde is not born as an independent being, but shares the body of his creator, Jekyll, and in fact is the embodiment of Jekyll's antisocial impulses. Interestingly, it is not until the final section of "The Great God Pan" that the reader learns Helen Vaughan is Mary's daughter. Before this point, she is described as having "Mary's face," but her expression holds "something else, something [Clarke] had not seen on Mary's features when the white-clad girl entered the laboratory with the doctor, nor at her terrible awakening, nor when she lay grinning in the bed."[56] This may well lead the reader to assume that Mary's body is being inhabited by another entity, something that emerges from within her as Hyde emerges from within Jekyll. Even Raymond, in the letter in which he confirms Helen's identity, describes her creation in terms that imply such an inhabiting or possession, saying that "when the house of life is . . . thrown open, there may enter in that for which we have no name, and human flesh may become the veil of a horror one dare not express."[57] As Roger Luckhurst has pointed out, the doubling that occurs in *Jekyll and Hyde* has implications within the scientific context of its time. The "ability of the human mind to split and fragment" had begun to be documented by the new science of psychology, and the mentally ill came to be viewed as "biological degenerates, moving lower down the evolutionary ladder with every symptom presented."[58] Criminals were also viewed as evolutionary degenerates. The narrative of *Jekyll and Hyde*, in one of its possible readings, presents us with the evolutionary past lurking within modern, "civilized" humanity. "The Great God Pan" features a similar scenario, but this time the past is pagan, and supernatural, corrupting soul as well as body.

The ways in which "The Great God Pan" adapts its sources bring to the fore the interplay and the tensions between the supernatural and the scientific. In the first chapter, Raymond describes himself as a practitioner of "transcendental medicine."[59] The conversation that follows oscillates between the language of mysticism and the occult, attributed to the distant past, and that of contemporary science and technology. Raymond insists that his experiment involves something transcendent and yet long-known: "the ancients," he tells Clarke, "knew what lifting the veil means. They called it seeing the god Pan."[60] A couple of paragraphs later, however, he employs the register of a surgeon. The procedure involves "a slight lesion in the grey matter . . . a trifling rearrangement of certain cells, a microscopical alteration."[61] The phrasing here also invokes the scientific discourse of degeneration. The French degeneration theorist Benedict Augustin Morel argued that drugs and alcohol, pollution, malnutrition, and disease could all cause brain lesions that would be passed down to subsequent generations, leading to physical and mental decline.[62] The Gothic trope of the scientific experiment about to go wrong, the scientific discourse of degeneration theory, and the classical image of Pan become intertwining threads, part of the same narrative tapestry, but also in tension. The experiment is meaningless without the figure of Pan and its supernatural consequences, but those consequences are themselves dependent upon the materiality of the experiment, and they manifest themselves in a physical fashion that clearly calls to mind the scientific and pseudo-scientific discourses of the late nineteenth century. The scientific and the supernatural are, in Machen's novella, interdependent, but also threaten at all times to undermine each other.

Similar tensions occur throughout the novella. The notion of Helen as unknowable "mystery" may draw to mind the mysterious rites of Bona Dea, forbidden to men and outsiders, but Clarke and Villers' piecing together of the evidence allows them to act like modern men of science, as well as echoing the nested narrative structures of *Frankenstein* and *Jekyll and Hyde*.[63] At the same time, the secular world of *Frankenstein* is replaced by something darker and less explicable. Clarke spends his time "reading, compiling, arranging and rearranging what he [calls] his 'Memoirs to prove the

Existence of the Devil'," but feels no similar call to prove the existence of God, and so his focus inverts the Christian structure.[64] Ultimately, Helen is destroyed, as Frankenstein destroys his female creature—but in her destruction, both mythic and evolutionary images are evoked, as she moves between sexes and species like Faunus and Pan, Blodeuwedd and Gwydion, and also like the degenerates of contemporary scientific theory. Mythological sources are adapted to the scientific and social concerns of their day, while contemporary Gothic narratives and scientific discourses are adapted to Machen's own philosophical concerns. Hutcheon's metaphor here appears in action.

This results repeatedly in moments where the divine and the mystical are invoked, and then seemingly undercut or brought down by their material explanations or effects. These moments echo the anxieties brought up by evolutionary theory and its undermining of the notion of divine creation. We see this first in the opening conversation between Raymond and Clarke, as mentioned above. Clarke questions whether "the knife is absolutely necessary"; Raymond insists that it is.[65] For all his talk of ancient wisdom and of a "world of spirit" inexplicable by contemporary scientists, Raymond's experiment remains inseparable from its material, biological basis.[66]

In the following chapter, Clarke recalls a story told to him by his friend Phillips concerning Helen's youth. Two other young people of the district where she grew up are adversely affected by contact with her. One is a young boy, Trevor, who suffers a fright after seeing Helen in the woods with "a 'strange naked man' whom he seemed unable to describe more fully."[67] Later, he identifies the man from the wood with a Roman artifact depicting the head of "a faun or satyr."[68] The man from the wood must, we understand, be Pan, and his nudity in the presence of his daughter recalls the incestuous story of Bona Dean and Faunus, though Helen, unlike her mythological predecessor, evidences no reluctance. The young Trevor, on the other hand, suffers medical consequences from the sight, developing "a weakness of intellect which gives but little promise of amending."[69] The discourse of mental illness here gives Faunus' mythical crime a biological consequence. The second incident in the story involves the disappearance of Helen's friend Rachel, the daughter of a family with whom she was staying. After accompanying Helen on one of her customary walks in the woods, Rachel is found weeping by her mother, and when asked what has happened, tells "a wild story."[70] The narrative is abruptly interrupted here, leaving it to the reader to imagine what bizarre experiences Rachel has undergone. Although Rachel is initially described as "deceased,"[71] Phillips later recounts her having "vanished in broad sunlight," accompanied by a mysterious figure.[72] Rather than simply dying, she has left the human world behind, entering into a supernatural, or perhaps divine, realm. And yet, intimations of the material remain. Rachel's mother finds her "lying, half undressed, upon the bed, evidently in great distress," hinting at the brutally physical possibility of sexual violence.[73] Clarke's reaction to the story, meanwhile, is horror at the physicality of Helen and of Pan: he is "appalled before the sight of such awful, unspeakable elements enthroned, as it were, and triumphant in human flesh."[74]

Elsewhere, the consequences of contact with Helen are similarly bodily. Though Herbert claims she has ruined him "in body and soul," it is the physical consequences of what has happened that are visible in the narrative.[75] Villiers remarks on how his face has been "altered and disfigured by poverty and disgrace," recalling the physical stigmata of degeneracy recorded by Morel, and believes that his story needs no proof because "he himself [is] the embodied proof of it."[76] The corruption may also be spiritual, but the proof is physical. The respectable gentleman who dies from fright at the Herberts' house also bears the proof of his experiences on his "hideously contorted" features, and the men who commit suicide after encountering Helen in her Mrs Beaumont guise are reduced to bare matter, "a living man in the evening and a dead body with a black swollen face in the morning."[77] The malaise experienced by Villiers after visiting the Herberts' former house manifests itself in clearly-described physical terms. He notices a "queer, heavy feeling about the air of the house" which "seem[s] to stop the breath"; he finds his "teeth grinding"; his "limbs tremble"; his heart "beat[s] as if [he] were at the hour of death"; and he staggers as though drunk.[78] Repeatedly, the spiritual horror visited by Helen manifests itself in concrete physical terms. Her final transformation into an "unspeakable shape, neither man nor beast" becomes as much the evolution of a super-evolved predator as the manifestation of a god, as much the descent of a criminal degenerate as the appearance of a devil.[79] Her preternatural powers, her adeptness at disguise and manipulation, are the means by which she adapts to her social world and insinuates herself into the lives of her victims, just as the text in which she appears adapts its intertexts to its cultural-historical context and its author's concerns.

In the figure of Helen, then, Machen's anti-materialism collides with the evolutionary notion of a life-driven universe in which human beings are the product of chaotic, impersonal forces. Mythical and religious allusions repeatedly insist on the existence of a spiritual world invisible to human eyes, while Gothic motifs and contemporary scientific discourses allow us to encounter that world only through its visceral, abject physical manifestations. The body of the text, blending mythic and scientific discourses and foregrounding the tension between them, rather than any easy synthesis, becomes itself a monstrous adaptation. Like Cohen's monstrous bodies, it refuses classification—as Gothic science fiction or resurgent myth. For Machen, scientific discourse is inadequate to describe the spiritual world, but in "The Great God Pan" the material world can never be fully transcended. Horror may be of the soul—but it is of the soul trapped in "human flesh."

NOTES

1. Arthur Machen, *The Great God Pan* (Cardigan: Parthian, 2010), 70.
2. Linda Hutcheon with Siobhan McFlynn, *A Theory of Adaptation*, 2nd ed. (London: Routledge, 2006), 31.
3. Peter Bowler, *Evolution: The History of an Idea*, 3rd ed. (Berkeley: University of California Press, 2003), 50–51.
4. Ibid., 57.
5. Ibid., 177.
6. E. Ray Lankester, *Degeneration: A Chapter in Darwinism* (London: MacMillan, 1880), 33.
7. Max Nordau, *Degeneration* (Lincoln: University of Nebraska Press, 1993 [1892]), 1–2, 7.
8. Charles Darwin, *The Descent of Man and Selection in Relation to Sex* (London: John Murray, 1883 [1871]), 140.
9. Lyndsay Andrew Farrall, *The Origins and Growth of the English Eugenics Movement 1865-1925* (Doctoral diss., Indiana University, 1969), 167.
10. Kirsti Bohata, "Apes and Cannibals in Cambria: Images of the Racial and Gendered Other in Gothic Writing in Wales," *Welsh Writing in English* 6 (2000), 126.
11. Jane Aaron, *Welsh Gothic* (Cardiff: University of Wales Press, 2013), 71.
12. James Machin, *Weird Fiction in Britain 1880-1939* (London: Palgrave, 2018), 147.
13. Chris Baldick, *In Frankenstein's Shadow: Myth, Monstrosity, and Nineteenth-Century Writing* (Oxford: Clarendon, 1990), 1–3.
14. Ibid., 2.
15. "Myth," *OED Online*, 3rd ed., https://www-oed-com.abc.cardiff.ac.uk/view/Entry/124670?rskey=EW7tXj&result=1 (accessed July 13, 2020).
16. Hutcheon, *A Theory of Adaptation*, xxvi.
17. Ibid., 31.
18. Ibid., 21.
19. Roland Barthes, "The Death of the Author," in *Image Music Text*, trans. Stephen Heath, 142–48 (London: Fontana, 1977), 146.
20. Kelly Hurley, *The Gothic Body: Sexuality, Materialism and Degeneration at the* Fin de Siècle (Cambridge: Cambridge University Press, 1996), 90.
21. Jeffrey Jerome Cohen, "Monster Culture (Seven Theses)," in *Monster Theory: Reading Culture*, ed. Jeffrey Jerome Cohen, 3–25 (Minneapolis: University of Minnesota Press, 1996), 7.
22. Hutcheon, *A Theory of Adaptation*, 7.
23. Stephen T. Asma, *On Monsters: An Unnatural History of Our Worst Fears* (Oxford: Oxford University Press, 2009), 165.
24. Richard J. Hand and Jay McRoy, "Monstrous Adaptations: An Introduction," in *Monstrous Adaptations: Generic and Thematic Mutations in Horror Film*, eds Richard J. Hand and Jay McRoy, 1–5 (Manchester: Manchester University Press, 2007), 1.
25. Hutcheon, *A Theory of Adaptation*, 9.

26. Arthur Machen, "Introduction," in *The Great God Pan and The Hill of Dreams* (New York: Dover, 2006), 6.
27. Machen, *The Great God Pan*, 7.
28. Ibid., 13.
29. Ibid., 26.
30. Ibid., 37.
31. Machin, *Weird Fiction*, 146.
32. Stephen Benko, *The Virgin Goddess: Studies in the Pagan and Christian Roots of Mariology* (New York: E. J. Brill, 1993), 4.
33. Ibid., 263–65.
34. See H. H. J Brouwer, *Bona Dea: The Sources and a Description of the Cult* (New York: E. J. Brill, 1989), 239, and Ariadne Staples, *From Good Goddess to Vestal Virgins: Sex and Category in Roman Religion* (London: Routledge, 1998), 28.
35. Staples, *From Good Goddess to Vestal Virgins*, 13–15.
36. Ibid., 43.
37. Ibid., 29.
38. Brouwer, *Bona Dea*, 340.
39. Ibid., 239.
40. Staples, *From Good Goddess to Vestal Virgins*, 34–35.
41. Ibid., 35.
42. Ibid., 34.
43. Brouwer, *Bona Dea*, 257.
44. Ronald Hutton, *The Triumph of the Moon: A History of Modern Pagan Witchcraft* (Oxford: Oxford University Press, 1999), 46.
45. Ibid.
46. Mihoko Suzuki, *Metamorphoses of Helen: Authority, Difference, and the Epic* (Ithaca: Cornell University Press, 1989), 18–19.
47. Ibid., 35.
48. Machen, *The Great God Pan*, 32.
49. Ibid., 39.
50. Suzuki, *Metamorphoses of Helen*, 68–69.
51. Ibid., 99.
52. Roberta Valente, *"Merched y Mabinogi": Women and the Thematic Structure of the Four Branches* (doctoral diss., Cornell University, 1986), 241–46.
53. Baldick, *In Frankenstein's Shadow*, 42.
54. Ibid., 43–44.
55. Ibid., 144.
56. Machen, *The Great God Pan*, 39.
57. Ibid., 75.
58. Roger Luckhurst, "Introduction," in Robert Louis Stevenson, *Strange Case of Dr Jekyll and Mr Hyde,* vii–xxxii (Oxford: Oxford University Press, 2006), xvii.
59. Machen, *The Great God Pan*, 4.
60. Ibid., 5.
61. Ibid., 5.

62. Benedict Augustin Morel, *Traité des Dégénérescences Physiques, Intellectuelles et Morales del'Espèce Humaine et des Causes qui Produisentces Variétés Maladives* (Paris: Baillière: 1857), 80–81, 365–66, 241–42, 48–49.
63. Machen, *The Great God Pan*, 38.
64. Ibid., 15.
65. Ibid., 5–7.
66. Ibid., 7.
67. Ibid., 18.
68. Ibid., 20.
69. Ibid.
70. Ibid., 22.
71. Ibid., 16.
72. Ibid., 22–23.
73. Ibid., 21–22.
74. Ibid., 22.
75. Ibid., 26.
76. Ibid., 24, 28.
77. Ibid., 31 and 51.
78. Ibid., 36–37.
79. Ibid., 70.

REFERENCES

Aaron, Jane. *Welsh Gothic*. Cardiff: University of Wales Press, 2013.

Asma, Stephen T. *On Monsters: An Unnatural History of Our Worst Fears*. Oxford: Oxford University Press, 2009.

Baldick, Chris. *In Frankenstein's Shadow: Myth, Monstrosity, and Nineteenth-Century Writing*. Oxford: Clarendon, 1990.

Barthes, Roland. "The Death of the Author." In *Image Music Text*, translated by Stephen Heath, 142–48. London: Fontana, 1977.

Benko, Stephen. *The Virgin Goddess: Studies in the Pagan and Christian Roots of Mariology*. New York: E. J. Brill, 1993.

Bohata, Kirsti. "Apes and Cannibals in Cambria: Images of the Racial and Gendered Other in Gothic Writing in Wales." *Welsh Writing in English* 6 (2000): 119–43.

Bowler, Peter. *Evolution: The History of an Idea*. 3rd ed. Berkeley: University of California Press, 2003.

Brouwer, H.H.J. *Bona Dea: The Sources and a Description of the Cult*. New York: E. J. Brill, 1989.

Cohen, Jeffrey Jerome (ed.). "Monster Culture (Seven Theses)." In *Monster Theory: Reading Culture*, edited by Jeffrey Jerome Cohen, 3–25. Minneapolis: University of Minnesota Press, 1996.

Darwin, Charles. *The Descent of Man and Selection in Relation to Sex*. London: John Murray, 1883.

Farrall, Lyndsay Andrew. *The Origins and Growth of the English Eugenics Movement 1865-1925*. PhD diss. Indiana University, 1969.

Hand, Richard J. and Jay McRoy (eds). "Monstrous Adaptations: An Introduction." In *Monstrous Adaptations: Generic and Thematic Mutations in Horror Film*, 1–5. Manchester: Manchester University Press, 2007.

Hurley, Kelly. *The Gothic Body: Sexuality, Materialism and Degeneration at the Fin de Siècle*. Cambridge: Cambridge University Press, 1996.

Hutcheon, Linda with Siobhan McFlynn. *A Theory of Adaptation*. 2nd ed. London: Routledge, 2006.

Hutton, Ronald. *The Triumph of the Moon: A History of Modern Pagan Witchcraft*. Oxford: Oxford University Press, 1999.

Lankester, E. Ray. *Degeneration: A Chapter in Darwinism*. London: Macmillan, 1880.

Luckhurst, Roger. "Introduction." In *Strange Case of Dr Jekyll and Mr Hyde*, edited by Robert Louis Stevenson, vii–xxxii. Oxford: Oxford University Press, 2006.

Machen, Arthur. *The Great God Pan*. Cardigan: Parthian, 2010.

———. "Introduction." In *The Great God Pan and The Hill of Dreams*. New York: Dover, 2006.

Machin, James. *Weird Fiction in Britain 1880-1939*. London: Palgrave, 2018.

Morel, Benedict Augustin. *Traité des Dégénérescences Physiques, Intellectuelles et Morales de l'Espèce Humaine et des Causes qui Produisentces Variétés Maladives*. Paris: Baillière, 1857.

"Myth." *OED Online*. 3rd ed. 2003. http://www.oed.com.abc.cardiff.ac.uk/view/Entry/124670?rskey=EW7tXj&result=1.

Nordau, Max. *Degeneration*. Lincoln: University of Nebraska Press, 1993.

Staples, Ariadne. *From Good Goddess to Vestal Virgins: Sex and Category in Roman Religion*. London: Routledge, 1998.

Suzuki, Mihoko. *Metamorphoses of Helen: Authority, Difference, and the Epic*. Ithaca: Cornell University Press, 1989.

Valente, Roberta Louise. *"Merched y Mabinogi": Women and the Thematic Structure of the Four Branches*. PhD diss., Cornell University, 1986.

Chapter 7

Lucian's *Ornaments in Jade*
Symbolist Decadence in Arthur Machen's Prose Poetry

Kostas Boyiopoulos

The slim volume of ten prose poems published under the title *Ornaments in Jade* in 1924 but composed in the 1890s is one of Arthur Machen's most elegant and polished works. It can be regarded as the pinnacle of prose poetry in English, a more baroque version of Ernest Dowson's "decorations" in prose. These poetic micro-narratives are highly elliptical in construction and riddled with deliberately planted hiatuses. They contain a decadent reservoir of culturally invested sculptural motifs, precious stones, and transfigured objects and environments. Machen's fetishistic materiality has not gone unnoticed by critics; Stefania Forlini has paid attention to the Welsh author's decadent fetish objects that populate his composite novel *The Three Impostors* (1895) in light of science and consumer culture.[1] The ornament in Machen's collection both refers to the text itself and is a magical object that also behaves like a text, a kind of illegible symbol that invites reconstruction and deciphering. Machen writes in *Hieroglyphics* (1902): "why do I find any pleasure in ornament? . . . But I can give no definite reason for liking the *Odyssey* or a curiously carved knife."[2]

These "ornaments" are quaint bedizenments that share an air of hermetic mystique and perilous sinfulness. They present variant scenarios in which a self-absorbed individual either taps into a hidden world of sensual wonder, or through epiphany acquires an alternative perspective on reality. They set the scene either for a *mirabile visu* or some terrifying insight. In a recent edition of Machen's work that includes four pieces from *Ornaments*, Dennis Denisoff compares the title of Machen's collection to Théophile Gautier's *Émaux et Camées* (1852) and sees in *Hieroglyphics* an adherence to Gautier's *l'art pour l'art*, the "cornerstone of decadent aesthetic theory," taken by Machen not to a "realist" but to a "symbolist" direction.³ But how are the autonomous sensuous images that make up *Ornaments* conducive to a symbolist process?

Prose poetry is a modern, urbane micro-genre popularized by Charles Baudelaire's milestone *Le Spleen de Paris* (1869). At once liminal and clear-cut, the prose poem became a nonpareil form of expression for the *fin-de-siècle* symbolists and decadents; it was especially cherished by Joris-Karl Huysmans. Vincent Starrett, Machen's friend and devotee, notes that only "Huysmans, in a really good translation suggests Machen better" and that both are "debtors to Baudelaire."⁴ For Jean des Esseintes, the hero of Huysmans's *À rebours* (1884), the prose poem is his favorite of all forms of literature.⁵ Des Esseintes prizes an anthology of prose poems he has built with stunning specimens by Aloysius Bertrand, Baudelaire, Mallarmé, and others. He comments that the prose poem contains "within its small compass and in concentrated form the substance of a novel."⁶ Each epithet, fastidiously chosen, is stamped with "finality,"

> and would open up such wide vistas that the reader could muse on its meaning, at once precise and multiple, for weeks on end, and also ascertain the present, reconstruct the past, and divine the future of the characters in light of this one epithet . . . [T]hus condensed in a page or two, [the novel] would become . . . an aesthetic treat available to none but the most discerning. [T]he prose poem represented . . . the ozmazome of literature, the essential oil of art.⁷

Des Esseintes's musings on the prose poem not as a text of sparse images but as a compact *multum in parvo* serve as the basis for the inner workings of Machen's *Ornaments*, which are even more condensed versions of the well-known "novels" in short story form intercalated in *The Three Impostors*. Each word and phrase in the prose poem emanates a jewel-like radiance as a *mot juste*, like a custom-built jigsaw piece. Similarly, Lucian Taylor, Machen's semi-autobiographical avatar and decadent hero of his Künstlerroman *The Hill of Dreams* (1907; composed in 1897), fetishizes text-making. He believes that sentences "must glow and burn, and be decked out as with rare work of jewellery."⁸

Through close textual reading, this chapter will examine ways by which the ornamental meshwork in Machen's prose poems transmutes alchemically into a mystical text. The ornament with its opacity arrests an inaccessible, ineffable world that teeters between the transcendent beyond and the subjective self. This peculiarity gives rise to Machen's brand of symbolist decadence and is governed by a particular incongruity: sensuousness of style is conducive to both the state of *l'art pour l'art* and the symbolist principle of suggestion. Lucian captures this incongruity in the dictum "sensations are symbols and not realities."⁹ Further, in his theory of literature, Lucian rejects the conventional use of language "as a means of expression," and instead proposes a reconfigured construal of words that is based on resonance "when [they are] exquisitely arranged"; he advocates "the secret of suggestion, the art of causing delicious sensation by the use of words."[10] Words, then, are treated as beautifully arranged objects that on a subconscious level suggest relational associations and unusual configurations. This subtle paradox in *Ornaments* is galvanized through the medium of the prose poem. With the example of "Midsummer" in mind (one of the volume's pieces), Jon Preece notes that "there are no wasted clauses" in Machen; we get "glimpses: the flint on the pavement, the face at the window, dry murmurings . . . anything more and the delicate candle flame will be extinguished."[11] But Machen pushes his poetics of economy to an extreme: suggestion itself is sublimated to the point that narrative is not just hidden but conjectured, and subsequently mirrored back in the textual signifier.

Under this paradigm, the self transforms into an ornament, as this chapter will demonstrate, fusing with, or even sucked into the surface of textual artifice. This can be better comprehended through a unique hypothesis: that the authorship of *Ornaments* could be ascribed to Lucian. Both *Ornaments* and *Hill* were drafted during 1895–1898 but were initially rejected by publishers. The two works stem from a common source, Machen's 1890s Notebook.[12] The recent publication of the Notebook by the Friends of Arthur Machen (2016) showcases the motivic and thematic affinities between the two works—such as dangerous lustfulness and obsession with idolatry—suggested by the contiguity of Machen's notes.[13] Many of the novel's episodes that convey Lucian's experiences of self-discovery in the ruin-strewn Welsh countryside and the labyrinth of London stand out as prose poems themselves that resemble variants of *Ornaments*. And, vice versa, the iconoclastic alienated daydreamers of *Ornaments*, especially the male author characters of "Psychology," "The Idealist," and "Midsummer," are Lucian's alter egos. This hypothesis can be extended and applied also to *Hill* as a vast site of scattershot prose poems.

The bulk of *Ornaments* consists of narratives of self-discovery through exotic and dangerous materialities. A coming-of-age narrative that reads like a compressed version of "The White People" (1904), "The Turanians" tells of Mary, a girl who strays into the woods—a typical Machenian topos—and comes into contact with the Turanians, "gipsies" or "metalworkers, degenerated into wandering tinkers."[14] The Turanians are the opposite of Mary's mother, who represents Victorian decorum and heeds against "the evils of 'exaggeration'."[15] Mary points out "a rose in the garden that 'burnt like a flame'"—a nod to Walter Pater's famous aesthetic credo to "burn" with a "hard, gem-like flame, to maintain this ecstasy"—with the mother disapproving of "such very strong expressions."[16] In symbolist writing, Clive Scott remarks, "[t]he precious image is one that is both outrageous and tactful";[17] it is this combination that informs what the tale props up as stylistic exaggeration. Drifting in the "shadowed path," Mary's body is transfigured: "her ankles were gently, sweetly kissed" by the "rich grass," a thought that her mother would deem inappropriate: "her own hands seem new, transformed into another likeness" and her hair turned "bronze and golden, glowing on her pure white dress."[18] Society regards the Turanians as "horrible people," but, primed for stylistic "exaggeration," Mary finds pleasure in their "indistinctly heard" voices and "unknown speech."[19] At the climactic moment of "The Turanians," Machen introduces a stark ellipsis to insinuate an undefined sexual act: a "strange smiling face peered out from between the leaves, and the girl knew that her heart leapt as the young man walked towards her."[20] Following this sentence, the narrative cuts abruptly to Mary's room. Details are entirely omitted with their absence, paradoxically, amplifying Mary's style of "exaggeration."

In her room, Mary is "caressing a small green stone, a curious thing cut with strange devices, awful with age," an ornament in jade, and so an obvious reference to the prose poem itself as such.[21] Absorbed and self-indulgent, Mary "laughed for joy, and murmured and whispered to herself, asking herself questions in the bewilderment of her delight."[22] Mary's green stone (an ornament in jade) is another aesthetic exaggeration, befuddling in its material opaqueness, and projected in her emotional reaction. It is a "sublime" object, in Karen Joan Kohoutek's words, emblematizing Machen's "desire to communicate the incommunicable."[23] *Hieroglyphics* contains the key to grasping the workings of "The Turanians" as an allegory of Machen's symbolist decadent textual style:

> a fine style, though it may carry suggestion beyond the bourne of thought, though it may be the veil and visible body of concealed mysteries, is always plain on the surface. It may be like an ingeniously devised cryptogram, which may have an occult sense conveyed to initiated eyes in every dot and line and flourish, but is outwardly as simple and straightforward as a business letter.[24]

The green stone "cut with strange devices" is an "ingeniously devised cryptogram." Its mysteries are revealed to Mary but we, the readers, are not directly let into its meaning. The prose poem may look like an incoherent cipher, plain as a "business letter." Once we become receptive to its surface associations as active readers, the text itself is transfigured in its "every dot and line and flourish" like an intricate textual festoonery that is full of evocative patterns.

Along similar lines, "The Turanians" can be compared to "Witchcraft," an admirably crafted piece that stands out in *Ornaments* untypically for its drawing-room atmosphere and sustained dialogue form. "Witchcraft" tells of a woman (Ethel Custance), who resorts to the black arts, coached by a knowing older woman (Mrs Wise), in order to bind the man she is infatuated with. The stunt Miss Custance has to perform involves a "loathsome" object handed to her by Mrs Wise, whose services she solicits. The object offends Ethel's sense of propriety to such a degree that when Mrs Wise "whispered her instructions," she "would have put a hand in illustration, but the girl pushed it away."[25] The elliptical economy of this story is so extreme that we do not even know what the "hidden . . . object in a drawer"[26] is, and even how it is used and in what manner it is supposed to have an effect. The narrative emerges as a cryptographic Pandora's Box that draws power from its vexing inaccessibility.

Returning to "The Turanians," in Machen's mind Mary could be conflated with Annie Morgan, Lucian's infatuation in *Hill*. In his 1890s Notebook, Machen jots down a note to "[m]ake the 'wonderful words' spoken by 'Annie' the ancient witch-speech—Turanian in origin."[27] Mary's type resembles Annie (as well as Lucian in her curiosity). Her murmurs and whispers to herself are no different than the "unknown speech" of the Turanians. Thus, Mary herself is transformed into a cipher, an ornament in jade. Her sensual adventure of occult discovery is incidentally a self-discovery, an inward adventure. In a composite allusion to Eve's pool-gazing scene in John Milton's *Paradise Lost* (1667) and Ovid's tale of Echo and Narcissus, Mary inspects herself in the mirror of the well's "dark water," "smil[ing] at the smiling nymph, whose lips parted as if to whisper secrets."[28] This suggestive *figura etymologica* marks the workings of the text in relation to subjectivity. Mary is the smiling nymph, or a chthonic version of herself reflected in the "dark water."

"The Ceremony" is similar to "The Turanians" as a poetic narrative of sexual awakening. The lynchpin of this narrative is a repeated pagan ritual involving a mysterious sculptural object: a grey stone in the woods, "something between the pillar and the pyramid in shape."[29] While Mary's curious green rock in "The Turanians" is grooved with "strange devices," here this eerie menhir stands out for the inscrutable indeterminateness of its shape. Machen masks reality in layers of subjectivity through the girl's stratified memory. As the girl recalls her confrontation with the "grey image," her "memory" transmutes into a "sensation" in which the sensory input of the topography is augmented: "The wide wood swelling like the sea," an arresting phrase that even anticipates Imagism, with "the gloom of the underglade rich, indistinct, gorgeous, significant as old tapestry." The lush, color-saturated cornucopia behaves like a web of signifiers, a "tapestry" of symbols. Then Machen further intensifies the already augmented sensations as there were "broken remnants of another and far earlier impression" about a woman interacting with the grey image and "red colour spilled upon it."[30] This is a memory of a memory or "the shadow of a shadow," when the girl was a little child.[31] The more memory tapers off in a fractal fashion and becomes more cryptic and impressionistic, the more the senses are distilled.

In one of the most provocative passages of the volume, when the girl turns eighteen she chances upon Annie Dolben (another reference to Annie Morgan), "the daughter of a labourer, lately a promising pupil at Sunday school," a "nice-mannered girl, never failing for her curtsy," who knows well the "Jewish Kings."[32] Annie Dolben's full name and respectable social profile emphasize her Victorian moral reputation. Annie's body then turns dangerously erotic when she approaches the grey image; "[h]er face had taken an expression" that "hinted strange things."[33] Concealed, the unnamed girl watches Annie. The final two paragraphs are racy and seductive:

> The lady hidden in hazels watched Annie come close to the grey image; for a moment her whole body palpitated with expectation, almost the sense of what was to happen dawned upon her. She watched Annie crown the stone with flowers, she watched the amazing ceremony that followed.
>
> And yet, in spite of all her blushing shame, she herself bore blossoms to the wood a few months later. She laid white hothouse lilies upon the stone, and orchids of dying purple, and crimson exotic flowers. Having kissed the grey image with devout passion, she performed there all the antique immemorial rite.[34]

In just a few sentences, Machen packs tightly an array of decadent topoi: voyeurism, sinfulness, lesbian undertones, titillation, aesthetic pagan ritual, occultism, fetishism, objectophilia, and, most of all, iconic hothouse flowers, lilies and orchids. These decadent images are further accentuated as they are sharply contrasted with Annie Dolben's façade of Victorian respectability. Through dexterous manipulation of ellipsis, Machen manages to suggest the sweet perils of an unfathomable moral transgression. As with "The Turanians," the nameless girl turns from contemplator to participator, from observer to observed. She is assimilated into a cipher-text of sensations, becoming herself a teasing ornament.

In other poetic prose pieces from the volume, Machen emblematizes the symbolist dimension of the ornament by focusing on male writers who are close resemblances to Lucian Taylor. In "Midsummer," a piece punctuated by stepwise spaces and thresholds, Leonard is a saunterer who moves from the hubbub of London to the countryside, to his own quarters in the farmhouse, to the garden, to the great wood in the night. Leonard's experience is a condensed version of Lucian's descent into "the dark and shady valley" of the Welsh countryside in Chapter Two of *Hill*.[35] Machen employs his characteristic technique of juxtaposition, segueing magically the everyday with the otherworldly. Leonard's senses in his picaresque adventure are heightened: in London, amidst the hansoms and the omnibuses, he observes the "turbid" streams of "thronging crowds," "the everlasting flux and reflux of white faces."[36] Such impressionistic images call to mind Arthur Symons's *flâneurie*—Machen's image here incidentally is a cross between Symons's "Pastel: Masks and Faces" (1890) and "In the Train" (1891). In his stroll, away from the cityscape and into the countryside, Leonard's sensations register the heavy scents and shapes of his surroundings in luxurious, flourishing detail. Leonard drifts into the heart of the wood, "in a new dark sphere that dreams had foretold. He had come to a place remote, without form or colour, made alone of shadow and overhanging gloom."[37] This new, plutonian vista of amorphous shadows is a conceit that reflects the expansion of Leonard's engulfing subjectivity.

The *flâneur*'s impressions in "Midsummer" go a long way, extending to nature, but aesthetically return in a sort of subtle textual folding. At the close of the piece, Leonard descries in chiaroscuro a summer solstice pagan ritual under a full moon. The farmer's daughter leads a procession of the village girls, "shameless" and "unabashed"; the concluding sentence is a fever-pitch moment, playing on what is termed as *ignis fatuus*: "The white writhing figures passed up towards the glade, and the boughs hid them, but he never doubted as to what he had seen."[38] Reprising the same technique as in "The Ceremony," Machen conveys through suggestion yet aestheticizes through ritual the repressed sexual desires seething under the surface of polite society. The "white writhing figures" in the wood counter-mirror "the everlasting flux and reflux of white faces" in the busy city near the beginning of the piece. This association prompts the conjecture that the flux of London's white faces is, too, a veneer of unutterable desire, or even that, in hindsight, resembles an orgiastic ritual similar to the one performed by the village girls. Typically, Machen ends his prose poems with an extraordinary espial. But part of the spectacle are its unavailable details and hence its aura of inaccessible meaning. We never become privy to the full spectacle. Yet the fact that Leonard "never doubted as to what he had seen" marks the unexpected procession of the village girls as paradoxically both hyper-real and unreal. The possible unreality of the sensual spectacle should be considered in conjunction with Leonard's sitting at his bureau midway the narrative: "[a]n idea flashed suddenly into his mind, and he began to write hurriedly, in an ecstasy."[39] This act, having no apparent narrative function, is another cipher (Machen provides no clue as to Leonard's creative idea). It spawns the suggestion that his straying into the wood is an embellishment of the imagination.

"The Idealist" is the volume's most emphatic statement of decadent style crystallized in the motif of the ornamental cipher. It is a city prose poem and one of the finest explorations of the artist-*flâneur* figure in English. Its unsettling psychological suggestiveness is such that in a contemporary review of *Ornaments*, the American poet William Rose Benét, noting Machen's ellipticism, singled it out unduly (together with "The Ceremony" and "Midsummer") for its "pronounced sadism."[40] The flippant banter between two unnamed clerks introduces us to the prosaic pragmatist Beever and the "idealist" Charles Symonds, the central character of the tale. Machen's use of this frame-narrative device, as with "The White People" and *The Three Impostors*, is effective in probing into Symonds's psychology in the ending, anchoring it in garish reality. Symonds is an unmistakable blueprint of Lucian Taylor: genteel and cultured, individualistic and cavalier, with an eclectic literary taste. He is disgusted by Beever's irreverent and vulgar storytelling style, and the latter's approval of the "good goods" of a deteriorated prostitute. He likens Beever and his audience, his mindless friends, "to plough-boys pawing and deriding an exquisite painted panel," "loathing at the three yahoos."[41] Symonds mirrors Lucian's social isolation, iconoclasm, and disdain toward uncouth ordinariness or what he calls "pigging" the "New Morality."[42]

Symonds is the epitome of what we might call an inverse *flâneur*. He is not interested in observing city life as such, but in his own imaginings: he transfigures the drab urban and suburban environment by projecting his aesthetic fantasies onto it. In his strolling, Symonds runs away from "the profane coarseness of the clerks," from "the stupid, the blatant, the intolerable."[43] He "escape[s] to his occult and private world" superimposed on his surroundings as he gazed "not on the pavement but on certain clear imagined pictures."[44] He drifts into a maze of streets that are "dull and gloomy and devoid of interest."[45] However, to Symonds

> these backwaters of London were as bizarre and glowing as a cabinet of Japanese curios; he found here his delicately chased bronzes, work in jade, the flush and flame of extraordinary colours. He delayed at a corner, watching a shadow on a lighted blind, watching it fade and blacken and fade, conjecturing its secrets, inventing dialogue for this drama in Ombres Chinoises.[46]

This passage indicates that the whole of *Ornaments* is an assortment of decadent artifacts fashioned as such by the power of the author's imagination which transmutes the imagery of dismal reality, calling to mind Baudelaire's prose poem "La Chambre double" (1869). Symonds is like an eclectic antiquarian; his London as "work in jade" is characterized by opulent, oriental exoticism. At the same time, his images emphasize visual presentation (display cabinet) and spectatorship (Chinese puppet shadow theater). Machen here builds a multi-storied edifice of a virtual materiality that bespeaks his poetics of symbolist decadence: prosaic reality turns into an exquisite display cabinet of curios, themselves populated with little shadow plays which invite deciphering. The Decadent *flâneur*'s observational and objectifying approach comes into focus when Symonds, "observing two children at play," regards them "with the minute scrutiny of an entomologist at the microscope."[47]

The piece cleverly folds in upon itself when Symonds ends his stroll at his home, in "a vast room, almost empty of furniture" where he labors away molding an "uncertain figure" (presumably female), beginning "to draw out incongruous monstrous things" as "white silk shimmered, laces and delicate frills hovered for a moment" while "[t]he old room grew rich, heavy, vaporous with subtle scents."[48] The self's imaginings superimposed on the topography of London here materialize privately in the form of sculptural art. Creative afflatus is tinged with Pygmalionic eroticism as "[p]assion had contorted his face."[49] Symonds's ideal, custom-built figure counter-mirrors Beever's lackluster prostitute. But in fashioning his ornament, the artist allows us a glimpse into its interior instability and ineffability. Elliptical language takes over the poem to the point where the text itself becomes psychologically pliable and cryptic in its trope of shape-shifting. When Symonds's sculpture is completed in the candlelight, "he forgot the effect of Ombres Chinoises, and those who passed and happened to look up at the white staring blind found singular matter for speculation."[50] Symonds is not an observer any more but he is observed by others through the veil of shadow theater. He has himself turned into an ornament, into an uncertain narrative. He is comparable to Lucian who, by the end of *Hill*, has written himself into his fiction. The final word of "The Idealist," "speculation," reverberates and is especially potent as in a well-tempered sonnet: it hints at plot deciphering as well as the divining of its hidden meanings. In addition, "speculation" here acquires a secondary sense: it points to the importance of the medium of presentation, the screen or *speculum*, as the lens through which to probe the story.

It is not only mysterious, fetish objects-ciphers littered in *Ornaments* that underpin Machen's process of self-aestheticization within his poetics of symbolist decadence. Transfigured spaces are equally important in representing hieroglyphic textualities. "The Rose Garden," the opening piece to *Ornaments*, in this respect, serves as a guide on how to approach the volume by setting up a paradox in which the subject is indistinguishable from his/her own subjectivity. If reality corresponds to "sensations" (that "are symbols and not realities"), the perceiving subject is a textual symbol as well, assimilated in his/her decorative milieu.

The nocturnal surroundings the unnamed lady perceives in "The Rose Garden" are sensuous and jewel-like. Conversely, they are spectral webs that gesture toward hidden worlds. A woman discerns "the faintest illusory glitter from the talc moons in the rich Indian curtain," "[t]he yellow silk draperies of the bed [that] were but suggestions of colour," and the white bedding that "glimmered as a white cloud in a far sky at twilight."[51] These bedimmed images are barely visible and hover between the tangible and the spectral. The woman observes the garden outside in a like manner. For example, "with eyes insatiable for wonder," "she found a strange eastern effect in the bordering of reeds, in their spearlike shapes, in the liquid ebony that they shadowed."[52] She then sat on "a divan of cushions on the Persian carpet . . . as motionless, as ecstatic as a poet dreaming under roses, far in Ispahan."[53] In this unmistakable iconography of decadent exoticism (a synthesis of *À rebours* and Oscar Wilde' *The Sphinx* [1894] with undertones of the Song of Solomon), the woman is both a "poet," a transfiguring perceiver and yet part of the tableaux. In what could be a nod to Plato's theory of Forms, she realizes that everything within sight is a "glimmering veil" and that "bodily rapture might be the ritual and expression of the ineffable mysteries, of the world beyond sense, that must be entered by way of sense."[54] Taking this idea to its logical conclusion, the lady-poet recognizes that "[h]erself was annihilated"; Machen's striking phrase here echoes Andrew Marvell's enigmatic couplet in "The Garden" (1681) where the mind "Annihilating all that's made / To a green Thought in a green Shade."[55] The lady's mind, or self, with all its everyday worries is expunged and she is assimilated in her own subjective reality—a kind of Marvellian *hortus conclusus*—as a symbol.

If in "The Rose Garden" Machen's symbolist-decadent epistemology comes as an epiphany, in "Nature" it comes as intuition. In this poetic vignette, Julian is "telling the story of his holiday" to his friend, who reminds him that "the earth . . . the hills, and even the old walls are a language, hard to translate."[56] Julian narrates a day-long perambulation in a landscape containing vestiges of the Roman past, with features such as the winding of the river and the flight of birds looking like "hieroglyphs."[57] The piece is essentially a luscious, impressionistic description of the natural landscape transfigured by the shifting sunlight, focusing on the effects of the sunrise and especially of the sunset. "Nature" contains one of the most phantasmagorical descriptions of the sunset (a signature Decadent motif established by Paul Verlaine in his sonnet "Langueur" [1884]). Julian describes the deep sunset in the horizon in its incremental gradation, from "pale blue" to "opal burning green," to a "purple wall," to "red glint . . . as if rose-hot metal were beaten and dinted on the anvil."[58] Julian does not stop there but dissects the sunset further when it is at the cusp of its refulgent extinction:

> Then I saw the sky was blossoming in the north. Rose gardens appeared there, with golden hedges, and bronze gates, and the great purple wall caught fire as it grew leaden. The earth was lit again, but with unnatural jeweled colours; the palest light was sardonyx, the darkness was amethyst. And then the valley was

aflame. Fire in the wood, the fire of sacrifice beneath the oaks. Fire in the level fields, a great burning in the north, and vehement flame to the south, above the town. And in the still river the very splendour of fire, yes, as if all precious things were cast into its furnace pools, as if gold and roses and jewels became flame.[59]

The saturated afterglow Julian describes here is the sunset of the sunset. He freezes the instant when a vision of beauty is about to be extinguished when it is analyzed into its constituents. The meteorological image of firmamental conflagration is also the frame motif that opens and concludes *Hill*: a "glow," "as if great furnace doors were opened"; however, although the first glow, in the novel, defines the sky, the latter is the "glow within," in the dead Lucian's brain.[60]

Mirroring Lucian's psychology in *Hill*, Julian's description of sunset in "Nature" operates as a metaphor for the workings of the prose poem in relation to style. Rendering something through its opposite (making the sky blossom into terrestrial landscape) is a figure that illustrates Machen's prose poem as carving a relief of material worlds out of mental processes. Nature is presented like an artificial handiwork, a vitrine of light-refracting gems and jewels. In its perfection, Machen's prose poem can arrest that sunset-of-sunset moment before everything can dissolve and be consumed into the "furnace pools." Julian is too engrossed in his own impressionist vision to realize what his friend points out: "without knowing, [you] have told me the story of a wonderful and incredible passion."[61]

"The Holy Things," the "ornament" that concludes the volume, transfigures space in a similar manner to "Nature," yet by aestheticizing not the sunset, but London. Both these pieces feature a materiality of artifice not in the form of mysterious narrative-driving objects, but as imagined metaphors. The hermetic cipher here is not an object (a rock or a statue), but the mind itself. Holborn Street in its mundane aspect transforms ecstatically into an aesthetic church interior: "The long aisle of the street was splendid in the full light of the summer, and away in the west, where the houses seemed to meet and join, it was as a rich tabernacle, mysterious, the cavern house of holy things."[62] The piece introduces the reader to the routine of a man who suffers from absolute ennui, weariness, and despondence. Then, as if the text itself undergoes a dramatic transformation, the man suddenly perceives the street as a tabernacle and himself as if attending a glorious religious service, with the "grind and jar of the wheels" turning into the "roll and swell . . . of the organ," and the "air" "blue with incense."[63] The trope of an apparitional, aestheticized version of the city superimposed on reality is also prominent in *Hill*. Lucian's imaginative transformation of Caermaen into "the splendid and golden city of Siluria" is one example.[64] In Machen's universe, space seems to be a tableau of ciphers by default. Its ordinary appearance turns into a visionary spectacle when the self is primed to read it in a certain way.

The transfiguration of the city in "The Holy Things" issues from the man's brain, of course, just like London in *Hill* which to Lucian seems "of the same substance as his own fantastic thoughts."[65] But what Machen indicates with this prose poem is a refined theology, so to speak, that reconciles subjectivity with objectivity: for Machen, the hidden realm of the marvelous is quiescent beneath the appearance of visible reality and can come to the fore only through imagination, the manner by which the subjective mind reads reality *actively* (despite the man's initial mood of passive resignation). And yet, if "The Holy Things" dramatizes the deciphering of drab reality as the veil of the marvelous, the man's psychology remains puzzling. This can be gleaned in the moment that triggers the transfiguration, when "a change fell."[66] When traffic stops, the miserable man experiences "a solemn hush that summoned remnants of a far-off memory."[67] Machen here uses diffused elipticism; this vague figure of metempsychosis renders the main character of "The Holy Things" a psychological enigma to be deciphered in turn.

The hypothesis that Lucian Taylor could be regarded as the author of *Ornaments* enhances our understanding of the authorial process of Machen's prose poetry in relation to his symbolist decadent style. "Psychology" serves as the link between *Hill* and *Ornaments*. It contains, in Andrew McCann's words, "a sort of endoscopic insight into the practices of composition."[68] It reads like a succinct summing-up of Lucian's, and by extension Machen's, literary mindset. Mr. Dale is the closest character in *Ornaments* to Lucian. He is a London writer who jots down "hieroglyphics" (in a metaphorical sense) on "little scraps of paper."[69] He observes the city from his window and notices everywhere in other people's windows "a quiet and comfortable respectability," a veneer of banal and stuffy Victorian normality: "marriage and birth and begetting were no more here than breakfast and lunch and afternoon tea."[70] Dale recalls a discussion on "the psychology of the novelists" he had the night before with a friend named Jenyns. By presumably referring the realist and naturalist tendencies, Jenyns says facetiously: "Do you call a description of the gilt tools on the morocco here an exhaustive essay on Shakespeare?"[71] Irrespective of realist detail, novels are exhausted on the shallow surface of hackneyed appearances. Although Dale thinks that there is nothing new under the sun, and that everything has been "laid open,"[72] Jenyns disagrees, offering an éclaircissement that prompts in Dale a profound epiphany:

> "Songs of the frantic lunapar; delirium of the madhouse. Not extreme wickedness, but the insensate, the unintelligible, the lunatic passion and idea, the desire

that must come from some other sphere that we cannot even faintly imagine. Look for yourself; it is easy."

Dale looked now at the ends and scraps of paper. On them he had carefully registered all the secret thoughts of the day, the crazy lusts, the senseless furies, the foul monsters that his heart had borne, the maniac phantasies that he had harboured. In every note he found a rampant madness, the equivalents in thought of mathematical absurdity, of two-sided triangles, of parallel straight lines which met.[73]

"Psychology" not only juxtaposes the tedium of conventional life with the "unintelligible" plastic realm of chthonic creativity beneath, but it does so in relation to mainstream realism and lurid fantasy, "the red storms of romance," respectively.[74] The prose poem in its undiluted form and driven by entrancing phrase-making, as it is suggested by Dale's "scraps of paper," is the ideal vehicle to tap into that realm. Dale's meditation on geometrical paradoxes evokes Machen's reflection in *Hieroglyphics* that "[a] proposition in Euclid is demonstrated and done with, since nothing can be added to a mathematical proof; but literature is different. It is many-sided and many-coloured, and variable always."[75] These mathematical figures indicate that, in reconfiguring reality, Machen's texts have a precise design which, like cut gems under light, can yield manifold patterns of association. The story highlights deftly the unintelligibility of "passion"; nevertheless, it never deciphers that passion to the reader. Even Dale, just like Julian in "Nature," is surprised that what is in front of him (the scraps of paper) is a hermetic passion in text, like a figure in a carpet. These hieroglyphics in script, which are detected though not necessarily unlocked represent Dale's own unfathomable self. In a little Jekyll-and-Hyde moment, Dale wonders: "we lead two lives, and the half of our soul is madness, and half heaven is lit by a black sun. I say I am a man, but who is the other that hides in me?"[76]

Similar to the case of Dale, the reality of Lucian's peregrinations is dichotomous, shifting between the dreariness of the real world and the phantasmatic realm of the projected mind. The juxtapositional tension generated between these two opposites is the basis for all of Machen's poetic "ornaments." *Hill* is studded with passages that hinge on this tension and can be extracted and isolated as prose poems.[77] Along the lines of his spatial poetics, Machen's prose poetry contained in *Hill* shares characteristics with the vignette, a generic variation of ornament that emphasizes the idea of an autonomous episode in a narrative continuum. A vignette is a little vine, in the sense of both an ornamental motif "on a blank space in a book" and a "brief verbal description of a person, place, etc.; a short descriptive or evocative episode in a play, etc."[78] Lucian aestheticizes nature in the form of jeweled foliation, employing the image of "trellised vines" which he compares to "rare green stones."[79] Curiously, in its early stage of composition, *Ornaments* were tentatively entitled "Vignettes." This information is in the 1890s Notebook, in which Machen notes: "A Book of Stories unfinished of things hinted 'story vignettes'."[80]

One of the novel's poetic vignettes that would not be out of place in *Ornaments* is "[t]he little tale of *The Amber Statuette*."[81] This is a story Lucian labors on. Its presumed text is not interpolated in full in *Hill*; instead, it is alluded to and sketched out as a distilled impression. The way it materializes as a prose poem showcases its formal and idiosyncratic intricacies. Hence the prose poem in question is this shorter impression of a longer (imagined) work, illustrating in practice Huysmans's view that the prose poem is a condensed, essential oil. Hence, for the purpose of this discussion, we can refer to this version as "The Amber Statuette" in roman lettering and not in italics.

To extract "The Amber Statuette," one could slice the text at more than two places, but the vignette could easily hold its properties as a poetic ornament in just three or four consecutive paragraphs.[82] Just as with Dale's dichotomous self in "Psychology," the passage juxtaposes Lucian's experience of the dismal urban environment with a phantasmagoric scene conjured by his imagination. For Lucian, "sunshine seemed but a gaudy light"; he habitually paints the city as a site of decay: "Always in the daylight it had been to him abhorred and abominable, and its grey houses and purlieus had been fungus-like sproutings, and the efflorescence of horrible decay."[83] However, on that particular morning, Lucian unperturbed returns to his "den," sits at his desk to write, blocking out external reality. Overcome by creative fever and engrossed in the realm of his imagination, he gives the barebones of his hierophantic tale. A cross between an Ovidian metamorphosis and a Gautierian archaeological fetish narrative, Lucian's synopsized story tells of the worship of the statue of "Amber Venus." One of the statue's adorers, a woman "in a fire of bronze hair"[84] devotes herself to the temple of Venus in a vividly seductive scene:

> She it was who stood forth from all the rest and fell down prostrate before the radiant form in amber, drawing out her pins in curious gold, her glowing brooches of enamel, and pouring from a silver box all her treasure of jewels and precious stones, chrysoberyl and sardonyx, opal and diamond, topaz and pearl. And then she stripped from her body her precious robes and stood before the goddess in the glowing mist of her hair, praying that to her who had given all and came naked to the shrine, love might be given, and the grace of Venus.[85]

Lucian's cornucopia of gems and jewels parallels Julian's precious stone imagery in rendering the sunset in "Nature." Yet, in the context of sacred sensuality, Lucian's tableau works as a metaphor for the amalgamation of self and textual imagination. This is further supported by and amplified in the rest of "The Amber Statuette" narrative. With characteristic ellipticism, after unspecified "strange adventures, her prayer was granted."[86] Then, Lucian uses an archaeological conceit that evokes a pagan version of the Christian Resurrection: in the "shrine, far in Britain,"

> they found the splendid and sumptuous statue of the Golden Venus, the last fine robe of silk that the lady had dedicated falling from her fingers, and the jewels lying at her feet. And her face was like the lady's face when the sun had brightened it on that day of her devotion.[87]

The woman of Lucian's tale, and by extension Lucian himself, invites comparison with the girl in "The Ceremony." In her metamorphosis, the woman, on the one hand, undergoes a sort of deification. On the other hand, by replacing the glorious statue of Venus she herself turns into a sacred, precious artifact of worship. Then stepping out of his interior narrative, Lucian mirrors the woman's initial consuming ecstasy by worshipping her in her new form as an exalted goddess. Amidst the "reek of cabbage water," his nostrils are "filled with the perfume of rare unguents"; he did "not contrive[e] a story with patient art, but rapt into another time, and entranced by the ardent gleam in the lady's eyes."[88] In a way, Lucian's mystical, hallucinatory rapture symbolizes his painstaking authorial process. The woman who turns from adorer-suppliant to object of adoration becomes a motif for Lucian who is likewise consumed and amalgamated with his own province of imagination, rendering himself a wondrous ornament in jade.

"The Amber Statuette" could end here, on a striking, positive, and teasing note, matching smoothly the rhetorical and narrative trappings of *Ornaments*. But if we annex to it the paragraph that follows, in which *The Amber Statuette* is issued from a "humble office" in humdrum fashion and is panned by the critics ("Where are the disinfectants?"),[89] Machen's prose poem is underpinned as decidedly decadent. In addition, it showcases its effects of dichotomous subjectivity through contrast of voices and a distanced perspective. Machen calibrates the interior mechanics of the prose poem in paragraph-long blocks, a method that can be extrapolated to *Ornaments*.

In *Ornaments*, Machen has refined and appropriated a micro-genre with clarity and distinctiveness. These pieces do not just reproduce a plethora of decadent motifs, tropes and materialities. Their jeweled preciousness comports with the principle of art for art's sake, but with a symbolist twist. They are ciphers that point to a hidden, reconfigured reality. They present objects and spaces that are *hermetic* while appealing to the field of *hermeneutics* (incidentally the two words share the same root). In sharing in this paradigm of symbolist decadence, they inevitably offer variant scenarios in which the writer's or artist's self is calcified as the ultimate precious object-symbol in a projected world of symbols. As Machen writes about Lucian, "the wild domed hills and darkling woods seemed symbols of some terrible secret in the inner life of that stranger—himself."[90]

NOTES

1. For an insightful study on decadent objects and artifacts and Machen, see Stefania Forlini, "Modern Narrative and Decadent Things in Arthur Machen's *The Three Impostors*," *English Literature in Transition, 1880–1920* 55, no. 4 (2012): 479–98.

2. Arthur Machen, *Hieroglyphics: A Note upon Ecstasy in Literature*, rev. ed. (1902; London: Martin Secker, 1912), 155.

3. Dennis Denisoff (ed.), *Decadent and Occult Works by Arthur Machen*, MHRA Jewelled Tortoise Vol. 4 (Cambridge: The Modern Humanities Research Association, 2018), 22 and 18.

4. Vincent Starrett, *Arthur Machen: A Novelist of Ecstasy and Sin* (Chicago: Walter M. Hill, 1918), 19. In a footnote, Starrett reveals that in private communication Machen admitted he had not read Baudelaire, yet Starrett's "own assumption is rendered clear" (19).

5. J.K. Huysmans, *Against Nature*, trans. Robert Baldick (London: Penguin, 1959), 198.

6. Ibid.

7. Ibid., 199.

8. Arthur Machen, *The Hill of Dreams* (Cardigan: Parthian, The Library of Wales, 2010), 74.

9. Ibid., 101.

10. Ibid., 10.

11. Jon Preece, "A Glow in the Sky: Some Observations on Machen's Style," in *The Secret Ceremonies: Critical Essays on Arthur Machen*, eds Mark Valentine and Timothy J. Jarvis (New York: Hippocampus Press, 2019), 126.

12. Arthur Machen, *The London Adventure* (London: Martin Secker, 1924), 71.

13. For Machen's notes for the composition of *Ornaments* see Arthur Machen, *Arthur Machen's 1890s Notebook*, eds The Friends of Arthur Machen (Leyburn: Tartarus, 2018), 137–67. His notes on the making of *Hill* come before.

14. Arthur Machen, *Ornaments in Jade* (1924; Milton Keynes: Snuggly Books, 2018), 19.

15. Ibid., 16.

16. Machen, *Ornaments*, 16; Walter Pater, *The Renaissance: Studies in Art and Poetry*, ed. Adam Phillips (1873; Oxford: Oxford University Press, 1998), 152; Machen, *Ornaments*, 16.

17. Clive Scott, "Symbolism, Decadence and Impressionism," in *Modernism: A Guide to European Literature 1890–1930*, eds Malcolm Bradbury and James McFarlane (London: Penguin, 1976), 211.

18. Machen, *Ornaments*, 16, 17.

19. Ibid., 18. Similarly, in *Hill*, Lucian "had descended into a dark and shady valley, beset and tapestried with gloomy thickets; the weird wood noises were the only sounds, strange, unutterable mutterings, dismal, inarticulate," 49.
20. Machen, *Ornaments*, 19.
21. Ibid., 20.
22. Ibid.
23. Karen Joan Kohoutek, "A Fit Symbol for His Meaning: Arthur Machen and the Inexpressible," in *The Secret Ceremonies: Critical Essays on Arthur Machen*, eds Mark Valentine and Timothy J. Jarvis, 161–69 (New York: Hippocampus Press, 2019), 162, 163.
24. Machen, *Hieroglyphics*, 68.
25. Machen, *Ornaments*, 32.
26. Ibid., 33.
27. Machen, *1890s Notebook*, 10.
28. Machen, *Ornaments*, 18.
29. Ibid., 35–36.
30. Ibid., 37.
31. Ibid., 36.
32. Ibid., 38–39.
33. Ibid., 39.
34. Ibid.
35. Machen, *Hill*, 49.
36. Machen, *Ornaments*, 56.
37. Ibid., 59.
38. Ibid., 60.
39. Ibid., 58.
40. Wesley D. Sweetser, "Arthur Machen: A Bibliography of Writings about Him," *English Literature in Transition, 1880–1920*, 11, no. 1 (1968): 1–33, 2.
41. Machen, *Ornaments*, 25, 22.
42. Machen, *Hill*, 102.
43. Machen, *Ornaments*, 23.
44. Ibid., 24.
45. Ibid., 26.
46. Ibid.
47. Ibid., 27.
48. Ibid., 27–28. Compare this paragraph from "The Idealist" with *Hieroglyphics*, 11–12.
49. Ibid.
50. Machen, *Ornaments*, 28.
51. Ibid., 9.
52. Ibid., 10.
53. Ibid., 9–10.
54. Ibid., 11.
55. Machen, *Ornaments*, 12; Helen Gardner (ed.), *The Metaphysical Poets* (1957; London: Penguin, 1985), 257.

56. Machen, *Ornaments*, 62.
57. Ibid., 64.
58. Ibid., 65, 64.
59. Ibid., 65.
60. Machen, *Hill*, 1, 219.
61. Machen, *Ornaments*, 65.
62. Ibid., 67.
63. Ibid., 71.
64. Machen, *Hill*, 98.
65. Ibid., 158.
66. Machen, *Ornaments*, 70.
67. Ibid.
68. Andrew McCann, *Popular Literature, Authorship and the Occult in Late Victorian Britain* (Cambridge: Cambridge University Press, 2014), 162.
69. Machen, *Ornaments*, 41.
70. Ibid., 42.
71. Ibid., 44.
72. Ibid., 45.
73. Ibid., 45.
74. Ibid., 44.
75. Machen, *Hieroglyphics*, 106.
76. Machen, *Ornaments*, 45.
77. For Starrett, the prose of *Hill* is "poetry of a high order." Starrett, *Machen*, 22.
78. "vignette," *n.*, *Oxford English Dictionary Online* (accessed June 1, 2020).
79. Machen, *Hill*, 105.
80. Machen, *1890s Notebook*, 137. See also 158.
81. Machen, *Hill*, 213.
82. See Machen, *Hill*, 211–13.
83. Machen, *Hill*, 211.
84. Ibid.
85. Ibid., 212.
86. Ibid.
87. Ibid.
88. Ibid.
89. Ibid., 213.
90. Ibid., 33.

REFERENCES

Denisoff, Dennis (ed.). *Decadent and Occult Works by Arthur Machen*. MHRA Jewelled Tortoise Vol. 4. Cambridge: The Modern Humanities Research Association, 2018.

Forlini, Stefania. "Modern Narrative and Decadent Things in Arthur Machen's *The Three Impostors*." *English Literature in Transition, 1880–1920*. 55, no. 4 (2012): 479–98.

Gardner, Helen (ed.). *The Metaphysical Poets.* 1957; London: Penguin, 1985.
Huysmans, J.K. *Against Nature*, translated by Robert Baldick. London: Penguin, 1959.
Kohoutek, Karen Joan. "A Fit Symbol for His Meaning: Arthur Machen and the Inexpressible." In *The Secret Ceremonies: Critical Essays on Arthur Machen*, edited by Mark Valentine and Timothy J. Jarvis, 161–69. New York: Hippocampus Press, 2019.
Machen, Arthur. *Arthur Machen's 1890s Notebook*, edited by The Friends of Arthur Machen. Leyburn: Tartarus, 2018.
———. *Hieroglyphics: A Note upon Ecstasy in Literature*, rev. ed. 1902; London: Martin Secker, 1912.
———. *The Hill of Dreams.* Cardigan: Parthian, The Library of Wales, 2010.
———. *The London Adventure.* London: Martin Secker, 1924.
———. *Ornaments in Jade.* 1924; Milton Keynes: Snuggly Books, 2018.
McCann, Andrew. *Popular Literature, Authorship and the Occult in Late Victorian Britain.* Cambridge: Cambridge University Press, 2014.
Pater, Walter. *The Renaissance: Studies in Art and Poetry*, edited by Adam Phillips. 1873; Oxford: Oxford University Press, 1998.
Preece, Jon. "A Glow in the Sky: Some Observations on Machen's Style." In *The Secret Ceremonies: Critical Essays on Arthur Machen*, edited by Mark Valentine and Timothy J. Jarvis, 117–27. New York: Hippocampus Press, 2019.
Scott, Clive. "Symbolism, Decadence and Impressionism." In *Modernism: A Guide to European Literature 1890–1930*, edited by Malcolm Bradbury and James McFarlane, 206–27. London: Penguin, 1976.
Starrett, Vincent. *Arthur Machen: A Novelist of Ecstasy and Sin.* Chicago: Walter M. Hill, 1918.
Sweetser, Wesley D. "Arthur Machen: A Bibiography of Writings about Him." *English Literature in Transition, 1880–1920.* 11, no. 1 (1968): 1–33.
"vignette," *n. Oxford English Dictionary Online.*

Chapter 8

"A Substance as Jelly"

Helen Vaughan as Pathogen and femme fatale *in "The Great God Pan"*

Loredana Salis and Laura Mauro

The Gothic fiction of the *fin de siècle* reflects the profound and pervasive societal unease of the era, with the body as the primary subject and space of manifest degeneration, mutation, and corruption. Stories written at the end of the nineteenth century are preoccupied with the often wild articulation of contemporary fears, transposing the strange and the horrific onto familiar settings, "from a safe remoteness to a frightening immediacy, from subjective to objective reality."[1] The shifting cultural landscapes that made Mary Shelley's *Frankenstein* (1818) so compelling to an audience struggling with the changes brought about by the Industrial Revolution proved likewise fertile ground, decades later, for authors seeking to make sense of the uncertainties of a mutable world, what the Hungarian sociologist Max Simon Nordau (1849–1923), in an apocalyptic and widely influential pronouncement, defined "the dusk of the nations."[2]

Arthur Machen's "The Great God Pan" (1894) is in such terms a typical anxious piece of *fin-de-siècle* fiction.[3] Denounced by some as "an incoherent nightmare of sex," this controversial novella created a stir, but was nevertheless well received both in the UK and the USA.[4] Thematically, it owed its debt to Machen's interest in medical matters and the occult, and to a literary *milieu* replete with narrative experimentation—most prominently George Eliot's *The Lifted Veil* (1859) and Robert Louis Stevenson's recent masterpieces, *The Dynamiters* (1885) and *The Strange Case of Dr Jekyll and Mr Hyde* (1886).[5] An avid reader of Stevenson's tales, Machen followed the narrative conventions of the Gothic to create a story of mystery, horror, and terror in which arcane forces become uncontrollable, moral and biological taboos are violated, the past revisits the present, human and divine blend, male and female become indistinguishable.

The story opens with a neurological procedure performed by a scientist upon a young woman, a recurring literary trope of the period, found as early as 1859 in Eliot's novella, and later also in H.G. Wells' *The Island of Dr Moreau* (1896) and Richard Marsh's *The Beetle* (1897), to cite a few examples.[6] Machen's use of a dubious medical experiment initiates a descent proper into the primordial where barriers between the human and divine regions are abated, and where a young female named Mary finds herself exposed to the dangers of a pagan obscure world. It is here that Pan lives, and it is here that he impregnates her. The child of this mystical conception is Helen Vaughan, the heir to an unspeakable horror that will result in an epidemic of fatal madness and mysterious deaths. Through oblique suggestions of sexual excess and decadent behaviors, Machen constructs Helen both as a degenerate and the propagator of contagious "social and sexual misrule."[7] He gives her distinctive physical traits that help define Helen as "a not-quite-human subject characterised by its morphic variability, continually in danger of becoming not-itself, [of] becoming other."[8] Helen, a character called Austin tells us, "*would be* called very handsome . . . Her features are exquisite, but *the expression is strange*."[9] Helen is indeed strange in her capacity to act as a disease vector in the guise of an intriguing human female. A pathogen and a *femme fatale*, that is, Machen's heroine is capable of unlocking the transgressive desires of those she comes into contact with, causing them irreparable damages, and ultimately liberating them from their repressed self beyond the normative conventions of their time. What follows looks at Helen's agency with special attention to Machen's engagement with panic mythology and with degeneracy discourses.

Degeneration theory, as popularized by physician Max Simon Nordau, set out to define deviations from the norm as a pathology or an illness of the modern age. Taking the view that "books and works of art exercise a powerful suggestion on the masses," Nordau maintained that authors and artists were themselves degenerates, who could determine the "morality and beauty" of their age and "exert a disturbing and corrupting influence on the views of a whole generation."[10] In his highly influential treatise, Nordau read through an array of nineteenth-century works by writers, artists, and composers to depict the wide-spread "stigma" of degeneracy of his time, namely the "contempt for traditional views of custom and morality."[11] He regarded city life and the ingestion of addictive substances (tainted foods) as the "poisons" from which degeneracy originates.[12] Exposure to urban contexts produced symptoms akin to outbreaks of virulent disease; consequently, people living in the city were liable to fall "victims to the same fatality of degeneracy and destruction as the victims of malaria."[13] Believing that degeneracy was hereditary, and thus could be passed from parent to child as any congenital condition, Nordau described an etiology more in keeping with mutagenesis than with transmissible illness.

The popularity of his ideas, and the notion that sexually assertive women can be "perverted in material instincts" and become dangerous proved crucial to Machen's characterization of Helen Vaughan as a degenerate and a pathogen.[14]

The late-Victorian pathologization of degeneracy was consonant with discourses on syphilis, "the symbolic disease of the fin de siècle."[15] As with degeneracy, syphilis became representative of the "sins of the fathers," a hereditary form of debilitating insanity whose primary cause was the patient's immoral behavior. Indeed, syphilis and degeneration theory were conflated by some proponents of social purity, who deemed responsible "otherwise 'respectable gentlemen' for contracting venereal diseases from prostitutes and introducing the seed of degeneration into their family line."[16] While feminists and moralists laid the blame at the door of negligent men, the Contagious Diseases Acts of 1864, 1866, and 1869 held women as major vectors of sexually transmitted disease and permitted the detention and medical inspection of any woman believed to be a prostitute. The same indignity was not imposed on male soldiers and sailors, primary clients of prostitutes[17] who were considered to be "reservoirs" of venereal diseases, capable of "invading via infection," and producing "malignancy" within the collective cultural imagination.[18] The Contagious Diseases Acts were reflective of patriarchal discourses of the time, and construed women as dangerous enemies and *femmes fatales*, capable of luring men "into sexual temptation only to destroy them."[19] Machen's characterization of Helen Vaughan thus emerges as a precious testimony to the *fin-de-siècle* anxiety with unchecked sexuality and degenerative disease.

A "terrible epidemic of suicide" sweeps through London's West End, claiming the lives of wealthy men of reputation.[20] As the story unfolds, and the mystery is solved, it becomes clear that all such "sordid murders" are linked to a woman called Helen, a *femme fatale* who lures men to their doom with her singing voice, her irresistible beauty, and enigmatic charm.[21] Her dispatch method is unusual. She is said to drive to suicide healthy men who did not suffer from depression nor had a reason to take their lives, prior to encountering her: Lord Argentine, for instance, dies "by slow strangulation" following an attack of "acute suicidal mania"; three gentlemen "perished miserably in almost precisely the same manner"; and another is found "hanging dead from the branch of a tree in his garden."[22] Suicide is promptly established among the fatalities ensuing from contact with Helen, who comes to be perceived as a hazard spreading across society, possibly worse than smallpox or any other type of virus.[23]

The case of Mr. Blank is emblematic. The man is found "stark dead" outside the house where Helen used to live when married to Charles Herbert.[24] The autopsy fails to reveal any sign of violence or poisoning, with the doctor's examination concluding that the man died from "sheer, awful terror."[25]

It remains unclear how the victim became acquainted with Helen, but there is a possibility that he may have been in the house at the time of his death. In a bid to find out more, sometime later, a character named Villiers visits the premises, and thus reports the experience to his friend, Mr. Clarke:

> I felt my teeth grinding as I put my hand on the door, and when I went in, *I thought I should have fallen fainting to the floor.* However, I pulled myself together, and stood against the end wall wondering *what on earth* there could be about the room to make my limbs tremble, and my heart beat *as if I were at the hour of death.*[26]

Upon leaving the house, the man recalls "staggering about from one side of the pavement to the other" and spending a week "in bed . . . suffering from . . . nervous shock and exhaustion."[27] Villiers' extraordinary reaction is written off by Clarke as "due to a vivid imagination," until the sight of a pencil drawing of Helen causes Clarke himself to suffer a nervous attack, and turn "white as death."[28] Villiers recounts the same episode to Austin, this time highlighting that what he had felt in Herbert's house was *"more physical than mental. It was as if I were inhaling at every breath some deadly fume, which seemed to penetrate to every nerve and bone and sinew of my body."*[29] Both descriptions leave no doubts as to what these men experience following their encounter, direct or indirect, with Helen. All of them are literally intoxicated (*breath, fume, physical, penetrate, body, sinew*); contamination occurring at times by way of traditional paths of infection (touch), or through other senses—sight and smell most especially. This reminds us that exposure by sight was central to Victorian gender bias discourse, with *femme fatales* considered capable of bewitching and killing their male beholders. It also reminds us of another Victorian trope, that of miasma, the belief that bad odor coming from corrupted or rotting matter was a source of infection.[30]

Bad odor, "the poison of atmospheric impurity" in the words of Neil Arnott, the Scottish physician, is associated with Helen on different and significant occasions.[31] As a child, she lived in a place by the forest where "the scent of wild roses . . . mixed with the heavy perfume of the elder . . . *is like the odour of the room of the dead, a vapour of incense and corruption."*[32] A walk into that forest is recalled by Clarke in a vision: while at Dr. Raymond's, the man becomes "half-conscious" as an "odd odour" fills the room where the experiment that brings Helen into this world is about to be performed—the disturbing olfactory experience clearly anticipating her conception and establishing, at an early stage, a connection between herself, an unpleasant smell and its ominous power.[33] "Bad odour" is recorded at Number 20, Paul Street, one of Helen's domiciles; and likewise, before she dies, "an odour of corruption" is said to "choke the breath" of he who stands firm watching that horrible scene.[34] The perception of Helen as an agent of atmospheric pollution, a woman who causes degeneration of the brain and the body confirms her subversive and incontrovertibly corrupt nature. She is held responsible for the West End suicides and also the fate befalling a seven-year-old boy called Trevor, and that of an adolescent, Rachel, both of whom have witnessed "some great terror" and have become fatally exposed to degeneracy. The former "saw Helen V. playing on the grass with a 'strange naked man' . . . he seemed unable to describe," while Rachel, a childhood friend of Helen's, is said to have entertained with her "a friendship of a peculiarly intimate character."[35] Machen does not provide additional details but suggests rather unequivocally that morally aberrant acts, perhaps an orgy of some sort were experienced by both. In Rachel's case, possibly a virgin at the time, she may have been involved in a Panic ritual, by way of Helen. The god Pan is associated with sex and instant gratification, which would however require a high price, such as derangement, heartbreak, loneliness.[36] Hence, the reaction of the once innocent country girl who turns "languid and dreamy," "different from herself," and is found one evening "weeping . . . lying, half-undressed, upon the bed, evidently in the greatest distress."[37] The tale of Rachel's sexual initiation is never fully unveiled: on the page this is significantly marked by a truncated sentence: "Rachel told her [*mother*] a wild story. She said ———."[38] Omissions such as this exemplify the narrative force of myths and of gothic devices toward moral ends and toward more sophisticated scopes. What remains unsaid or half-said, that is, serves to introduce the specter of unspeakable acts in the text, thus drawing readers into an unfamiliar territory of speculations and fantasies, to confront them with their own most hidden desires, fears, and uncertainties. In the novella, this alien and alienating territory is recreated in both urban and rural contexts that become places of Panic possession, where Machen's Great God manifests himself—London's Whitechapel area, the West End, the Welsh fields and the forest where Helen encounters her victims, where Trevor "peeps through the branches," and Rachel entertains her excursions with her.[39]

Of necessity, a reading of Helen as a pathogen, a "typhoid Mary" of some sort, takes us back to the moment of her conception and, therefore, to the roots of her infectious nature.[40] As a young woman, Helen's mother Mary undergoes vivisection at the behest of Dr. Raymond and witnessed by Mr. Clarke. Depicted as an innocent teenager who acquiesces to the doctor's will to alter her brain surgically, Mary is left in a near-vegetative state. The operation is nevertheless pronounced to be a success by Dr. Raymond, who considers damages to Mary's cerebral functions as merely unfortunate side-effects. It is later revealed that the actual result is her unholy union with Pan, when "a devil was made incarnate. And a human being produced."[41] Having seen Pan, Mary is left "a hopeless idiot," while her "flesh," as Raymond puts it, is intoxicated and becomes *"the veil of a horror* one dare not express," the "unspeakable" here being Helen herself.[42]

Dr. Raymond raises the infant until he finds himself unable to bear the "constant and incarnate" horror and decides to send her away.[43] In doing so, he refrains from taking responsibility as her creator and surrogate father, thereby releasing Helen (and everything she stands for) into the world. Though he claims ownership and thinks that Mary's "life is mine, to use as I see fit,"[44] Raymond abdicates responsibility of both Helen's birth and of her dispatch, much in the same way as Helen's victims will abdicate to her, consenting to her intrusion in their lives, even as they pay a high price for it. In the end, all blame is laid at Helen's feet, a woman doomed from inception who is eventually forced to commit suicide. Significantly, Machen names his heroine after Homer's Queen, *casus belli* of the legendary Trojan war, and equally shapes his Helen as a beautiful but fatal woman, who remains largely unvoiced.[45] For all her centrality, Helen Vaughan never speaks for herself—not a word literally comes from her in the entire text. Her voice being unheard or silenced, except when she sings, Machen's protagonist reflects the kind of hostility toward anything deemed subversive (and degenerate) on the part of *fin de siècle* patriarchal apprehensions and aspirations.[46] Yet, while being denied the possibility to express herself verbally, she holds powers of intervention that are superior to the force of the spoken word: for Machen she is a "door open [*into*] the house of life."[47] This pathogen is a woman who needs no voice to bring about change.[48] Ultimately, her agency is necessary, however painful, to individual and collective regeneration, if not resurrection.[49]

Emblematic of the emerging category of women that are no longer and easily victimized, Helen is a "New Woman" in her own right.[50] She is a sophisticated female type, "a Womanly Woman" who is oversexed, maneating, anti-domestic, revolutionary, an agent of decline but also of social regeneration.[51] Helen differs from Mary; she differs also from the kind of woman represented in other *fin de siècle* works across the continent. A *femme fatale* proper, Helen is a "sister to the many Salomés and Judiths whose lust to decapitate derives from male anxiety about increasing female empowerment."[52] She is not "the noble woman, driven only by her altruism,"[53] nor is she the self-abnegating type; she does not embody passivity nor innocence, she is not an "old Eve seduced by the serpent" but rather "a New Eve who has appropriated the serpent's phallic power, making her extremely dangerous to the patriarchal status quo."[54]

Her "olive skin" and "Italian appearance" identify this outsider, conveniently and efficaciously, and turn her into the source of an alluring exotic threat. Born of a scientist's act of transgression, a child to a god from a foreign mythology, Helen belongs to an arcane world that is alien to traditional (medical) knowledge and which can only be accessed at one's peril. Just as Pan is a pagan force, so does Helen, his offspring, share in that same intrinsically ambivalent and liminal quality. She recalls Coleridge's Abyssinian harpist whose "symphony and song / to such a deep delight 't would win me," and in that vision enrapt the poet in a heightened sensory and sensual experience.[55] Helen recalls also Bertha Grant in *The Lifted Veil*, the "daughter of an aged river," "a sylph," "an oriental alphabet" that cannot and will not be deciphered. Bertha is "the very opposite of *the ideal woman*" writes Eliot,[56] questioning the validity of extant normative notions of femininity while seeking to dismantle them.[57] Similarly, Machen's heroine bears traits that reflect and challenge gender prejudices to assert diverse modes of femininity. She belongs to "the rising generation of well-educated, free-thinking, assertive New Women" who are sexually confident, fascinating, and yet somehow repulsive.[58]

A menace to "be expelled (if not destroyed)" so the "disorder" can be deactivated, this type of woman is antithetical to the norms of a period that is attracted to and intimidated by prospects of change, and which to a significant extent remains obsessed with "degeneration discourses, invasion anxieties, and an increase in the classification of the abnormal and the pathological."[59] In these terms, Machen's tale and the construction of Helen as a pathogen and a *femme fatale* are not only a valuable testimony but also a critique of analogous discourses as they were still deeply rooted in the culture of the *fin de siècle*.

Helen's assertive qualities are established at an early age, when Dr. Raymond rejects her and leaves her free of making her own choices. As a young girl she spends long days alone in the forest, returning home after dusk, to the discomfort of her foster family, for whom her lifestyle is inappropriate. Comfortable in her independence, Helen finds herself at odds with orthodox female roles that are central to the Victorian value system, occupying an anomalous space outside the sphere of domesticity and closer to the margins, where other "improper" or unconventional female types are also located, who "invade female sexuality [*and are*] seen as the bearer of corruption and disease."[60]

A key to Machen's fascination with Panic mythology and the occult, taboos concerning sexuality are central to dominant misogynist practices.[61] In "The Great God Pan," sexual taboos are articulated through omissions and ambivalences—what characters wish but cannot express. In recounting his wedding night, for instance, Mr. Herbert finds it hard to talk of an unconventional wife who ends up corrupting his soul:

> The night of the wedding I found myself sitting in [*Helen's*] bedroom in the hotel, *listening to her talk*. She was sitting up in bed, and *I listened to her as she spoke in her beautiful voice, spoke of things which even now I would not dare*

whisper in blackest night, though I stood in the midst of a wilderness . . . In a year . . . I was a ruined man, in body and soul, in body and soul.[62]

The scene by the marriage bed, the place of consummation, is where the spouse is said to utter unspeakable words and do "such things" which are clearly beyond the acceptable boundaries of conjugal sex. Appalled and enthralled, mesmerized by the sound of Helen's "beautiful voice," Herbert is literally intoxicated by her words and eventually corrupted by them. In his recollections, he spares the details in an act of self-denial and repulsed drives which, as Stephan Karschay notes, confirms "Herbert's self-recognition of his own darker impulses."[63] As with Clarke and his "memoirs," the duality of normative and degenerate is undermined to assert the possibility of their coexistence. The veil that separates them in daylight (the public sphere) is lifted within the confines of the bedroom (the private sphere), where everything becomes licit, however temporarily. In the process, Helen acts as a catalyst for Herbert's latent transgressive desires; she allows for his most basic impulses to be liberated and become somehow acceptable, like a new norm, contrary to the standard that would otherwise classify them as animal deviations.

The implication is doubly interesting. On the one hand, Herbert's reaction reveals the uncomfortable truth that this outwardly "respectable" gentleman, like other men of reputation, incubates sordid inclinations. On the other, it confirms Helen's role as a liberating force, one which legitimates basic instincts, brings them to the surface, fatally displays the innate dual nature of all human beings. Sidney Crashaw, another of Helen's "victims," provides an eloquent instance of Machen's insightfully provocative narrative. The man is spotted in a dark London street by Villiers who reports that though his "outward form remained . . . all hell was within it. Furious lust, and hate that was like fire, and the loss of all hope and horror that seemed to shriek aloud to the night, though his teeth were shut."[64] The man appears to be overcome by some superior, unmanageable force, and eventually gives up to a form of dementia that is akin to neurosyphilis, which at the time was held "responsible for a large proportion of the cases of lunacy and idiocy in . . . asylums."[65] The man's horrific demise points to the analogy between Helen's agency and the effects of syphilitic insanity, which, as Showalter observes, "seemed to violate and subvert all of the society's most potent moral norms, to break the bourgeois rules of sexual and social conduct."[66] Through Helen, in other words, Crashaw's lust breaks the rules of decency, causing him to trespass imaginary lines beyond which lies the insanity of Coleridge's pure and "deep delight."

Crucial to Helen's function as instigator of a man's inmost nature and repressed instincts is her ability to masquerade under various guises and names. Her multiple identities (Helen V., Helen Vaughan, Miss Raymond,

Mrs. Herbert, Mrs. Beaumont) allow her to act freely while avoiding detection, at least until connections are traced between her different personas. Managing to hide, Helen is granted protection and escapes the fate of most fallen women who "got what they deserved" for not being "asexual beings."[67] Her furtive, often nocturnal movements suggest how for Machen the exploration of sexuality and of desire facilitated a powerful indulgence in one's own hidden vices. Helen thus makes it possible for her lovers (and for readers of this story) to become aware of their desires, to face their "syphilophobic fantasy," to acknowledge their "monstrous sexual self,"[68] and come to terms with that "primitiveness in woman which can be released through an unbalanced and perverted carnality."[69]

The prospect lies at the heart of theories disseminated in the late 1850s by William Acton. Warning women against the dangers of "taking pleasure in sex," which could induce "cancer of the womb or insanity," that prominent medical expert believed that (happily for society) "the majority of women are not very much troubled with sexual feelings of any kind."[70] In *The Functions and Disorders of the Reproductive Organs* (1857), he went as far as taking a rather dim view of sexually assertive women, and advised that excess of "sexual indulgence brings out *our* brutal biological heritage."[71] Men can be degraded "to the level of animal," whereas "wanton women are like lionesses or spiders, *dangerous aggressors who dominate males . . . and make them their victims.*"[72] By those standards, Helen Vaughan is a typical "wanton woman": more serpent than Eve, she is a dialectical whore to Mary, her quasi-Madonna mother figure.[73] The analogy is again significant. As with her biblical namesake, Mary's pregnancy results from an encounter with the divine, but contrary to the Biblical God, the pagan Pan is a symbol of decadence and degeneracy, traits which Helen inherits and which she clearly displays.[74]

Pan, who is classically associated with unrestrained sexuality, is a gleefully promiscuous divinity often "depicted sexually accosting other deities, nymphs, shepherds and shepherdesses."[75] There is a "darker and more sinister side of the god," however, which causes youths to fly as they may be suffering from a real attack of *panic*.[76] As Panic imagery became shorthand for uncanny horror in late-Victorian texts, Machen's works of the *fin de siècle* also featured satyrs and other unholy presences.[77]

Pan can inflict death to his beholders; likewise, Helen, his daughter, spreads a disturbing (Panic) frenzy among those who establish as little as visual contact with her.[78] Her deadly powers are worth exploring further insofar as they enable us to pose the question of what *really* dies, and for what reasons, in consequence of her agency. To this aim, it is interesting to note Machen's use of the physical body as a contested site, at once the cause and effect of dominating ideologies. In "The Great God Pan," the body is taken to represent a materiality easily repressed, if not suppressed, a manifestation of a deeper and darker self (individual and collective) waiting to be unleashed. Physical transformations become inevitable; they are forced upon the body as it reaches a point of no return, usually insanity or death, a sacrifice of the flesh which becomes necessary to redemption. Helen herself is not immune to a dramatic modification of her material self, a metamorphosis that alters her body as she dissolves into a jelly-like substance. The dismal episode is reported in fragments compiled by Dr. Matheson, the sole witness to the woman's death:

> I saw that which was on the bed, lying there like black ink, transformed before my eyes. The skin, and the flesh, and the muscles, and the bones, and the firm structure of the human body that I had thought to be unchangeable, and permanent as adamant, began to melt and dissolve . . . *Here was something that caused dissolution and change.*[79]

Before the doctor's eyes an alchemical process takes place that kills Helen's satanic self, saves her as a human, only to kill her again in the end as her body "wavers from sex to sex, dividing itself from itself, and then again reunited":

> I watched, and at last I saw nothing but a substance like jelly . . . I saw a Form, shaped in dimness before me which I won't farther describe. *But the symbol of this form may be seen in ancient sculptures, and in paintings which survived beneath the lava, too foul to be spoken of, as a horrible and unspeakable shape, neither man nor beast* was changed into human form, there came finally death.[80]

The symbol seen in ancient sculptures is clearly the effigy of the god Pan, who does not really die but is rather born again in an endless ritual of self-regeneration.[81] There are clear echoes of occult practices of which Machen was a devotee at the time, and which are used conveniently to tackle cultural biases of the late nineteenth century period. One most prominently is that concerning the "New Woman" as a "desexualised half-man," possibly to assert her original place and true nature, and to mediate between human and divine, sacred and profane, spirit and matter.[82] The encounter of separate worlds would lead to the totality of all things, through the liberating force of the senses and their delight, which Machen saw as the true legacy of the Great God Pan (the capitalized spelling is Machen's). Helen's dissolution into a jelly-like substance recalls images of degradation as described by Nordau, though in Machen's conception of the process, the abject body returns to a basic and primordial state to accomplish its restorative and transformative function.[83] Helen, by these terms, becomes a vehicle for physical and metaphysical mutations of the repressed.

To conclude, Helen's story is a romantic narrative of great aspirations and irresistible desires. Through it, Machen pursues and conjures up an otherworldly status beyond the veil of normativity, of moral and material stringencies, where contamination kills habit, intoxication gives new life to the soul and the body, madness becomes creative, and sexual exuberance is no longer inhibited. "The Great God Pan" records and confronts us with the diverse preoccupations dominating discourses on gender and sexuality of the *fin de siècle*, when, as Martin Tropp notes, "men and women faced new anxieties that threatened the cult of Respectability."[84] Among them was the specter of degeneration, partially borne of the Decadent movement to which Machen's novella was somehow connected, though he later tried to distance himself from what he termed "Yellow Bookery."[85] The advent of the "New Woman" and the ensuing threat that the model of femininity posed to late-Victorian values and normative system is another key aspect. Machen was aware that a constant fear of contagion remained crucial to the rhetoric of degeneracy and that this, in turn, affected the role of both men and women, within the private and the public spheres. At the turn of the century, the Victorian obsession with contagion, disease, and death was still strong, lending itself to narratives of horror and terror in which, as with Helen Vaughan, fear of diversity and of change justifies her being de-humanized, silenced, and eventually discarded with. Her passivity, however, is only apparent, as is her gratuitous evil nature and fatal intent. This child of the Great God Pan dies a victim to a repressed and repressive society, her bodily sacrifice and substantial mutation being a potent metaphor of the kind of radical transformation to which several *fin de siècle* writers aspired. Fascinated with pagan mythologies and early Romantic ideals, Machen's literary imagination was molded by the mysteries, the natural beauty, and the ancient legends of his native Wales, the land of his formative adolescent years. He was enthralled by the occult, which would become central to his life, including his married life, and which helped shape his sophisticated aesthetics.[86] A curious explorer of unchartered territories of the self in its entirety, in the 1890s he engaged in a type of literature that could record the "interior tale of the soul and its emotions,"[87] aim for a "*participation mystique* with nature"[88] and break down the ideological boundaries between the inner and the outer self. Machen was a keen observer of society at a time of profound transformations. As a writer, he pursued a new and modern sensibility beyond mainstream decadent dissent, and took an active role in undermining disciplinary structures, including popular notions of gender, sexuality, and degeneracy. Drawing attention to dynamics of infection and of self-containment, he made his Helen a pathogen and a *femme fatal* to defy broadly unquestioned norms and envision individual and collective regeneration. Spiritual and cultural healing demanded a return to the roots of which the Great God Pan was to him a mighty and crucial agent.

NOTES

1. Martin Tropp, *Images of Fear: How Horror Stories Helped Shape Modern Culture (1818-1918)* (Jefferson, NC: McFarland Classics, 1990), 5.
2. Max Simon Nordau, *Degeneration* [1892], trans. Howard Fertig (Frankfurt: Outlook Verlag, 2018), 8.
3. "The Great God Pan" was first published in *The Whirlwind*, London, 1890. An expanded and a revised version appeared in John Lane's *Keystone Series*, Vol. V, London, 1854, and Boston, Roberts Bothers, 1894. John Lane published it again in 1895. In 1901, the novella was translated into French. Subsequent editions include 1906, London, Richards, repr. in 1910; 1916, London, Simpkin Marshall; 1922, London, Knopf; 1923, London, Seeker, 1923; 1941, London, Random House; and 1948, Knopf. All references to the text are taken from Arthur Machen, *The Great God Pan and Other Horror Stories*, ed. Aaron Worth (Oxford: Oxford University Press, 2018).
4. Review appeared in the *Westminster Gazette*, qtd. in Machen, *The Great God Pan*, xiv. Machen cites some of the reviews in the introduction to the 1916 edition of "The Great God Pan" (London: Simpkin, Marshall), vii-xxiii, reprinted in Dennis Denisoff, *Decadent and Occult Works by Arthur Machen* (Cambridge: MHRA, 2018), 300–07. Negative reception of Machen's work was counterbalanced by H.P. Lovecraft's often quoted appreciation of his work: "Of living creators of cosmic fear raised to its most artistic pitch, few if any can hope to equal the versatile Arthur Machen." Lovecraft, *Supernatural Horror in Literature*, qtd. in Machen, *The Great God Pan*, x.
5. See Corinna Wagner, *Gothic Evolutions: Poetry, Tales, Context, Theory* (Peterborough: Broadview Press, 2014), 387; Susan Johnston Graf, *Talking to the Gods. Occultism in the Works of W.B. Yeats, Arthur Machen, Algernon Blackwood, and Dion Fortune* (New York: SUNY Press 2015), 57–78.
6. See Jack Holland, *A Brief History of Misogyny: The World's Oldest Prejudice* (London: Robinson, 2006), 189–195. See also Coral Lansbury, "Gynaecology, Pornography, and the Antivivisection Movement," *Victorian Studies* 28, no. 3 (1985), 413–37.
7. Lynn Pykett, *Engendering Fictions. The English Novel in the Early Twentieth Century* (London: Edward Arnold, 1995), 38.
8. Kelly Hurley, *The Gothic Body. Sexuality, Materialism, and Degeneration at the Fin de Siècle* (Cambridge: Cambridge University Press, 1996), 4.
9. Machen, *The Great God Pan*, 40. References to faces and facial expressions are numerous and highly significant throughout the narrative. The face mirrors one's inner self, with the eyes being a key into a person's soul: as Clarke puts it: "the woman's soul looked out of the eyes, and the lips parted with a strange smile" (30).
10. Nordau, *Degeneration*, viii.
11. Ibid., 6.
12. Ibid., 41.
13. Ibid.
14. Ibid., 413.

15. Elaine Showalter, "Syphilis, Sexuality, and the Fiction of the *fin de siècle*," in *Sex, Politics, and Science in the Nineteenth-Century Novel*, ed. Ruth Bernard Yeazell, 88–115 (Baltimore, MD: The Johns Hopkins University Press, 1986), 88.

16. Heidi Rimke and Alan Hunt, "From Sinners to Degenerates: The Medicalization of Morality in the 19th Century," *History of the Human Sciences* 15, no. 1 (2002), 59–88, 16. Social purity movements were active in England as early as the 1690s. According to their philosophy "sex and sexuality are deeply problematic drives, which unless tightly controlled will spill out into society and cause untold harm." Margaret Hunt, "The De-eroticization of Women's Liberation: Social Purity Movements and the Revolutionary Feminism of Sheila Jeffreys," *Feminist Review* 34 (Spring 1990), 23–46, 25. At the start of the 1860s social purity discourse was incorporated in feminist discourse, with special impact upon the Contagious Disease Acts, and the double-standard implicit in these anti-vice laws that tended to blame prostitutes, not their male clients, who were not hampered for spreading venereal disease, nor were they isolated to prevent contagion.

17. Inspecting soldiers was an unthinkable procedure that may have caused them potential demoralization. See Margaret Hamilton, "Opposition to the Contagious Diseases Acts, 1864-1886," *Albion: A Quarterly Journal Concerned with British Studies* 10, no. 1 (1978), 14–27.

18. Rebecca Stott, *The Fabrication of the Late Victorian Femme Fatale* (Hampshire: Macmillan, 1992), 47.

19. Showalter, "Syphilis," 89.

20. Machen, *The Great God Pan*, 41.

21. Ibid., 38. Machen calls them "the sordid murders of Whitechapel," a clear reference to Jack the Ripper and to the mysterious crimes that occurred in that area.

22. Ibid., 38 and 41.

23. Ibid.

24. Machen's character is possibly drafted upon the Welsh poet and clergyman Charles Spencer (1593–1632), whom he cites at the start of the story. Dr Raymond describes the unreality of the material world using Herbert's line "chases in Arras, dreams in a career," from "Dotage," in *The Temple* (10 and note 10 of the Explanatory Notes [by Aaron Worth], 353). Another possible source is Machen's contemporary Herbert Spencer (1820-1903), the English sociologist and philosopher who forged the concept of the "survival of the fittest" and promoted social Darwinism. See https://www.britannica.com/biography/Herbert-Spencer (accessed April 23, 2021).

25. Machen, *The Great God Pan*, 26. Emphasis added.

26. Ibid., 29.

27. Ibid.

28. Ibid., 30 and 31.

29. Ibid., 33. Emphasis added.

30. Stephen Halliday, "Death and miasma in Victorian London: an obstinate belief," *British Medical Journal* 323, no. 7327 (2001), 1469–71, www.ncbi.nlm.nih.gov/pmc/articles/PMC1121911 (accessed January 29, 2021).

31. Ibid. Emphasis added.

32. Machen, *The Great God Pan*, 52. The place is called Caermaen, Machen's fictionalized birthplace of Caerleon on Usk.

33. Ibid., 13.

34. Ibid., 26 and 50.

35. Ibid., 18 and 19.

36. On the theme of panic mythology, on the modern cult of Pan, and on Pan's archetype as a method of revelation and transformation see James Hillman, "An Essay on Pan," in *Pan and the Nightmare* (New York: Spring, 1972).

37. Machen, *The Great God Pan*, 20.

38. Ibid.

39. This reminds us that with Pan categories are confused, and that his "mythical connection were to the rural, but the divine laughter of chaos might also erupt in the middle of the polis." Ingvild Saelid Gilhus, *Laughing Gods, Weeping Virgins: Laughter in the History of Religion* (London: Routledge, 2013), 44.

40. Machen may have had in mind Mary Mallon (1869-1938), an Irish emigrant who moved to the USA, in 1884, and there worked as a cook. As a healthy carrier of *Salmonella typhi* her nickname of "Typhoid Mary" had become synonymous with the spread of disease, as many were infected due to her denial of being ill. She was forced into quarantine on two separate occasions and died alone without friends. See Filio Marineli, Gregory Tsoucalas, Marianna Karamanou, George Androutsos, "Mary Mallon (1869-1938) and the history of typhoid fever," *Annals of Gastroenterology* 26 (2013), 132–34.

41. Machen, *The Great God Pan*, 21. "Et Diabolus Incarnatus Est. Et Homo Factus Est."

42. Ibid., 53. Emphasis added. In a letter to Clarke the doctor refers to the child Helen multiple times as "it"; in spite of his paternal role Dr Raymond too does not deem Helen fully human. This stark misogyny harks back to his assertion that he owns Mary's life, and it is further confirmed when Raymond is asked for Helen's name, to which he responds: "Only human beings have names" (23).

43. Ibid., 54.

44. Ibid., 12.

45. Helen of Sparta, who is traditionally held responsible for the outbreak of the first large-scale conflict between the Western and the Eastern civilizations. There is an echo of Euripides's characterization of Helen in his homonymous play in which the gods, not the woman, are responsible for creating the illusion of her guilt though images misconstrued by humans. In Euripides' play, and possibly in Machen's understanding of the protagonist's role, unveiling the truth about Helen serves to expose facile and deeply-rotted prejudices in social and cultural dynamics. As to Helen's surname in the novella, Vaughan is probably a reference to Thomas Vaughan, a hermetic philosopher and an alchemist (1621–66), "the brother of the Silurist," the Welsh poet, whose works Machen knew and whom he mentions in his *Autobiography*.

46. Helen's silencing has not gone unnoticed, nor has it remained unchallenged. Rosanne Rabinowitz's novella "Helen's Story" (2015) is a clear attempt to even out the scales and let Machen's voiceless heroine account for herself in a way that nineteenth-century *fin de siècle* culture seemed to deny her. This is typical of feminist and

post-colonialist reworkings of Victorian misogynist narratives, such as, for instance, Jean Rhys' *Wide Sargasso Sea* (1966), based on Charlotte Brontë's *Jane Eyre* and centred on the character of Bertha Mason, to whom George Eliot owes the name of her female protagonist in *The Lifted Veil*.

47. Machen, *The Great God Pan*, 53.

48. Helen's power to bring about change is remarked by Dr Matheson, cited here (note 96).

49. See Hillman, "An Essay on Pan." The term "regeneration" owes to contemporary writers George Egerton and Alfred Egmont Hake. Resurrection is used by Machen with reference to London, "the city of resurrections" (*The Great God Pan*, 21).

50. A definition of the "New Woman" is complex, contested, if not contradictory. As Lynn Pynkett argues, "the New Woman was by turns a mannish amazon and a Womanly Woman; she was over sexed, undersexed, or same sex identified, or man-hating and/or man-eating, or self-appointed saviour of benighted masculinity; she was anti-domestic, or she sought to make domestic values prevail; she was radical, socialist or revolutionary, or she was reactionary and conservative; she was the agent of social and/or racial regeneration, or symptom and agent of decline." See Lyn Pykett, "Foreword," in *The New Woman in Fiction and Fact: Fin de Siècle Feminism*, ed. Angelique Richardson and Chris Willis (New York: Palgrave, 2001), xii.

51. Ibid.

52. Nicholas Ruddick, "The Fantastic Fiction of the Fin de Siècle," in *The Cambridge Companion to the fin de siècle*, ed. Gail Marshall, 189–206 (Cambridge: Cambridge University Press, 2007), 193. This is in contrast with Denisoff's suggestion of a "sustained misogynistic strain in [Machen's] attitude," while also acknowledging that the Welsh author "perceived women as strong forces in contemporary British culture and politics." See Denisoff, *Decadent and Occult Works*, 6.

53. Holland, *A Brief History of Misogyny*, 192.

54. Ruddick, "The Fantastic Fiction of the Fin de Siècle," 193.

55. Samuel Taylor Coleridge, "Kubla Khan," in *Selected Poems* (London: Routledge, 2002), 178. Machen claimed to have had a vision, as Coleridge also had before he wrote the fragment entitled "Kubla Khan."

56. George Eliot, *The Lifted Veil and Brother Jacob* (Oxford: Oxford University Press, 2009), 26 and 35. Emphasis added.

57. Loredana Salis, "'The Alchemy of Writing': George Eliot's Representations of Gender in *The Lifted Veil*," *Rivista di Studi Vittoriani* 45 (2018), 77–90, 81.

58. Ruddick, "The Fantastic Fiction of the Fin de Siècle," 193.

59. Stott, *The Fabrication of the Late Victorian Femme Fatale*, 49 and 30.

60. Lyn Pykett, *The "Improper" Feminine: The Women's Sensation Novel and the New Woman Writing*, 1st ed. (London: Routledge, 1992), 154.

61. Machen's first encounter with occultism occurred as early as 1855, at the time when George Redway, the bookseller, asked him to compile a catalogue entitled *The Literature of Occultism and Archaeology: Being a Catalogue of Books on Sale Relating to Ancient Worships, Astrology, Alchemy*. See Machen, *Autobiography*, 165. In 1887, the Welsh writer married his muse, Amelia (Amy) Hogg, with whom he

shared occult interests and practices. Amelia's death in 1899 was to Machen an irreparable loss that altered his views on religion and spiritual philosophy and changed his aesthetics. "The Great God Pan" ought to be read in the light of his private life and especially of his bond with the woman who nourished his creative genius throughout that decade. As Susan Johnston Graf maintains, "Machen was taken in hand by an independent woman, thirteen years his senior," whose presence in the writer's life accounts for "the sexuality inherent in [much of the power of his 1890s narratives]." Graf, *Talking to the Gods*, 66.

62. Machen, *The Great God Pan*, 23.

63. Stephan Karschay, *Degeneration, Normativity and the Gothic at the Fin de Siècle* (London: Palgrave Macmillan, 2015), 106.

64. Machen, *The Great God Pan*, 43.

65. Joanne Townsend, "Marriage, Motherhood and the Future of the Race: Syphilis in Late-Victorian and Edwardian Britain," in *Syphilis and Subjectivity: From the Victorians to the Present*, ed. Kari Nixon and Lorenzo Servitje, 67–91 (London: Palgrave Macmillan, 2017), 74.

66. Showalter, "Syphilis, Sexuality, and the Fiction of the *fin de siècle*," 88.

67. Holland, *A Brief History of Misogyny*, 207. This was in keeping with following the Victorian contention that sexual desire on a woman's part was a sign of "disease."

68. Showalter, "Syphilis," 93.

69. Adrian Eckersley, "A Theme in the Early Work of Arthur Machen: 'Degeneration'," *English Literature in Transition, 1880–1920* 35, no. 3 (1992), 277–87, 285.

70. Quoted in Holland, *A Brief History of Misogyny*, 187.

71. Quoted in Tropp, *Images of Fear*, 137. Emphasis added.

72. Ibid. Emphasis added.

73. For an in-depth study of the theme, see Gemma Persico, *Madonne, maddalene e altre vittoriane: modelli femminili nella letteratura inglese al tempo della Regina Vittoria: i testi e il contesto*, vols. 1–5 (Sarzana: Agorà & Co., 2011).

74. Early Victorian texts tend to portray Pan as a kind of benevolent god of nature. In these depictions, the Greek god resides in a *locus amoenus*, an edenic place far removed from Machen's sterile laboratories or dark, dismal London streets. In texts such as Keats' *Endymion* (1818), Pan is variously represented as a benign overseer, or a giver of life. Later texts present Pan more frequently as an almost Bacchic figure, a lustful, phallic being as in D.H. Lawrence's *The Plumed Serpent* (1926), or else an arcane, diabolic creature with tendencies towards the malevolent, as alluded to by Robert Louis Stevenson in *Virginibus Puerisque* (1881).

75. Catherine Johns, *Sex or Symbol? Erotic Images of Greece and Rome* (London: British Museum Press, 1999), 48.

76. Ibid.

77. In "The Inmost Light" the glimpse on Mrs. Black's face is described as "the visage of a satyr." See Machen, *The Great God Pan*, 60.

78. Machen's vision of Pan as too terrifying for mortal eyes may be influenced by Eusebius' *De Praeparatio Evangelica:* "Being one of the good daemons [Pan] appeared once upon a time to those who were working in the fields ... Those to whom

this blessed sight was vouchsafed all died at once." See Patricia Merivale, *Pan the Goat-God: His Myth in Modern Times* (Cambridge, MA: Harvard University Press, 1969), 162.

79. Machen, *The Great God Pan*, 50. Emphasis added.

80. Ibid.

81. Machen's use of Pan in a story that is about decadence and regeneration echoes an earlier tale by another prominent literary figure of that decade, Jean Lorrain. In "Magic Lantern" (1891) a character called Monsieur laments the effects of science on man and his "capacity for passion": "A yes—he says—great Pan is dead, and you are numbered among those who have killed him—yes, you Monsieur Physicist." In the exchange Pan is taken as an emblem of the passions and of poetry, "which is Fantasy," killed by "Modern Science" and its "horrid mania to explain everything." Jean Lorraine, "Magic Lantern," in *Late Victorian Gothic Tales*, ed. Roger Luckhurst (Oxford: Oxford World's Classics, 2005), 171–76, 172.

82. Hugh E. M. Stutfield, "From Hugh E. M. Stutfield, 'Tommyrotics' (1895)," in *The Fin de Siècle: A Reader in Cultural History c.1880-1900*, ed. Sally Ledger and Roger Luckhurst, 120–26 (Oxford: Oxford University Press, 2000), 124.

83. Decline, in Nordau's view, is a radical decadence by which the degenerate "sinks somatically to the level of fishes, nay to that of the arthropoda, or, even further, to that of rhizopods not yet sexually differentiated . . . perhaps even to the bristles of worms" (*Degeneration*, 535).

84. Tropp, *Images of Fear*, 8.

85. Machen, *The Great God Pan*, xv. Machen's attempt in 1916 to distance himself from the movement and literary productions was not "to erase his connections . . . with Decadent aesthetics" but rather, as Denisoff suggests, "to distance himself from the caricature of Decadence developed by critics and parodists of the period" (*Decadent and Occult Works by Arthur Machen*, 8). See Machen's introduction to the 1916 edition of "The Great God Pan" (repr. in Denisoff, 300–07). It may be added that it was also an attempt to "come further," define his place and claim his value as a professional writer within the British literary canon of the *fin de siècle*. For an insightful analysis of the expression "to come forward," see Carol A. Bock, "Authorship, the Brontës, and *Fraser's Magazine*. 'Coming Forward' as an Author in Early Victorian England," *Victorian Literature and Culture* 29 (2001), 56–69.

86. For influences of Machen's childhood landscapes, see his introduction to the 1916 edition of "The Great God Pan." For his experience of the occult while married to Amy Hogg, see Graf, *Talking to the Gods*, 66.

87. William Francis Gekle, *Arthur Machen, Weaver of Fantasy* (Millbrook, NY: Round Table Press, 1949), 132.

88. Hillman, "An Essay on Pan," 24.

REFERENCES

Acton, Harry Burrows. "Herbert Spencer." *Encyclopedia Brittanica*, Jan. 13, 2021. http://www.britannica.com/biography/Herbert-Spencer.

Bock, Carol A. "Authorship, the Brontës, and *Fraser's Magazine*. 'Coming Forward' as an Author in Early Victorian England." *Victorian Literature and Culture* 29 (2001): 56–69.

Dionisio, Fiammetta. *New Women. Ansie di degenerazione e profezie di rinascita nell'Inghilterra di fin de siècle*. Roma: Aracne, 2017.

Eckersley, Adrian. "A Theme in the Early Work of Arthur Machen: 'Degeneration.'" *English Literature in Transition, 1880-1920* 35, no. 3 (1992): 277–87.

Gilhus, Ingvild Saelid, *Laughing Gods, Weeping Virgins: Laughter in the History of Religion*. London: Routledge, 2013.

Eliot, George. *The Lifted Veil and Brother Jacob* [1859]. Oxford: Oxford University Press, 2009.

Gekle, William Francis. *Arthur Machen, Weaver of Fantasy*. Millbrook, NY: Round Table Press, 1949.

Hake, Alfred Egmont. *Regeneration: A Reply to Max Nordau*. Westminster: Archibald Constable, 1895.

Halliday, Stephen. "Death and Miasma in Victorian London: An Obstinate Belief." *British Medical Journal*, 323, no. 7327 (2001): 1469–71, https://www.ncbi.nlm.nih.gov/pmc/articles/PMC1121911/.

Hamilton, Margaret. "Opposition to the Contagious Diseases Acts, 1864-1886." *Albion: A Quarterly Journal Concerned with British Studies* 10, no. 1 (1978): 14–27.

Hillman, James. "An Essay on Pan." In *Pan and the Nightmare*. New York: Spring, 1972.

Holland, Jack. *A Brief History of Misogyny: The World's Oldest Prejudice*. London: Robinson, 2006.

Hunt Margaret. "The De-eroticization of Women's Liberation: Social Purity Movements and the Revolutionary Feminism of Sheila Jeffreys." *Feminist Review* 34, Perverse Politics: Lesbian Issues (Spring 1990): 23–46.

Hurley, Kelly. *The Gothic Body Sexuality, Materialism, and Degeneration at the Fin de Siècle*. Cambridge: Cambridge University Press, 1996.

Johns, Catherine. *Sex or Symbol? Erotic Images of Greece and Rome*. London: British Museum Press, 1999.

Johnston Graf, Susan. *Talking to the Gods. Occultism in the Works of W.B. Yeats, Arthur Machen, Algernon Blackwood, and Dion Fortune*. New York: SUNY Press, 2015.

Karschay, Stephan. *Degeneration, Normativity and the Gothic at the Fin de Siècle*. London: Palgrave Macmillan, 2015.

Lansbury, Coral. "Gynaecology, Pornography, and the Antivivisection Movement." *Victorian Studies* 28, no. 3 (1985): 413–37.

Machen, Arthur. *The Autobiography of Arthur Machen*. London: The Richards Press, 1951.

———. *The Great God Pan and Other Horror Stories*, edited by Aaron Worth. Oxford: Oxford University Press, 2018.

Merivale, Patricia. *Pan the Goat-God: His Myth in Modern Times*. Cambridge, MA: Harvard University Press, 1969.

Nordau, Simon Max. *Degeneration* [1892], translated by Howard Fertig. Frankfurt: Outlook Verlag, 2018.
Persico, Gemma. *Madonne, maddalene e altre vittoriane: modelli femminili nella letteratura inglese al tempo della Regina Vittoria: i testi e il contesto*, vols. 1–5. Sarzana: Agorà, 2011.
Pykett, Lynn. *Engendering Fictions. The English Novel in the Early Twentieth Century*. London: Edward Arnold, 1995.
———. "Foreword." In *The New Woman in Fiction and Fact: Fin de Siècle Feminism*, edited by Angelique Richardson and Chris Willis, xii. New York: Palgrave, 2001.
———. *The "Improper" Feminine: The Women's Sensation Novel and the New Woman Writing*. London: Routledge, 1992.
Rimke, Heidi and Alan Hunt. "From Sinners to Degenerates: The Medicalization of Morality in the 19th Century." *History of the Human Sciences* 15, no. 1 (2002): 59–88.
Ruddick, Nicholas. "The Fantastic Fiction of the Fin de Siècle." In *The Cambridge Companion to The Fin De Siècle*, edited by Gail Marshall, 189–206. Cambridge: Cambridge University Press, 2007.
Showalter, Elaine. "Syphilis, Sexuality, and the Fiction of the Fin de Siécle." In *Sex, Politics, and Science in the Nineteenth-Century Novel*, edited by Ruth Bernard Yeazell, 88–115. Baltimore, MD: The Johns Hopkins University Press, 1986.
Stott, Rebecca. *The Fabrication of the Late Victorian Femme Fatale*. Hampshire: Macmillan Press, 1992.
Stutfield, Hugh E.M. "From Hugh E.M. Stutfield, 'Tommyrotics' (1895)." In *The Fin de Siècle: A Reader in Cultural History c.1880-1900*, edited by Sally Ledger and Roger Luckhurst, 120–26. Oxford: Oxford University Press, 2000.
Townsend, Joanne. "Marriage, Motherhood and the Future of the Race: Syphilis in Late Victorian and Edwardian Britain." In *Syphilis and Subjectivity: From the Victorians to the Present*, edited by Kari Nixon and Lorenzo Servitje, 67–91. London: Palgrave Macmillan, 2017.
Tropp, Martin. *Images of Fear: How Horror Stories Helped Shape Modern Culture (1818-1918)*. Jefferson, NC: McFarland Classics, 1990.
Wagner, Corinna. *Gothic Evolutions: Poetry, Tales, Context, Theory*. Peterborough: Broadview Press, 2014.

Part III

SPIRITUALITY

Chapter 9

"[A] Mystic, Ineffable Force and Energy"

Arthur Machen and Theories of New Materialism

Adrian Tait

This chapter explores the work of Arthur Machen from the perspective of new materialist theories; in particular, it relates his fiction to Karen Barad's theory of agential realism. As the discussion of works such as "The Terror" (1917), *The Hill of Dreams* (1907), and *A Fragment of Life* (1904) demonstrates, Machen's ideas about the reintegration of the spiritual and material worlds align his views with Barad's monistic theory of material entanglement in sometimes surprising ways. With their emphasis on the vitality of the material world, theories of new materialism such as Barad's have readily found a place within the environmental humanities.[1] As Barad has explained, the aim of an agential realism is to shift the theoretical focus back toward a now neglected, subordinate material world, while also emphasizing the extent of our entanglement with it, and by extension, "the real consequences . . . and responsibilities of intra-acting within and as part of the world."[2] For Barad, "*values are integral to the nature of knowing and being*" (emphasis in the original), a message that resonates strongly with environmentalist concerns.[3] As Barad also insists, "the entanglement of matter and meaning calls into question [the] set of dualisms that places nature on one side and culture on the other."[4] These dualisms constitute what Val Plumwood has described as an oppressive "logic of colonization" that is integral to Western thinking.[5] In addition, and while Barad's theory reasserts the importance of matter, it does not exclude "discursive practices" from consideration, since discourse is itself caught up in the co-constitution of the material world.[6] Rather, Barad's theory is concerned with "material-discursive"—or "naturalcultural"—practices.[7]

In turn, Barad's theory suggests a fresh way in which to approach Machen's work. Arthur Machen has variously been described as a writer of horror stories and supernatural tales, and as one of "the 'modern masters' of weird fiction."[8] Of late, his work has prompted "a veritable explosion" of critical interest, not least in relation to his engagement with the occult.[9] As critics have also stressed, Machen "was pre-eminently a writer of place," and of the spirit of place, or the "pagan . . . *genius loci.*"[10] Like theories of new materialism, with their emphasis on "the world's radical aliveness," Machen's narratives insist on the agentiality of the nonhuman and more-than-human worlds.[11] In "The Terror," for example, Machen's narrative specifically attributes "agency" and even the possibility of a "malignant design" to "non-human creatures," and claims that they have "revolted against men," in so doing blurring one of the most fundamental of the dis-associative dualisms to which Plumwood refers: the separation between (human) culture and (nonhuman) nature.[12] This "conspiracy against the human race" is terrifying not only because of the very real threat it poses to human life, but because, more insidiously, it destroys the comfortable certainties on which a distinctively human civilization is raised, and in particular, the foundational belief that humans alone possess sufficient intelligence to act in a concerted and coordinated fashion.[13] Furthermore, and while "The Terror" works from within a broadly realist framework, the narrative suggests at its conclusion that the meaning of nature's apparent revolt can only be found in the realm of mysteries that lie beyond the powers of reason to explain, or realism to depict. Machen's comment on the agency of matter is also, therefore, a response to the discursive practices of his day, and the limitations those practices imposed on writers with the imagination to see beyond a narrowly materialistic interpretation of the world's meaning.

As this example suggests, Machen's work offers a suggestive critique of Western ways of thinking—and in particular, its dualistic logic of colonization—that also overlaps with Barad's own arguments. While agential realism offers a potentially persuasive way of reevaluating Machen's works at the level of both content *and* form, however, the example of "The Terror" also exposes the obvious conceptual difficulty of bringing one to bear on the other. At the end of the story, the narrator hazards a guess that "the beasts" have risen up against their masters because they recognize that "man" has sacrificed his spirituality to rationalism, and in so doing, conceded their sovereignty over the animal world.[14] This emphasis on the spiritual is typical of Machen's "view of the world."[15] As Machen affirmed in the "Novel of the White Powder," "[t]he whole universe . . . is a tremendous sacrament; a mystic, ineffable force and energy, veiled by an outward form of matter."[16] Moreover, Machen's work reflects not only his spiritual concerns but his lifelong resistance to "science and materialism" and "the scientizing of the supernatural."[17] Clearly, these aspects of Machen's thought suggest a fundamental discontinuity or disjuncture between his own outlook, and a theory of new materialism such as Barad's, which is rooted in quantum physics, and specifically intended to reassert the importance of the material world.[18]

At the same time, however, Barad's account of "technoscientific and other naturalcultural practices" does not in and of itself rule out dimensions of experience that might also be termed "spiritual."[19] Nor is Machen's religiosity rigidly conventional. As Nicholas Freeman suggests, Machen's religious views were idiosyncratic and anti-dogmatic: the universe may be a sacrament, but as the narrator in the "Novel of the White Powder" also insists, "man, and the sun and the other stars, and the flower of the grass, and the crystal in the test tube, are each and every one as spiritual, as material, and subject to an inner working."[20] Views such as these bear out Susan Johnston Graf's observation that, at least during the 1890s, Machen was "deeply immersed in occult studies," and more concerned with an autonomous, personal form of mysticism than with orthodox belief.[21] Indeed, it might even be argued that Machen's idiosyncratic and allusive expression of that mysticism itself emerges as a form of eco-spirituality: as the self merges with the totality of existence, as Lucian's consciousness does during the hallucinatory experiences that Machen describes in *The Hill of Dreams*, the dizzying result seems to be a (dismaying) version of the deep ecological vision proposed by Arne Naess.[22]

Consequently, the next step in this rereading of Machen's work is to explore the agential realist perspective in more detail, and, mindful of the potential for differences between the two, relate it to Machen's own strong sense of a world that is itself alive. In so doing, it becomes clear that Machen's ideas are more idiosyncratic—and the implications of Barad's theory more radical—than might at first be apparent. As this chapter argues, the two perspectives converge in what might be described as "hypernaturalism—an expanded sense of what the material cosmos contains."[23]

As Barad's use of neologisms such as "naturalcultural" underlines, a theory of agential realism is intended as a counter to the pervasive but also divisive logic of Western thought, which privileges reason and culture at the expense of nature and matter. In *Feminism and the Mastery of Nature*, published in 1993, Plumwood argued that "the western concept of progress and development" is rooted in the "continual and cumulative overcoming of the domain of nature by reason," and reason has in turn been established as a "privileged domain" from which "the sphere of materiality" is separated out and constructed as "subordinate other."[24] This dualistic opposition between "reason" and "nature" has formed the basis for a series of "interrelated and mutually reinforcing dualisms," such as human/nature, mind/body, civilized/primitive, and male/female, all of which serve "the construction of a devalued and sharply demarcated sphere of otherness."[25] A theory such as Barad's—a theory which emphasizes the complex entanglements that bind together nature and culture, matter and discourse, mind and body—is also one, by extension, that contends with this dualistic and oppressive logic, and challenges the very basis of what has been thought of in the West as ineluctable "progress."

Machen unfolds a similar argument. He was strongly critical of "the course of modern civilization" and of the rationalist, dualistic structures that underpinned it; he also saw reality as lively and dynamic.[26] From the "dry mutter of the trees" and the "wind shrilling through the wood" to the "murmur of the brook" and the "pale light flowing from the mouldered trunks," the world that Machen describes in (for example) *The Hill of Dreams* is alive and agential.[27] For Machen's human protagonists, however, such a world is also one in which they are "at risk of losing agency": it is "unknown, terrible," and humans respond with "panic terror."[28] Indeed, Machen's story "The Great God Pan" (1894) goes to the root of that phrase, "panic terror," by invoking the state of fear induced by the sudden reappearance of Pan, the mythic demi-God associated with nonhuman nature. Like the agential materiality for which he might be said to stand, Pan is, as Dennis Denisoff notes, not singular but "multiple and all-pervasive," and while Pan is sensed rather than seen in the story, he is sufficiently material to leave a trail of death in his wake.[29] As such, Pan bridges "the world of matter and the world of spirit," or, as Jake Poller argues, the "noumenal and phenomenal worlds," once again collapsing dualistic oppositions; indeed, Pan's human embodiment, Helen, is revealed in death to come from "*prima materia*, the fundamental matter from which all forms derive."[30] In *The Hill of Dreams*, by contrast, Lucian's imbrication in a landscape of memory and affect blurs the dualistic divide between subject and object: looking back over his visionary experience of Caermaen and its surroundings (discussed in more detail below), it seems to Lucian that "his very soul was being moulded into the hills."[31] Nor does Lucian's subsequent life in London re-encode a further dualistic opposition—that of the city, as symbol of human culture, and country, as symbol of "Nature." On the contrary, his experiences in the city culminate in visionary experiences that are no less immersive: "he could not shut out the sight of an orgy of dusky figures whirling in a ring, of lurid naptha flares blazing in the darkness."[32]

In spite, however, of these obvious parallels between a theory of agential realism and Machen's work, the obvious difficulty remains: Barad's theory insists on the importance of matter, while Machen—as S.T. Joshi notes—consistently relates his critique of modernity to the spiritual.[33] Yet Machen's belief in what Denisoff calls "the reality of the supernatural" is itself suggestive.[34] Machen is often described as a writer of occult or weird tales, terms which carry within them the suggestion of the supernatural or mystical, but "occult" may simply mean hidden or concealed, while "weird" can simply refer to what is unusual. As Mark Fisher argues, "weird" tales are preoccupied with what is strange: they have to do with "a fascination for the outside, for that which lies beyond standard perception, cognition and experience," and while there are "terrors to be found there," they "are not all there is to the outside."[35] As Fisher contends, a further mode—the eerie—can be distinguished from the weird.[36] While weird is "constituted by . . . the presence of *that which does not belong*," Fisher suggests, the eerie is "is constituted by a *failure of absence* or by a *failure of presence*."[37]

This distinction between the weird and the eerie is a helpful way in which to approach Machen's fiction. In "The Terror," for example, a man is found dead with his open mouth crowded with moths.[38] However, the moths have not settled there after his violent death; it is they who have suffocated him. To the characters in the novella, this is weird: an active, agential, even malevolent nature has no place in a modern world. In Fisher's terms, it is "*that which does not belong*."[39] Yet Machen's own argument is different. Nature is always already agential, but as Machen's narratives suggest, it has been subjugated so successfully that modern society has forgotten that it was ever anything other than passive, pliable, and inert. It has receded into the background. Nature resurgent—the nature described in Machen's tale—is not something that does not belong (the definition of weird) but something that has, to the consternation of all those affected by it, failed to remain absent (the definition of eerie). And by failing to remain dormant, hidden, or forgotten, it has revealed the inadequacy of "our conceptions."[40]

The significance of Fisher's distinction lies in the fact that, in Machen's tales, the weird thing is "not wrong, after all"; it belongs.[41] Often, it will transpire, Machen is attacking materialistic, rationalistic modernity, but doing so by referring back to what he perceives to be forgotten ways of seeing, understanding, and being, which in turn relate directly to our entanglements with the more-than-human world. These entanglements are so profound, however, that the more-than-human world is not necessarily registered as external; for those of his characters who recover the modes of perception to which Machen refers, that world is integral, internal. Like a "collective cultural memory," it waits within.[42]

This is, for example, the way in which Machen's protagonists experience the eerie in *A Fragment of Life*. Outwardly, the Darnells live a thoroughly conventional, lower-middle-class life in a London suburb; Darnell is described as "an English City clerk, 'flourishing' towards the end of the nineteenth century."[43] But as the narrative insists, the Darnells are actually living "in the grey phantasmal world, akin to death, that has, somehow, with most of us, made good its claim to be called life."[44] Yet Darnell is repeatedly haunted by a dream of an "ancient wood, and of a clear well" that awakes in him memories of his ancestral identity, and of "the forgotten country in the west."[45] Amidst everything that is prosaic and ordinary, Darnell begins to piece together a deeper, more spiritual existence. His mystical education transforms him, and it also transmutes the world of which he is a part.[46] Traipsing the London streets, Darnell comes to see the city as itself "strange and wonderful."[47] As his walks take him further afield and out into "open country," however, Darnell realizes that his "voyage of discovery" is in fact a voyage of rediscovery.[48] His wife, Mary, is similarly entangled with the half-remembered "rapture [of a] deep and happy valley."[49] For both, the recovery of an eerie, "deep past" reflects its continued hold over them, and what they feel is "not horror but *fascination*" at the thought of half-remembered but radically different ways of being.[50]

As Machen's narrative suggests, recovering these lost ways is not just an ontological challenge, but a conceptual and representational one, and it lies beyond the capacity of the conventional, realist narrative. Whether or not the Darnells depart London is left for the reader to guess; the narrative simply announces that "[i]t would be impossible to carry on [their] history . . . since from this point their legend is full of impossible events."[51] The narrator of "The Terror" is in a similar difficulty. Rightly concluding that animals are in revolt against human mastery, he nevertheless sees evidence of a greater mystery—a "trembling vibration of the air," trees that visibly grow, and "the apparition of secret fires among them"—that defies rational (and hence his own) understanding.[52] Constrained by his own rationalism, and by the associated limits of the realist narrative, the narrator is simply powerless to explain what these strange signs might mean. In effect, the narrative confesses its own powerlessness. Perhaps Lucian is right when, in *The Hill of Dreams*, he concludes that, far from winning "the secret of words" or the "great secret of language," he has in fact reached their limits: "he no longer believed that language could present the melody and the awe and the loveliness of the earth."[53]

Here, there is a further, powerful parallel between the challenge that Machen set himself—that of depicting "a reality beyond immediate experience, and beyond the conventions of realism"—and the difficulties raised by Barad's own relational theory.[54] For those who recognize in agential realism a way in which to interrogate the subject-object divide, the difficulty lies in conceptualizing, comprehending, and hence representing the mutual entanglement to which Barad refers. Barad's theory suggests a continuous, iterative process of co-constitution, as what we think of as our "selves" are continuously reconfigured through our entanglement with the environment which we in turn affect, and from which we are in fact, inseparable except in the moment; only in the moment does the self-emerge as an independent entity ("[w]hich is not to say," as Barad adds, "that emergence happens once and for all").[55] Yet Western thought has long asserted the autonomy and persistence of the sovereign self, which is invariably conceived of as distinct from its surroundings (a distinction that is itself an essential element in the dualistic structures to which Plumwood refers). In turn, this kind of individualistic thinking has its corollary in the stories we tell about ourselves, stories that tend to reinforce the idea that humans have their own distinct paths and satisfying destinies that are their own to control and dictate. Reason itself supports this mode of story-telling, in which events proceed logically, and are narrated reasonably; they coincide with "our 'natural attitude' about the world."[56] Indeed, there is a strong relationship between the emergence of the realist novel in the nineteenth century, and the rise of science, with its insistence on the importance of facts in a world shaped by immutable but also logical laws.

Consequently, it is significant that Machen's most distinctive narratives depart from the realist mode, and instead adopt an "anti-realist Decadent style of writing."[57] There are, for example, strong resemblances between Machen's "masterpiece," *The Hill of Dreams*, and the Decadent "devotion to exquisitely crafted style in literature, and in life to the quest for new sensations, involving variously the exploration of the occult, the exotic, the sexually unorthodox, the bohemian way of life, and a taste for strong drugs and drink."[58] In *The Hill of Dreams*, Mark Valentine argues, Machen "allies himself with the Decadents."[59] It is notable, nonetheless, that the novel's Decadent tropes—its focus on Lucian's experiences, his sensations, his fascination with the mysterious, and his increasingly tormented attempt to "make the form of it and the awe of it in prose"—emerge as if organically from the novella's thematic emphasis on the entanglement of people and place.[60] Lucian's life is both literally and metaphorically overshadowed by the hill to which the title refers, "the black sheer height rising above the valley," with its "weird wood noises."[61] Once again, nature is shown to be strangely agential—"stem and root began to stir; the wood was alive"—but nature is never shown to be a thing apart from the human world, or more precisely, apart from Lucian's experiences.[62] To Lucian, it seems as if his experiences "upon the fairy hill" have merged him with his surroundings: "a changeling had gone down into the hill, and now stirred about the earth."[63]

Entrapped by "the mesh of the hills," Lucian's highly subjectivized experiences form the substance of a novella in which, like *A Fragment of Life*, little happens, but what happens is deeply significant and exhaustively detailed.[64] As Lucian seeks "the true science of the exquisite," sensation is prioritized over plot.[65] Lucian's mental recreation of Caermaen, "once the glorious capital of [Roman] Siluria," is a case in point.[66] Raising a "rare and wonderful city" in his imagination, he calls it "Avallaunius."[67] Absenting himself from "dull modern life," Lucian instead inhabits his imaginary town:

> Lucian wandered all day through the shining trees, taking shelter sometimes in the gardens beneath the dense and gloomy ilex trees, and listening to the plash

and trickle of the fountains. Sometimes he would look out of a window and watch the crowd and colour of the market-place, and now and again a ship came up the river bringing exquisite silks and the merchandise of unknown lands.[68]

In mocking echo of the realist novel's emphasis on facticity, the physical fabric of Lucian's invented world is described in great detail: Lucian maps and names "every villa," and dwells lovingly on the physical details of the life he describes.[69] But as the reader must recognize, this world is not real, except to Lucian, whose immersion in it is so disturbingly total that his day-to-day life recedes from him and itself become unreal, so much so that Lucian's physical frame begins to waste and starve; "entranced in the garden of Avallaunius," he grows "thinner and thinner."[70] At this point, it is no longer so clear what constitutes the reality with which the novella is engaged or which it sets out to describe. "Truth and the dream were now so mingled that he could not divide one from the other."[71] The only certain things in this confusing landscape are the sensations and experiences that the narrative attributes to Lucian as he loses himself ever more completely in his own creation.

In Machen's provocative fiction, therefore, the real world is shown to be a pretense, and Lucian's fictive world is shown to be real. How, then, can that world be related to a theory of new materialism, with its insistence on the physical plane? Strictly, materialist philosophy discounts the existence of mind apart from matter, just as it also rejects a supernatural dimension to human existence. But this is not (or not quite) the implication of Barad's theory of agential realism. As Barad argues, all matter emerges as itself only through an unending process of "entangled intra-relating," "dynamic" and "iterative."[72] It follows that what we think of as the world is also the world as it emerges from and through our own being—and vice versa—a point that Barad explains by highlighting the way in which, at the quantum level, the observer of an experiment affects the outcome of it: necessarily, Barad's emphasis on "the entanglement of matter and meaning" implies the entanglement of mind and matter.[73] In other words, the concept of intra-activity readmits the role of the mind—but also and equally the role of emotions, feelings, or sensations—as themselves agential. Each affects what we experience, because what we experience is not separable from us. Thus, Lucian's vision of Avallaunius is not simply an imaginative recreation of a real Roman city, "real" only insofar as it is a self-enclosed "vision." In the moment of its resolution, as Lucian recognizes, an ancient reality exists and is itself entangled with his own, nineteenth-century world.

Another way of attempting a paraphrase of Lucian's experience is by suggesting that time itself has become fluid. In "Arthur Machen and the Horrors of Deep History," Aaron Worth draws attention to Machen's imaginative response to the scalar challenge of deep or geological time, as the Victorians had begun to encounter it, but Machen's response was not to regard it as in some way annihilatory: Machen, for one, did not dwell on his own utter inconsequentiality when confronted with the vast timescales of the planet's history. On the contrary, the Welsh writer conceptualized time as a fluid dimension, or perhaps even as a series of dimensions, each persisting and overlapping. The trope of the "little people," a savage but not entirely primitive survival of an earlier stage in human evolution, is one of the ways in which Machen expressed that sense of time as something other than predictable, singular, linear, evolutionary, or even progressive.[74] Our own recognition of the inseparability of time and space—a recognition that Machen may have in very general terms intuited—makes it possible (if no less difficult) for us to conceive of the kind of transgressive coevality that Machen entertained, and to which Lucian's story gives expression. Here, the narrative suggests, time has folded back on itself, and through the mesh that we mistake for a single, coherent, monolithic "reality," we glimpse further realities beyond it. As Barad has herself suggested, "time and space, like matter and meaning, come into existence, are iteratively reconfigured through each intra-action, thereby making it impossible to differentiate in any absolute sense between . . . beginning and returning, continuity and discontinuity, here and there, past and future."[75] "The past is never finished," a point borne out by Lucian's trans-historical experiences, as he is commanded by the voices of "his far-off ancestors": "[t]he Celt assailed him, beckoning from the weird wood he called the world."[76]

As it may now be clear, Barad's claims are themselves radical; a concept of co-constitutive, quantum intra-activity enacts a decisive shift away from the "naïve realism" that classical science takes for granted (i.e., the assumption that matter exists, is independent of us, but is also accessible to us).[77] As such, agential realism represents a marked departure from the kind of scientific understanding to which Machen himself objected. What is more, Machen's imaginative exercises in thinking again about the relationship between an individual and his or her lived experience gave rise to statements about the nature of reality which today seem much less unscientific than Machen could, perhaps, have anticipated. The modern concept of multiple universes (or of a "multiverse") is not in or of itself spiritual—although it is nevertheless debatable whether it is a philosophical as opposed to a scientific hypothesis—but it opens the door to the possibility that "otherworldly" dimensions do exist. Similarly, the growing recognition of matter's agentiality (but also of humankind's limitations in recognizing the timescales—exceptionally long or short—over which matter may operate) suggests a reinterpretation of the supernatural not as a realm or dimension beyond nature, but as a part of a nature that is itself infinitely more extensive, heterogeneous, and active than any proponent of nineteenth-century science would have accepted. Since

Machen's work is concerned with a much-expanded sense of what constitutes nature, theories such as these beg the question of whether Machen's tales are after all supernatural, or whether they offer an insight into the kind of expanded consciousness and "deepened realism" proposed by deep ecologists.[78] Perhaps "it is only our ignorance of certain 'natural laws'"—or, as Machen suggests, our forgetfulness of them—"that creates the illusion of supernaturalism."[79] "Our great loss," argues Machen's narrator in *The Secret Glory* (written in 1907; first published in 1922), "is that we separate what is one and make it two; and then, having done so, we make the less real into the more real."[80] The "life of bodily things is *hard*," the narrator continues, and as a consequence we accept its existence, its naturalness, its inevitability, yet "the air about us is just as substantial as a mountain or a cathedral."[81] The fault or failing lies in our inability to see beyond the limits of our senses, and recognize the eerie in everyday life.[82] But as Machen's narrator also insists, a truly spiritual state is one that collapses these conceptual divides through our own bodily experience: "[t]hrough the joy of the body I possessed the joy of the spirit."[83]

There is one final point of contact between Machen's views, and Barad's theory. In Machen's opinion, fiction itself has a part to play in bridging the divides that he had identified, by offering what Christine Ferguson describes as "ecstasy, awe, and the opportunity for direct encounter with a hidden ancient wisdom tradition associated contemporarily with occult experience."[84] "It may turn out after all that the weavers of fantasy are the veritable realists," Machen would later observe, but not just because those weavers were capable of describing a lost reality: Machen believed that the right kind of writing could itself "induce a spontaneous and epiphanic encounter."[85] For Machen, literature was active, not passive, and not simply mimetic: it offered "an alternative way of viewing the world" because, as Barad has herself argued, discourse is itself agential.[86] In Barad's terms, stories such as Machen's are among the "material-discursive factors" responsible for "reconfiguring the material-social relations of the world."[87]

"[D]oes scientific knowledge accurately represent an independently existing reality?" Barad has asked; "[d]oes language accurately represent its referent?"[88] The answer, she insists, is that neither does. Given the nature of quantum entanglement, subject and object are no more clearly distinguishable than matter is independent of discourse. Dualism itself is a fiction, a falsity on which the Western world's logic of domination has been raised. It also follows, however, that fiction itself may act substantively, shaping the world, and shaping our understanding of it: even a "dry plot," as Machen observed, may reveal "itself as a living thing, stirring and mysterious, and warm as life itself."[89] For those who work within the environmental humanities, theories such as Barad's agential realism are profoundly important for the way in which they readmit the material world while simultaneously insisting on the importance of the discursive. When seen from a new materialist perspective, Machen's idiosyncratic fiction itself represents an important and agential response to conventional, dualistic structures of understanding. As Machen wrote in "the anti-realist polemic" *Hieroglyphics* (1902), "man" is "a sacrament, soul manifested under the form of body," and "art has to deal with each and both and to show their interaction and interdependence."[90]

On the one hand, therefore, Machen's narratives point to the entanglements that bind his subjects to their surroundings, blurring what we understand by matter, by mind, but also by spirit; these entanglements are, his narratives suggest, immersive, operative, and as Lucian discovers, inescapable. Immersed in his surroundings, psychically, psychologically, and physically, his death (as a form of dissolution) becomes almost inevitable. On the other hand, Machen's narratives also highlight how difficult it is to conceptualize and represent these entanglements—entanglements that lie "outside theory, outside our theory"—particularly from within a realist framework.[91]

Lucian's own restless and ultimately futile search for new and more perfect forms of literary expression is, in this sense, an expression of Machen's own difficulty: "strange, amazing, ineffable things seemed to have been presented to him, not in the form of ideas, but actually and materially, but . . . he could not, even vaguely, image to himself what he had seen."[92] The ineffable is that which lies beyond expression, but perhaps it may be implied; Lucian himself suspects that it is in "suggestion [that] all the chief secrets of literature" lie, and that "impressions [might] transcend altogether the realm of the formal understanding."[93]

Yet the word "ineffable" can also mean that which must not (as opposed to cannot) be uttered (*OED*), and Machen's willingness to consider both senses of the word is part of his enduring importance as a writer, and relevant not only to a new materialist rereading of his work but to new materialist reinterpretations of human existence. Arguably, theories such as Barad's agential realism point inevitably toward a loss of self (and in its most complete form, as Lucian's fate makes clear, that loss means death), or toward the recognition of an agentiality that lies beyond us, beyond our control, beyond even our ability to comprehend. Neither possibility is necessarily liberatory; each may in fact be terrifying. There is horror in loss, or in loss of self, and there is horror in Machen's work, as his characters reconnect with and surrender to forgotten, primitive, and sometimes brutal realities.

Nevertheless, and as Machen implies in his story of the Darnells, there are also more positive possibilities associated with this expanded sense of self, possibilities that far exceed the terms of new materialist philosophy, but which nevertheless anticipate deep ecological thinking. For Machen, the recognition that an individual is part of a wider totality from which he or she is not, strictly speaking, separate, is a first step toward a sense of the mysterious and the spiritual; for environmental philosophers such as Naess, it is the basis for a "deepened perception of reality" from which sustainable attitudes will naturally flow, and while these are possibilities that a theory of agential realism does not venture to consider, they have their basis in a sense of entanglement that it too shares, and Machen's narratives articulate with compelling intensity.[94]

NOTES

1. Serpil Oppermann and Serenella Iovino (eds), "Introduction," *Environmental Humanities: Voices from the Anthropocene*, 1–21 (London: Rowman & Littlefield, 2017), 12.

2. Karen Barad, *Meeting the Universe Halfway: Quantum Physics and the Entanglement of Matter and Meaning* (London: Duke University Press, 2007), 37.

3. Ibid., 37.

4. Karen Barad, "Interview with Karen Barad," in *New Materialism: Interviews & Cartographies*, by Rick Dolphijn and Iris van der Tuin, 48–70 (Ann Arbor: Open Humanities Press, 2012), 50.

5. Val Plumwood, *Feminism and the Mastery of Nature* (London: Routledge, 1993), 41.

6. Barad, *Meeting the Universe Halfway*, 34, 133.

7. Ibid., 169, 32.

8. S. T. Joshi, *The Evolution of the Weird Tale* (New York: Hippocampus Press, 2004), 7.

9. Aaron Worth, "Introduction," in *The Great God Pan and Other Horror Stories*, by Arthur Machen, ed. Aaron Worth, ix–xxx (Oxford: Oxford University Press, 2018), xi. Recent critical responses include Christine Ferguson's discussion of Machen's centrality to the "late Victorian occult revival," Jake Poller's analysis of the influence of alchemy on Machen's transmutations, Aaron Worth's evaluation of Machen's response to "the depths or abysses of temporality," and Nicholas Freeman's timely reconsideration of "instances of epiphany and ecstasy in Machen's work." See Christine Ferguson, "Reading with the Occultists: Arthur Machen, A. E. Waite, and the Ecstasies of Popular Fiction," *Journal of Victorian Culture* 21, no. 1 (2016): 40–45, 40; Jake Poller, "The Transmutations of Arthur Machen: Alchemy in 'The Great God Pan' and *The Three Imposters*," *Literature & Theology* 29, no. 1 (2015): 18–32; Aaron Worth, "Arthur Machen and the Horrors of Deep History," *Victorian Literature and Culture* 40 (2012): 215–27, 216; and Nicholas Freeman, "Arthur Machen: Ecstasy and Epiphany," *Literature & Theology* 24, no. 3 (2010): 242–55, 243.

10. Worth, Introduction, xi; Dennis Denisoff (ed.), "Introduction," *Decadent and Occult Works*, by Arthur Machen, 1–28 (Cambridge: Modern Humanities Research Association, 2018), 15.

11. Barad, *Meeting the Universe Halfway*, 33.

12. Arthur Machen, *The White People and Other Weird Stories*, ed. S. T. Joshi (London: Penguin, 2011), 349, 355, 352, 352.

13. Ibid., 351–52.

14. Ibid., 357.

15. S. T. Joshi (ed.), "Introduction," *The White People and Other Weird Stories*, by Arthur Machen, xi–xxiv (London: Penguin, 2011), xviii.

16. Machen, *The White People*, 80.

17. S. T. Joshi, *The Weird Tale* (Holicong: Wildside Press, 1990), 14; Poller, "The Transmutations of Arthur Machen," 29.

18. Barad, *Meeting the Universe Halfway*, 36.

19. Ibid., 32.

20. Freeman, "Arthur Machen," 243; Machen, *The White People*, 80.

21. Susan Johnston Graf, *Talking to the Gods: Occultism in the Work of W. B. Yeats, Arthur Machen, Algernon Blackwood, and Dion Fortune* (Albany: State University of New York, 2015), 59.

22. Naess's deep ecological philosophy emphasizes the need for self-realization, but the "wider Self" in question is not the individual; Arne Naess, *Ecology of Wisdom*, eds Alan Drengson and Bill Devall (London: Penguin, 2008), 90. It is, instead, the collective totality of which the individual being forms just one part; self-realization is, by definition, the realization that we are a part of (and not apart from) nature, thereby removing the basis for all forms of divisive, dualistic thought. Once this level of self-realization has been achieved, Naess argues, properly ecological thinking will result, with everything this might mean for a fully sustainable relationship between humankind and its environment. Naess's philosophy has been profoundly influential, but it is also highly problematic, not least because the nature we may encounter through "Self-realization" could in fact be indifferent, even hostile to our needs; Patrick Curry, *Ecological Ethics: An Introduction* (Cambridge: Polity, 2006), 71–72, 77.

23. Mark Fisher, *The Weird and the Eerie* (London: Repeater Books, 2016), 18.

24. Plumwood, *Feminism and the Mastery of Nature*, 3.

25. Plumwood, *Feminism and the Mastery of Nature*, 42, 41.

26. Joshi, *The Weird Tale*, 14.

27. Arthur Machen, *Decadent and Occult Works*, ed. Dennis Denisoff (Cambridge: Modern Humanities Research Association, 2018), 234, 157.

28. Denisoff, "Introduction," 19; Machen, *Decadent and Occult Works*, 234, 312.

29. Denisoff, "Introduction," 43.

30. Machen, *Decadent and Occult Works*, 46; Poller, "The Transmutations of Arthur Machen," 21, 24.

31. Machen, *Decadent and Occult Works*, 196.

32. Ibid., 243.

33. Joshi, *The Weird Tale*, 1–3, 6–7.

34. Denisoff, "Introduction," 11.

35. Fisher, *The Weird and the Eerie*, 8, 9.

36. Ibid., 8.

37. Ibid., 61.

38. Machen, *The White People*, 324, 326.

39. Fisher, *The Weird and the Eerie*, 61.
40. Ibid., 15.
41. Ibid.
42. Curry, *Ecological Ethics*, 7.
43. Machen, *The White People*, 205.
44. Ibid., 170.
45. Ibid., 148 (also 169, 222), 156.
46. Ibid., 217.
47. Ibid., 179.
48. Ibid., 178, 179.
49. Ibid., 157.
50. Fisher, *The Weird and the Eerie*, 16, 17.
51. Machen, *The White People*, 220.
52. Ibid., 303, 308.
53. Machen, *Decadent and Occult Works*, 133, 232, 233.
54. Denisoff, "Introduction," 9.
55. Barad, *Meeting the Universe Halfway*, ix.
56. Peter Gratton, *Speculative Realism* (London: Bloomsbury, 2014), 15.
57. Denisoff, "Introduction," 4.
58. Ibid.; Mark Valentine, *Arthur Machen* (Bridgend: Seren, 1995), 22.
59. Valentine, *Arthur Machen*, 22.
60. Machen, *Decadent and Occult Works*, 232.
61. Ibid., 143, 234.
62. Ibid., 121.
63. Ibid., 120, 217.
64. Ibid., 218.
65. Ibid., 182.
66. Ibid., 124.
67. Ibid., 171, 176.
68. Ibid., 175.
69. Ibid.
70. Ibid., 165, 189 (also 189).
71. Ibid., 247.
72. Barad, *Meeting the Universe Halfway*, ix, 35, 35.
73. Ibid., 32; Barad, "Interview with Karen Barad," 50.
74. Worth, "Arthur Machen and the Horrors of Deep History," 220–25.
75. Barad, *Meeting the Universe Halfway*, ix.
76. Ibid.; Machen, *Decadent and Occult Works*, 145–46.
77. Gratton, *Speculative Realism*, 15.
78. Fisher, *The Weird and the Eerie*, 18; Naess, *Ecology of Wisdom*, 93.
79. Joshi, *The Weird Tale*, 7.
80. Arthur Machen, *The Secret Glory* (Rookhope: Aziloth, 2014), 81.
81. Ibid., 81.
82. Ibid., 81.
83. Ibid., 81.

84. Ferguson, "Reading with the Occultists," 42.
85. Quoted in Joshi, *The Weird Tale*, 38; Ferguson, "Reading with the Occultists," 43.
86. Freeman, "Arthur Machen: Ecstasy and Epiphany," 243.
87. Barad, *Meeting the Universe Halfway*, 35.
88. Karen Barad, "Posthumanist Performativity: Toward an Understanding of How Matter Comes to Matter," *Signs: Journal of Women in Culture and Society* 28, no. 3 (2003): 801–31, 804.
89. Machen, *Decadent and Occult Works*, 149.
90. Freeman, "Arthur Machen: Ecstasy and Epiphany," 246; Arthur Machen, *Hieroglyphics* (London: Grant Richards, 1902), 84.
91. Machen, *The White People*, 346.
92. Machen, *Decadent and Occult Works*, 201.
93. Ibid., 197, 198.
94. Naess, *Ecology of Wisdom*, 93.

REFERENCES

Barad, Karen. "Posthumanist Performativity: Toward an Understanding of How Matter Comes to Matter." *Signs: Journal of Women in Culture and Society* 28, no. 3 (2003): 801–31.

———. *Meeting the Universe Halfway: Quantum Physics and the Entanglement of Matter and Meaning*. London: Duke University Press, 2007.

———. "Interview with Karen Barad." In *New Materialism: Interviews & Cartographies*, by Rick Dolphijn and Iris van der Tuin, 48–70. Ann Arbor: Open Humanities Press, 2012.

Curry, Patrick. *Ecological Ethics: An Introduction*. Cambridge: Polity, 2006.

Denisoff, Dennis. "Introduction." In *Decadent and Occult Works*, by Arthur Machen, edited by Dennis Denisoff, 1–28. Cambridge: Modern Humanities Research Association, 2018.

Ferguson, Christine. "Reading with the Occultists: Arthur Machen, A. E. Waite, and the Ecstasies of Popular Fiction." *Journal of Victorian Culture* 21, no. 1 (2016): 40–55.

Fisher, Mark. *The Weird and the Eerie*. London: Repeater Books, 2016.

Freeman, Nicholas. "Arthur Machen: Ecstasy and Epiphany." *Literature & Theology* 24, no. 3 (2010): 242–55.

Graf, Susan Johnston. *Talking to the Gods: Occultism in the Work of W. B. Yeats, Arthur Machen, Algernon Blackwood, and Dion Fortune*. Albany: State University of New York, 2015.

Gratton, Peter. *Speculative Realism*. London: Bloomsbury, 2014.

Joshi, S. T. "Introduction." *The White People and Other Weird Stories*, by Arthur Machen, edited by S. T. Joshi, xi–xxiv. London: Penguin, 2011.

———. *The Evolution of the Weird Tale*. New York: Hippocampus Press, 2004.

———. *The Weird Tale*. Holicong: Wildside Press, 1990.

Machen, Arthur. *Decadent and Occult Works*, edited by Dennis Denisoff. Cambridge: Modern Humanities Research Association, 2018.
———. *Hieroglyphics*. London: Grant Richards, 1902.
———. *The Secret Glory*. Rookhope: Aziloth, 2014.
———. *The White People and Other Weird Stories*, edited by S. T. Joshi. London: Penguin, 2011.
Naess, Arne. *Ecology of Wisdom*, edited by Alan Drengson and Bill Devall. London: Penguin, 2008.
Oppermann, Serpil and Serenella Iovino (eds). Introduction. *Environmental Humanities: Voices from the Anthropocene*, 1–21. London: Rowman & Littlefield, 2017.
Poller, Jake. "The Transmutations of Arthur Machen: Alchemy in 'The Great God Pan' and *The Three Imposters*." *Literature & Theology* 29, no.1 (2015): 18–32.
Plumwood, Val. *Feminism and the Mastery of Nature*. London: Routledge, 1993.
Valentine, Mark. *Arthur Machen*. Bridgend: Seren, 1995.
Worth, Aaron. "Arthur Machen and the Horrors of Deep History." *Victorian Literature and Culture* 40 (2012): 215–27.
———. "Introduction." *The Great God Pan and Other Horror Stories*, by Arthur Machen, edited by Aaron Worth, ix–xxx. Oxford: Oxford University Press, 2018.

Chapter 10

Occult Investigations in Arthur Machen's Detective Stories

Deborah Bridle

When "The Great God Pan"—Arthur Machen's most notorious work—was published in 1894 in Lang's edition, the volume featured another story, entitled "The Inmost Light." The character of Dyson, an amateur detective, is introduced in that narrative. Over 1894 and 1895, Machen published two more stories centered on Dyson—"The Shining Pyramid" and "The Red Hand"—and crowned the series with the novel *The Three Impostors*. The latter pieces together a large number of previously published short stories that Machen adapted to make them fit in this new Dyson narrative, creating a vast patchwork delineating a complex investigation.

In the four volumes of what we may call the Dyson series, the detective is faced with various weird phenomena calling for his investigative skills. He is thus led down the paths of occultism and magic as he uncovers dark deeds and even darker truths. As a result, Dyson will be forced to call into question rational techniques of ratiocination and to dabble with the dark discipline to understand and try to solve the mysteries at play. Consequently, will the supernatural thwart the investigation or will it give special insight to the detective? Keeping in mind that occultism concerns that which is hidden (from the Latin *occulere*: to conceal), how can it work alongside the task of detection, whose goal is precisely to reveal and to explain the workings of mystery?

Analyzing how occultism can be weaved into the diegetic fabric of a work of detective fiction will finally lead to an investigation on how occultism can also be seen as a deliberate tool for the writer. Indeed, on the extra-textual level, the narratives function as occult works in which Machen uses fragmentary viewpoints and a multi-layered narration in combination with horror and magic, always playing with the readers by giving them a partial description of the events, particularly in the tour de force *The Three Impostors*. Occultism thus works as a literal motif and a metatextual symbol in all those stories, ultimately leading to the failure of the detective.

No work of detective fiction can happen without one—or several—case(s) to solve, the most common form being that of murder. The crime is the initial cause that will allow the detective to come into play and the narrative to unfold, and the Dyson stories are no exception. In "The Inmost Light," for example, a woman is killed by her husband in the aftermath of a horrific scientific experiment which turns her into an inhuman fiend; "The Shining Pyramid" relates the case of the disappearance of a young woman leading to the discovery of the fact that she was murdered by a group of mysterious and primitive people living in underground caves; "The Red Hand" presents the convoluted investigation following the murder of a respected physician in a London alley; and, finally, *The Three Impostors* is made of a series of apparently disjointed stories of horror and/or murder in which the three eponymous characters are pursuing a young man for dark purposes. In each of those stories, a perfectly rational explanation can initially be found, but the reader soon finds out, thanks to Dyson, that all the crimes are steeped into the occult and the supernatural.

Before diving any deeper into those crimes, it is worth taking the time to describe more precisely what form of occultism and magic is displayed in those stories. While it is true that Machen was involved for a short while with the Hermetic Order of the Golden Dawn, it is also accurate to say, as R.A. Gilbert suggests, that he "had a wide and deep knowledge of the subject-matter [i.e., occultism], but was content to take a purely scholarly and bibliographical interest in it."[1] Early on in his career, in 1885, the Welsh writer was offered a job as a cataloger for George Redway, a publisher and second-hand bookseller who wished to create a catalog of his numerous volumes pertaining to the subject of occultism.[2] The collection was a trove of knowledge for Machen and certainly a source of inspiration for many of his subsequent works. To complete this succinct picture of Machen's attachment to occultism, Edward Gauntlett also suggests that the author's affinity with the occult and magic was entrenched in his love for his native Welsh country and its history:

> In terms of magic, taking that word in its widest sense, it is the countryside that inspired him; his connexions with landscape and place were profound. . . . Machen, who seems to have had a natural tendency towards experiencing the numinous through nature, spent a large part of his youth [taking solitary walks in remote areas], [seeking out ancient buildings, standing stones and the like].[3]

The magic that Machen liked to explore in his stories thus plunged its roots in ancient Sabbatic rituals more than it did in the form of esoteric occultism that was popular at the end of the nineteenth century,[4] and to which his attitude could very much be "playful and irreverent."[5] As a result, even though he was a member of the Hermetic Order of the Golden Dawn, Machen's occultism was that of an observer more than that of a practitioner, especially at the time he wrote the Dyson stories, which precedes his involvement with the Order.

This is the reason why the kind of occultism we can find in the Dyson stories is different from the esoteric and symbolic brand which Machen later develops with Waite in *The House of the Hidden Light* (1904), for instance. In that exchange of letters, the two men develop a cryptic mode of writing which uses a slew of alchemical metaphors and occult symbols more akin to the type of so-called magic studied and developed by members of hermetic orders and societies at the turn of the century. Furthermore, the goal of the two writers was to pierce the Veil and reach the Light in the manner of alchemists seeking for the perfect transmutation. There is admittedly something alchemical and occult as well in how the characters of the Dyson stories can see and interpret the world around, as if the initiate could see and access an alternate reality. A comparison between *The House of the Hidden Light* and *The Three Impostors* can attest to a certain affinity between the two visions. In the former volume Machen affirms:

> With great awe this day have I seen some matter of the Work in the transmutation of the world. For something is added which gives vastness and a certain splendour and immensity to the material universe in all its parts, so that when I came down the stairs in this house, I did so with the sense that I passed through immense distances, as if I came down the stair of a cathedral spire. And when I went out into the street, it seemed to me that I saw in a happy and shining air, a new, glorious and unknown city, builded of radiant and living stones.[6]

Similarly, in the 1895 novel Miss Lally and Mr. Leicester, respectively, state:

> I looked down and saw the pure white mist tracking the outline of the river like a shroud, and a vague and shadowy country; imaginations and fantasy of swelling hills and hanging woods, and half-shaped outlines of hills beyond, and in the distance the glare of the furnace fire on the mountain, glowing by turns a pillar of shining flame and fading to a dull point of red.[7]

> Look at the afterglow; why it is as if a great city were burning in flames, and down there between the dark houses it is raining blood fast.[8]

But while the vocabulary of alchemy and transmutation—particularly visible in the lexical field of fire and intense light—is used to express the search for the Light[9] and for ecstasy in *The House of the Hidden Light*, the visions found in *The Three Impostors* always announce some evil deed or the discovery of occult truths. In the Dyson stories, the Veil is present but the mysteries it reveals are dark and dangerous. As Sophie Mantrant notes, there is a distinction between Machen's early stories and his later writings, which she names respectively "black tales" and "white tales."[10] Even though all his career as a writer was devoted to the exploration of what is hidden behind the Veil and to finding the perfect way to express ecstasy, the stories Machen wrote prior to the very end of the nineteenth century resolutely belong to the subgenre of supernatural horror and they revolve around the vision of the past as a *Visio malefica*.[11]

In the Dyson stories, occultism is thus present as a means to represent the resurgence of a primal past, with its rituals and its dangers, its horrors and its magic. Most of the stories of the cycle are built on the premise that a primitive and devilish people has survived for millennia in underground tunnels and caves in places like the West country. They worship pagan gods and practice dark magic through rituals, sacrifices, and Sabbaths. "The Shining Pyramid" and "The Red Hand" therefore link seemingly ordinary crimes to the existence of those "little people"—as they are named throughout Machen's writings. This theme is also present in one of the short tales featured in *The Three Impostors* ("Novel of the Black Seal"), in which the reader understands that a young woman was abducted by the very same little people and impregnated by a kind of ancient god. The centerfold role played by paganism and an ancestral past is further reinforced through the profusion of artifacts and hieroglyphic carvings that are left behind as so many clues for Dyson to interpret: flints arranged in various patterns and eye symbols crudely drawn on pillars in "The Shining Pyramid," all constituting a means of communication for the little people; a murder weapon that is a ten-thousand-year-old knife, the recurrent drawing of an evil sign on the wall, a stone tablet covered in cuneiform writing, and an enigmatic obscene gold item in "The Red Hand"; a Roman coin bearing the face of a faun, an ancient seal of black stone with curious engravings which turn out to be a formula for a transgressive ritual of transformation, and a strange powder which can turn water into the wine of the Sabbath in *The Three Impostors*.

All the stories therefore feature crimes which may seem "normal" at first, but soon turn out to be the work of evil forces, or of human beings under the influence of those ancient occult powers that still roam the world underneath the surface of the earth. A supernatural agent of evil is always at work, occurring in the forms of the little people and of a primal and corrupting force that Machen also associates with the image of the God Pan. Even the mission of the three evil characters in *The Three Impostors*—finding the young man with spectacles and torturing him to death in a hideous way—has a link with the occult.[12] This mission was given to them by a Dr. Lipsius who sought to punish the young man for betraying him after sharing in the corrupting pleasures of the Sabbath, which reintroduces the primordial occult at the heart of the motive, as illustrated by the following excerpt taken from Joseph Walters's notebook and describing his first experience of the Sabbath:

> my initiation began . . . they gave me red wine to drink, and a woman told me as I sipped it that it was wine of the Red Jar that Avallaunius had made. Another asked me how I liked the wine of the Fauns, and I heard a dozen other fantastic names, while the stuff boiled in my veins, and stirred, I think, something that had slept within me from the moment I was born. I was no longer a thinking agent, but at once subject and object; I mingled in the horrible sport, and watched the mystery of the Greek groves and fountains enacted before me, saw the reeling dance and heard the music calling as I sat beside my mate . . . Thus with strange rites they made me drink the cup, and when I woke up in the morning I was one of them, and had sworn to be faithful.[13]

As Dennis Porter indicates in *The Pursuit of Crime* (1981), detective fiction is normally founded on a definition of crime as an "antisocial act committed by one member of a human group against the group as a whole or another member of the group."[14] Such a transgression of the social rule, embodied as a transgressive act in the law, is resolved through the arrest and prosecution of the criminal. No such thing is possible with Machen's brand of detective fiction because the choice of an occult and supernatural agent dispenses with a rational explanation or motive and does not lead to reconciliation through arrest and/or conviction. The crimes go unpunished because they cannot be punished. But it does not mean that they cannot be interpreted and deciphered.

To solve those occult puzzles, one needs a detective whose mind is open to these kinds of weird phenomena and is ready to accept them as plausible. Dyson is one such character. Nevertheless, he also bears some resemblance to the classic detectives of his time, the prime example being Edgar Allan Poe's Dupin. As Stephen Knight notes in his work *Form and Ideology of Crime Fiction* (1980), "Poe was the first to create the intelligent, infallible, isolated hero so important to crime fiction of the last hundred years . . . The isolated intellectual and imaginative life is a sufficient and successful response to the world and its problems."[15] Dyson is similarly presented as an intellectual man whose only company is the valuable sidekick who will provide him with the momentum he needs for his analytical process. Like Dupin and Sherlock Holmes before him, Dyson is always paired with a partner (not necessarily the same, however: Salisbury in "The Inmost Light," Vaughan in "The Shining Pyramid," and Phillips in both "The Red Hand" and *The Three Impostors*). The partner's role is to make the detective shine through a dynamic of opposition that mainly expresses itself through a radically antagonistic frame of mind. Since the crime is rooted in the occult, it is easy for Machen to conjure up a foil to the detective, one whose only purpose is to present a mind steeped in the rational world and resistant to the possibility of the supernatural.

The realm of literature is one field in which the two mindsets are most clearly opposed, revealing their different approaches to reality. Dyson is an amateur detective solving murders and mysteries when he is not busy trying to write. As an aspiring man of letters, his taste for literature nourishes his disposition and allows him to accept the possibility of the improbable. In the opening of "The Red Hand," he admonishes Phillips for not keeping his mind open: "Possibly, but as I said just now, you go to work at the wrong end. You neglect the opportunities that confront you and await you, obvious, at every corner; you positively shrink from the chance of encountering primitive man in this whirling and mysterious city."[16] Phillips's rational and therefore limited—in the eyes of his companion—thinking prevents him from understanding that Dyson could not be more serious and literal when he mentioned the "primitive man":

> "There are certainly people about here whose ideas are very primitive."
>
> "I wish, Phillips, you would not rationalise my remarks . . . I meant exactly what I said. Who can limit the age of survival? The troglodyte and the lake-dweller, perhaps representatives of yet darker races, may very probably be lurking in our midst, rubbing shoulder with frock-coated and finely draped humanity, ravening like wolves at the heart and boiling with the foul passions of the swamp and the black cave."[17]

As expected, Phillips, who "neglect[s] the opportunities that confront [him]," is not ready to believe unless he meets one such creature.[18]

But being "a man of letters" and believing in what others would call mere fantasies of the imagination does not prevent Dyson from being a rational thinker and "a man of science" as well, as he tells his friend Salisbury at the beginning of "The Inmost Light": "I told you I was a man of letters; it would, perhaps, be more correct to describe myself as a man of science."[19] It is undeniable that his investigation methods are modern and that he believes in science. Of course, this is not specific to Machen's brand of detective fiction. Dyson shares his reliance on hard evidence and facts with Sherlock Holmes. Just as the latter could be seen as a pioneer in forensic science—finding invaluable information and clues in minute observation of fingerprints, footprints, handwriting, with the help of various sciences such as chemistry, mathematics, biology, and physics[20]—the former is also a connoisseur in the latest sciences and a keen observer of crime scenes. The emergence of the detective fiction genre corresponds to a period of intense scientific progress that managed to plunge its roots in the collective imagination and become part of the readers' expectations, as explained by Dorothy L. Sayers in her introduction to *The Omnibus of Crime* (1937): "In place of the adventurer and the knight errant, popular imagination hailed the doctor, the scientist, and the policeman as saviours and protectors."[21] As religious faith lost ground with the rise of new scientific disciplines and knowledge, there was also at the same time a peak in the popularity of policemen and detective characters in fiction. Those were no longer the laughing stock or the targets of distrust they used to be but rose instead to the role of cunning and intelligent figures able to thwart the criminals' designs and to protect the population thanks to their skills in detection, as Judith Flanders explains in *The Invention of Murder* (2011).[22]

Therefore, the different stories feature the reports and opinions of various specialists on certain clues and evidence (as with the autopsy of Mrs. Black in "The Inmost Light," the thorough analysis of the drug administered to Mr. Leicester in "The Novel of the White Powder," or the opinion of a specialist working at the Museum on a mysterious carving in a stone in the same story). Dyson himself analyzes the concrete clues that he has at his disposal and is a keen observer as well as a relentless investigator. In "The Shining Pyramid," he inspects every square inch of the place where his friend Vaughan has been seeing weird patterns made of flints next to his house, in what is described as a "[minute] inquisition."[23]

Similarly, every piece of paper or object that comes his way is treated as a potential clue, however unrelated to the current case it may initially appear. The efficiency of his investigative method lies in the fact that he is ready to accept anything as possible. In that sense, Dyson is once again related to Dupin, for whom, according to Stephen Knight, "the material known is real, sense-available, though its analysis is projected at an ideal and theoretical level. The epistemology is at once based on facts and developed through ideal categories. Dupin is both in and above the real world."[24] Likewise, Dyson follows the principle enunciated by Holmes in Doyle's *The Sign of the Four* (1890): "when you have eliminated the impossible, whatever remains, however improbable, must be the truth."[25] The main difference between Dyson and Poe's and Doyle's arch-detectives is that the realm of the improbable includes the supernatural which consequently becomes utterly possible. Therefore, Dyson can be seen as rational because his mind strictly follows the clues that he is given, but his rationality is different from the stubborn and material skepticism of his various sidekicks. In all the different stories under study, there always comes a point when Dyson's companion offers his own interpretation of the mystery under investigation, only to be shot down by Dyson's explanation—which invariably takes into account the existence of an occult reality, and which always happens to be the right one. For instance, when Phillips offers a seemingly plausible explanation of vendetta to account for the murder of Sir Vivian in "The Red Hand," Dyson rules out his friend's ideas based solely on the facts of the investigation and decides to keep an open mind to a more unusual explanation than the one provided by his friend: "I cannot do as you do, and fortify myself with cast-iron propositions to the effect that this or that doesn't happen, and never has happened."[26] Spurred by his literary inclinations, Dyson is characterized by a mind prone to accept things out of the ordinary, and it is precisely his open-mindedness that makes him a good detective: "A fervent curiosity and an innate liking for the obscure were great incentives."[27] At the beginning of *The Three Impostors*, he uses his literary disagreement with Phillips to explain his own understanding of reality. Indeed, while Phillips is an admirer of realism, Dyson believes in the marvelous, and each man firmly defends his own stance based on his own vision of the world:

> You know, Phillips . . . that I have always battled for the marvellous. I remember your maintaining in that chair that one has no business to make use of the wonderful, the improbable, the odd coincidence in literature, and you took the ground that it was wrong to do so, because as a matter of fact the wonderful and the improbable don't happen, and men's lives are not really shaped by odd coincidence.[28]

Dyson's strong belief in the improbable and in odd coincidences sometimes leads precisely to those chance events that, in all objectivity, seem too fortunate to be true. In "The Inmost Light," for instance, a sudden rainshower forces Salisbury to take shelter in a dark archway. Precisely then, a couple stumbles into that same passage from the other end and after a quick argument, the woman throws away a piece of paper and both characters leave the scene. As it turns out, the paper contains an invaluable clue which, after deciphering, will enable Dyson to come into possession of a strange crystal into which Dr. Black has transferred the soul of his wife during his terrible experiment. In an all-too-similar fortunate combination of events, Dyson gets his hands on a crucial black stone in "The Red Hand" during a bizarre encounter in a pub. But there is actually a method, not to his madness, but to his luck. Knowing that the black stone has been lost or stolen, he decides to spend most of his time in pubs and at pawnbrokers in the hope that the stone might reappear to be sold or exchanged. He thus explains this method—the theory of improbability—to his friend Phillips:

> I will tell you how I work. I go upon the theory of improbability. The theory is unknown to you? I will explain. Suppose I stand on the steps of St. Paul's and look out for a blind man lame of the left leg to pass me, it is evidently highly improbable that I shall see such a person by waiting for an hour. If I wait two

hours the improbability is diminished, but it is still enormous, and a watch of a whole day would give little expectation of success. But suppose I take up the same position day after day, and week after week, don't you perceive that the improbability is lessening constantly—growing smaller day after day? Don't you see that two lines which are not parallel are gradually approaching one another, drawing nearer and nearer to a point of meeting, till at last they do meet, and improbability has vanished altogether? That is how I found the black tablet: I acted on the theory of improbability.[29]

As Sophie Mantrant explains, the concept of coincidence as sign of a hidden truth is something that can be found in different works by Machen: "coincidence finds its place in a vision of the world as a series of hieroglyphs—it is the sign revealing an invisible design . . . There are no coincidences, only signs that have to be identified as such."[30] The image of the detective as a reader and decipherer of those signs is also to be found in the work of decryption which takes place in all the stories given the profusion of coded notes and ancient alphabets coming up in the investigations. Language can thus also be seen as a series of symbols that have to be interpreted before they can reveal an alternate reality.

The work of detection, deciphering, and interpretation ultimately leads to the phase of understanding and illumination: that which was hidden—occulted—is exposed to the light by the detective for all to see. However, Geoffrey Reiter explains that it is perplexing to notice that the eureka moment is never followed by a real sense of victory or justice. There is no solace to be found because the usual arrest of the culprit cannot take place: "none of Machen's paranormal detective tales end on reassuring notes, concluding instead with open-ended dread."[31] In "The Inmost Light," Dr. Black, who has killed his wife, is already dead when Dyson uncovers the truth and the story ends with the detective overwhelmed with horror and crushing the crystal containing Mrs. Black's soul; "The Shining Pyramid" closes on Dyson's avowal of his powerlessness to save Annie from the little people's ritual; in "The Red Hand," Dyson and Phillips are seized with revulsion when Selby shows them the jewel he brought back from the caves of the little people. Even more interestingly, the novel *The Three Impostors* ends on the complete failure of the two men to save the young man with spectacles. In the previous short stories, the various crimes have already been committed when Dyson gets involved and his task is simply to unravel the mystery, but the longer novel follows the pursuit of the young man by the three impostors who fool Dyson and Phillips all along, and when the amateur detective finally understands the whole story, it is too late. The three villains have caught up with their prey and have killed him in the most abject fashion. There is no reassuring meaning to be found to compensate for the horror of the crime and the murderers walk away free at the end of the story.

The absence of legal punishment of the perpetrators stems mainly from the prevalence of the supernatural over the nature of the crimes committed. The dead ends in which Dyson finds himself even after solving the mysteries are mirrored in the structure of the narratives themselves, which take the form of labyrinthine compositions, culminating in the schizophrenic maze of *The Three Impostors*. A work of detective fiction is chiefly a narrative in which the author follows a particular strategy that differs from that of a more classic narrative since it is founded on the withholding of information from the detective and, of course, from the reader. Machen chooses to turn his short stories into veritable puzzles that further complicate the original narration of the crime and the investigation.

As mentioned before, several of the stories contain reports and accounts made by a third party, whether in verbal form (the autopsy report explained by the doctor to Dyson in "The Inmost Light," or the confession of Selby to Dyson and Phillips in "The Red Hand"), or in a written form later integrated into the main frame of the narrative for the reader (as is the case for Dr. Black's notebook in "The Inmost Light," the lengthy notes left by Professor Gregg in "The Novel of the Black Seal" or Joseph Walters's pocket book in *The Three Impostors*). As a result, the reader is faced with polyphonic stories in which the omniscient narrator appearing at the beginning willingly gives way to temporary narrators.

Indeed, retelling and rephrasing play a major part in the stories, so much so that a lot of the information that the reader learns is actually not transmitted by a descriptive narration but by the account that Dyson makes of his discoveries to his various companions. Consequently, dialogues occupy a vast portion of the stories, replacing the third-person narrative with a first-person one and therefore switching the focalization on the speaker. To quote but one example, the first section of "The Inmost Light" is made of eight pages almost entirely composed of a dialogue between Dyson and Salisbury, during which Dyson explains to his friend the mysterious circumstances of Mrs. Black's death. If we add to Dyson's voice those of the different authors of notes and reports and diaries and letters, we end up with a multitude of first-person narrators and several layers of embedded tales. A process which was hardly new of course, but that Machen took to a paroxysm with *The Three Impostors*. That novel, as explained in this chapter's introduction, is a patchwork of different short stories written independently and collaged together in a larger narrative. Inside the novel, the reader finds a prologue, eight stories (the last of which can be considered an epilogue), and five of those stories contain further embedded units of narratives (one or two each). The only link between those seemingly independent and separate narratives is the recurring reference to "the young man with spectacles," who appears to be involved in different weird or horrific narratives and is therefore looked for by the different characters at the origin of the eight stories.

Contrary to the previous three short stories, Dyson is not investigating anything here. There is no murder or disappearance to solve and he and Phillips simply become the narratees of those new storytellers. Those narratives involve death by dissolution, weird bodily transformations, the obsessive quest for the discovery of an ancient people which leads to death and madness, the theft of an old mysterious Roman coin—so many themes that regularly reappear in Machen's fiction. But the careful reader should not be long to understand that the characters at the origin of all those stories are none other than the three people introduced under different names in the Prologue. Certain physical features[32] are indeed carefully placed by Machen for the reader to understand that the three impostors from the title are actually the ones who weave those intricate and strange stories around Dyson and Phillips, and that their sole purpose is to find the young man with spectacles. As Reiter accurately notes, for the first time ever "it is the reader who is consistently one step ahead of the detectives, Dyson and Phillips remain oblivious to the connections that the audience makes with each passing chapter, realizing that they are being told stories by impostors."[33] Of course, the reader has had access to the information as early as in the Prologue and he knows that the three individuals are up to no good, but Dyson's incredible skills in deduction should tell him that something is off in all the tales that he is told.[34] It is only too late that he finally pieces everything back together. Once Dyson has had access to the young man's notebook, he understands that he and Phillips have been duped all along. Unfortunately, he is too late, and Joseph Walters has been tortured to death by the time he and his companion find him.

This casts a whole shadow of doubt upon the status of the story as a work of reported information. The novel is founded on the premise that everything inside the main frame is a lie, putting into question the reliability of the narrators and therefore highlighting Dyson's credulity. From perspicacious and intelligent detective, he turns into gullible victim of the impostors' lies. Only four parts out of the fourteen subdivisions can be considered true: the Prologue, in which the three villains leave a dilapidated house and talk about their mission, the next part in which Dyson witnesses a deadly chase in a dark street and subsequently picks up an old Roman coin that the fugitive (Walters) has lost, and the very end, with the transcription of Joseph Walters's pocket book, and Dyson's discovery of the dilapidated house from the beginning where the poor young man has been killed. Interestingly, the prologue and the epilogue are narrated by an omniscient third-person narrator and they validate the other two sequences that cannot be doubted, but the rest of the novel is only founded on the accounts spoken by the three impostors, therefore confirming their dubious quality.

Consequently, one could also question the validity of the supernatural in this novel, since all the occult and magical events that are told are actually part of the liars' tales. However, the reader and Dyson discover through the reading of Walters's pocketbook that before being chased by the three criminals, he was a member of their secret society. This group appears to be a mysterious order led by a Dr. Lipsius who initiated Walters to all kinds of occult and orgiastic rituals. It therefore makes perfect sense to assume that all the horrific stories told by the three impostors are very likely to have happened in one form or another in the course of the characters' involvement with Lipsius's order.

In terms of narrative construction, *The Three Impostors* has been criticized for its lack of integrity and cohesion but it is precisely what makes it stand out as a true work of art among Machen's *fin-de-siècle* works. It constitutes a puzzle that the reader has to solve while carefully avoiding the traps of deceit, becoming a sort of metatextual object of detective fiction that celebrates the work of the detective reader at the same time as it marks the utter failure of the detective. A work of detective fiction calls for a solution, and with the solution comes the reestablishment of normality through a restoration of the social order. Introducing the variable of the supernatural in the equation leads to a profound imbalance that makes it impossible to find this restoration of order, whether it be social or more generally metaphysical. Allowing for the existence of creatures and phenomena that can be investigated but that will never be fully grasped by the human mind contributes to the prevailing sense of *malaise* to be found in the Dyson stories. Indeed, as good a detective as Dyson can be, there is only so much he can comprehend, and oftentimes it is the sensation of horror and disgust that reigns supreme at the end of the stories. Occultism is sensed and most of the time decoded by Dyson, but ultimately, it is meant to remain concealed because the reality it reveals is too much to bear.

Such thinking is not surprising in works that belong to the *fin de siècle* period and that are associated to the Decadent movement. Reiter links Dyson's investigative efforts to his aesthetic vision of the world (mainly expressed through his repeated references to literature and the beauty of the marvelous), and the horror that prevails is caused by the realization that there is no meaning behind the awful discoveries that he makes. The moral distinction between good and evil has disappeared, only to leave us in a world where such atrocities can happen and go unpunished: "The reason Machen's early stories are often considered his best, the reason writers like Lovecraft praised them so highly, is that they spring from the pen of a man who at the time had the soul of a mystic but the mind of an atheist, who could not bear the possibility that there might be nothing beyond 'the abyss of all being'."[35]

As noted earlier, this gloomy vision was not meant to last, and Machen would soon be able to consider the occult in a more radiant and positive light through his search for forms of ecstasy. But in the Dyson cycle, Machen achieves the feat of writing detective stories which are both an homage to the tradition of the genre and a manifesto of the spirit of his age—they are a statement on the human mind's helplessness before powers stronger than itself, forces that are extremely compelling but dangerous to uncover.

NOTES

1. R.A. Gilbert, "Introduction," in *The House of the Hidden Light*, ed. R. A. Gilbert, v–viii (Leyburn: Tartarus Press, 2017), Ebook edition.

2. Ibid.

3. Edward Gauntlett, "Transmutations of Good and Evil: Alchemy, Witchcraft and the Graal in the Work of Arthur Machen," in *Abraxas* 1 (Lopen: Fulgur Press, 2009), 20.

4. Ibid., 19. Gauntlett explains that, after publishing "The Great God Pan," Machen wrote to his French translator that he had undergone certain occult experiences, on the subject of which he added that "none of the experiences I have had has any connexion whatever with such impostures as spiritualism or theosophy."

5. Jake Poller, "The Transmutations of Arthur Machen: Alchemy in 'The Great God Pan' and *The Three Impostors*," in *Literature & Theology*, vol. 29, no. 1, 18–32 (Oxford: Oxford University Press, 2015), 25.

6. Arthur Machen, *The House of the Hidden Light*, ed. R. A. Gilbert (Leyburn: Tartarus Press, 2017), Ebook edition, Letter XIX.

7. Arthur Machen, *The Three Impostors*, in *The Dyson Chronicles*, 95–238 (Greenville: Coachwhip Publications, 2014), 143.

8. Ibid., 199.

9. The word is capitalized in *The House of the Hidden Light*, thus showing that it is the main object of the two writers' quest and akin to a sort of Holy Grail. The coded correspondence between Machen and Waite profusely uses alchemical imagery and esoteric language in the two men's search for the Light.

10. Sophie Mantrant, *Arthur Machen et l'Art du Hiéroglyphe* (Cadillon: Le Visage Vert, 2016), 16. My translation.

11. Ibid., 27.

12. Interestingly, all the stories the impostors tell involve evil deeds steeped in the supernatural and dark magic, whereas the torture they impose on the young man with spectacles is as down-to-earth and physical as can be, involving no occult intervention.

13. Machen, *The Three Impostors*, 225.

14. Dennis Porter, *The Pursuit of Crime. Art and Ideology in Detective Fiction* (New Haven: Yale University Press, 1981), 120.

15. Stephen Knight, *Form and Ideology in Crime Fiction* (London: Macmillan Publishers, 1980), 39.

16. Arthur Machen, "The Red Hand," in *The Dyson Chronicles*, 65–94 (Greenville: Coachwhip Publications, 2014), 65.

17. Ibid., 66.

18. Ibid.

19. Arthur Machen, "The Inmost Light," in *The Dyson Chronicles*, 11–40 (Greenville: Coachwhip Publications, 2014), 12.

20. See for instance James O'Brien, *The Scientific Sherlock Holmes: Cracking the Case with Science and Forensics* (Oxford: Oxford University Press, 2013), 48, 87, 88, 116, 121, 144.

21. Dorothy L. Sayers, *The Omnibus of Crime, Volume One* (New York: Garden City Publishing, 1937), 13.

22. See Judith Flanders, *The Invention of Murder, How the Victorians Revelled in Death and Detection and Created Modern Crime* (London: Harper Press, 2011), 176, 177, 299, 379, 380.

23. Arthur Machen, "The Shining Pyramid," in *The Dyson Chronicles*, 41–64 (Greenville: Coachwhip Publications, 2014), 49.

24. Knight, *Form and Ideology in Crime Fiction*, 42.

25. Arthur Conan Doyle, *The Sign of the Four*, 2000, http://www.gutenberg.org/ebooks/2097 (accessed May 12, 2020).

26. Machen, "The Red Hand," 76.

27. Ibid.

28. Machen, *The Three Impostors*, 100–01.

29. Machen, "The Red Hand," 84.

30. Mantrant, *Arthur Machen et l'Art du Hiéroglyphe*, 121. My translation.

31. Geoffrey Reiter, "'Man is Made a Mystery': The Evolution of Arthur Machen's Religious Thought," PhD diss. (2010), 68. https://baylor-ir.tdl.org/baylor-ir/handle/2104/8049 (accessed May 22, 2020).

32. See, for example: ". . .said the smooth, clean-shaven man to his companion, an individual . . . who had chosen to make his ginger-coloured moustache merge into a pair of short chin-whiskers," "a girl . . . quite young, with a quaint and piquant rather than a beautiful face . . . her eyes were of a shining hazel" (95); "a pair of bulbous chin-whiskers of a ginger hue, into which moustaches of like colour merged imperceptibly" (107); "She was a young girl with a quaint and piquant rather than a beautiful face . . . she looked at him with a pair of charming eyes of a shining hazel" (129); "a smooth, clean-shaven, and smiling gentleman entered" (175); "she was dressed in deep mourning, but the piquant smiling face and charming hazel eyes ill accorded with the heavy garments" (196); "the smooth-tongued and smooth-shaven Burton" (219). All previous quotations are from Machen, *The Three Impostors*.

33. Reiter, "Man is Made a Mystery," 71–72.

34. Interestingly, he does have a strange feeling when he meets each of the three impostors, but surprisingly he never acts on his suspicions: "Dyson walked off smartly, pondering the strange story chance had brought him, and finding on cool reflection that there was something a little strange in Mr. Wilkins's manner, for which not even so

weird a catalogue of experiences could altogether account" (126); "In the first place, [Dyson] cherished a profound conviction that the words of truth were scattered with a too niggardly and sparing hand over the agreeable history of Mr. Smith and the Black Gulf Cañon; and secondly . . . the idea of a man going about London haunted by the fear of meeting a young man with spectacles struck Dyson as supremely ridiculous" (175); "For many revolving weeks Mr. Burton delighted Dyson by his agreeable conversation, diversified by anecdote, and interspersed with the narration of singular adventures. Finally, however, he vanished as suddenly as he had appeared . . . Dyson, considering . . . certain glaring inconsistencies in the talk of his late friend, arrived at the conclusion that his stories were fabulous" (192); "Mr. Dyson looked shyly at the young lady before him. She was dressed in deep mourning, but the piquant smiling face and charming hazel eyes ill accorded with the heavy garments and the mouldering surface of the crape . . . 'Sir I will not waste your time . . . Learn, then, that I am a fugitive, and in hiding here; I place myself in your power; you have but to describe my features, and I fall into the hands of my relentless enemy'. Mr. Dyson wondered for a passing instant how this could be, but he only renewed his promise of silence" (196). All previous quotations are from Machen, *The Three Impostors*.

35. Reiter, "Man is Made a Mystery," 86.

REFERENCES

Doyle, Arthur Conan. *The Sign of the Four*. 2000. http://www.gutenberg.org/ebooks/2097.

Flanders, Judith. *The Invention of Murder, How the Victorians Revelled in Death and Detection and Created Modern Crime*. London: Harper Press, 2011.

Gauntlett, Edward. "Transmutations of Good and Evil: Alchemy, Witchcraft and the Graal in the Work of Arthur Machen." In *Abraxas* 1, 18–30. Lopen: Fulgur Press, 2009.

Gilbert, R. A. "Introduction." In *The House of the Hidden Light*, edited by R. A. Gilbert, v–viii. Leyburn: Tartarus Press, 2017. Ebook edition.

Knight, Stephen. *Form and Ideology in Crime Fiction*. London: Macmillan Publishers, 1980.

Machen, Arthur. "The Inmost Light." In *The Dyson Chronicles*, 11–40. Greenville: Coachwhip Publications, 2014.

———. "The Shining Pyramid." In *The Dyson Chronicles*, 41–64. Greenville: Coachwhip Publications, 2014.

———. "The Red Hand." In *The Dyson Chronicles*, 65–94. Greenville: Coachwhip Publications, 2014.

———. "The Three Impostors." In *The Dyson Chronicles*, 95–238. Greenville: Coachwhip Publications, 2014.

Machen, Arthur and A. E. Waite. *The House of the Hidden Light*, edited by R. A. Gilbert. Leyburn: Tartarus Press, 2017. Ebook edition.

Mantrant, Sophie. *Arthur Machen et l'Art du Hiéroglyphe*. Cadillon: Le Visage Vert, 2016.

O'Brien, James. *The Scientific Sherlock Holmes: Cracking the Case with Science and Forensics*. Oxford: Oxford University Press, 2013.

Poller, Jake. "The Transmutations of Arthur Machen: Alchemy in 'The Great God Pan' and *The Three Impostors*." In *Literature & Theology*, vol. 29, no. 1, 18–32. Oxford: Oxford University Press, 2015.

Porter, Dennis. *The Pursuit of Crime. Art and Ideology in Detective Fiction*. New Haven: Yale University Press, 1981.

Reiter, Geoffrey. "'Man is Made a Mystery': The Evolution of Arthur Machen's Religious Thought." PhD diss., 2010. https://baylor-ir.tdl.org/baylor-ir/handle/2104/8049.

Sayers, Dorothy L. *The Omnibus of Crime, Volume One*. New York: Garden City Publishing, 1937.

Chapter 11

Through the Ancient Wood

Envisioning Apophatic Mysticism in A Fragment of Life

Geoffrey Reiter

If there is one thing all scholars of Arthur Machen can agree on, it is that he was, at least in some manner, a mystic.[1] He famously identifies "ecstasy" as the defining characteristic of great literature in his manifesto *Hieroglyphics* (1902), a roundabout, quasi-narrative book in which a literary hermit lectures amicably to a frame narrator on the nature of art. In attempting to clarify what he means by ecstasy, Machen's hermit-narrator declares,

> I have chosen this word as the representative of many. Substitute, if you like, rapture, beauty, adoration, wonder, awe, mystery, sense of the unknown, desire for the unknown. All and each will convey what I mean; for some particular case one term may be more appropriate than another, but in every case there will be that withdrawal from the common life and the common consciousness which justifies my choice of "ecstasy" as the best symbol of my meaning.[2]

"Ecstasy" in this context clearly means more than just mystical experience, but it is certainly not less. And yet, throughout *Hieroglyphics*, Machen struggles to make any clearer than this statement just exactly what he *does* mean. His roundabout, conversational tone cycles through repetitions, and he returns again and again to the same dozen or so examples (positive or negative) to illustrate his theory. Aidan Reynolds and William Charlton aptly observe that "he is more concerned with the symbolism of ecstasy, than with explaining succinctly what he means by it."[3] S. T. Joshi finds the book flawed "as a handbook of aesthetic theory" and appears to second Machen's own suspicions that his "ecstasy is too nebulous to define."[4]

Yet, Machen's inability fully to put his notion into words is not just part of the problem—it is, in a sense, part of his literary and philosophical project as well. Wesley Sweetser has commented on Machen's lifelong quest "to express the inexpressible,"[5] and herein lies the fundamental paradox of his literary project. As a writer, Machen must operate in the realm of the sensory world to communicate through concrete imagery; as a mystic, however, he desires to evoke an ecstatic experience that is incommunicable in sensory and linguistic terms. This is because Machen's understanding of the supernatural world toward which his mysticism inclines is primarily "negative," or *apophatic*—that is, best described in terms of what it is *not*.[6] At the same time he was formulating his aesthetic and metaphysical theories about otherworldly ecstasy, Machen was also trying to depict these theories in his fiction, and so in looking at his fictional output from the *Hieroglyphics* period, readers should expect to find among his most conscious intentional attempts "to express the inexpressible" in narrative terms.

One of the most obvious places to look is in his novella *A Fragment of Life*. The writing of *A Fragment of Life* runs directly parallel to that of *Hieroglyphics*: they were both begun in 1899, the latter published in 1902, the former in 1904. First appearing in *Horlicks Magazine* in 1904 and then collected with several of Machen's best-known pieces in the 1906 book *The House of Souls*, *A Fragment of Life* is an account of the life of the middle-class London couple Edward and Mary Darnell. Edward, a city clerk, has been married to Mary for about a year, and the details of their life are exceptionally mundane. Much of the book's "plot" follows the couple's debates as they quietly argue over humdrum matters: the uses and décor of their spare bedroom, their maid's relationship to her beau's mother, Mary's aunt's fear that her husband is unfaithful. All the while, however, Edward begins to have mystic musings and dreams and visions, experiences that cluster with increasing frequency as the story proceeds and as he learns more about his Welsh heritage. And gradually, tentatively, he is able to sway his more conservative wife to join him. The story ends ambiguously, the narrator saying only that "their . . . legend is full of impossible events, and seems to put on the semblance of the stories of the Graal."[7]

Joshi, who is often critical of Machen's metaphysical project, nonetheless maintains that *A Fragment of Life* "captures the essence of Machen's whole world view,"[8] considering it "Machen's most finished and satisfying work."[9] Other readers may not be quite so enthusiastic; *A Fragment of Life* is hardly among Machen's more widely known tales even now. Yet, Joshi may not be inaccurate in praising the piece: rightly understood, it represents perhaps Machen's most successful effort among his later fictions of mediating his seemingly disparate roles as mystic and author—of finding a way to use concrete sensory imagery to point readers toward a transcendent, ecstatic (and apophatic) spiritual experience.

If determining what Machen meant by "ecstasy" can prove a challenge, so too is categorizing that process by which such ecstasy is discovered—mysticism. Late in *A Fragment of Life*, Machen draws his protagonist to discover "that they must read not 'science' books, but mass-books, and that the soul is made wise by the contemplation of mystic ceremonies and elaborate and curious rites."[10] This assessment follows closely with the assertion in *Hieroglyphics* "that there are, speaking very generally, two solutions of existence; one is the materialistic or rationalistic, the other, the spiritual or mystic."[11] But even though he read widely (and eclectically), Machen was not necessarily systematic in his application of his learning. So while mysticism has a long and well-defined history in the Christian tradition (to say nothing of its application in other religions), it can be a little more difficult to demarcate Machen's usage of the term. That is not to say, however, that his mysticism is without precedent or outside the bounds of religious classification entirely.

Broadly speaking, Christian tradition has divided mysticism into two branches, each of which is itself an extension of a particular approach to theology and knowledge of the divine. The *via affirmativa* (or "affirmative way") represents a *cataphatic*[12] approach. Cataphatic theology stresses the (often rational) communicability of God and his attributes, and the ability of his creatures to know about him and his character. According to the *Encyclopedia of Religion*, "The affirmative way of theology, *theologia kataphatika*, uses terms from one's own experience to describe God and his qualities. According to the affirmative theology, every term that refers to the good and the beautiful in this world can be applied analogously to God."[13] Cataphatic mysticism thus places emphasis on the experience of the divine through external means—words, images, symbols, rites.

Apophatic theology, on the other hand, is the *via negativa* (the "negative way"): it underscores the transcendence of God, positing that he may be best understood by describing what he is *not*. According to the *Encyclopedia of Religion*, this approach "refuses to identify God with any concept or knowledge, for God transcends all that can be known of him. Yet, the term points to the possibility of union with God and the experience of his presence."[14] That experience, proponents suggest, may be achieved through apophatic mysticism, which, according to Harvey Egan, "stresses that because God is the ever-greater God, so radically different from any creature, God is best known by negation, elimination, forgetting, unknowing, without images and symbols, and in darkness. God is 'not this, not that.' All images, thoughts, symbols, etc. must be eliminated."[15]

Most scholars of Christian mysticism would trace its origins back to the earliest days of the faith and especially highlight eastern patristic theologians like Origen or Gregory of Nyssa. Still, there is widespread agreement that the traditional divisions of cataphatic and apophatic mysticism find their fullest early expression in the writings of Pseudo-Dionysius the Areopagite.[16] Writing in the late fifth or early sixth centuries, Pseudo-Dionysius's relatively small corpus included two significant works for subsequent mystical thinkers. *The Divine Names* represents a more affirmative, cataphatic approach to theology. Perhaps more influential, though, is *The Mystical Theology*, a brief explanation of apophaticism: "In *The Divine Names*," Pseudo-Dionysius writes:

> I have shown the sense in which God is described as good, existent, life, wisdom, power, and whatever other things pertain to the conceptual names for God ... But my argument now rises from what is below up to the transcendent, and the more it climbs, the more language falters, and when it has passed up and beyond the ascent, it will turn silent completely, since it will finally be at one with him who is indescribable.[17]

The fact of Pseudo-Dionysius's influence across Christian history is unchallenged among church historians, and while the nature of his influence varied across east or west, Catholic, Orthodox, or Protestant, his call to apophatic mysticism was one of the defining features of his thought. Yet, as Egan has observed, "to sever the link between apophatic and kataphatic theology is to render the former empty. Pseudo-Dionysius teaches implicitly that a purely apophatic theology is a contradiction."[18]

That said, however, in the centuries after Pseudo-Dionysius, the apophatic and cataphatic paths tended to diverge more overtly. The late medieval period saw a significant proliferation of texts about mystical experience, with the bifurcation between the two approaches becoming more evident. In Machen's England during this period, the split could be exemplified by two noteworthy texts, Julian of Norwich's visionary, cataphatic *Revelations of Divine Love* and the anonymous apophatic manual for mystics, *The Cloud of Unknowing*.[19] In the ensuing centuries, Christian mystics continued to write about and analyze their experiences, especially in the Roman Catholic and Eastern Orthodox traditions (but also within Protestantism to a certain extent). Around Machen's own times, one of the seminal studies on the subject was Evelyn Underhill's book *Mysticism*, first published in 1911, though running through a dozen editions across two decades. Underhill's study is expansive and proved influential. Though well-researched, it is more than a systematic academic treatment; as Colleen M. Griffith has observed, "The five hundred page volume established Underhill's reputation and gave exposure to a treasury of mystical literature in the Christian tradition that was largely unknown in the English-speaking world."[20] Underhill never uses the technical terms "cataphatic" or "apophatic" in *Mysticism*, yet she clearly distinguishes between the two concepts: what she calls the "contemplation of transcendence" and "the contemplation of immanence."[21] Yet, Underhill collapses (or at least problematizes) this distinction between contemplative forms shortly after making it:

> Both are necessary if we are to form any idea of that complete reality, imperfect as any such idea must be . . . Since it is the essence of the Christian religion to combine personal and metaphysical truth, a transcendent and an incarnate God, it is not surprising that we should find in Christianity a philosophic and theological basis for this paradox of the contemplative experience.[22]

Perhaps even more pertinently, Underhill follows up this discussion with a chapter entitled "Ecstasy and Rapture." "All mystics agree," she writes, "in regarding such ecstasy as an exceptionally favorable state; the one in which man's spirit is caught up to the most immediate union with the divine."[23]

Such emphasis on ecstasy naturally brings us back to Machen, which is hardly surprising, since Underhill biographers have long acknowledged the influences of the Welsh writer on her early thought. The two knew each other—probably through the Hermetic Order of the Golden Dawn—and corresponded, and Underhill thought highly enough of Machen to dedicate her 1909 novel *The Column of Dust* to him and his second wife, Purefoy. The exact nature of their relationship is not entirely clear, however, for the admiration does not appear to have been fully reciprocal. In a 1924 letter to Colin Summerford, Machen writes in a matter-of-fact postscript that *The Column of Dust* is "not very good."[24] Underhill, writing to Nancy Paul in 1913 about her latest book, laments, "so far the outstanding results of *The Mystic Way* have been a rather harrowing letter from Arthur Machen, making it obvious that he no longer considers me a Christian; some objectionable flattery from unbelievers, and the amazing deduction of *The Times* reviewer, that I have proved that mystics value the sacraments highly, as an elaborate sham."[25]

If Machen was critical of Underhill's literary accomplishments and later writings, her specific discussions of apophatic and cataphatic (transcendent and immanent) mysticism, in such close proximity to her discussion of ecstasy, nonetheless suggest a way of understanding what Machen was attempting to achieve in the fiction he wrote at the turn of the century at the same time he penned *Hieroglyphics*. In her book *God and the Gothic*, Alison Milbank specifically links Machen and Underhill (along with eventual Inkling Charles Williams) as examples of what she calls the "mystical Gothic."[26] As she notes, all three writers were onetime members of the *fin-de-siècle* magic society the Hermetic Order of the Golden Dawn, yet all three were also Christians who fold a doctrinal religious component into their approach to magic and mysticism. Milbank specifically connects all three back to the theology of

Pseudo-Dionysius, contending, "Darkness is . . . in these stories a mystical path, rather in the manner of [Pseudo-]Dionysius the Areopagite, whose writings would be central to the development of ideas and practices of Christian mystical ascent. Dionysius valorizes the dark and the obscure . . . activating the paradoxes of knowledge and mystery, affirmations and denials."[27]

Perhaps unsurprisingly, Milbank takes as her primary Underhill text *The Column of Dust*. Her analysis of Machen focuses on his more evidently "Gothic" works, "The Great God Pan" (1894) and *The Three Impostors* (1895). In doing so, she helpfully sets the precedent for applying Pseudo-Dionysian categories to Machen. Yet, these categories ring even truer for *A Fragment of Life*, which was written at a time in Machen's life he was clearly attempting to articulate sensations or intuitions that defy the boundaries of language. One could infer as much from *Hieroglyphics*, a text as didactic about its insistence on artistic ecstasy as it is nebulous about what the term ought to mean. The period of late 1899, following his wife Amy's death, saw Machen begin to experience states of consciousness that he could never satisfactorily put into words. Writing allusively about this period in his much later memoir, *Things Near and Far* (1922), Machen would later claim that he would see "the world . . . presented to me at a new angle."[28] But as in all his 1920s-era memoirs, the descriptions of his changing perceptions and esoteric techniques are more oblique and poetic than straightforward.[29] Writing to his French friend (and translator) P. J. Toulet, Machen would compare his life as a *de facto* skeptic earlier in the decade to his newfound appreciation of life's mysteries: "Alors je n'aurais pu croire un instant que d'aussi étranges événements fussent jamais arrives dans la vie réelle ou meme aient jamais été susceptibles de s'y produire. Mais depuis, et tous récemment, il s'est produit dans ma proper existence des *expériences* qui ont tout à fait changé mon point de vue à ce sujet" (Then, I could not believe for a moment that such strange events had ever happened in real life or have ever been likely to occur. But since then, and all recently, there have been in my own existence *experiences* that have completely changed my point of view on this subject).[30] Here again, Machen struggles to put into (French) words what he means; his newfound encounters with the supernatural are first and foremost *expériences*, on which he does not elaborate. But they have changed his perspective: "Mais je crois que nous vivons dans un monde de grands mystères, de choses insoupçonnées et tout à fait stupéfiantes" (But I believe we live in a world of great mysteries, of unsuspected and absolutely amazing things.)[31]

Machen penned the letter to Toulet on October 1, 1899. That date is significant, given the nature of his other 1899 productions, for it places them all within a distinctly apophatic matrix: Machen the writer cannot put into words what Machen the mystic is now beginning to feel. *A Fragment of Life* is Machen's most successful literary attempt to bridge this divide. It does so in part by depicting a protagonist who, like Machen himself, cannot articulate what he can intuit: silence itself is embedded in the narrative. Leading into the story's events, Machen tells his readers that in their first year of marriage, Edward and Mary "had got on excellently, rarely sitting silent for more than an hour."[32] Yet, since Machen wishes to privilege the contemplative mystical life over the meaningless noise of modern workaday existence, this apparent sociability on their part is not necessarily intrinsically commendable. The opening paragraphs begin with Darnell experiencing a vision that he dares not speak of to his "grave and quiet" wife.[33] Later in the first chapter, in which the two have debated almost *ad nauseam* about spare rooms and furniture, they find themselves together in the outside yard:

> A warm, scented gale came to them from beyond the walls. He longed to ask her to stay out with him all night beneath the tree, that they might whisper to one another, that the scent of her hair might inebriate him, that he might feel her dress still brushing against his ankles. But he could not find the words, and it was absurd, and she was so gentle that she would do whatever he asked, however foolish it might be, just because he asked her. He was not worthy to kiss her lips; he bent down and kissed her silk bodice, and again he felt that she trembled, and he was ashamed, fearing that he had frightened her.[34]

There is an intimacy in their quietness in this scene that transcends the bland domestic conversations that precede it. Yet, in the interstices of this intimate quiet is also Edward's recognition that "he could not find the words" to speak to her.

Such silences of incommunicability, however, become less frequent as the novella progresses. Edward grows more conscious about his mystical quest, and he becomes more confident in speaking of it to Mary, who herself is increasingly intrigued. Even here, though, apophatic silence plays a role. When Edward finally works up the courage to speak to Mary about one of his mystical walking tours, Machen is careful to distinguish his descriptions from the mundane conversations the couple has had in the past, maintaining that Edward "went on, as if continuing the thoughts that had filled his mind *while his lips were silent.*"[35] Edward's meditations on these long walks are punctuated by travels to environments that are likewise characterized by silence, beginning with "a hush in the world"[36] at the early morning. Mary's response to her husband's excursions demonstrate her own receptivity, while underscoring at the same time the difficulty that he has in putting his thoughts into words:

> She was silent for a little while, and then she spoke—
>
> "Oh, my dear, why have you waited so long to tell me these wonderful things? I think it is beautiful."[37]

But if the silences hint at the difficulty in articulating mystic experiences, how then does Machen go about trying to do so in *A Fragment of Life*? And how does the character of Edward do so in his more substantive conversations with Mary? The answer, which has already been suggested here, is that he arrives at apophatic mysticism by a cataphatic route. This is entirely consistent with the Christian mystical tradition as it has been rightly understood. Pseudo-Dionysius himself saw his more apophatic *Mystical Theology* as building upon the foundation of *The Divine Names*, and, as Egan notes in this context, "a purely apophatic theology is a contradiction."[38] Underhill too stresses the interdependence of what she calls the "transcendent" and "immanent" approaches. Machen's ultimate goal (and through him Edward Darnell's) might be an unspeakable, ineffable experience of the divine, but the only way to achieve—and then to communicate—that experience is through the world of the senses.

This is precisely the point he makes in *Hieroglyphics*—fine literature must generate ecstasy, but doing so requires the words and events in its pages to function above all symbolically, like hieroglyphics: "things made by ecstasy and for ecstasy, things that are symbols, proclaiming the presence of the unknown world."[39] He acknowledges that literature cannot be too abstract, that it must have a cataphatic element to it. Aspects of plotting makes up the second and third of Machen's four elements necessary in a literary work—something must indeed happen. But of most vital importance is the first element, "the Idea or Conception, the thing of exquisite beauty which dwells in the author's soul."[40]

A Fragment of Life accomplishes this effect through a technique of careful juxtaposition.[41] Large swaths of the narrative are, in fact, nothing more than Edward and Mary talking with each other about tediously ordinary events, the kind of raw material most people spend their lives talking about: family, friends, jobs, possessions. This is the subject matter that occupies the artificers whom Machen discredits as literary authors in *Hieroglyphics*, novelists like Jane Austen, George Eliot, and William Makepeace Thackeray. Structurally, his work is for much of its length the most commonplace of realistic dramas, and if readers find the book unappealing, it is very likely for this reason. But then, Machen *desires* for his readers to find such a work unappealing since his Christian mystic project is to set up this lifestyle (and the writers who purport to reflect it) as tragically flawed. Most moderns, Machen asserts, live shallow, materialistic lives like Edward Darnell, who "was sincerely of opinion that he was a City clerk, living in Shepherd's Bush—having forgotten the mysteries and the far-shining glories of the kingdom which was his by legitimate inheritance."[42]

Reynolds and Charlton appear to find this juxtaposing effect arbitrary and Machen's "mysterious phenomena" to be "random"[43]—yet they are anything but. His proactively cataphatic imagery is in fact part of a carefully modulated effect, one that will move toward imagery increasingly suggestive of *apophaticism* as the work progresses. One of the primary sources of his imagery is, unsurprisingly, his home environment of Wales. The story begins and ends with Edward Darnell's vision "of an ancient wood, and of a clear well rising into grey film and vapour beneath a misty, glimmering heat."[44] Edward learns that he has Welsh ancestry so that for him, as for Machen, the dream of the wood carries connotations of returning home, even as its natural beauty contrasts favorably with the shallow suburban purgatory in which the Darnells live. The fact that the vision carries suggestions that Machen would associate with his physical home is important—for on the deeper level, it is meant to represent the mystical state that is the Darnells' (and all people's) true spiritual home. Thus, when Edward returns to this symbolic site at the end of the work as a true mystic himself, it has replaced London as his true home: "So I awoke from a dream of a London suburb, of daily labour, of weary, useless little things; and as my eyes were opened I saw that I was in an ancient wood, where a clear well rose into grey film and vapour beneath a misty, glimmering heat."[45]

The image of the well is also significant, as it is an image that conveys the idea of thirst. Thirst-related imagery naturally pushes the reader closer to Machen's underlying apophatic purposes, since it implies absence and longing. Edward's vision is presumably of an actual well from his family's history, one which Machen describes on exactly the spiritual terms one might expect:

> Here, then, he read of the Holy Well, hidden in the Wistman's Wood—*Sylva Sapientum*—"a fountain of abundant water, which no heats of summer can ever dry, which no flood can ever defile, which is as a water of life, to them that thirst for life, a stream of cleansing to them that would be pure, and a medicine of such healing virtue that by it, through the might of God and the intercession of His saints, the most grievous wounds are made whole." But the water of this well was to be kept sacred perpetually, it was not to be used for any common purpose, nor to satisfy any bodily thirst, but ever to be esteemed as holy, "even as the water which the priest hath hallowed."[46]

But Wistman's Well is not the only mystic image of thirst, for Machen increasingly draws in another of his favorite symbols: the Holy Grail (or Graal, as he names it). The Graal—the legendary cup or dish from Christ's Last Supper—was always a vessel for mystical ecstasy in the medieval Arthurian tales so beloved by Machen. He would return to the image again in his story "The Great Return" (1915) and novel *The Secret Glory* (published in 1922, but first begun in 1899). Both the ancient Welsh well of spiritual water (also an evident allusion to John 4) and the Graal, a chalice for wine, may evoke a sense of thirst.[47]

More significantly still, however, is Machen's increasing use of sacramental images. The Graal is no ordinary wineglass but a medieval emblem of the Eucharist, and those subtexts are quite apparent in the final lines of the poem Edward is said to have written:

The sullen river rolls all gold,
The desert park's a faery wold,
When on the trees the wind is borne
I hear the sound of Arthur's horn
I see no town of grim grey ways,
But a great city all ablaze
With burning torches, to light up
The pinnacles that shrine the Cup.
Ever the magic wine is poured,
Ever the Feast shines on the board,
Ever the song is borne on high
That chants the holy Magistry—
Etc. etc. etc.[48]

The progress of the imagery here is worth noting, as it moves from the more explicitly pagan (or at least non-dogmatic) realm of the "faery wold" to the poetic invocation of the Eucharist.[49] While Machen had employed Christian allusions throughout his earlier work, never in any prior piece is it this obviously privileged, for *A Fragment of Life* was written even as he was more consciously adopting the Christian faith as his own. This usage would pave the way for his subsequent, more thoroughgoing Christian treatments of the Graal as a conduit for mystical ecstasy in *The Secret Glory* and "The Great Return." Mark Valentine speculates that *A Fragment of Life* may have been written to imagine what his life with Amy could have been if she had survived,[50] making it a deeply personal work to him, but returning to the faith of his childhood—this time with a distinctly ritualistic flair—was also deeply personal. As Underhill notes, "For the Christian mystics, the sacraments and mysteries of the faith have always provided a *point d'appui*; and these often play a large part in the production of their ecstasies."[51] Machen's lyrical terminology defamiliarizes the sacrament, doubtless to wrest it from becoming watered-down by low-church Protestantism, but its importance to the Darnells' own turn toward mysticism is unmistakable.

The ending of *A Fragment of Life* seems somewhat abrupt and can no doubt be frustrating to readers desiring more closure, or at least more rich depiction of Edward and Mary's "New Life" with its "semblance of the stories of the Graal."[52] Yet, given his ultimate project, it is difficult to imagine Machen successfully ending the tale in any other way. It is, indeed, a fragment—not a horrific antimetaphysical fragment like the final chapter of "The Great God Pan" but a numinous apophatic fragment. John Howard notes that this is truly the culmination of Machen's juxtapositions in the story, giving "the effect of fragmenting the story as if there had been no alternative."[53] This final fragmenting was not what Machen had written in his first pass at the story, instead a product of the revision before its eventual publication. Unlike the "'false' ending," Howard observes, the new ending

> is in fact anything but hasty and clumsy . . . [I]n the revised chapter he strains as ever to express that which cannot be expressed, and even if the result was still far from successful in his eyes, Machen harnessed this inherent inability to point toward what he wants to say. This is appropriate in a story of yearning and transmutation.[54]

Machen, that is, has traveled the *via affirmativa* as far as he can go in good conscience, but the true destination was always ineffable, unspeakable, incommunicable. It is a challenging needle he must thread: too much imagery could risk giving the impression that these mysteries were more comprehensible than in fact they are. Yet, as a work of literature (not philosophy or theology), *A Fragment of Life must* work in the realm of the senses, at least to some extent. In his poorly-regarded final novel, *The Green Round* (1933), Machen would surrender too easily, leading to a climax so apophatic that the only imagery he provides is bland and generic; the reader is then left with a mysticism too abstract to be compelling.[55]

For that reason, Machen continues to deploy cataphatic-style imagery up to the end; these images—the silence, the wood, the well, the Graal—function as spiritual landmarks as far as he can post them. But to follow the Darnells to their true home, readers must abandon intelligible signs altogether. That is because, to use Howard's terms, *A Fragment of Life* is indeed "a story of yearning and transmutation." Milbank makes a similar observation about the "mystical Gothic" project in which she locates Machen's oeuvre. Unlike occult knowledge, mysticism "through purgation and illumination is a real change in being: it is ontological rather than merely epistemological or, rather, this mode of knowledge is one of transformation. The difference is that that the will to know is taken up into the will to love."[56]

These interpretations fit well with the final fate of Edward and Mary Darnell as Machen describes it. The symbols Machen chooses also suggest absence or "yearning." Yet, though Machen sometimes employs the term "magical" about the Darnells' increasingly mystic consciousness, this yearning is not simply Hermeticism, a magician's *curiositas*: they do not simply want to "know" in the intellectual sense. Rather, they want to "know" in the more intimate sense,[57] to join with each other but also the divine source of their mystic yearnings. Near the book's end, Darnell experiences this in the sacraments of the church, "the mystic dance that signifies rapture and a joy above all joys, and when he beheld Love slain and rise again victorious he knew that he witnessed, in a figure, the consummation of all things, the Bridal of all Bridals, the mystery that is beyond all mysteries, accomplished from the foundation of the world."[58] So readers know that the final experience Machen has been describing through Edward's poem, just before it fades into its last apophatic "Etc. etc. etc."—the cup, the wine, the feast, the song, the magistry—all point back to this divine Christian sacramental Love. And that love "transmutes" and "transforms" them: "It is certain, indeed, that in this world they changed their lives, like King Arthur, but this is a work which no chronicler has cared to describe with any amplitude of detail."[59]

So their mystical experience, described when necessary through poetic images, finds its consummation in a union that *transcends* language and *transforms* its subjects. However much readers may *not* know about the Darnells after their experiences in the book, Machen makes clear the one things his readers *can* know—this couple has "changed," "awoke from a dream of a London suburb"[60] to a very different (and perhaps linguistically inexpressible) form of life. How many readers will join them? Machen never seemed optimistic that his perspective would become popular. But the hieroglyphics of *A Fragment of Life* remain in print, awaiting those few readers willing to interpret them and start along the way.

NOTES

1. This essay was made possible in part through discussions with my 2016 Senior Seminar class on Fairy Tales (Rachel Miller, Katlynne Waldrop, and Samantha Raney) and the assistance of my student graders, Samantha Raney and Rebekah Van Landingham Mann.
2. Arthur Machen, *Hieroglyphics: A Note upon Ecstasy in Literature* (New York: Alfred A. Knopf, 1923), 18–19.
3. Aidan Reynolds and William Charlton, *Arthur Machen: A Short Account of His Life and Work* (London: Baker, 1963), 67.
4. S. T. Joshi, *The Weird Tale* (Holicong, PA: Wildside, 2003), 13.
5. Wesley D. Sweetser, *Arthur Machen* (New York: Twayne, 1964), 31, 107.
6. The nature of apophatic theology will be discussed in more detail below.
7. Arthur Machen, *A Fragment of Life*, in *The White People and Other Weird Stories*, ed. S. T. Joshi (New York: Penguin Books, 2011), 220.
8. Joshi, *The Weird Tale*, 27.
9. Ibid., 29.
10. Machen, *A Fragment of Life*, 166.
11. Machen, *Hieroglyphics*, 63.

12. This term is variously spelled "cataphatic" and "kataphatic."
13. Veselin Kesich, "Via Negativa," in *Encyclopedia of Religion*, 2nd ed., ed. Lindsay Jones, vol. 14, 9586–88 (Farmington Hills, MI: Macmillan Reference, 2005), 9587.
14. Ibid., 9586.
15. Harvey Egan, "Christian Apophatic and Kataphatic Mysticisms," *Theological Studies* 39, no. 3 (September 1978), 403.
16. The theologian's real name is unknown. He wrote under the name of Dionysius, a first-century Christian convert of the Apostle Paul during his visit to the Athenian site of the Areopagus (as described in Acts 17).
17. Pseudo-Dionysius the Areopagite, *Pseudo-Dionysius: The Complete Works*, Classics of Western Spirituality, trans. Colm Luibheid (New York: Paulist, 1987), 139.
18. Harvey Egan, *An Anthology of Christian Mysticism* (Collegeville, MN: Liturgical Press, 1991), 94. Egan extensively examines the symbiotic (rather than adversarial) relationship between the two forms in his essay "Christian Apophatic and Kataphatic Mysticisms."
19. Here, too, the distinctions between approaches may not be as sharp as they initially appear. See Egan, "Christian Apophatic and Kataphatic Mysticisms," 405–13. Nonetheless, the overall divergent trajectories of these works are clear.
20. Colleen M. Griffith, "Underhill's *Practical Mysticism*: One Hundred Years Later." *New Theology Review* 27, no. 1 (September 2014), 26.
21. Evelyn Underhill, *Mysticism*, 12th ed. (New York: Image, 1990), 337–44.
22. Ibid., 344.
23. Ibid., 358.
24. Arthur Machen, *Selected Letters: The Private Writings of the Master of the Macabre*, eds Roger Dobson, Godfrey Brangham, and R. A. Gilbert (Wellingborough: Aquarian, 1988), 93.
25. Evelyn Underhill, *The Letters of Evelyn Underhill*, ed. Charles Williams (London: Longmans, 1943), 140.
26. Alison Milbank, *God and the Gothic: Religion, Romance, and Reality in the English Literary Tradition* (Oxford: Oxford University Press, 2018), 269–85. Milbank also invokes weird fiction writer Algernon Blackwood (270), whose work is often compared with Machen's and who was also a member of the Golden Dawn, though because Blackwood is not operating from a Christian theistic or mystical framework, he is not her focus.
27. Milbank, *God and the Gothic*, 285.
28. Arthur Machen, *Things Near and Far* (New York: Knopf, 1923), 176.
29. Mark Valentine does, however, believe "that the mystical state [Machen] describes is an almost classic account of the characteristics of similar experiences recorded in many ages and cultures, especially the quality of ineffability, the sense of things taking on a new significance, the transiency, the astonishment, or bewilderment at what has transpired, and the enhanced identification with all things encountered." Mark Valentine, *Arthur Machen* (Bridgend: Seren, 1995), 72. Valentine's description here serves to show that Machen truly is discussing mysticism and not something

altogether different; yet such a vague or clinical cataloging could hardly be to Machen a satisfactory communication of his experiences.

30. Henri Martineau, "Arthur Machen et P. J. Toulet: Une Correspondance Inédite," *Mercure de France* 281 (January 1, 1938): 54, italics in the original, my trans.

31. Ibid., 54, my trans.

32. Machen, *A Fragment of Life*, 148.

33. Ibid.

34. Ibid., 167.

35. Ibid., 181, italics added.

36. Ibid.

37. Ibid., 183.

38. Egan, *An Anthology of Christian Mysticism*, 94.

39. Machen, *Hieroglyphics*, 49.

40. Machen, *Hieroglyphics*, 68–69.

41. For more discussion on this juxtaposition, see Geoffrey Reiter, "'Man Is Made a Mystery': The Evolution of Arthur Machen's Religious Thought" (PhD diss., Baylor University, 2010), 127–43.

42. Machen, *A Fragment of Life*, 170.

43. Reynolds and Charlton, *Arthur Machen*, 77.

44. Machen, *A Fragment of Life*, 148.

45. Ibid., 222.

46. Ibid., 216.

47. Machen likewise employs thirst-related imagery to parallel mystical experience in the climax of his later novella "The Terror." See Reiter, "Man," 186–88.

48. Machen, *A Fragment of Life*, 221.

49. While the references at the end of this poem of the Wine, the Feast, and the "chants of holy Magistry" use terminology that abstractly could still be conceived of as pagan, their context in the story strongly favors a Christian reading, proceeding out of Darnell's discovery of a church earlier in the story and following lines invoking Arthur, the king who legendarily oversaw the Christianization of Britain.

50. Valentine, *Arthur Machen*, 68.

51. Underhill, *Mysticism*, 364.

52. Machen, *A Fragment of Life*, 220.

53. John Howard, "The Impossible History: Machen's 'A Fragment of Life,'" in *The Secret Ceremonies: Critical Essays on Arthur Machen*, ed. Mark Valentine and Timothy J. Jarvis, 333–43 (New York: Hippocampus, 2019), 341.

54. Howard, "The Impossible History," 341–42.

55. For further discussion of *The Green Round*'s failed apophaticism, see Reiter, "Man," 200–10.

56. Milbank, *God and the Gothic*, 280.

57. In Hebrew, for instance, "to know" is a euphemism for joining in loving sexual union specifically, or intimate communion more broadly.

58. Machen, *A Fragment of Life*, 216.

59. Ibid., 220.

60. Ibid., 222.

REFERENCES

Egan, Harvey D. (ed.). *An Anthology of Christian Mysticism*. Collegeville, MN: Liturgical Press, 1991.

———. "Christian Apophatic and Kataphatic Mysticisms." *Theological Studies* 39, no. 3 (September 1978): 399–426.

Griffith, Colleen M. "Underhill's *Practical Mysticism*: One Hundred Years Later." *New Theology Review* 27, no. 1 (September 2014): 25–32.

Howard, John. "The Impossible History: Machen's 'A Fragment of Life.'" In *The Secret Ceremonies: Critical Essays on Arthur Machen*, edited by Mark Valentine and Timothy J. Jarvis, 333–43. New York: Hippocampus, 2019.

Joshi, S. T. *The Weird Tale*. Holicong, PA: Wildside, 2003.

Kesich, Veselin. "Via Negativa." In *Encyclopedia of Religion*. Vol. 14. 2nd ed., edited by Lindsay Jones, 9586–88. Farmington Hills, MI: Macmillan Reference, 2005.

Machen, Arthur. *A Fragment of Life*. In *The White People and Other Weird Stories*, edited by S. T. Joshi. New York: Penguin Books, 2011.

———. *Hieroglyphics: A Note upon Ecstasy in Literature*. New York: Alfred A. Knopf, 1923.

———. *Selected Letters: The Private Writings of the Master of the Macabre*, edited by Roger Dobson, Godfrey Brangham, and R. A. Gilbert. Wellingborough: Aquarian, 1988.

———. *Things Near and Far*. New York: Knopf, 1923.

Martineau, Henri. "Arthur Machen et P. J. Toulet: Une Correspondance Inédite." *Mercure de France* 281 (January 1, 1938): 47–61.

Milbank, Alison. *God and the Gothic: Religion, Romance, and Reality in the English Literary Tradition*. Oxford: Oxford University Press, 2018.

Pseudo-Dionysius the Areopagite. *Pseudo-Dionysius: The Complete Works*. Classics of Western Spirituality, translated by Colm Luibheid. New York: Paulist, 1987.

Reiter, Geoffrey. "'Man Is Made a Mystery': The Evolution of Arthur Machen's Religious Thought." PhD diss., Baylor University, 2010.

Reynolds, Aidan, and William Charlton. *Arthur Machen: A Short Account of His Life and Work*. London: Baker, 1963.

Sweetser, Wesley D. *Arthur Machen*. New York: Twayne, 1964.

Underhill, Evelyn. *The Letters of Evelyn Underhill*, edited by Charles Williams. London: Longmans, 1943.

———. *Mysticism*. 12th ed. New York: Image, 1990.

Valentine, Mark. *Arthur Machen*. Bridgend: Seren, 1995.

Chapter 12

A "Miracle" in No Man's Land?
Arthur Machen and the Angels of Mons
Andrew R. Lenoir

In arguably the most iconic scene of the 2017 Warner Brothers' film *Wonder Woman*, the protagonist Diana is brought to the Western Front to see the grim realities of the then-unfolding World War I.[1] She is told that this is "no man's land," and after a year's struggle "no man can cross" the space between the trenches. Victory is "impossible." Taking this as a challenge, the heroine removes her civilian clothes and reveals her otherworldly, supernatural armor—a magical bulletproof shield and bracers along with a sword handed down to her by the Gods. As Diana draws the full brunt of the German machine-gun fire, the allied forces follow her example and surge over the top, finally succeeding in taking the enemy position. A strikingly similar scene plays out in the fifth issue of Alan Moore's 1999 comic series *Promethea*, "Weapon For Liberty." A British soldier at the Battle of Ypres finds himself alone in his trench, surrounded by the bodies of his dead comrades. As he begins to openly despair, a naked woman wrapped with a white cloth, wearing Athena's helmet and holding a Greek shield—nearly identical to the one used in *Wonder Woman*—descends, saying she is "come to take [him] home." "I've gone already, haven't I?" the soldier responds. "I'm dead and you're an angel. I-I've heard of chaps who've seen 'em . . ."[2]

Many people—especially in Great Britain—have heard of "chaps who've seen" angels on the battlefields of World War I. The tales of "The Angels of Mons" are strangely persistent, appearing in seemingly authoritative sources like 1992's *The World War One Source Book* and websites with names like WorldWar1.com and Warfare History Network.[3] As recently as 2002, British tabloids were flooded by rumors that a film reel of angels on the Western Front had not only been found but that Marlon Brando had acquired the rights to make a big-budget movie on the subject. When this was proved to be a hoax, the BBC noted the surprising staying power of what it deemed "the first example of an Urban Myth." Having established its continued popularity more than a century later, this chapter will explain how this story came to be, what the myth of the Angels of Mons meant and may mean for contemporary and modern supporters, and how the man behind it all felt about the "monster" he had created.

Writer Arthur Machen (1863–1947) would probably prefer to be remembered for his novels, novellas, and perhaps even his short acting career, but it is his 1914 short story, "The Bowmen," and its resultant "Angels" that have had the greatest longevity. Although his horror stories are routinely cited as inspirations for authors like Lovecraft and Stephen King, the lasting legend of angels appearing on the battlefield might be Machen's most successful, if inadvertent, creation, a fiction that has for many become a matter of faith and fact.

In early August 1914, the 80,000–130,000 strong British Expeditionary Force (BEF) was deployed to Belgium to help defend the smaller nation's neutrality and to stop the German march toward France. Less than a week after the BEF's arrival on August 17, British and French Forces coordinated an attempt to cut off the German advance.[4] The French Fifth Army under General Lanrezac arrived first and was quickly devastated by the full brunt of the superior German artillery. Overwhelmed, Lanrezac ordered a retreat leaving the unaware BEF to face an enemy who outnumbered them more than two to one.[5] Arriving at a fortified canal outside the city of Mons, Belgium, British commander Sir John French opted to hold the line, hoping his troops could slow the Germans long enough for the Allies to regroup. On the morning of August 23, German troops attempted to cross the canal's bridges and the two armies engaged.[6] In all, the BEF suffered 1,600 casualties, compared to the German's 5,000–10,000, before being forced into a hasty retreat. The exhausted British troops marched 25-miles over the next two days without sleep or rest, losing another 2,600 men in subsequent skirmishes before finally regrouping with the French.[7] At the Battle of Le Cateau on August 26, the last battle to ever use Napoleonic era tactics, the BEF finally managed to stop the German advance at the cost of another 7,800 men.[8] In all, 12,000 BEF troops, at least a tenth of all its men, had been killed or wounded in nine days.

News was slow to come back from the front, but as it did, the extent of the destruction—the inhuman horror of it—set in. The sheer number of soldiers killed and wounded in so little time was inconceivable to the British public. The world had never before seen anything like "The War to End All Wars"—a name and sentiment loaded with an excess of symbolic meaning. In September 1914, the same month Machen's "The Bowmen" was published, Reverend Henry Charles Beeching of Norwich Cathedral told his congregation, "The battle is not only ours, it is God's, it is indeed Armageddon.

Ranged against us are the Dragon and the False Prophet."[9] By the spring of 1915, at least two distinct pamphlets by different authors entitled "The Great War—In the Divine Light of Prophecy: Is It Armageddon?" and "Is It Armageddon? Or Britain in Prophecy?" were circulating around England. Ralph Shirley, editor of *The Occult Review* magazine, wrote articles asking whether German Kaiser Wilhelm II was the anti-Christ, complete with numerological "evidence" based upon the leader's name. This thinking was so prevalent and seductive, it even began to affect the names of individual clashes, like 1918's "Battle of Megiddo," a title chosen by General Edmund Allenby to directly invoke the final battle of Revelations (and origin of the word "Armageddon," from "Har Megiddo" or "Mount Megiddo") itself.

To the religiously minded, a worldwide struggle of such magnitude could only be explained as part of a divine plan. Surely, so much death and destruction must attract the attention of heaven. How could an all-powerful and all good God stand aside at his people's suffering? According to newspaper reports, he was not, or, at least, his intermediaries were not. In early September 1914, the Virgin Mary was said to have answered the prayers of French Catholics through the Allied victory at the Battle of the Marne.[10] That October, newspapers reported the Virgin appearing to Russian troops the night before the Battle of Augustov.[11] There were other stories of St. Michael and the still-unsanctified Joan of Arc urging Allied troops onward.[12] It could be that this was nothing more than mass hysteria. On the other hand, in 1917 the Marian Apparitions at Fatima, Portugal took place, including the so-called "Miracle of the Sun" were witnessed by 30,000 people, the only one of these incidents officially recognized by the Catholic Church. In comparison to the reports of their Catholic and Orthodox comrades, the accounts from the protestant British soldiers seemed rather drab and conventional. It was against this backdrop of renewed religiosity and paranoia that Machen's "The Bowmen" first appeared, and it was perhaps because of this climate that the myth of the "Angels of Mons" was able to take flight.

By then fifty-one years old, and more than two decades after "The Great God Pan" had secured his reputation as one of the foremost horror writers of the era, the aging Machen found himself boxed in by material concerns. Struggling to make ends meet, he took a position with the London-based *Evening News* where his creative powers were constrained by deadlines as he reported current events, wrote editorials, and, occasionally, wrote fiction. With a first-hand look at the news coming back from the front, including the details government censors deemed too sensitive or depressing for public consumption, Machen was, like most observers of his generation, deeply moved and disturbed by events both at home and on the continent. In September 1914, he first weighed in on the then widespread reports and rumors of a "phantom army" that were consuming the British public's imagination. This phantom army, however, was not angelic, and it was not on the battlefield. Instead, it was purported to have arrived in England by way of Arkangel, the North Russian seaport. In his September 15 *Evening News* column entitled, "What About Those Russians!," Machen made quick work of the second- and third-hand stories of train-loads of Russian troops supposedly stopping at a variety of British railway stations. Dismissing the stories as products of overactive and overtaxed public imagination, the Welsh writer affirmed: "It strikes me that it will remain in history as one of the most remarkable delusions that the world has ever harbored."[13] In fact, he would prove himself wrong exactly two weeks later when "The Bowmen," his first "legend of the war," was published on September 29, the feast of Saint Michael and All Angels.

On paper, "The Bowmen" purports to be the first-hand account of an unnamed soldier's experience on a presumably Belgian battlefield. Pinned down by German gunfire, outnumbered, and with no hope of escape, the protagonist recalls "a queer vegetarian restaurant in London," with "cutlets made of lentils and nuts that pretended to be steak."[14] Most importantly, though, he remembers the strange decoration on their flatware, "a figure of St. George in blue, with the motto, *Adsit Anglis Sanctus Georgius*—May St. George be a present help to the English."[15] The soldier quietly murmurs the Latin prayer as he stands and opens fire on the approaching enemy forces. Suddenly, an otherworldly vision begins to play out before the protagonist.

> For as the Latin scholar uttered his invocation he felt something between a shudder and an electric shock pass through his body. The roar of the battle died down in his ears to a gentle murmur; instead of it, he says, he heard a great voice and a shout louder than a thunder-peal crying, "Array, array, array!"
>
> His heart grew hot as a burning coal, it grew cold as ice within him, as it seemed to him that a tumult of voices answered to his summons. He heard, or seemed to hear, thousands shouting: "St. George! St. George!"
>
> "Ha! messire; ha! sweet Saint, grant us good deliverance!"
>
> "St. George for merry England!"
>
> "Harow! Harow! Monseigneur St. George, succour us."
>
> "Ha! St. George! Ha! St. George! a long bow and a strong bow."
>
> "Heaven's Knight, aid us!"
>
> And as the soldier heard these voices he saw before him, beyond the trench, a long line of shapes, with a shining about them. They were like men who drew the bow, and with another shout their cloud of arrows flew singing and tingling through the air towards the German hosts.[16]

The other British soldiers continue fighting, apparently unaware of the spectral archers. Several comments on how fast the German soldiers are falling. Finally, miraculously, the British soldiers win the day. Perplexed by their enormous losses and the number of bodies without "discernable wounds," German high command theorizes that their army fell victim to some new poisonous gas, "But the man who knew what nuts tasted like when they called themselves steak knew also that St. George had brought his Agincourt Bowmen to help the English."[17]

In Machen's own estimation, "The Bowmen" was not his finest story. Unsatisfied with his first efforts at composing what would later become "The Soldier's Rest," he tried his hand at another, simpler story. He handed the hastily written draft off to his editor, who thought only to ask why English archers would use French terms like, "Monseigneur." Machen remarked that they "struck [him] as picturesque."[18] What neither of them realized was the chord this story would strike with the sympathetic public, its popularity turning the tale into Machen's personal nightmare. As he wrote in his column "NO ESCAPE FROM "THE BOWMEN," on July 30, 1915, "Frankenstein made a monster to his sorrow . . . I have begun to sympathize with him."[19]

The chain reaction started with Ralph Shirley, editor of *The Occult Review*, author of *Prophecies and Omens of the Great War* (1915), and proponent of the theory equating the Kaiser to the anti-Christ. Perhaps surprisingly, he took Machen at his word when, after asking if there was any truth to "The Bowmen," Machen said he had made it all up. Shortly after that, David Gow, the editor of another spiritual journal, *Light*, wrote to ask the same question and received the same answer. He too seemed satisfied. Writing on October 10, Gow described "The Bowmen" as "a little fantasy," while simultaneously citing his own supernatural beliefs: "as far as we can see the unseen world does not work that way . . . the spiritual hosts are probably better employed in ministering . . . to the wounded and dying."[20]

With the paranormal enthusiasts put to rest, Machen probably thought that was the last he would hear of "The Bowmen." What he had not counted on was the Church of England. In November, Father Edward Russell, Deacon at the Church of St. Alban the Martyr in Holborn, wrote and received permission to reprint the story in his parish magazine.[21] In the Spring, Russell wrote again reporting that the issue with "The Bowmen" had sold out. Hoping to appease his curious congregation, he asked Machen for his sources and if he had any more corroborating information about the miraculous events in Belgium. Machen explained, once again, that "The Bowmen" was fiction. But while that answer had pacified the occultists, the priest was more persistent. Recounting the response he received that April, Machen quotes Russell as saying, "That I must be mistaken, that the main 'facts' of 'The Bowmen' must be true, that my share in the matter must surely have been confined to the elaboration and decoration of a veridical history."[22] In hindsight, Machen marks this as the moment that "the snowball of rumor was . . . set rolling . . . growing bigger and bigger."[23]

Before the end of 1915, letters had begun appearing in newspapers across the country from soldier's claiming to have seen strange things during the battle and retreat from Mons. Some reports spoke of Saint George, a few versions even including the plates from the vegetarian restaurant, but the stories of archers were far fewer than those of angels saving the British army. The stories were so prevalent that the Society for Psychical Research, the foremost and most "respectable" of organizations exploring extraordinary phenomena conducted their own investigation, reporting in 1915, "the result of our enquiry [into the Apparitions] is negative . . . all our efforts to obtain the detailed evidence upon which an enquiry of this kind must be based have proved unavailing."[24] Despite this, the public did not seem to notice, and neither did they heed Machen's similar assessment. Instead, his protests and public statements fell on deaf ears at best, and open rebuke and mockery at worst. Edward Begbie, author of *On the Side of the Angels, A Response to Mr. Arthur Machen* (1915), went so far as to accuse his Machen of "sacrilege," stating, "Mr. Machen in his quieter and less popular moments will feel a very sincere regret and perhaps sharp contrition."[25] Although the Welsh writer fought back with his own response, the public had already chosen a side. By 1916, there was already an Angels of Mons piano solo by Sydney C. Baldock; an Angel of Mons Waltz, by composer Paul Paree; and an Angels of Mons silent film by director Fred Paul. Postcards depicting angels ministering to fallen soldiers began to proliferate, and the term was even adopted as a title for posters and pamphlets promoting young female volunteer nurses as "The Real Angels of Mons."

Although Machen had his own theories about the origins of "angelmania," no one is quite sure how to explain what transpired between the story's publication and the cementing of the "Angels of Mons" myth. It has been repeatedly claimed, such as in David Clarke's 2004 *The Angel of Mons*, that "The Bowmen" was published without being properly marked as fiction, and that its quasi-journalistic tone fooled readers into taking it for fact.[26] This assertion falls apart, however, when one considers that Machen's other fiction stories printed in the *Evening News* before and after had never carried any such genre label. Further, regular readers could have encountered Machen's story "The Ceaseless Bugle Call," only twelve days earlier. That simple narrative shares many obvious connections to "The Bowmen," centering around a British soldier at a training camp contemplating a statue of Saint George and reciting the same Latin prayer. Although this rather mundane, uneventful plot stretches no one's credulity, it was never confused for anything other than Machen's imaginings.

It could be that the answer was archetypical. Just as soldiers and average citizens on the continent seemed to experience a resurgence of almost medieval religious phenomena, it is possible the answer lies in the English unconscious. In the United Kingdom, traditions reaching back into antiquity told of the "Wild Hunt": a group of dead soldiers who rode behind a figure variously identified, depending upon the period, as Odin, King Arthur, and Sir Francis Drake.[27] In 1642, the English Civil War battle at Edgehill was noted for the appearance of two phantom armies fighting in the sky above the battlefield for two days. In fact, Machen acknowledges the fifteenth-century Battle of Agincourt, as the direct inspiration for "The Bowmen."[28] *The Brut Chronicle* account states King Henry V prayed on the way into battle, "In the name of almighty God and Saint George, avant banner!" and ends, saying, "Thus almighty god and saint George brought our enemies to the ground."[29]

Another popular theory, also explored by David Clarke, is the question of whether the angels were a product of intentional government propaganda efforts. Though the Angels of Mons stories predate the formal creation of the War Propaganda Bureau, it coincides exactly with the exaggerated news reports of the "Rape of Belgium." In the most famous example, the story of the Crucified Soldier, German troops were said to have bayonetted a Canadian soldier to a barn door or, sometimes, a tree. Although the story is immortalized to this day with memorial statues, to date, there is no definitive evidence that the incident actually occurred.[30]

Perhaps the most tantalizing piece of circumstantial evidence for this theory comes from the involvement of Brigadier General John Charteris. In addition to his claim of having heard about the angels before "The Bowmen" was published, Charteris is most famous for his own fictitious creation: the story of the German "corpse factories." An inspired piece of propaganda, eerily prescient of the similar rumors that emerged from World War II's concentration camps, Charteris leaked reports to newspapers claiming the Germans were processing the bodies of their own dead soldiers into animal feed and weapon grease.

Most pertinent to our current question is Charteris' claim to have written a postcard about the angel rumors on September 5, 1914—two weeks before the publication of "The Bowmen." Although Charteris said he had only heard about the apparitions and had not seen them himself, his account suffers from a common problem among "Angels of Mons" sources. There is no evidence of the postcard's existence outside a quote Charteris provided in his 1931 memoir *At GHQ*. Perhaps most fatal to this theory is the fact no orders or documentation from Charteris or any other government figure to spread the stories of the angels has yet been found. But did there need to be such an order?

As Edward Bernays, father of modern public relations, noted in his 1923 book, *Crystalizing Public Opinion*, "When real news breaks, semi-news must go. When real news is scarce, semi-news returns to the front page."[31] Torn between the slowness of actual reporting, the limits placed upon them by government censors, and the overwhelming demand from the public for news of the war, British newspaper editors found themselves printing spurious stories to fill their pages. As such, the government might never have needed to actively push the angel stories to reap their benefits. As Clarke suggests, this same phenomenon might explain the phantom Russian Army Machen covered in the weeks before publishing "The Bowmen."[32] The reports of unexpected Russian troop movements confused German spies in Britain, leading the commanders to move troops from the front in preparation for a false invasion from the North Sea.[33]

Perhaps no single person is as responsible for the spread and acceptance of the rumors as Edward Begbie, author of the already mentioned *On the Side of the Angels*. At the time, a famous journalist and Christian apologist in his own right, Begbie's acquaintance with John Charteris is suspiciously suggestive, but nothing concrete can be made out of his motives. Machen himself, commenting on Begbie's book in a letter to an American fan wrote: "*On the Side of the Angels* was a publisher's commission; I don't think that Harold believes a word of it. I don't think he's fool enough to do so."[34] Still, even if Begbie did not believe the stories himself, the fact remains that among believers today, *On the Side of the Angels* serves as the biggest source of "eyewitness accounts" and other quotations.

Begbie's 1915 book consists largely of reports from anonymous soldiers describing the appearances of three angels in the sky, a yellow mist, and some even more abstract phenomena like disembodied voices and phantom lights. At times resorting to the popular belief in spiritualism and telepathy ("No man of science who has examined the phenomena of telepathy would dispute [it]."), Begbie's "main quarrel" and chief aim is to establish that "beyond the widest circumference of equivocation, is the now definite fact that some of our soldiers, officers as well as men, believe they saw visions in France long before Mr. Machen published his story."[35]

Perhaps the most famous and prototypical account from *On the Side of the Angels* is that of volunteer nurse Phyllis Campbell, taken from her essay "The Angelic Leaders" published in the August 1915 edition of Ralph Shirley's *The Occult Review*. In the most widely quoted scene, Campbell describes her encounter with a Lancastershire Fusilier who is brought to her attention after asking a French nurse for some sort of holy picture. As the sole English speaker, Campbell seeks to clarify, and learns that the soldier wants an icon, medal, or any sort of image of Saint George. She promises to help but, intrigued and confused, asks the man if he is Catholic. He answers that he is a Wesleyan Methodist, but he believes in Saint George now because he has seen him in person. Citing the newspaper testimony of another nurse, Miss Courtney Wilson, in his narration Begbie goes on to say that he actually tracked down and spoke to one such anonymous soldier who had seen the angels and found him, not only reliable, but "a man . . . who would resent injustice . . . you can see that he might be terrible with a bayonet in one moment and quite tender with a child in the next."[36]

At the time, Machen responded to the story by citing the same legal precedent he had laid against the second- and third-hand accounts of Russian soldiers in England. "I would remind [Miss Campbell] of that famous (and golden) ruling of Stareleigh, J.: to the effect that you mustn't tell us what the soldier said; it's not evidence."[37] Later, in his contribution to the 1938 anthology, *The Great War—I was There*, he allowed his criticism to be more cutting: "There was not one word of truth in [them] . . . these stories were lies."[38] Although Machen seems almost patronizingly "sympathetic" to Phyllis Campbell, as if he considers her confused, in his rebuttals he seems much more frustrated by Begbie. This is perhaps because *On the Side of the Angels* was written, explicitly, not for Machen but accusatorily at him. In addition to suggesting Machen did not so much write "The Bowmen" as receive it through telepathic connection with dying soldiers, Begbie states in his introduction: "My own interference in the matter, is concerned with what seems to me a most lamentable failure upon [Machen's] part to realize the acuteness of human suffering and the intense eagerness for consolation which are now lying at the heart of English existence."[39]

This same sentiment is echoed by the individuals Machen blamed most for the spread of the angels: the clergy and priests of modern Christian churches, like Father Russell with his parish magazine, who through editorial liberties turned fiction into fact and the archers of "The Bowmen" into angels. In an interview for this chapter, Prof. Owen Davies, author of *A Supernatural War* (2018), suggested that the change emerged from the desire to emulate the ecstatic responses the purported sightings of the Virgin Mary were receiving in Europe. Machen's story made for a solid framework, but its quasi-Catholic focus on Latin prayers and saintly intervention was a sticking point for British Protestants. By transforming St. George and his Agincourt archers into the more ambiguous angels, the story was made more palatable and appropriately Anglican. This also goes some way toward explaining the stories of a "Comrade in White," a mysterious figure reported to be ministering to wounded soldiers who would then be discovered to be Jesus in disguise. Although this too had begun as fiction, specifically as W.H. Leathem's 1915 story "In the Trenches," by the end of that year it too was treated as an actual occurrence, and even reprinted as such in a 1918 American Lutheran magazine. For those church men who knew that they were spreading falsehoods, it seems that, for them, the ends justified the means.

As one observer from the *Christian Commonwealth* put it, the angel stories "strengthen religious faith . . . and . . . reinforce the belief in the justice of the cause for which so many men fell during that magnificent retreat."[40] In many ways, this is the other side of the coin from the apocalyptic hysteria which painted the Germans as devils. "These stories," the theologian Dr. R.F. Horton wrote, "are the unveiling of the real power on which we depend . . . if God is for us, who can be against us?"[41]

Machen, for his part, was entirely opposed to this style of religious self-conception among the British public. Although as the *Times Literary Supplement* quipped, he was "the last man to be skeptical of miracles."[42] Machen's own faith defies easy definition and explanation. In some ways, it seems that was the point. As he phrased it in the introduction to *The Bowmen and Other Legends of the War*, "Christianity . . . is a great Mystery Religion; it is *the* Mystery Religion."[43]

Following the death of his first wife, Machen experienced a series of "waking visions" (perhaps similar to those described in so many of his stories) in November 1899, which led him out of skepticism and his occult dabbling with the Hermetic Order of The Golden Dawn into a full Christian conversion. Although he felt "theology [was] the only true and exact science," Machen's Christianity held little in common with the anemic Anglicanism that he felt characterized the modern Church of England.[44] "Its priests . . . pass their time in preaching, not the eternal mysteries, but a two penny morality, in changing the Wine of Angels and the Bread of Heaven into ginger beer and mixed biscuits."[45] The result, he opined, spoke for itself: "Separate a man from good drink, he will swallow methylated spirit with joy."[46] For Machen, there were no more methylated spirits than the Angels of Mons.

As the French literary theorist and linguist Roland Barthes wrote, "Myth is a form of speech."[47] That is to say that a myth is made up of two parts: the signifier, it is obvious, immediately apparent, constituent parts; and the signified, the greater meaning that those apparent parts stand in for and represent. As we have seen, the appearance of angels on the battlefield saving English troops was suggested to mean that God was on the English side and that their cause was just. That might be good for wartime patriotism and church attendance, but it is not good for faith. In fact, it is its opposite. In some ways, this issue echoes Jesus' exchange with the skeptical Pharisees in Matthew 12:39: "An evil and adulterous generation seeketh after a sign; and there shall be no sign given to it but the sign of the prophet Jonas." In effect, the Gospel has Jesus arguing that his own death and resurrection will be the only proof needed that he is the Messiah. To the conventional mind, the escape from and reversal of physical death is impossible, it simply cannot happen. And yet, as Paul writes in 1 Corinthians 15:14, "If Christ be not risen, then is our preaching vain and your faith is also vain." As Machen put it in his own response to Dr. Horton, "It has often struck me that the most awful disaster that could happen to the world would be the scientific 'proof' of the Christian religion

... A religion must be impossible to the ordinary, practical understanding—or it would not be a religion at all."[48]

For Machen, the "mystery" of faith was its purpose. Inspired by the legends of King Arthur and the Holy Grail, featuring heavily in his writings like *A Fragment of Life* (1904) and *The Secret Glory* (1922), mystical truth was something to be quested for and tasted. Finding the secret for oneself was the escape from the mundane and often cruel reality of modern existence. By contrast, worse even than expecting proof of the divine and the justice of one's cause, was to desperately accept any cheap and easily debunked "proof" provided by suspect sources. Not only was this reliance on evidence in effect a denial of faith, it was a denial of personal agency and the responsibility that it implies.

The two places where Machen grapples with these questions and the Angels of Mons controversy most clearly, are in his horror story *The Terror* (1916) and *War and Christian Faith* (1918), an extended meditation on how a good God could allow this war to happen. Not terribly well regarded, *The Terror* holds the dubious distinction of being Machen's most brutally violent story. According to critics like Geoffrey Reiter, it is needlessly so. Like "The Bowmen," *The Terror* is written in a journalistic style. In several places, the reporter narrator laments the nature of censorship and rumor in war time, directly referencing "The Angels of Mons" and "The Russians" numerous times throughout the text. Following a string of mysterious and gruesome civilian deaths involving animals, the reader is first lead to the false conclusion the attacks are the result of a "Z ray," a German secret weapon which provokes animals into murderous rage by conveying fear along the "material ether."[49] Not only does this mirror the Germans' gas theory from *The Bowmen*, but the provided explanation for the "Z ray" borrows directly from Begbie's reasoning in *On the Side of the Angels*, stating: "Telepathy, you know, is well established."[50] In the end, it is revealed that the real explanation for the attacks is supernatural—it is an act of divine judgment, the charge of which is first laid out in a channeled letter beginning "Incipit liber iræ Domini Dei nostri (Here beginneth The Book of the Wrath of the Lord our God)."[51]

> The answer to the mystery—the random mass deaths of innocents, a reflection of the war itself—is laid out in the final pages: "The animals had revolted against men."[52]
>
> Man has dominated the beasts throughout the ages, the spiritual has reigned over the rational through the peculiar quality and grace of spirituality that men possess, that makes a man to be that which he is . . . But the beasts also have within them something which corresponds to the spiritual quality in men—we are content to call it instinct. They perceived that the throne was vacant—vacant—not even friendship was possible between them and the self-deposed

monarch. If he were not king he was a sham, an imposter, a thing to be destroyed.[53]

Read alongside *War and the Christian Faith*, it is clear that the moral of *The Terror* extends beyond its own narrative, both to the Angel controversy and to the grim facts of a world at war. The apocalypse, in this case, is not the source of comfort that the church of Machen's day made it out to be. Instead, "The Wrath of the Lord our God" takes the form of a natural world in revolt against the failed leadership of humankind. The loss of the "grace of spirituality" and descent into irrationality, perhaps another comment on the war itself, casts man's "self-depos[ition]" as a further rejection of the natural order—akin almost to a second fall from grace. As Machen explains in *War and The Christian Faith*, man's confusion stems from his lack of instinct, the means by which animals implicitly know their purpose, because "it is we, not the beasts, who were driven out of paradise. They were not driven out; they are still in paradise."[54]

In this sense, the destruction of *The Terror* is not an act of God, but the natural world's reaction to man's rejection of what he is and his responsibilities. God is not on the side of the animals. Instead, the animals are on God's side, and there will be no divine intervention to save humankind from its self-created peril. As Machen writes in *War and the Christian Faith*,

> There is no God of infinite amiability—infinite love is a different matter—and the world of the natural order isn't a very pleasant place, never has been a very pleasant place, and never will be a very pleasant place, so long as water drowns and fire burns and steel cuts flesh, and lightning destroys this body.[55]

The key distinction Machen presents here is the difference between infinite love and infinite amiability. An infinitely amiable God might take an active role in human affairs, correcting mistakes or picking a "righteous" side in a conflict. But, an infinitely loving God does not, because to love infinitely is to love equally, regardless of the human consequences. Just as the God of *The Terror* allows the animals to usurp the human kingdom, a God of infinite love allows nations to commit mass murder because they have chosen to. As horrible as that choice is, the suffering it inspires might show those nations the error of their ways.

This, ultimately, is the problem Machen found with the Angels of Mons, as well as the key reason for the myth's seductive longevity. By serving as apparently immediately accessible proof of a divine order and preference for the Allied cause, not only do the angels serve as a kind of religio-political propaganda, they remove human responsibility for the conflict and its eventual resolution, as well as the solace of religion. If God were to be an active participant in the war, it would, Machen writes, "make the world so much more horrible than it already is," because confining the infinite to a limited human perspective would deprive it of what makes it worth seeking.⁵⁶ The point of religious mystery, of art, for Machen was not to reinforce any moral position within the apparent world, but to provide an escape from it, "for art is but a search for that hidden beauty which is God."⁵⁷

In many ways, this position is a culmination of Machen's earlier thoughts and fears, found in "The Great God Pan" and "The Inmost Light," where the progression of materialist science reveals either an absence of a benevolent eternity or the capacity to destroy it. A God who chooses sides and sends angels to save armies is no longer an escape from the misery and horror of the mundane world but its principal cause. In this sense, the same reasons the British public and the Church of England wanted to believe in the "Angels of Mons" are exactly why Machen, the mystic, was so offended by the myth. It was not just that the story was not true, and he knew it, but that it deprived others of potential access to the truth he thought was most important.

What is striking as one reads the accounts of soldiers who claimed to have seen the angels, is the fact that, without fail, all such stories emerge nearly a year after the publication of "The Bowmen" and well after the start of its distortion by the church. Although some men who retreated from Mons had reported sleep-deprived hallucinations, the consistent image of "angels" does not solidify until after the myth had started and spread. Instead, what emerges, if one takes these "eyewitnesses" at their word, is a variety of psycho-spiritual experiences in a moment of exhaustion and terror being overwritten and replaced with a provided shape constructed for its easy consumption. By inadvertently giving people a legend to believe in, the story Machen inspired may actually have separated these individuals from their profound personal experiences and the lessons they may have actually provided.

More than once, Machen called "The Bowmen" his Frankenstein's monster. Perhaps it was. Considering how central Machen's mystical experiences were both to his personal spirituality and his fiction, what is the deception he is referencing in his comment that "it began to dawn on me that if I had failed in the art of letters, I had succeeded, unwittingly, in the art of deceit"?⁵⁸ Was it convincing others to believe in angels or the creation of yet another false and poisonous grail?

NOTES

1. *Wonder Woman*, dir. Patty Jenkins (Burbank, CA: Warner Brothers Films, 2017).
2. Alan Moore, *Promethea* (New York: DC Comics, 2000), 3–4.

3. "World War I Miracle? The Angels of Mons." *Warfare History Network*, Warfare History Network, www.warfarehistorynetwork.com/daily/military-history/world-war-i-miracle-the-angels-of-mons/ (accessed December 15, 2018).

4. George Stuart Gordon, *The Retreat from Mons* (New York: Houghton Mifflin Company, 1917), 12–14.

5. Ernest Hamilton, *The First Seven Divisions, being a detailed account of the fighting from Mons to Ypres* (London: Hurst and Blackett, 1917), 8.

6. John Terraine, *Mons, The Retreat to Victory* (Ware, UK: Wordsworth Editions Limited, 2002), 78–83.

7. David Clarke, *The Angels of Mons* (Chichester: J. Wiley, 2004), 47.

8. Ibid., 55.

9. Henry Beeching, *Armageddon: A Sermon Upon the War Preached in Norwich Cathedral* (London: Society for Promoting Christian Knowledge, 1914), 14.

10. Alain Denizot, *Le Sacre-Coeur et la Grande Guerre* (Paris: Nouvelles Editions Latines, 1994), 140–43.

11. Owen Davies, *The Supernatural War: Magic, Divination and Faith during the First World War* (Oxford: Oxford University Press, 2018), 65.

12. Phyllis Campbell, "The Angelic Leaders," in *Occult Review* XXII, edited by Ralph Shirley (London: William Rider and Son, 1915), 76.

13. Arthur Machen, "What about Those Russians?," in *London Evening News*, edited by Walter Evans (1914), 2.

14. Arthur Machen, *The Angels of Mons: Bowmen and Other Legends of the War* (New York: The Knickerbocker Press, 1915), 27.

15. Ibid.

16. Ibid., 27–29.

17. Ibid., 31.

18. Ibid., 8.

19. Arthur Machen, "NO ESCAPE FROM THE BOWMEN," in *London Evening News*, edited by Walter Evans (1915), 2.

20. David Gow, "The Invisible Allies," *Light* 34, edited by E. Dawson Rogers (London: London Spiritualist Alliance, October 1914), 490.

21. Clarke, *The Angels of Mons*, 105.

22. Machen, *The Angels of Mons*, 10.

23. Ibid.

24. W.H. Salter, "An Enquiry Concerning 'The Angels of Mons'," in *The Journal of the Society For Psychical Research* 28 (Glasgow: Robert Maclehose Company, 1915), 118.

25. Harold Begbie, *On The Side of the Angels* (London: Hodder & Soughton, 1915), 12.

26. Clarke, *The Angels of Mons*, 100.

27. K. M. Briggs, *The Fairies in English Tradition and Literature* (London: University of Chicago Press, 1967), 49.

28. Machen, *The Angels of Mons*, 8.

29. Friedrich Brie, *The Brut, or, the Chronicles of London* (London: Trüber and Co, 1906–1908), 379–80.
30. James Hayward, *Myths & Legends of the First World War* (Stroud, UK: The History Press, 2005), Loc. 1834.
31. As quoted by Edward Bernays, *Crystallizing Public Opinion* (New York: Liveright Publication Corporation, 1961), 114.
32. Clarke, *The Angels of Mons*, 84.
33. Ibid.
34. From Michael Murphy's edited collection *Starrett vs. Machen: A Record of Discovery and Correspondence* (St. Louis: Autolycus Press, 1971), 51.
35. Begbie, *On the Side of the Angels*, 8.
36. Ibid., 33.
37. Machen, *The Angels of Mons*, 79.
38. Arthur Machen, "The True Story of the Angels of Mons," in *The Great War–I Was There*, vol. 2, edited by Sir John Hammerton (London: The Amalgamated Press, 1938), 86–87.
39. Begbie, *On The Side of the Angels*, 9.
40. Anonymous, "War and Miracles," in *Japan Daily Mail Weekly Edition* LXIV, no. 17 (October 30, 1915), 290.
41. R.F. Horton, "Do Miracles Still Happen?," Reprinted from *The Daily Chronicle* in *The London Evening News*, edited by Walter Evans (June 21, 1915), 2.
42. Harold Hannyngton Child, "The Birth of a Legend," *Times Literary Supplement* 709 (August 19, 1915), 276.
43. Machen, *The Angels of Mons*, 21.
44. Donald Hassler, *Arthur Machen & Montgomery Evans: Letters of a Literary Friendship, 1923–1947* (Kent, OH: Kent State University Press, 1994), 70.
45. Machen, *The Angels of Mons*, 20–21.
46. Ibid.
47. Roland Barthes, *Mythologies*, translated by Jonathan Cape (New York: The Noonday Press, 1972), 109.
48. Arthur Machen, "Dr. Horton and 'The Bowmen'," in *London Evening News*, edited by Walter Evans (1915), 2.
49. Arthur Machen, *The Terror* (New York: Robert McBride and Company, 1917), 70.
50. Ibid.
51. Ibid., 193.
52. Ibid., 213.
53. Ibid., 226–27.
54. Arthur Machen, *War and the Christian Faith* (London: Skeffington and Sons, 1918), 29.
55. Ibid., 11.
56. Ibid., 14.
57. Ibid.
58. Machen, *The Angels of Mons*, 10.

REFERENCES

Anonymous. "Alleged Visions on the Battlefield." *Journal of the Society for Psychical Research* 27, 95. Glasgow: Robert Maclehose and Company, 1914–15.

Anonymous. "War and Miracles." *Japan Daily Mail Weekly Edition* 64, no. 17, 290. October 30, 1915.

Barthes, Roland. *Mythologies*, translated by Jonathan Cape. New York: The Noonday Press, 1972.

Beeching, Henry Charles. *Armageddon: A Sermon upon the War Preached in Norwich Cathedral*. London: Society for Promoting Christian Knowledge. 1914.

Begbie, Harold. *On the Side of the Angels*. London: Hodder & Stoughton, 1915.

Bernays, Edward. *Crystalizing Public Opinion*. New York: Liveright Publishing Corporation, 1961.

Bleiler, Richard. *The Strange Case of "The Angels of Mons"*. Jefferson, NC: McFarland & Company. 2015.

Brie, Frederich W.D. *The Brut, or The Chronicles of England*. London: Trübner & Co., 1906-08.

Briggs, K. M. *The Fairies in English Tradition and Literature*. London: University of Chicago Press, 1967.

Campbell, Phyllis. "The Angelic Leaders." *The Occult Review* XXII, 76–82. August 1915.

Child, Harold Hannyngton. "The Birth of a Legend." *Times Literary Supplement* 709, August 19, 1915.

Clarke, David. *The Angel of Mons: Phantom Soldiers and Ghostly Guardians*. Chichester: J. Wiley, 2005.

Davies, Owen. *The Supernatural War: Magic, Divination and Faith during the First World War*. Oxford : Oxford University Press, 2018.

———. Personal Interview with Andrew Lenoir. November 1, 2018.

Denizot, Alain. *Le Sacre-Coeur et la Grande Guerre*. Paris: Nouvelles Editions Latines, 1994.

Gordon, George Stuart. *The Retreat from Mons*. New York: Houghton Mifflin Company, 1917.

Gow, David. "The Invisible Allies." *Light* 34, October 10, 1914.

Hamilton, Ernest. *The First Seven Divisions, Being a Detailed Account of the Fighting from Mons to Ypres*. London: Hurst and Blackett, 1917.

Hassler, Donald. *Arthur Machen & Montgomery Evans: Letters of a Literary Friendship, 1923-1947*. Kent, OH: Kent State University Press, 1994.

Hayward, James. *Myths & Legends of the First World War*. Stroud, UK: The History Press, 2005. Kindle Edition.

Horton, R.F. "Do Miracles Still Happen?" *Daily Chronicle* column from June 15, 1915, reprinted in *Evening News*, June 21, 1915.

Lomas, David. *Mons 1914 The BEF's Tactical Triumph*. Oxford: Osprey Publishing, 1997.

Machen, Arthur. "Dr. Horton and 'The Bowmen.'" *Evening News*, June 12, 1915.

———. "NO ESCAPE FROM THE BOWMEN! My Sympathies with Frankenstein'." *Evening News*, June 12, 1915.

———. *The Angels of Mons: Bowmen and Other Legends of the War*. New York: The Knickerbocker Press, 1915.

———. *The Terror*. New York: Robert M. McBride & Company, 1917.

———. "The True Story of 'The Angels of Mons'." In *The Great War—I Was There*, vol. 2, edited by Sir John Hammerton. London: Amalgamated Press, 1938.

———. *War and the Christian Faith*. London: Skeffington & Son, 1918.

———. "What About Those Russians!" *Evening News*, September 15, 1914.

Moore, Alan, et al. *Promethea*. New York: DC Comics, Vertigo, 2000.

Murphy, Michael (ed.). *Starrett vs Machen: A Record of Discovery and Correspondence*. St Louis: Autolycus Press, 1977.

Reiter, Geoffrey. "Man is Made a Mystery: The Evolution of Arthur Machen's Religious Thought." PhD diss. Baylor University, 2010.

Salt, W. F. T. *The Great War—in the Divine Light of Prophecy: Is it Armageddon?* Bristol, UK: F. Walker, 1915.

Salter, W.H. "An Enquiry Concerning 'The Angels of Mons'." *Journal of the Society for Psychical Research* XXVII, 106–18. Glasgow: Robert Maclehose, 1915.

Terraine, John. *Mons, The Retreat to Victory*. Ware, UK: Wordsworth Editions Limited, 2002.

Wonder Woman, directed by Patty Jenkins. Burbank, CA: Warner Brothers Films, 2017.

"World War I Miracle? The Angels of Mons." *Warfare History Network*, Warfare History Network, www.warfarehistorynetwork.com/daily/military-history/world-war-i-miracle-the-angels-of-mons/.

Index

acting, 1, 10–12, 16, 17, 242
adaptation, 26, 34n97, 135–46
agential realism, 193–204
The Anatomy of Tobacco (1884), 3–4, 28n18
Ancient Romans, 2–3, 12, 15, 83–84, 98–99, 106, 140, 160, 199, 200, 212, 219
The Angels of Mons, The Bowmen and Other Legends of War (1915), 12–13, 25, 27, 241–53
apophatic/cataphatic, 27, 225–36, 237nn18–19, 238n55

Bakhtin, Mikhail, 25, 44, 54n11
Barad, Karen, 193–204
Barthes, Roland, 138, 250
Baudelaire, Charles, 32n76, 152, 158, 166n4
Begbie, Edward, 246–51
The Birds (1952), 60, 67, 70n6
"The Bowmen" (1914), 12, 17, 27, 242–53
Bridle and Spurs (1951), 23, 87

Caerleon-on-Usk, 2, 46, 98, 184n32
The Canning Wonder (1925), 19
cataloguer, 4, 5, 16, 17, 29n22, 185n6, 210, 223n34
Catholicism, 11, 228, 243, 248, 249

"The Ceremony" (1924), 18, 33n81, 81, 99–101, 105–6, 155–58, 165
Chamber, Robert, 103, 116
"The Children of the Pool" (1936), 21, 88, 92n62
The Children of the Pool and Other Stories (1936), 21, 23
Christian faith, 14, 18, 31n64, 227, 234, 249–52
The Chronicle of Clemendy (1888), 4
chronotope, 43–54, 54n11
chronotopia, 26, 77, 80
Coleridge, Samuel Taylor, 177, 178, 185n55
Contagious Diseases Acts, 173, 183nn16–17
The Cosy Room and Other Stories (1936), 22–23, 80
cryptozoology, 126–28, 131n55

Darwinism, 26, 102, 116, 120, 136–38, 143, 183n24
decadence, 6, 8, 26, 52, 84, 126, 151–66, 172, 179, 181, 187n81, 187n83, 187n85, 199, 220
degeneration, 26, 84, 90n29, 98, 135–46, 171–81, 187n83
detective fiction, 6, 9, 22, 27, 85, 102, 116, 123, 209–21
Dickens, Charles, 17, 18, 23, 34n98, 49

disease, 26, 101, 117, 144, 172–73, 177, 181, 183n16, 184n40, 186n67
Dog and Duck: A London Calendar Et Cætera (1924), 14, 17–18, 32n80
Don Quixote (1605), 9, 15
Doyle, Arthur Conan, 20, 123, 128, 215
Dreads and Drolls (1926), 19, 122
Dr. Stiggins: His Views and Principles (1906), 11
Dyson, 6–8, 47, 85–86, 102, 105–6, 116, 121–23, 209–21, 222n34

ecstacy, 9, 18, 22, 27, 33n84, 79, 100, 137, 153, 157, 160, 165, 202, 204n9, 211, 212, 221, 225–36, 249
eerie, 26, 59–69, 72n48, 197–98, 202
"Eleusina" (1881), 3
euhemerism, 115–29
Evolutionary theory, 96, 102–5, 116, 120–29, 135–46, 201

Fairies. *See* "the little people"
fantastic, 64, 68, 69, 70n25, 71n27, 119, 129
Far Off Things (1922), 15–16, 48, 51, 56n48, 106
femme fatale, 171–81
fin de siècle, 26, 29n26, 135–39, 152, 171–81, 184n46, 187n85, 220, 229
Fisher, Mark, 26, 59–69, 71n30, 197
folklore, 2, 7, 59, 72n45, 72n47, 85, 115, 118, 120–28
Foucault, Michel, 26, 75–88, 89n11
A Fragment of Life (1904), 9, 10, 27, 31n48, 41, 193, 197, 199, 225–36, 251
Frankenstein (1818), 7, 137–39, 142–45, 171, 245, 253
Freud, Sigmund, 88, 98

Gautier, Théophile, 68, 151, 164
geology, 136, 200
ghosts, 12, 19, 22, 27, 79–80
The Glorious Mystery (1924), 18
God, 31n64, 67, 69, 138, 139, 143, 227–30, 233, 242, 243, 247, 250–53

Gothic, 1, 16, 24, 41, 48, 52, 68, 84–86, 97, 102–3, 135, 138–39, 143–46, 171, 229, 230, 235
"The Great God Pan" (1894), 6, 7, 24, 26, 31n48, 48, 70n9, 72n47, 83–84, 91n44, 98, 130n29, 135–37, 139–46, 171–81, 182nn3–4, 182n9, 184nn45–46, 186n61, 186n78, 187n85, 196, 209, 221n4, 230, 235, 243
"The Great Return" (1915), 13, 23, 77–79, 89n14, 233, 234
The Green Round (1933), 20, 235, 238n55

"The Happy Children" (1920), 23, 79, 90n24
Hermetic Order of the Golden Dawn, 9, 11, 25, 30n40, 210–11, 229, 250
heterotopia, 26, 75–89, 91n44
Hieroglyphics (1902), 9, 100, 151–66, 203, 225–36
hierophanies, 99–103, 164
The Hill of Dreams (1907), 9, 12, 26, 31n53, 47, 52, 99, 105–6, 152, 193–99
history, 11, 16, 17, 65, 80, 97, 99, 103, 106, 115–29, 136, 146, 200–201, 210, 228
Hoggs, Amelia, 4, 9, 185n61, 187n86, 230, 250
Holmes, Sherlock, 116, 123, 213–15
Holy Grail legend, 11, 13, 15, 18, 20, 23, 27, 30n45, 78, 221n9, 226, 233–35, 251, 253
Homo floresiensis, 126–29
The House of Souls (1906), 11, 31n48, 226
The House of the Hidden Light (1904), 10, 211–12, 221n9
Howard, Robert E., 123–25, 129, 131n42, 132n67
Huddleston, Dorothie Purefoy, 9, 23, 229
human beings, 25, 31n64, 59–68, 85, 98, 101–4, 116, 136, 142–43, 146, 178, 184n42, 212

Hurley, Kelly, 24, 30n35, 102, 138
Hutcheon, Linda, 135–45
Hyltén-Cavallius, Gunnar Olof, 120, 127, 132n60

imperialism, 135–36
"The Inmost Light" (1894), 6–7, 24, 27, 102, 106, 186n77, 209–18, 253

James, M.R., 70n9, 71n30
Joshi, S.T., 2, 15, 24, 28n9, 29n27, 31n55, 72n49, 83, 85, 91n40, 196, 225, 226
journalism, 1, 3, 5, 6, 9, 11, 12, 14–16, 20, 31n55, 50, 59

knowledge, 6, 7, 10, 14, 18, 41, 46, 52–54, 62, 67, 71n27, 82, 84, 141, 177, 202, 210, 215, 227, 230, 235

language, 26, 53–54, 103–6, 124, 144, 153, 198, 202, 217, 228, 230, 236
Lankester, E. Ray, 136
The Lifted Veil (1859), 171, 177–78, 185n46
literature, 1, 9, 11, 12, 15–17, 19, 33n90, 42, 45–46, 51–53, 64, 68, 71n27, 100–101, 135–43, 155, 163, 181, 187n85, 199, 202, 203, 214, 216, 220, 225, 226, 228, 232
"little people", 7, 8, 10, 16, 18, 20, 21, 26, 32n80, 85–88, 95, 96, 99, 104–6, 115–29, 129n11, 201, 212, 217
London, 2–23, 25, 28n10, 32n76, 41–54, 56n46, 61, 79, 84, 89n14, 91n44, 99, 122, 137, 139, 140, 153, 156–62, 173, 175, 178, 185n49, 186n74, 196–98, 210, 223n34, 233, 236, 244
The London Adventure, or the Art of Wandering (1924), 16, 25, 41–54
London cognita/incognita, 43–54
loneliness, 2, 3, 7, 12, 15, 28n18, 31n53, 61, 70n25, 86, 175
Lorraine, Jean, 187n81
Loukaki, Argyro, 95, 98–100

Lovecraft, H.P., 1, 29n27, 70n9, 72n48, 83, 124–25, 127, 129, 131n42, 182n4, 220, 242

MacRitchie, David, 121–22, 126
matter, 7, 95–107, 180, 193–203
minerals. *See* stones
modernity, 25, 44, 50–51, 67, 69, 71n27, 72n47, 83, 85, 91n40, 98–100, 103, 172, 181, 196, 197, 199, 214, 231, 232, 251
monsters, 21, 26, 103, 104, 119, 123–29, 135–46, 163, 245, 253
"Munitions of War" (1926), 22, 23, 80
murder, 8, 18, 19, 21, 64, 68, 105, 122–28, 173, 180, 183n21, 210–21
mysticism, 4, 9, 10, 12, 26, 27, 29n22, 30n40, 50, 56n46, 66, 75, 77–79, 90n29, 99, 137, 143–46, 151, 152, 165, 181, 194–98, 220, 225–36, 237nn18–19, 26–29, 238n47, 251, 253

"N" (1936), 22–23, 56n46, 79
nature, 5, 15, 18, 25, 26, 51, 59–69, 71n25, 75, 78–84, 91n40, 96, 100, 119, 136, 139, 157–63, 181, 193–204, 205n22, 210, 233, 252
new materialism, 27, 193–204
New Woman, 6, 29n26, 176–81, 185n50
Nordau, Max, 90n29, 135–36, 171–72, 180, 187n83
Notebook (1890), 26, 153, 155, 164
Notes and Queries (1926), 19–20
"Novel of the Black Seal" (1895), 9, 104–6, 115–25, 212, 218
"Novel of the White Powder" (1895), 8, 98, 102–3, 106, 194–95, 215

occultism, 4, 9, 11, 17, 24, 25, 27, 29n22, 30n40, 50, 82, 101, 102, 104, 119, 139, 144, 154–58, 171, 177, 180–81, 185n61, 187n86, 194–99, 202, 204n9, 209–21, 221n4, 221n12, 235, 243, 245, 248, 250

Ornaments in Jade (1924), 9, 18, 22, 23, 26, 81, 151–66
"Out of the Earth" (1923), 17, 27, 70n25, 115, 117, 124
"Out of the Picture" (1936), 21

paganism, 5, 10, 18, 29n27, 30n45, 33n84, 70n9, 83–84, 90n32, 96–100, 119, 140, 144, 155–57, 165, 172, 177, 179, 181, 194, 212, 234, 238n49
paleontology, 26, 115–29, 129n1
Pan, 6, 83, 84, 88, 130n29, 141, 144, 172, 175, 177, 179–81, 184nn36–39, 186n74, 186n78, 187n81, 196
past, 6, 12, 44, 47, 49–52, 70n9, 77, 79–89, 90n24, 91n40, 95–107, 115, 131n41, 137, 141, 144, 152, 160, 171, 198, 201, 212
pathogen, 26, 171–81
Plumwood, Val, 193–95, 199
Poe, Edgar Allan, 19, 64, 213
posthumanism, 95–107
Protestantism, 2, 11, 19, 228, 234, 243, 249
Pseudo-Dionysius the Areopagite, 228–32, 237n16
psychogeography, 16, 22, 32n76, 51, 56n53

rationality, 2, 7, 13, 19, 20, 27, 64, 69, 71n27, 78, 85, 90n24, 101, 103, 194–98, 209–10, 213–15, 227, 251
realism, 1, 9, 17, 79, 152, 162–63, 193–204, 216, 232
"The Red Hand" (1895), 8, 27, 31n48, 122, 209–18

science, 16, 26, 27, 50, 56n48, 71n27, 84, 101, 115–18, 123, 126, 127, 129, 136–39, 142–46, 172, 194, 195, 199, 201, 202, 214–15, 248, 250, 253
Scott, Walter, 23, 119–20, 127, 132n60

The Secret Glory (1922), 12, 14–15, 31n54, 202, 233–34, 251
sexuality, 6, 10, 29n26, 83–84, 99, 135, 140, 141, 154, 155, 157, 171–81, 183n16, 185n50, 186n61, 186n67, 199, 238n57
"The Shining Pyramid" (1895), 7, 27, 70n25, 85–86, 98, 105–6, 115–17, 121, 125, 209–17
The Shining Pyramid (1923), 17
"The Soldier's Rest" (1915), 245
spiritualism, 16, 23, 27, 30n40, 34n95, 221n4, 248
spirituality, 2, 7, 10, 12, 16, 27, 29n27, 67–69, 77, 97, 146, 181, 186n61, 193–204, 226, 227, 233, 235, 251–53
Starrett, Vincent, 1, 14, 17, 18, 29n27, 152, 166n4, 168n77
Stevenson, Robert Louis, 7, 8, 26, 32n76, 72n47, 123, 143, 171, 186n74
stones, 7, 18, 26, 63, 71n25, 81, 84, 86, 95–107, 117–21, 124, 151, 154–56, 164, 210–12, 215, 216
"The Strange Case of Dr Jekyll and Mr Hyde" (1886), 7, 123, 131n41, 143–44, 163, 171
Strange Roads. With The Gods in Spring (1923), 16, 86–87
"The Strange Tale of Mount Nephin" (1951), 23, 87–88
supernatural, 6, 11, 13, 19, 21, 22, 26, 28n9, 60–69, 71n30, 72nn41–48, 75–89, 91n44, 100–102, 117–18, 120, 135–38, 142–44, 194, 196, 200–202, 209–21, 221n12, 226, 230, 241, 245, 251
symbolism, 17, 26, 72n49, 151–66, 225
Symonds, Charles, 158–59
syphilis, 173, 178–79

Taylor, Lucian, 12, 52, 99, 101, 152–56, 158–59, 162–65, 167n19, 196, 198–203

The Terror (1917), 13–14, 26, 27, 31nn63–64, 59–69, 70n6, 70n9, 70n14, 70n25, 72n41, 193–98, 238n47, 251, 252
Theosophical Society, 16, 101, 221n4
Things Near and Far (1923), 9, 15, 41, 47–48, 230
The Three Impostors: or, The Transmutations (1895), 7–8, 18, 24, 27, 31n48, 45, 47, 52, 117, 151, 152, 158, 209–21, 222nn32–34, 230
time, 25, 42–54, 54n11, 66, 76–77, 79–81, 87, 97, 129, 200–201, 204n9
Tom O'Bedlam and His Song (1930), 20
topophrenia, 42, 44
translations; *Casanova's Memoirs* (1888), 5, 14; *Heptameron* (1885), 4; *The Way to Attain* (AKA *Fantastic Tales*) (1888), 5

Valentine, Mark, 1, 25, 199, 234, 237n29
Vaughan, Helen, 6, 26, 29n27, 48, 83–84, 91n44, 135, 138–46, 172–81, 184nn42–46, 185n48, 196

Waite, Arthur Edward, 4, 7, 9–11, 211, 221n9
Wales, 3, 12, 22, 41, 61, 83, 84, 86, 88, 117, 118; countryside, 2–3, 7, 10, 16, 17, 20, 21, 24, 27, 78, 105–6, 153, 156, 175, 210, 233; heritage, 27, 142, 181, 210, 226, 233
War and The Christian Faith (1918), 14, 31n64, 252
weird, 59–60, 71n30, 197, 209, 213, 219
weird fiction, 1, 23, 59, 194, 237n26
The White People (1904), 9–10, 30n43, 70n25, 81–82, 84, 90n29, 90n32, 153, 158
Wilde, Oscar, 6, 8, 26, 160
woods, 10, 18, 21, 26, 44, 61, 65, 71n25, 75, 77, 81–85, 99–101, 121–22, 125, 127, 139, 145, 153, 155–57, 161, 166, 167n19, 174, 175, 177, 196–99, 201, 211, 233, 235
World War I, 13, 14, 59, 65, 67, 78, 80, 241, 243, 245, 249

About the Contributors

Emiliano Aguilar is an MA who graduated at the Universidad de Buenos Aires (UBA)—Facultad de Filosofía y Letras (Argentina). He has published about science fiction in journals such as *Lindes* and *Letraceluloide* and chapters in *Orphan Black and Philosophy*, edited by Richard Greene, *The Man in the High Castle and Philosophy*, edited by Bruce Krajewski, *Giant Creatures in our World: Essays on Kaiju and American Popular Culture*, edited by Camille Mustachio and Jason Barr, among others.

Kostas Boyiopoulos is a teaching associate and Honorary Fellow in the Department of English Studies at Durham University. He has published essays on Oscar Wilde, Arthur Machen, and others. He is the author of *The Decadent Image: The Poetry of Wilde, Symons, and Dowson* (2015), partly funded by the Friends of Princeton University Library. He has coedited the essay collections *Decadent Romanticism: 1780–1914* (2015) and *The Decadent Short Story: An Annotated Anthology* (2014). His most recent works are the coedited volumes *Literary and Cultural Alternatives to Modernism: Unsettling Presences* (2019) and *Aphoristic Modernity: 1880 to the Present* (2019).

Deborah Bridle currently teaches at the Science Faculty at Université Côte d'Azur (Nice, France) while continuing her research work in British and American literature. Her research focuses on fiction dealing with the fantastic. After defending a doctoral dissertation on the image of the mirror in a selection of Victorian fairy tales, her interests have expanded and are now turned to specific subgenres of the fantastic, such as weird fiction and supernatural horror. She is particularly interested in occultism and mysticism in the works of authors from the end of the nineteenth century, as well as in the nihilistic philosophical approaches in the works of twentieth-century writers of horror such as H.P. Lovecraft and Thomas Ligotti. She is also a member of the editorial board of *Journal of the Short Story in English*.

Amanda M. Caleb, PhD, is an associate professor of English and director of Medical and Health Humanities at Misericordia University. She specialized in nineteenth-century British literature, particularly the novel and short story, and the intersection of science, medicine, and literature. She has published several articles on science and literature, specifically on the works of H.G. Wells, Arthur Machen, and Robert Louis Stevenson. She is the editor of *(Re) creating Science in Nineteenth-Century Britain* (2007) and *Teleny* (2010), an anonymous novel associated with Oscar Wilde.

Francesco Corigliano completed his PhD at the University of Calabria (Italy) in 2019 with a research project about weird fiction in the literary works by Howard Phillips Lovecraft, Stefan Grabiński, and Jean Ray. In October 2013, he earned a Master's Degree in Modern Philology at the University of Calabria, where, in 2014, he also attended a Master's Program in Didactics for Teaching Italian Language to Foreigners. In 2020 he published *La letteratura weird. Narrare l'impensabile* (Mimesis).

Jessica George received her PhD from Cardiff University in 2014. Her doctoral research focused on evolutionary theory in the fiction of Arthur Machen and H. P. Lovecraft, and she has also published on plant horror and contemporary horror TV. She has interests in literature and science in the long nineteenth century and contemporary Welsh writing in English. She is also a published fiction writer and recently participated in the Literature Wales mentoring scheme.

Andrew R. Lenoir is an independent researcher and speechwriter. He presented at the first Lovecraft Emerging Scholarship Symposium and his academic work on writers Ambrose Bierce and HP Lovecraft have been published in *The Brown Journal of History* and *Lovecraftian Proceedings*, respectively. Andrew studied semiotics at Brown University and holds an MFA from Columbia University where he designed and taught a writing course exploring history and psychogeography. His popular history writing has appeared in *Atlas Obscura*, *Mental Floss*, and *America Magazine*. He is currently working on a survey of alcohol's religious associations for a forthcoming Bloomsbury cultural history anthology.

Laura Mauro is a writer of short fiction who holds an MA in Modern and Contemporary Literature from Birkbeck, University of London. She has previously spoken about the influence of Gothic fiction on her work at the Manchester Gothic Festival, an annual event run by Manchester Metropolitan University. Her fiction has been shortlisted for a Shirley Jackson Award, and in 2018 she won the British Fantasy Award for Best Short Story.

Justin Mullis is a PhD candidate at Bowling Green State University in Ohio. He has an MA in Religious Studies from the University of North Carolina at Charlotte where he previously lectured on topics relating to the intersection of religion with science fiction and horror fiction. His published work includes explorations of H.P. Lovecraft's Cthulhu Mythos in *The Journal of the Fantastic in the Arts* 26.3, Japanese monsters and superheroes in *Giant Creatures in Our World*, *Star Wars* in *The Myth Awakens*, and cryptozoological science fiction in *The Paranormal and Popular Culture*. His current research involves the role of cryptozoology in the life of Thomas Jefferson.

Fernando Gabriel Pagnoni Berns (PhD) works as a professor at the Universidad de Buenos Aires (UBA). He teaches seminars on international horror film and he has published chapters in the books *Divine Horror*, edited by Cynthia Miller, *and To See the Saw Movies: Essays on Torture Porn and Post 9/11 Horror*, edited by John Wallis, among others. He has authored a book about Spanish horror TV series *Historias para no Dormir* and has edited books on Frankenstein bicentennial and director James Wan.

Geoffrey Reiter is Associate Professor and Coordinator of Literature at Lancaster Bible College and Associate Editor at the website Christ and Pop Culture. He holds an MA in Church History from Gordon-Conwell Theological Seminary and a PhD in English from Baylor University. His research focuses on the intersection of religion and science in genre fiction from the Victorian and Edwardian periods. He has previously published essays on writers such as Arthur Machen, George MacDonald, and Bram Stoker.

Loredana Salis is an associate professor in English and Irish Literature at the Università di Sassari. She has published monographs on contemporary uses of myth (2009) and stage representations of the migrant other (2010) with special attention to the Irish context. Her research interests include gendere(d) and exile narratives, and the remediation and adaptation of the English canon. She has published articles on Marlowe, Edna O'Brien, Marina Carr, Frank McGuinness, Mary Morrissy, and Seamus Heaney. She has contributed to the Italian translation of Dickens' theater (2013) and of Yeats' prose (2015). Her most recent work is a critical edition of *Lettere dal carcere* by Constance Markievicz (2017).

Antonio Sanna completed his PhD at the University of Westminster in London in 2008. His main research areas are English literature, Gothic literature, horror films and TV, epic and historical films, and cinematic adaptations. In the past thirteen years, he has published about ninety articles and reviews in international journals. Antonio is the co-editor, with Adam Barkman, of the Lexington Books' series *Critical Companions to Contemporary Directors*, which includes his coedited volumes on Tim Burton (2017), James Cameron (2018), Steven Spielberg (2019), and Robert Zemeckis (2020). He has also edited the volumes *Pirates in History and Popular Culture* (2018) and *Critical Essays on Twin Peaks: The Return* (2019). Antonio teaches in Sassari (Italy) and is currently working on a volume on *Alice in Wonderland*.

Dr. Adrian Tait is an independent scholar and environmental critic with a particular interest in the long nineteenth century. He has contributed to a number of scholarly journals, including *Green Letters*, the *European Journal of English Studies*, and the *Australian Humanities Review*, and to essay collections such as *Thomas Hardy, Poet: New Perspectives* (2015), *Nineteenth-Century Transatlantic Literary Ecologies* (2017), *Victorian Ecocriticism* (2017), and *Enchanted, Stereotyped, Civilized: Garden Narratives in Literature, Art and Film* (2018).

www.ingramcontent.com/pod-product-compliance
Lightning Source LLC
Chambersburg PA
CBHW020113010526
44115CB00008B/806